MW00933366

Why We Failed: 40 Years of Education Reform

Why We Failed: 40 Years of Education Reform

A SOLUTIONS-BASED ACCOUNT OF THE LAST 40 YEARS OF K-12 EDUCATION IN THE U.S.

● ● ●

Find out how to improve student achievement, why school choice discriminates against vulnerable students and where all the money has been spent in a book by scientist turned educator turned author Lonnie Palmer who spent 40 years working in public schools first as a science and math teacher and later as a superintendent of schools.

Lonnie Palmer

Copyright © 2016 Lonnie Palmer
All rights reserved.

ISBN-13: 9781539677956
ISBN-10: 1539677958
Library of Congress Control Number: 2016950108
Guaranteed Press, Clifton Park, NEW YORK

This book is dedicated to Beautiful.

"Failure is success if we learn from it."

-- Malcolm Forbes

Scientist Turns Educator Turns Author

● ● ●

IN 1970, LONNIE PALMER, AUTHOR of the solutions-based book "Why We Failed: 40 Years of Education Reform," graduated from Union College in Schenectady, NY, with a Bachelor's Degree in Physics and planned to continue on to a Ph.D. program but was interrupted by a notice from the U.S. Government – a draft notice. Knowing his low number would preempt plans to continue his education, Palmer took a temporary teaching position at a nearby middle school — and a reluctant education reformer was born.

Within a year Palmer was drafted into the U.S. Army. It was during the Vietnam War and Palmer was sent to Edgewood Arsenal in Maryland, where he worked as a Science Research Assistant calibrating radiation detection devices in the physics, health and safety office.

Even though his sights were set on eventually becoming a physicist, the time Palmer spent teaching – the students he met – prompted him to take a teaching job at Spackenkill High School when two years later he was discharged from the U.S. Army.

Over the next seven years at Spackenkill, Palmer taught physics, AP Physics, earth science, chemistry, algebra, geometry, trigonometry and precalculus. In 1980, he left Spackenkill to become principal of Averill Park High School outside of Albany, NY.

In 1993, Palmer became Assistant Superintendent for Secondary Education in the City School District of New Rochelle, NY. An urban environment with a diverse population, New Rochelle was a hot bed of reform. Using a Mellon Foundation Grant for educational innovation, Palmer implemented New York State Education Department approved variances on Regents exams that allowed teachers to substitute portions of 13 different exams with rubric-based research projects. One example: 20 percent of the Biology Regents Exam was a research project students completed with the aid of medical doctor mentors from the Sound Shore Medical Center.

Then in 1997, Albany City School District recruited Palmer to take over a district that had been run by the Albany political machine for decades. Palmer was hired by a majority reform board to move the school district away from decades of patronage, nepotism and cronyism and toward a results-based school district.

In 2003, following his tenure in Albany, Palmer started a consulting business that analyzed and compared school district performance data with similar districts and established benchmarks for effective school spending and academic performance. It wasn't long before he heard from another urban school district. Troy School District, in Troy, NY, was in dire straits and needed a leader to turn things around.

Within two years with Palmer at the helm, Troy schools were upgraded by Standard and Poor's and both the middle and high school were removed from the State's Schools In Need of Improvement (SINI) list.

Palmer was recruited again in 2013 to lead a rural school district with several outstanding labor contracts. Palmer settled two contracts in one year and helped implement the new Common Core standards. Part of the Common Core implementation effort included freeing up funds from places where they weren't effectively improving the program and reinvesting those dollars in programs, curriculum and teachers. During that year, Palmer also researched a contract between the school district and administrators union tying raises for general education and special education administrators with academic performance improvement targets.

While the Vietnam War forced Palmer to put his formal education on hold, he eventually obtained his Master's in Physics Education (1975) and a Certificate of Advanced Study in Educational Administration (1982) from the State University of New York at New Paltz. Palmer is also an American Society of Energy Engineers certified Energy Conservation Specialist.

Table of Contents

Acknowledgements

● ● ●

IF YOU EVER THINK ABOUT writing a book, I have a few words of advice.

First, try to pick a subject less complicated than education.

Second, be sure to have you have a team of intelligent and supportive friends, family and work colleagues who will take the time to provide excellent research articles, valuable insights and concrete suggestions that will make your book more readable, relevant and effective. I was lucky enough to have such an outstanding team.

My brother Robert Palmer, Jr., my sister Kathy Ordonez, my son David Palmer, my daughter Sarah Siedlik (just now starting her first year as a high school math teacher) and my friend and former work colleague Kilmer Heighton all reviewed sample chapters and offered critical comments and suggestions. All also offered essential words of encouragement. Another friend, Mac Saunders, gave me a number of news articles that also provided valuable research for this book. My friend Kevin Kronau read two chapters and provided encouragement and suggestions.

Charles Winters is in many ways the author of the scatterplots I reference throughout the book. His system for comparing schools and school districts, based on free and reduced lunch percentages, U.S. Census poverty and household income, is invaluable to the solutions-based theme of the book.

Work colleagues Audrey Wood and Dr. Gerald Kirschenbaum offered excellent insights on effective elementary education programs. My step-daughter Nicole "Kit" Jelonek guided me through the process of converting color charts into black and white and without her help I would never have finished this project. Friends and work partners Mark Kellett and Brian Corey offered encouragement and great ideas.

Writing this book took more than two years and there were many days in that time period when I was discouraged and floundering, uncertain about whether I'd ever be able to successfully finish the book with the quality, attention to detail and clear writing I knew was necessary if it was to achieve my goals. Encouragement from all of these individuals helped enormously.

My son Jason Palmer and I exchange multiple emails every week on news items frequently related to the topic of education. We argue in the best way about everything. Jason offered helpful critical comments and suggestions about multiple chapters and emailed me numerous news articles and research studies that ended up as footnotes in this book. Jason has also worked in education related fields for much of his career and his views provide a critical, albeit alternative, lens that clarifies my thinking and understanding of many issues featured in this book.

And lastly, if you want your book to have any chance for success get yourself a great editor, someone you totally respect who is just as immersed in the topic you are writing about as you are and someone who can effectively re-direct and challenge your ideas and your writing to make it much better than your original drafts indicated possible. If I have an authentic and clear voice and value as a writer in this book, my editor, Sheila Carmody, owns the credit for that success.

I love her but we argued about every page…but in a good way.

Finally, I have to acknowledge all of the students I've come in contact with over my 40 years in education.

Introduction

● ● ●

ON JUNE 1, 2013, I started a one-year stint as interim schools superintendent for the rural Berne-Knox-Westerlo (BKW) Central School District located 25 miles southeast of Albany, NY.

The first item on my list of things to do during that school year was to settle the teacher union contract. The second was to settle the support staff union contract. Both had expired five years earlier.

Preparing for contract negotiations was tricky and time consuming (they had become acrimonious over those five years) and began immediately after I was hired. The school board knew their failed attempts to reach a settlement made them appear weak. What they didn't know was that every day that went by was costing them money.

Meanwhile, the teachers had little motivation to move forward as they continued to receive salary step increases and over-priced, school district funded health insurance under the old contract.

Also on my agenda for that year was BKW's academic program. Standardized test scores for BKW's students were well below average for the state and for similar school districts with 35 percent of students eligible for free or reduced price lunch. In an effort to improve the academic program and understand many of the curriculum changes that came about as a result of the new Common Core standards, I attended three days of curriculum training with my principals and other administrators.

The Common Core was already under attack by teachers unions, parents and conservative politicians. A new teacher and principal performance evaluation system implemented by the New York State Education Department required superintendents and principals to complete meticulously detailed classroom teacher observations and principal observations recorded and written in a maze-like computer filing system that defied logic and years of my experience with these tasks. I had to complete a week-long training on the new teacher observation process while simultaneously completing all the other tasks in the school district including hiring five teachers and a principal.

Additionally, a new edict from the New York State Education Department required integrating student test score results into teacher evaluations for the school year that just ended and the school year about to begin. Complicating matters, the district had apparently selected an inappropriate scale for integrating state and local test results into teacher evaluations, resulting in more teachers than expected (18 out of 80) being identified as ineffective or performing at levels that indicated a need for improvement.

Some of the district's weakest teachers were not identified as ineffective or performing at levels that indicated a need for improvement and vice versa.

Then, in late August, I received an invitation along with 100 other New York State school superintendents to hear the New York State Education Commissioner speak at a regional school building 50 miles north of BKW in Saratoga Springs, NY. It was August 26, 2013, and I had so much on my plate I almost passed on the invitation. School was starting in one week and taking a whole afternoon to drive to Saratoga from Berne, NY, seemed like a waste of time.

From what I had read about Commissioner John King – a former charter school principal from New York City who had never dealt with a school board and had no experience as a school district superintendent – I doubted he would provide any information that might make my long and difficult to-do list any shorter or easier to accomplish. But I'm a good soldier so I made the 50-mile drive north to the Washington-Saratoga-Warren-Hamilton-Essex BOCES.

I milled around with many colleagues I hadn't seen for several years until the commissioner arrived – 15 minutes late. He was introduced by one of the local BOCES Superintendents. BOCES is short for Board of

Cooperative Educational Services and is a regional consortium of school districts and provides special education, vocational education and staff training services to school districts.

Commissioner King planned to speak on the new Common Core tests and their link to teacher evaluations. He spent 45 minutes reading almost entirely from his notes while zipping through a PowerPoint presentation. He spoke quickly and made no effort to connect with the audience of superintendents.

He seemed to embody the disconnect between the New York State Education Department and those charged with leading the 733 school districts in the state.

"The Common Core is here to stay," he said. "Get used to it."

He told us that teacher evaluations tied to student test scores were the best answer to our concerns about teacher tenure and poor teacher performance.

There were audible groans followed by whispers. The fact that we were already struggling with poorly designed teacher evaluations that improperly integrated test scores into teacher evaluations did not deter the commissioner from his task at hand, which consisted of reading his PowerPoint notes aloud and verbatim.

The New York State Board of Regents, he told us, was fully supportive of this teacher evaluation model and our parents, taxpayers, and politicians expected us to implement it effectively. His comments were divorced from reality. Teachers were already fighting this and parents were already opting out of testing for their children.

The 80-plus superintendents in the room were incredulous and at the same time stunned by Commissioner King's brazen ability to totally ignore the reality of the situation.

By the end of the 2014-15 school year, Commissioner King had moved on to his next job in Washington, D.C., where he took Arnie Duncan's place as the U.S. Department of Education Secretary.

He left behind Meryl Tisch, the Chancellor of the New York State Board of Regents (state level board of education), to defend herself saying the Board of Regents had to act fast because the schools were performing so badly and had been for so long.

It was a tough afternoon in Saratoga as the commissioner barreled through his 25-page PowerPoint in 45 minutes. He took three questions from the shell-shocked superintendent audience, which he answered in single sentences that restated his mantra. Then he fled the building.

I feel safe in saying that none of my colleagues wanted to be there to hear the commissioner that day. I feel equally safe in saying that he didn't want to be there delivering his PowerPoint to a totally disbelieving audience.

We both knew this ship had sailed and would not ever arrive in port. It was only a matter of time before the Common Core/teacher evaluation/ required state test regime collapsed like another of China's five-year Great Leaps Forward. It was doomed and we would all play it out while hoping it didn't hurt too many students and teachers in the process.

Meanwhile, New York State Governor Andrew Cuomo who had initially supported the Common Core implementation and the teacher evaluations tied to student test scores did a complete 180. First, he bellowed with anger threatening all kinds of retribution when only one percent of New York teachers were evaluated as ineffective during that first year, while well over 50 percent of the students performed below expectations on the new Common Core tests. Then when the pushback from angry teacher unions and upset parents about teacher evaluations tied to the tests and the large number of students performing below expectation levels began to put the squeeze on him and other politicians, he flipped his position to support eliminating the use of student test scores in teacher evaluations for the next few years.

And over the next two years, parents sent a clear signal by having their children opt out of the required state English language arts and math tests given to students in grades three to eight. The "opt out" movement gained steam in 2013-14 and peaked in 2014-15, when almost 25 percent of grade three to eight students statewide skipped tests with "opt out" percentages of more than 50 percent in several school districts.

When I took the job as interim schools superintendent at BKW I was already considering writing a book about education. I had been in education for 40-plus years, starting out teaching middle school science, high school physics, AP Physics, chemistry, algebra, geometry, trigonometry and pre-calculus and later progressing through the roles of science department chairman, assistant principal, principal, assistant superintendent and superintendent. I thought I had learned enough about education, what works and what doesn't work, that it was worth sharing with others.

As I moved through my career, I reverted to the role of teacher many times. Frequently, I slipped into the teacher role without even realizing it. For example, when I was an assistant principal I often used a Socratic questioning technique with students who were in my office as a result of some behavioral infraction.

When I observed teachers in their classrooms as a principal, I tried to ask the right questions that would lead them to "discover and own" improvements in their instruction. As a superintendent I tried to ask my principals and school board members questions that would lead them to see the problems we faced and potential solutions in a new and more productive light. And in every case, I tried to use data, the best information we could assemble about the world around us, to frame and increase the insightfulness of my questions.

As I worked with other school administrators and school board members who were part of the school district leadership teams, I came to realize that in asking these questions and playing the "teacher" role I had become a mentor to many education leaders.

I also came to realize that this was a role I enjoyed and was good at. Many of the education leaders I mentored have told me that my incessant questions, particularly the questions about our long-held assumptions, and my personal and provocative perspective on thorny educational issues, helped them grow as leaders. This book is a way for me to raise those important questions with a wider audience and hopefully help more education leaders move closer to achieving their full leadership potential.

Have we failed?

Some have suggested I change the book title to something more positive. I carefully considered the suggestion, as the last thing I wanted to do was select a book title that discourages potential readers from giving the book serious consideration. But the truth is those in my generation who are leaving the educational leadership roles now need to appreciate that while we worked hard and achieved many great things during our careers, the public we serve is asking and will continue to ask the question: "Why are we failing?"

After an undeniable and large increase in after-inflation per pupil spending on education in the U.S. (89 percent more than CPI inflation from 1970 to 2015 in states with weak public unions and 163 percent more than CPI inflation in strong public union states)[i], our schools are ranked 35th and 27th internationally in math and science, respectively.[ii] [iii]

It begs the question: How could we spend so much more and not see a reasonably comparable increase in student achievement?

And isn't failure one of the best teachers? This book is my honest attempt as one education leader to face the question of why we failed head on and provide some of what I see as solutions.

I've tried to select the best data, the best stories and the best questions to effectively illustrate our educational leadership failures and how we might be more successful in the future.

That afternoon in Saratoga with Commissioner King and 80 of my fellow superintendents gave me unforgettable insight into why we have failed to ignite a long overdue improvement in student achievement.

The politics, the shortsighted and simplistic solutions, the widget counters and superfluous data that override the agenda, the budgets that prioritize the needs of the adults who are always angling to increase their power, improve their position, make their jobs easier, increase their pay and benefits, decrease their responsibilities and allow them to blame someone else – they are all there for us to see and deal with every day in schools.

The topics for this book – including teacher tenure, charter schools/school choice, standardized testing, union negotiations, poverty, special education, and the Common Core, among others – were culled from a long list I created during my time at BKW. I chose these topics because I thought they would best explain the nature of our failures, the reasons for those failures and how we could more productively tackle these issues and create significantly greater success for our students. The list of topics is not intended to be comprehensive or complete. Much more could be written on a number of related topics.

The italicized stories in each chapter were created from fictionalized characters and settings that reflect my 40-plus years of experience in education. The stories are meant to bring to life our failures and potential solutions and enhance our understanding of the difficult issues we need to resolve. I resorted to fictionalized characters to avoid lawsuits about legitimate confidentiality concerns and to more efficiently combine important ideas and issues into a reasonably-sized book.

Many who read this book including lifetime successful educators might well be disheartened by the book's primary message, which is: We have a lot of work to do and much of it will be very hard. Our schools have many warts. The removal and eradication of those warts will be at least another lifetime's work for the educators and school board members who follow me. But we can't give up.

We can't give up because our students – children – deserve a world class education. Students like the boy in the blue parka.

The boy in the blue parka

● ● ●

AS WITH MOST SOPHOMORE STUDENTS *in one of my three geometry classes, Gary Allerdyce chose his own seat on the first day of class. I never argued with students about where they sat unless it distracted from the ebb and flow of instruction. Gary parked himself in the student desk right up against the desk high heater between two bay windows at the side of my classroom.*

Gary was a "low rider," sitting slumped down low in his seat, leaning on the heater. Every day he wore the same dark blue parka with a fur-fringe hood that made him appear bigger and more ominous than he was. A mix of smells – pot and body odor – emanated from the jacket. I don't know whether it was because of his odor or his surly demeanor, but his classmates kept their distance.

Gary and I reached an uneasy and unspoken agreement early on: He didn't bother me and I didn't bother him. I attempted a couple of times to engage him in one-on-one conversations. When he failed to write anything but his name on tests, I made a few calls to his home. When no one returned my calls or responded to computer progress reports and report cards that showed his lack of progress, naturally, I stopped calling.

At the end of the first quarter I gave Gary a 50 on his report card. Many public schools have a school-wide grading system that won't allow for less. The hope is the student will do better the second quarter and numerically they'll be able to pass by year's end. A zero won't allow for that and a report card zero is just a way for frustrated teachers to write kids off for the year.

YEAR TWO OF TEACHING

I was in year two of teaching and the first year of preparing students for the New York State Geometry Regents exam, which was a big deal in this suburban community populated mostly by IBM employees. They had high expectations for their children, especially in math. Earning acceptance to competitive colleges was the norm.

So my mind was not on Gary Allerdyce. My attention was directed toward the students who were motivated...for whatever reason.

Like most rookie teachers, I used the textbook as a framework for my curriculum and lesson plans with only a few minor edits based on advice from other more experienced math teachers, advice I rarely sought due to the fact that I didn't want to appear ignorant in front of my students, my principal or other teachers.

While my instructional approach failed to produce stellar results, it kept me in good standing with the school principal, parents and most of my students... until one gray April day when we struggled through a challenging unit related to right triangles with similar shapes and different sizes.

I was trying to explain why the length of the altitude drawn to the hypotenuse is the mean proportional between the segments of the hypotenuse and get the students to prove why that was true and solve numerical problems based on different dimensions for the triangles.

It was an archaic, convoluted, abstract, abstruse bit of math no one would ever use anywhere except for in geometry class, but that didn't stop the state education department from requiring it.

The students — many of whom had class averages of 95 percent or above — were confused, as well as lost and frustrated.

I tried to explain the concepts for what felt like the tenth time using my most effective teaching technique (SPEAK MUCH SLOWER AND VERY LOUDLY). I was gesturing wildly at my elaborate chalk diagram on the chalkboard when I asked a question, hoping someone — ANYONE — would give me the right answer.

"So for this right triangle with the altitude drawn to the hypotenuse and the altitude as the mean proportional what must be the length of the altitude?" I asked.

Silence.

"C'mon guys this isn't that hard. What's the length of the altitude?"

That's when I heard it: "Eight."

I turned around to face the class: "Who said that?"

The answer came from Gary Allerdyce.

I ignored the obvious and blurted back: "Correct!"

To this day I have no idea why Gary jumped in with the correct answer. My best guess is he was tired of hearing me say the same thing over and over slower and more loudly than the time before and just wanted me to move on.

When the class ended, I tried to corner Gary, but he beat me to the door and disappeared into the noisy, crowded hallway.

That night I couldn't sleep. I kept thinking: "What have I done? I let this kid sit slouched next to the heater for seven months and all this time he had the potential to do well in math and in school."

I knew I was an inexperienced teacher with a lot to learn, but I never thought of myself as someone who didn't care if students fell through the cracks.

All night I laid awake trying to come up with a plan.

The next morning I began class with a review problem on the chalkboard and asked Gary to follow me into the hall, which he did, obediently. I closed the classroom door and made my best pitch: "Look Gary you obviously know a lot more than you've shown in class," I said. "You knew the answer yesterday when no one else did. I made a mistake by writing you off and I want to set things straight by giving you a second chance right now.

"We both know that with the three 50 percent quarterly averages you already have on your report card numerically you can't pass Geometry unless you get a 100 percent for the fourth quarter and a 100 percent on the Regents final exam. Let's put all that behind us. If you pass the Regents exam I will give you a passing grade for the year and I'll help you any way I can between now and the final exam. What do you think?"

I held my breath. It was the best option I could come up with. I had a strong feeling I cared a lot more about Gary's answer than he did.

Gary hesitated. Then, he smiled a little (maybe it was a smirk) and said: "If I pass the test, I pass for the year. Right?"

"That's right," I said.

He nodded in agreement.

Now we were playing by Gary's rules. He still wore the fur-fringe hooded parka, and he still sat slumped in his seat near the heater. He still had an air of pot and body odor about him. He never did homework as far as I could tell, but he started trying on tests and quizzes. He even asked and answered a few questions in class.

He passed only a single unit exam all year and that was late in May, but his Regents review book was all marked up with what looked like his attempts to solve geometry problems. When I saw his review book splayed open on his desk during review, I had high hopes we'd both pull this rabbit out of a hat on the June Geometry Regents exam.

Then two days before the test the New York State Education Department reported that a copy of the New York State Geometry Regents exam was stolen from a school in New York City, and the New York State Education Department was cancelling the year-end Geometry Regents exam – statewide.

Schools were instructed to use students' four quarterly grades to determine their final grade in place of the Geometry Regents exam grade. Our math department disagreed with the state's decision, and we tried to circumvent them. We administered the purloined Geometry Regents exam anyway to gauge student performance, but the word on the street was the exam didn't count.

On the day of the exam, only a fraction of students showed up to take the test. Gary wasn't one of them.

I called his home but this time the number was disconnected.

Gary never showed up the following school year. I never saw him again.

Common Core is Not the Problem

●　●　●

JIM MCMAHON TAUGHT ENGLISH AT a small, suburban high school in upstate New York where I was assistant principal. He was a rookie so he taught a "school group," a label for students with weak academic skills and a proclivity for social and school discipline problems.

Due to the teacher "seniority pecking order," rookies like Jim McMahon were usually saddled with the most challenging students and expected to keep them from breaking the furniture while hopefully getting them to read a few books slightly more challenging than the easiest comic book.

As assistant principal I saw more than one student from Jim's school group class for typical behavioral issues: smoking in school, skipping class or ditching the entire day, fighting in the cafeteria, cursing out a teacher, etc.

After a year or two of teaching, Jim decided to buck the trend of weekly spelling tests, diagramming sentences and rewriting "essays" and have this "school group" perform a play, a move that was immediately viewed as heresy among the faculty room glitterati. Didn't he know that these students had to take and pass a required Basic Competency Test? What was he thinking?!

THE SKY IS FALLING, THE SKY IS FALLING

The Basic Competency Test (BCT) in the mid-1970s was the first of what would become a testing movement that continues today. And, as with today's standardized state tests, BCT tests elicited panic in teachers who didn't think the "school groups" could pass the tests.

But the tests were a joke. In fact, I overheard one math teacher say: "Give me two weeks, 2 pounds of bird seed and a grey squirrel with above average dexterity so I can teach him to hold the pencil, and I'll get him to pass the BCT."

And, of course, over 95 percent of the "school group" did pass with ease on the first try.

Given the fact that teachers taught their own homegrown less-than-challenging curriculum to "school groups" in New York State at the time it was little wonder the Basic Competency Test was designed with such low standards. Without knowing what was being taught (every teacher had her/his own curriculum), test developers had to allow for a low degree of difficulty.

Meanwhile, the college bound students took Regents exams with a more challenging and structured curriculum and very predictable tests administered in June, August and January.

TALK ABOUT A REBEL

With little or no guidance and a groundswell of criticism, English teacher Jim McMahon threw caution to the wind and invested nearly two months of class time preparing for a public presentation of the Broadway play adaptation of Ken Kesey's novel "One Flew over the Cuckoo's Nest," which at the time was a hit movie starring Jack Nicholson. The theme of the movie – rebel with a bad attitude in a mental hospital strikes a blow for humanity – didn't sit well with some of the faculty room crowd, and I myself was doubtful Jim could pull this off with the motley crew assembled in his "school group" English class. Remember, these were students selected because they couldn't read and write well enough to be considered candidates for college. And they had to take the BCT test at the end of the year.

They also were not drama students and this was a very difficult play for students to perform well.

One particularly sullen, long-haired boy who had been to my office several times would play the lead role of Randle McMurphy. While his personality fit the role, I couldn't see him being successful with the discipline and teamwork required for the role. (At that time I, like most everyone else in education, was convinced a segment of the school population was not going to succeed for whatever reason.)

A school-wide assembly during the last class period of the day gave Jim's class a chance to show their stuff to their high school peers with the performance of a single scene from the play as a teaser for the entire play which was to be performed later that evening.

I was backstage in my assistant principal role trying to make sure things ran smoothly. Jim's students were obviously scared to death of looking stupid in front of their peers but it was also obvious they were well prepared. The audience started out a bit rowdy and more than a bit restless. But within three minutes the student actors had them paying close attention to every word, gesture and sigh. When the scene ended there was a roar of applause and appreciation from the students in the audience and smiles, hugs and slaps on the back for all the cast including "Mr. Sullen."

I still remember the goose bumps I had when the applause erupted at the end of the scene. But I was still uncertain about how these students would do with the full play and an audience of adults including their parents whose previous contacts with the school came only when their children were in trouble.

Later that night the students put on an outstanding play with a minimum of slip-ups, flubbed lines and recoveries and some truly remarkable and effective student acting performances.

The audience was as appreciative as the students earlier in the day. The teaser performance appeared to have boosted Jim's students' confidence and the students in Jim's class were beaming when they took their bows and still beaming a full week later when I saw them in the cafeteria or in the halls in our school. It was a total success.

Even the weekly spelling test proponents in the faculty room quieted down briefly, grudgingly acknowledging that something meaningful had happened in our school.

Jim left our school at the end of the year and I never saw him again. But his impact on me as an educator was significant.

A few years later in my role as a high school principal, when I was reading books by Ted Sizer and John Goodlad and materials from the Coalition of Essential Schools, I realized what Jim McMahon's class performed was technically called an "authentic assessment" of their English skills. An authentic assessment is a real test like an athletic contest or a concert performance by the band as contrasted with the inauthentic fill-in-the-bubble tests made by commercial test-making companies.

As the psychometricians who develop the inauthentic tests will tell you the bubble tests are statistically more reliable – the results can be repeated with different versions of the tests administered to the same test takers. Would Jim's class have done as well, better, worse with a second play? Who knows?

Evaluating the academic success of individuals who participated in Jim's play is cumbersome and tricky. Did the student who designed the sets really learn anything of value? Can any of these students read, write or speak better as a result of their work on this play? There are rubrics (complicated scoring systems) for evaluating essays, projects and even acting performances, but they are all approximations and they all involve subjective analysis by the teacher.

Three highly trained teachers evaluating the same acting performance using the same rubric on the same student in the play would come up with three different scores. On the other hand, rubrics and the bubble sheets cannot measure intangibles like student motivation and confidence or how students see themselves as learners and as people.

CHARACTERISTICS OF EFFECTIVE LEARNING

The bubble sheet test proponents frequently miss a key point in the discussion on assessments: The ultimate goal of Jim's English class is to make his students better readers, writers, listeners and speakers, more confident in their communication skills and hopefully more adept at understanding and dealing effectively with the subtleties of communication.

Jim's students' theater performance is a more valid measurement of knowledge and skill gains in these areas than psychometrically reliable substitute skills measured by bubble sheet tests. If you are acting in the role of rebel Randle McMurphy, and the lines you must deliver require you to show anger and sensitivity at the same time, your acting task will be challenging and your audience will know immediately if you have succeeded or failed. How could anyone fit that skill set in a bubble sheet test question? You can't.

And Jim's theater performance has the added benefit of providing motivation, structure and purpose to student learning, as anyone who has performed in a play, a band or orchestra concert or for a school sports team in an athletic contest knows.

Have the bubble sheet tests and the endless prep exercises for those tests had a positive impact on student motivation to learn? Not likely. An overemphasis on testing definitely leads to problems. We could easily replace failing instruction in many classrooms with failing, prescriptive and even more boring instruction for the benefit of testing.

Jim's play had one other characteristic that bubble sheet tests don't. Jim's class performed that play in 1978, more than 35 years ago, and his students are now in their early 50s. How many of them still remember that play and their role in its success? No doubt, every one of them.

How many of them were impacted in some positive and meaningful way as learners, as parents and as workers by their experience in that play? My guess, probably more than one and maybe more than a handful. How many of us can remember anything meaningful coming from our preparation for and participation in any of the many bubble sheet tests we encountered in our years in school?

One of the characteristics of all effective learning experiences in our lives – including those learning experiences that occur outside the classroom – is that they are memorable. Many teachers do their best to make classroom instruction memorable. But if teachers limit themselves to traditional lectures and bubble sheet test prep activities as their entire instructional tactical arsenal, their efforts will be forgotten. There are many ways to create memorability:

authentic assessments with an audience, academic contests, experimental activities, school/workplace collaborations, etc. Effective learning and teaching requires a combination of those strategies.

At the same time, we need reliable, believable, numerical measures of student learning. Without these reliable academic measures, children from poverty would almost certainly experience more inequity than they're already experiencing in our educational [iv]system.[4] Bubble sheet tests with their reliable essays and simple extended problems that include packaged scoring rubrics provide us with data that can help us make decisions about how to proceed with academic improvement efforts. Without these tests and some common standards that guide the test and curriculum development, we're guaranteed to have a disjointed system of mostly weak standards and tests across the country. And our race to the top will quickly become a race to the bottom.[v]

Anyone who says we don't need standardized tests is kidding themselves. The question is: How do we marry those two different measurement systems into something that helps our students learn and increases the odds they'll develop the "soft" less easily measured but very important skills and values that came from Jim's class play?

(Sections in italics are fictional stories made from composites of multiple actual experiences.)

A district resting on its socioeconomic laurels

In 2013, I was approached about serving as interim school superintendent in the suburban Candle Central School District. I reviewed the district's student test performance data on the New York State Education Department website, which isn't sophisticated enough to make true comparisons as it compares apples to oranges, high poverty school districts to low poverty school districts.

So I used a sophisticated measurement of school performance developed by Charles (Charlie) Winters, a New York State School Business Official and respected colleague I had worked with on multiple projects.

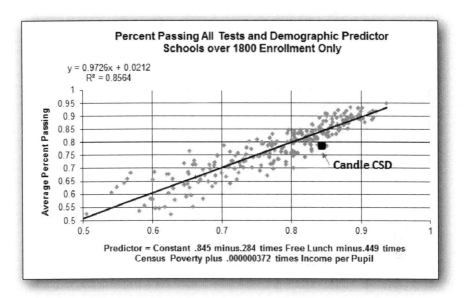

As the Business Official for the Newburgh Enlarged City School District and as a consultant for the New York State Association of Small City School Districts, Mr. Winters compiled extensive data sets on student outcomes, demographics, local costs and state support. Mr. Winters used the "scatterplot" graph to display the results because he found it was an effective visual for illustrating multivariate data.

Mr. Winters's school district comparison data became a key element in the Campaign for Fiscal Equity lawsuit and a companion lawsuit filed by several small cities in New York State that ended in 2006 with a plan to redistribute $5.5 billion in new aid to school districts in the state with the primary focus on serving the largest poverty populations.

I'd come up with a similar measurement based on free and reduced lunch data while I was an urban schools superintendent and before I met Mr. Winters as a way to rate the performance of elementary schools within a district. His much more comprehensive and mathematically accurate system was based on three criteria: free and reduced school lunch percentages, U.S. Census data on poverty and income data from New York State income tax filings. He found a combination of all three that was the best predictor of student performance on the state tests.

When I used Mr. Winters's system of measurement, the Candle Central School District revealed itself to be a weak performer in comparison with other districts with similar demographics, relatively low poverty and multiple resources.

Judging by Candle Central's test scores from the previous year (the first year of Common Core testing in the state) teachers hadn't adjusted to new test expectations. They needed a better handle on curriculum.

I took the job and almost immediately contacted the head of the local school district consortium BOCES (Board of Cooperative Education Services) and arranged for teacher and administrator training. I booked myself and three of the four district principals available during the summer into a three-day-long session of sixth grade math Common Core curriculum training for teachers.

The Candle elementary and middle school math teachers opted out of the training (no pun intended). A lot of that had to do with the fact that they weren't informed of the training until a couple of weeks before it took place. The elementary school principal and the superintendent who preceded me were both consumed with trying to find new jobs at the time and, as a result, no planning was done to have the teachers available for the summer training.

The training emphasized the new Common Core sixth grade math expectations in ratio and proportion, algebra, coordinate and plane geometry and number line graphs and the more complicated and intricate word problems students were expected to solve with the new Common Core tests.

After all I had read and heard about the Common Core and how much anger it produced in schools and communities, I was struck by the fact that it wasn't all that different from the previous math curriculum. It had fewer topics that were dealt with in greater depth, including more pre-algebra and graphing and pictorial/preliminary equation problem solving tasks. The curriculum presented a higher level of challenge than the old curriculum, but the challenge levels and approach to instruction made sense and aligned with expectations in other countries that outperformed the U.S. on international measures of student academic performance. In short, the Common Core asked students and teachers to do what they should be doing. It was a good curriculum, better than the one it had replaced.

As a former math and science teacher, I could understand the changes in expectations, so I used the training time to evaluate the outlooks and thought processes of my principals, as well as those of teachers from other districts in attendance.

Teachers from the other school districts illustrated the contrast between teachers who have been teaching to a lower standard and teachers using strategies that allow students to meet higher Common Core standards.

The blame game

One of the teachers at the training was Ruth Weiss who had 20-plus years of experience teaching sixth grade math in one of the several smaller urban and socioeconomically diverse school districts in the area. She loved students and loved her job.

She peppered the trainer with questions over all three days of training. Most related to how she could effectively retain the creative projects she used with her students and still bring about high scores for her students on the Common Core tests.

For example, Ruth's sixth graders used proportions and similar triangles with averages of multiple data measurements to estimate the height of the flagpole in front of the school. They also predicted the time it would take the district's grounds team to mow the lawn inside the track by computing the area and measuring mowing rates with the grounds team in other areas of the school campus.

She had them estimate the daily average revenue for the cafeteria by surveying lunches and snacks purchased in a set time period, computing revenue estimates based on posted prices and discounts available to students with pre-purchased meal cards as well as students who received free and reduced price lunches and comparing it to the actual weekly revenue reported by the cafeteria staff.

She had students estimate the time it would take three different electric-powered model cars to traverse terrain in the school's parking lot based on previous measurements for cars. Ruth ended the school year with an elaborate project that required her students to predict flight-to-ground contact times and distances for water balloons shot from a toy cannon set to different angles to the horizon.

Ruth was clearly concerned she had too much new and unfamiliar material to cover in sixth grade Common Core math, and she worried about her students who were weak in basic math facts (7 X 9 = 63) and computational skills (713/23 = 31).

New curriculum expectations would interfere with the real-world projects that typically motivated her students.

At lunch on our third and final day of training Ruth confided in me while holding back tears. The first year of the new teacher evaluation system in which 20 percent of teacher performance was based on their students' standardized test scores had just passed, and Ruth was rated as a "developing" teacher, which was just barely above the lowest teacher performance category – "ineffective."

Ruth said the low rating was caused by two things. First: She chose a challenging local assessment that pulled down the scores. Each teacher, with school district approval, chose a local student assessment that counted as 20 percent of the teacher's evaluation and some chose poorly. Second: She refused to replace her customary student projects with test prep activities.

During training Ruth learned some strategies that would allow her to keep the best of her projects and simultaneously improve her test scores on the new Common Core tests.

The strategies included:

- *Completing several projects after the standardized tests were given in April.*
- *Figuring out which projects help teach skills students need to know.*

     *   Accumulating a portfolio of project work that's effective, tried and tested.*

     *   Sharing projects with other teachers and trying out their projects later in the year after the standardized tests are administered.*

TIMING IS EVERYTHING

At the same time that the new Common Core standards were being implemented, a new teacher evaluation system was being implemented with 40 percent of teacher evaluations being based on new Common Core and locally selected tests and the rest on principal observations, documented staff development and training activities completed plus lesson planning.

New York State split the 40 percent for testing into two parts with 20 percent for a "local" test selected by teachers with principal approval and 20 percent coming from the year-end state tests for grades three through eight. In the first year of implementation many teachers and districts chose the wrong test – either too easy or too hard – to make up the local portion of the testing for teacher evaluations, which ultimately led to unreliable teacher evaluations.

For the local portion, most teachers and districts erred on the side of selecting local assessments that were too easy, resulting in all of the teachers being evaluated as "effective" or "highly effective" on the local portion.

In addition, principals rated almost all of their teachers as effective or highly effective on the parts of the teacher evaluations that did not relate to test scores. The result: Statewide less than 1 percent of the teachers were rated as ineffective and fewer than 5 percent fell in the lowest two categories of "ineffective" and "developing." [vi]

A few districts erred on the other side with local assessments that were much too difficult and had 20 percent or more of their teachers rated "ineffective." Many of these "ineffective" teachers had produced good test results for their students for many years prior to the new teacher evaluation system and the new Common Core tests.

Not shockingly, New York State Governor Andrew Cuomo was incensed that less than 1 percent of teachers statewide were rated "ineffective" while

60 to 65 percent of the students scored below "proficient" on the new Common Core-based state tests in their first year of implementation. [vii]

Of course Gov. Cuomo and many others conveniently forgot that most of the students taking the new Common Core tests had been exposed to the new curriculum for only one or two years, while they had worked with a less challenging curriculum for three to eight years prior to the new standards and tests. It was too much change, initiated too quickly and tied to teacher evaluations before anyone had a chance to reasonably make the adjustments required.

It was no surprise when Gov. Cuomo announced plans to introduce legislation that would increase the weight of student test results in teacher evaluations to 50 percent and exclude the local test component. His proposal also required teacher observations by administrators outside the school district, illustrating politicians mistrust for school principals and creating an administrative nightmare for the folks who actually complete the teacher observations.

Later, Gov. Cuomo (and later U.S. Education Secretary Arne Duncan) [viii] totally backed off on these proposed changes. Under significant political pressure from the state teachers union, New York State United Teachers (NYSUT), and from droves of parents who refused to let their children take the new Common Core exams, both Gov. Cuomo and the New York State Board of Regents (state level board of education) decided to temporarily forgo teacher evaluations tied to the new Common Core test results. [ix]

Prematurely changing directions when predictable change implementation problems develop and trying the fad of the week to reform U.S. education is a pattern that repeats itself regularly in K-12 education. The pattern has been noted by many educators.[x]

THE TRUTH ABOUT TESTING

I learned the truth about testing when I was assistant superintendent in the New Rochelle City School District, a diverse school district 15 miles north of New York City. Ellin Rossberg was the chairperson for the English

Department for New Rochelle High School and two middle schools in the city of New Rochelle, NY.

Ellin knew more about children's literature and effective English instruction than anyone I ever met. She was also capable of withering imperiousness when she felt I stepped over the line with my many disruptions and changes for the academic program.

Like most school districts at the time, when students arrived at New Rochelle's two middle schools from six different elementary schools they were grouped into three skill level groups. The problem is the six elementary schools defined the three categories differently, and we needed a quick, simple, easy-to-grade test to measure student performance.

I expected to see another fill-in-the-bubble test, but Ellin had a different, time-tested, reliable method I had never seen before.

She went to each fifth grade classroom and wrote on the chalkboard in her meticulous handwriting a Shakespearean sonnet with all the Old English spellings, capitalizations and punctuation and asked the students to copy it exactly as it had been written.

Teachers collected the copies, reviewed them and sorted students based on the number of errors they made when copying the sonnet. Students with zero or one error went to the "high" group in sixth grade, students with two to three errors went to the "middle" group and students with more than three errors to the "low" group.

Relying on elementary schools for recommendations on group placement was 80 to 85 percent accurate, while Ellin's placement rate based on this simple test was 95 percent accurate. Initially, I didn't believe her but she convinced me with data on student transfers that resulted – or didn't result – from her initial placements.

When it was introduced, the much vilified English language arts (ELA) Common Core exam administered to students in grades three through eight in New York State was an ordeal taking four-and-a-half hours spread out over three school days. (In 2016, New York State began to rein in test times.[xi])

I saw students vomit over fears about the Common Core tests. The tests take months to grade and the results sort students into four skill groups: excel or well above proficient; proficient; partially proficient; and well below proficient with 98 percent reliability.

Ellin's test sorted students into three groups instead of four and took little time to produce. She gave [xii]students 15 minutes to copy the sonnet and each teacher spent an hour reviewing and scoring an entire class assessment. And Ellin's test had 95 percent reliability. So to gain 3 percentage points we spent billions of dollars nationally and invested enormous amounts of teacher and student time. This is part of the reason why the public and especially parents have become increasingly unsupportive of the new testing expectations, opting out and using other tactics to demonstrate their displeasure.

And these new English language arts exams have none of Jim McMahon's play's enthusiasm, "soft skill" development and memorability.

I am certain if we could identify one of the key English language arts (ELA) test designers from the international corporation Pearson, which receives (or received) most of the millions of dollars spent nationally on newly required testing, and compel her/him to provide us with a one-hour, one-day ELA test that sorted grade three through eight students into four performance groups based on their ELA skills s/he could do it, reluctantly, but s/he could do it.

The cost and time savings would be enormous. Pearson wouldn't like it but we need to remember: We pay them and they work for us. We design the tasks and they complete them as we expect.

Wouldn't test reliability suffer? Yes, reliability would drop from the present 98 percent to between 96 and 97 percent, and we can all live with that. Pearson[xiii] and a few other companies have controlled the test design process across the country with little competition[xiv] and (surprise!) they have designed a high-priced, over-engineered monster that makes them millions in profits. As a profit-making enterprise that is their goal. We should not be surprised.

TEST SECRECY BEGETS FEAR

The roll-out of the Common Core in New York failed for multiple reasons. Besides overcomplicating the process, the teachers were unable to review sample tests, which produced fear among teachers, parents and students.

What exactly are they asking the students to do? How will the questions be worded? How can I make certain my students will be ready when I can't see the test? Such secrecy also prevents teachers from uncovering the errors that always creep into even the best standardized tests.

The reason teachers can't see the tests is not just for exam security; it's because of cost. If the tests become public after they're given, then Pearson and test companies like them have to design completely new tests every year and that costs more money for an already expensive enterprise.

Another reason for the secrecy: Pearson uses the actual tests as a way to integrate potential future test questions that don't count in student scores (field testing them on the students).[xv] Making the tests public is incompatible with test security.

Why not keep the field test questions secret and reveal the questions that count in student scores? We'd save enough with a switch to a one-hour-long test from a four-and-a-half hour test, and then we could release the tests to everyone. It's a move that would calm a lot of fears.

Releasing the tests would also facilitate work going on in many school districts right now to gear up for the new Common Core standards and test expectations. The smartest districts, principals and teachers are already well on their way to adjusting the curriculums, and the huge drop in student proficiency rates seen in the first two years of Common Core test implementation in New York State[xvi] and other early implementation states will largely be made up in the next 10 years. We could make this process much more efficient and cut the transition time to five years by releasing the tests.

Instructional strategies that make the Common Core work

Anthony Tompkins, a sixth grade teacher in the Common Core training group I attended with Candle Central School District educators, was a tall, slender, 28-year-old African American math teacher. He had been teaching math for seven years and during our three-day-long training session offered some excellent tips on how he'd produced outstanding results on the new Common Core sixth-grade math test — a test students statewide found impossibly difficult.

One of the teachers in our training voiced concern over her students' weak math fact and computational skills and the time she had to invest to help these students improve these key skills while the students who knew these skills sat on their hands.

"This is one of the few areas where technology can really help," Anthony told her.

He explained how all of his students use five computers set up in a corner of his classroom in rotating groups during five-minute sessions throughout the class period. During the brief sessions students complete quick math fact and computational challenges at the appropriate level based on their previous performance on the program.

The software program Anthony recommended works on leftover computers found in closets in most schools, and gives the teacher diagnostic information on each student. With that diagnostic information, Anthony zeros in on student weakness and with one or two minutes of focused one-on-one tutoring, while the other students are working on other math activities, moves them past their mini math roadblock. Anthony likened this work on the computer to athletes working out in the weight room every day to gain strength.

Several teachers in the training mentioned not having enough time to cover all the material expected by the new curriculum and the difficult challenge level of the math concepts.

Anthony shook his head: "Man, you guys are stressing way too much and letting these students off too easy," he said.

For each unit Anthony told them he covered only the topics in the curriculum. And that meant weeding out extraneous topics in the math textbook and in his old lesson plans that were not in the new curriculum, which amounted to about 50 percent of what he had previously taught his students prior to the Common Core standards.

Anthony also said he limited the days he spent on each required topic to the number of days suggested on the state education department's online curriculum map. For example: Ratios and unit rates, 35 days.

Some teachers objected and said this amounted to spending all their time teaching to the test. Anthony responded that his textbook included every conceivable topic any sixth grade math teacher in the country might address and no one could do justice to all of that curriculum material. Trying to cover the whole textbook was a guaranteed way to ensure the curriculum was a mile wide and an inch deep.

"By focusing solely on the topics in the curriculum and on the tests, I do a much better job of ensuring students master the critical and more intellectually challenging skills," Anthony said. And, he said, this approach leaves the teaching of other critical skills to teachers at other grade levels where they belong.

When teachers argued that 35 days for this unit was insufficient, he told them his sixth graders finished the test for the ratios and unit rates on day 28. The trainer, who knew Anthony personally and had planned to use him as a plant to improve the training all along, smiled and asked Anthony to explain how he did this. Anthony described an elaborate and very scientific approach to his work in the classroom.

During the first 20 days of instruction on a unit, each week included three days of what teachers would normally call "instruction."

Each 40-minute math class began with a two-minute math challenge on the front board based on the previous day's or week's lesson. This warm-up activity was collected and graded by Anthony before the next day's class.

He followed with an eight to 12 minute lecture on the new content and skills he wanted students to understand and use for the rest of that class period. The eight to 12 minutes of lecture included one or two minutes of preview to tie what he was saying into previous lessons and one or two minutes of wrap-up and summary.

"Talk less and teach more" was Anthony's motto.

What Anthony meant by "teach more" became apparent as he described his methods and what happened in his classroom on a typical day in greater detail. Following his initial mini lecture on the ratio and unit rates unit, he divided his students into groups of four or five, grouping them based on ability and personality type.

These groups then solved math problems related to Anthony's mini lectures, but with a few problems mixed in from mini lectures from previous days, weeks and months.

Every five minutes, Anthony's phone alarm sounded and one or two students from each group of four or five would head to the computers to practice math computational and math fact skills for five minutes. When they returned to the group, one of their peers in the group helped them get up to speed on what the group had done during their absence. With five minutes to go in the period Anthony announced he would collect the group's work in two minutes. When the time came, all of the students handed in their work to Anthony in a group packet.

Anthony reviewed student work every day, returned it to students the next day with feedback and gave bonus points on major tests to each group based on the number of correct answers given by the entire group.

If the weaker students performed poorly, their performance negatively impacted the group's bonus opportunities so the better performing students had an incentive to help their weaker peers. But because the students were working for bonus points on the test, no one was penalized if her/his group did not do well on the tests. Anthony used the errors he saw students making in this group work and on their daily start-up challenges and adjusted the next day's mini lecture accordingly.

"I figured out early on when I was talking at the front of the room my students weren't really doing the math; I was doing the math,"

Anthony said. "They're the ones who need to do it with me there to monitor and help them if they're going to learn."

This process – a kick-off activity followed by group work – went on each day for the first three days of the week. On day four students completed a 20-minute review activity in groups and took a 20-minute independent test covering the content and skills taught in the three lessons from days one, two and three of the week (with a few review questions from previous units thrown in).

Anthony collected the tests and graded them that night and used the results to break the students into three bigger groups of six to nine students.

The next day in class (the fifth and last day of the week or mini unit) the group of six to nine students with the highest scores on the mini unit test were assigned "challenge" activities requiring them to go beyond what had been taught in class that week with the possibility of earning bonus points for correct solutions to the challenge activities. Some of the students worked on these tasks individually and others worked in groups. They all turned in their completed work at the end of class to be graded.

The six to nine mid-level scorers on the mini unit test were given "extension" activities that reinforced the content and skills at the same level of difficulty demonstrated on the mini unit test.

This same group also worked in small groups of two and three students or singly as they chose and their work was collected at the end of class and graded. Correctly completed "extension" activities could be used to replace incorrect answers on mini unit tests for grading purposes.

Anthony took the remaining six to nine weakest mini unit test performers to the side of the classroom and retaught some of the key concepts they missed on the exam using a different approach. After 12 to 15 minutes of working with the "re-teach group," Anthony circulated in the room to check on student progress for the other groups while the re-teach group completed tasks he would collect and grade to determine whether or not his re-teach efforts were successful.

Again, corrected work on the re-teach activities was used to replace incorrect answers on the mini unit exam for grade book purposes.

MATH: NOT A SPECTATOR SPORT

I had the same experience as Anthony when I was a math teacher in the 1970s. After a long day of teaching at the blackboard and overhead projector, I turned around and realized my math students were just sitting back and watching and listening while I did all the work in the front of the classroom.

Their test scores on unit after unit showed that my hard work was not resulting in their understanding and being able to apply what I had taught. It was discouraging to say the least. I remember one day in frustration blurting out to one of my classes: "Math is not a spectator sport. You can't just sit there and watch me do it."

I assigned and collected homework to be graded, but the students who needed the practice the most didn't usually do the homework or did it in a rush, all wrong but "completed." Going through the motions with their homework was no help to their learning. So I made a huge shift in my teaching approach that paid big dividends in student learning.

I limited myself to two to four days of traditional lecture at the overhead or the blackboard. Then I had the students working on a "practice test" in groups in the classroom with me circulating to offer hints and suggestions. I gave no answers just hints and suggestions.

The practice test was challenging and took the best students in the class two hours or more in the classroom and at home to complete. It had the hardest questions I could find on the topic being taught and I graded these tests (one composite test from each group) and gave bonus points to the groups in the classroom with the best overall practice test score.

These bonus points were used by all the group members as an add-on to their scores on the actual unit test (40 minutes in length or one full class period and including questions of moderate difficulty, similar to the questions students would encounter on the Regents exam at the end of the year).

Frequently, the practice test took one whole week of instructional time and when the week was done as a way to prepare for the actual unit test I gave each student a copy of the practice test's answer key so they could make their own corrections.

Initially, students worked on the practice test only in my classroom. Then one student who wanted to improve his grades convinced me he could learn more if I let him work on the practice test at home. Turns out he received help from his older sister who was a math whiz.

My first reaction on finding this out from another student who felt disadvantaged was horror that I was letting him cheat with help from another student. Then I realized that if he was able to learn the math this way, why not encourage it. So the "practice test" rules changed. It was "anything goes." I didn't care if your sister helped you, your older brother at college, if students worked in groups at home or if parents contributed. All I cared about was whether they could demonstrate on the actual test they had learned the math and could apply it themselves.

All of a sudden my students were arguing over the correct solutions to math problems in the cafeteria, on the bus and in the hallway before school. They were also much more engaged in their math study and more successful on the unit tests.

Anthony's prep test
On day 21 of instruction for the unit on ratios and unit rates, Anthony said he handed out a copy of a preparation test. The prep test included the most challenging problems his students would possibly face on the end-of-unit ratios and unit rates test.

Groups worked together for the next five class periods completing the preparation test. Each student had a copy of the prep test and the group as a whole produced a handwritten copy with answers written by all members of the group on a rotating basis.

Anthony circulated as students worked, offering hints and questions but no answers. They were allowed to use textbooks, notebooks, parents and older siblings, evening phone calls to each other and to older siblings away at college, and even use the Internet to help them complete the prep test.

At the end of class on day five of prep test week (day 25 of the unit), Anthony collected each group's prep test. He graded it that night (learning requires immediate feedback) and returned it to the group with corrected copies for each group member and an answer key for the preparation test. The group grade on the preparation test would correspond to a set of bonus points on the actual individual end-of-unit test.

HOW A 5" X 8" INDEX CARD HELPS INSTRUCTION

Anthony's instructional tactics reminded me of a special education teacher whose classes I observed when I was a high school principal. Her students had trouble remembering details from each unit and organizing the ideas so they could make sense of them for essays that were part of the state exams they had to pass. She encouraged them to create a "cheat sheet" for every subject.

They wrote the details they might need during a unit test and organized them by unit topic on the 5" X 8" card for each corresponding subject. Each student's card was unique based on her/his own memory and test taking issues. They used pictures or diagrams, wrote down words they found difficult to spell, made notes of dates and names. Whatever they needed. And she allowed students to use their 5" X 8" cards when they took their unit test.

I was certain this was cheating and students wouldn't retain enough information to pass the state exam where the "cheat sheets" would be prohibited. But in the end she convinced me that when the end of the year arrived her students would have the information on their 5" X 8" cards committed to memory.

She was right. Her "struggling students" aced the state exam and proved me wrong, ultimately internalizing the information on the cards through repeated use. The 5" X 8" cards were worn and well used by the time the state exam arrived.

Anthony's cards
Using the grading key Anthony provided for the prep test and their own mini unit tests, class notes and corrected copies of the prep test, students worked in groups in class on day 26 of the unit, creating a two-sided

5"X 8" index card with "cheat sheet" type notes for the upcoming individual unit test on ratios and unit rates.

Students crammed in as much information as possible using black ink to fill side one with reminders, notes and problem examples and red ink on the top half of the back to summarize their corrections from key errors on the mini unit tests and the prep test.

The bottom half of the back of the 5" X 8" card was purposely left blank. Anthony circulated and explained errors and corrections from the prep test and shared with the whole class on the overhead good notes he had seen on student 5" X 8" cards.

On day 28, Anthony administered a full period (40 minute) test on ratio and unit rates to all of his sixth grade math classes. This test included questions that reflected Anthony's best guess at what they might encounter on this topic on the end-of-year state math test plus a sprinkling of questions on topics from previous units. Students referred to their 5" X 8" index cards for the unit on ratios and unit rates and for all previously completed units as they took the test.

Some of the teachers in the training were skeptical of his practices, but Anthony explained that he included questions from previous units on all of his unit tests. By having students create these cards and use them throughout the year to study for and take each unit exam they were forcing themselves to remember what was on the cards.

By the end of the year and before the state tests they had committed the cards to memory. In addition, time spent reviewing material was much more efficient when done in short bursts throughout the year rather than all at once at the end of the year.

Unfortunately, despite Anthony's clear understanding of the new Common Core standards and his careful study of the curriculum on the state education department website what he thought would be on the state test was a best guess because Anthony couldn't see real examples of the sixth grade test due to exam security policies.

Anthony said he corrected all of his students' tests that evening, an arduous task of about five hours for the 120 students assigned to his five classes, but he emphasized that this quick turnaround for graded student work was key to his success.

On day 29, Anthony said he divided his class into three groups based on unit test scores.

The "extra challenges" group used the lower half of the back of their 5" X 8" cards to record in blue ink notes on the unit test questions they had missed. They used the remaining time during the next six class days to complete two "expansion" projects similar to those Ruth Weiss did with her class.

Anthony said these projects were selected due to their interesting and motivational nature, their "soft skill" development and their memorability.

Each project included a rigorous scoring rubric students had to familiarize themselves with as they completed independent learning tasks in small groups of two to four students. They earned grade book bonus points for accurately completed project work.

The second group completed the same 5" X 8" card and then completed several sample problems similar to those found on the prep test for the topics they had missed on the unit test, selecting their specific questions from a bank of problems pre-selected by Anthony. Correct answers replaced missed questions on their unit exam for grade book purposes. After this work was done in one to three class periods, this second group completed at least one "expansion" project.

Anthony pulled the last group of six to nine students to the side and retaught one of the pre-selected key concepts many of them had missed on the unit test. He did this every day for the next four days and helped students as they completed the final corrections for their 5" X 8" cards.

They took a quiz every day on the retaught material with review questions and questions from other parts of the unit mixed in and while this quiz was being completed Anthony circulated to offer help to students working on "expansion" projects.

Anthony collected the final quizzes and all the work completed by the other two groups every day and graded it and returned it the next time class met. Correctly completed questions replaced incorrect answers on the unit test in Anthony's grade book. Completed project work earned bonus points for students regardless of which group they were in.

Lastly, Anthony explained that his room was always open for his students before school, during lunch and after school to retake any portion of any exam or quiz and replace any question any student had missed on a test or quiz with a replacement question preapproved by Anthony.

This process could be repeated until the student answered a question correctly or until they were satisfied with their grade. The only expectation was students had to show up in his room with their math notebook showing all the completed homework, quizzes, notes, prep tests, unit tests and 5" X 8" cards. Almost half of Anthony's students had a 4.00 grade-point average for sixth grade math.

"I could never do that," one of the teachers in training said. "I believe in high standards for students and besides these students will have you giving them make-up tests and questions forever if you let them. You're doing too much for them. They need to work harder."

"It's true; I'm working harder to provide added testing opportunities. But they're working harder too," Anthony said. "Actually, the harder I work, the harder they work," he said.

"This new Common Core curriculum and these new tests are difficult and that means students and teachers have to work harder. Students who try a tough test question five times before they get it right work harder than students who get it right on the first try. And in the end the student who tried to answer the question five times knows as much as the student who answered it right on the first try.

"If they have worked harder and they know just as much, why shouldn't they get the same grade?" Anthony asked. "I like to think what I am doing is the definition of having high expectations for all my students."

NOT THE ONLY WAY

Anthony's approach is not the only way to be successful with the Common Core or any challenging set of academic standards. Many theme-based schools, magnet schools and charter schools and many effective teachers in regular public schools combine instructional approaches.

Some common instructional elements are found in all these successful approaches, including:

- Daily multilevel instruction that provides extra challenges for students who are ready for them and re-teaching for students who need it.
- Limited time in whole group lecture.
- More time in individual and small group student work with teachers circulating to coach and support students as they work.
- Authentic assessments that encourage student creativity, problem solving and teamwork.
- Opportunities for students to improve their grades through re-testing.
- Daily corrections of group work and individual student work to provide feedback for student improvement.
- Diagnosis of student learning for instructional adjustments by the teacher.

You have to assess students every day, diagnose learning needs every day and adjust instruction every day. Instruction and assessment are the same thing. You have to know where learners are.

The teachers talk

At 3 p.m. on Friday, the training ended and about a third of the teachers left, but many stayed behind to ask questions of the trainer and Anthony.

I sat in the back of the room with my three principals as quiet as a mouse. When one of my principals started to make a comment, I gestured silently for her to sit back and listen, and we did.

These teachers had grown accustomed to our sitting there. We were not their bosses so my guess was we were hearing real and valuable teacher thoughts and fears about the new Common Core standards, the new tests based on those standards and the teacher evaluation system tied to them. This is what we heard.

First, Ruth, the teacher who wanted to continue using her cadre of expansion projects, expressed her fears about giving up her projects as she switched over to Anthony's approach.

Anthony reassured her that his students did many similar projects and that he would be glad to help her adjust her projects in order to fit as many as possible into his suggested time schedule. Three others asked if they could be part of that ongoing conversation, and they all exchanged email addresses.

Another teacher spoke up. "I want to first apologize if I say this wrong, but I think Anthony's suggested teaching approach amounts to all test prep all the time. Anthony, don't you want to have any say in what you teach these students? You're spending all your time preparing them for this test."

Anthony responded: "Before the Common Core I pretty much followed my textbook and reviewed for the test in March and April. I threw in a few projects I liked at the end of the year after the state test.

"Now, I follow the Common Core guidelines and throw in many of the same projects after the unit tests and at the end of the year. What I'm teaching is not that different from before. It's actually less content now. It's more challenging content and skills but fewer topics. What is really different is how I am teaching with more group work, more re-teaching and a lot more extra challenges and expanded projects for the students who are ready for them."

Anthony admitted that he didn't think he was the one who should be setting the standards for the curriculum and that, that was a job for the state education department. He did, however, want to determine how to teach the standards. He thought his students were working harder and doing more challenging math in his classroom than they were before the Common Core.

Another teacher came back to the grading issue. "Anthony, don't your students just take advantage of you with this constant re-testing and all the chances to improve their grades. Aren't you just giving high grades to students who really don't understand the math?"

"Look, I know it's hard to believe but try it," Anthony said. "Teach one section using this approach for one marking period and review your results. I bet you'll move all your classes to the grading-and-instructional approach I'm advocating after one marking period. You'll see the results in student motivation.

"Yes, some of the students will take advantage," he said, "more than I like to admit, but overall it's worth it because I get so much more out of them on a daily basis."

The proof was in the test scores. Students Anthony initially expected to score 1's or 2's achieved 3's and even 4's on the tests.

"I can set up a grading system where students sometimes take advantage of me but are working hard all the time and learning higher level math or I can set up a grading system that makes certain they don't ever take advantage of me and learn less."

One teacher asked a question I knew from experience was probably a concern for several in our training group. "When I try group work and projects where students are doing more independent tasks on their own without my direct guidance, my students misbehave, joke around and waste time. They don't complete the tasks I set up for them to do. Anthony's approach requires a kind of student that isn't showing up in my classroom."

Ruth responded to the question/comment. "I struggled with the same problem for years until I signed up for a teacher training session offered here by BOCES called Classroom Management for Open-Ended Instruction," she said. "The instructor is great and she provides real strategies that will help you and your students better manage open-ended tasks more effectively. I could never do the projects I do now without those strategies."

Several others who had taken the same training agreed.

A quiet teacher who hadn't spoken at all in three days chimed in. "I wish this training had been available last summer. My students and I would have done better with the state test. But I'm concerned about finding time in my schedule to create three different *lesson plans for three levels of student for every topic and grading all the quizzes and test papers and returning them to students the next day. And unless I missed something, this is necessary to make Anthony's system work."*

Anthony responded. *"The first year is a killer, but I'll be able to re-use 70 percent of what I created for lesson plans last year again this year. The other 30 percent will be new strategies and content. By the way I plan to talk a lot with Ruth about her excellent projects because integrating some of what she has created will be a good part of that 30 percent of the change I'm envisioning."*

Anthony made another suggestion: *"Share lesson planning tasks with the other teachers,"* he said. *"One can produce 'challenge tasks' for this unit, another can produce 'expansion projects' and another can work on organizing activities for re-teaching. Also, I have most of my stuff in Word documents. I can share it electronically."*

The trainer assured everyone she would share Anthony's email address.

"And I spend every available minute during the school day correcting papers so that at night I don't have to take as much home as you might think," Anthony added.

I sit in front of the television with papers to be corrected and correct at every commercial. If I have leftover papers at bedtime I set the alarm a little early to finish them off in the morning. I average one minute per student a day of paper correction time or two hours for my 120 students. And my prep time this first year, without the help of other teachers, was about 90 minutes per day and that was for all three levels. It's hard work, but it's doable."

Then another teacher spoke up. *"Look, I know these new tests and this new curriculum are probably what we should be teaching but this teacher evaluation system isn't fair."*

Another agreed. *"We had no warning and no time to prepare. The new curriculum arrives and with it the new tests and — boom! — our evaluations are pulled down because of student test scores on a test we've never even seen. On top of that, this was the first year our students ever* experienced the Common Core standards. For seven years from pre-k to grade five we have one expectation and all of a sudden in grade six they drop this test on them and on us?! That's not right."

Meanwhile another teacher said her district picked the wrong local tests and 25 percent of the teachers were deemed "ineffective." And this happened in a school district with some of the highest state test scores in the region.

One teacher was obviously angry. "More than half our teachers have no state tests to worry about in their evaluations," she said. "That's totally unfair!"

The first teacher who had spoken on this issue spoke again. "If there's a problem with tenure then fix the tenure law. Why do they have to tie teacher evaluations to brand new tests?"

And her angry friend sitting next to her spat out: "They set the cut scores where they did just to make us all look bad. They knew before the test was given how many students would achieve below proficient. This was rigged. I read it in the newspaper." [xvii]

Then the trainer responded: "You're right this isn't fair, but it is reality. And we can make it work if we follow the curriculum, use the tactics we've talked about these past three days and maintain a positive, professional attitude."

On that note: They all headed home.

LET'S UNPACK AND ANALYZE TEACHER CONCERN

Ruth's concern that she will have to lose all of her creative and motivational projects is real but probably overstated. Anthony integrated a number of projects into his approach and will likely use Ruth's ideas to integrate more.

In the past, Ruth used 100 out of 180 class periods for her projects. Some of this was time wasted.

Meanwhile, Anthony used about 40 class periods for project completion in his first year with the Common Core and will be increasing this to 60 periods with year two's improvements.

If Ruth improved her classroom management and her procedures for moving students through the project work more efficiently, she could keep most of what she does with her projects in this 60-period allotment and at the same time align the projects more closely with the Common Core expectations.

Many teachers need training in classroom management and procedures for open-ended student projects and group activities and a wise principal would organize this type of classroom management training for teachers.

Another place where Anthony manages time well is in his mini lectures. Too many teachers spend too much time lecturing to their students when the students learn better working individually and in groups on the content and skills the curriculum requires. This means fewer and more focused, brief lectures.

Ultimately, Anthony's methods are more time consuming and more challenging for the teacher, but there's no way around it. The daily grind of grading papers and readjusting instruction are a requirement of the job and the job may take more than eight hours a day.

Gains in teacher effectiveness will only come with better planning, daily feedback to students about their learning and fewer long, boring lectures. That goes for every kind of education, every kind of learning, whether it's a doctor trying to educate her/his diabetic patients on how to live healthier lives and mitigate the damage to their overall health and well-being or the algebra teacher trying to educate students in her/his classroom.

PERSONALIZED INSTRUCTION

Anthony's two hours of daily paper correction provides each student in his class with 25 to 30 minutes of individual personalized feedback before the end-of-unit exam is given. That's the data that really needs to be produced and analyzed so that instruction can be differentiated and the education system improved.

As Anthony circulates in his classroom, while his students are completing individual and group work, his students receive more targeted feedback that improves their understanding. Teachers who lecture can try to check for student understanding with oral group and individual questions and verbal and nonverbal responses from students, but nothing beats leaning over a student's shoulder and asking the right question to diagnose student understanding and identify learning roadblocks.

Anthony's daily classroom circulation interactions with his students allow him to offer his students exactly the right personalized hint, encouragement or correction.

Anthony's students have opportunities to improve and correct their errors before the end-of-unit exam and even after that exam because of his re-testing procedures. Contrast Anthony's approach with what happens in most classrooms where students take a unit exam, receive a grade and then move on, and you'll understand why Anthony's a more effective teacher.

Teachers frequently complain students seldom really even read or react to their comments and corrections after hours of paper grading. Why would they? They can't change the past in a test-and-move-on culture.

Anthony's response to the "succumbing to test prep all the time" accusation is on target. This is a very common and important teacher concern.[xviii] His classroom is NOT all test prep all the time. In fact, he's getting students ready for the test by having them take the test and giving them feedback so they can correct their errors. This is how we've all learned everything we know. It's not a new idea.[xix]

The picture Anthony paints of his classroom is a high-energy, not-a-minute wasted, teamwork-oriented learning environment. Yes, class time is focused clearly on the topics and skills that will be measured on the sixth grade Common Core math test. But do we really want Anthony or any other sixth grade math teacher teaching something else?

Anthony is also on target with regard to who should set the standards for the curriculum. The sixth grade math teacher in your local middle school is not the person who should be determining what math skills sixth graders should be learning and the appropriate challenge level of that learning.

Yes, that local math teacher should be as creative and inspiring as possible in seeing to it that her/his students meet and exceed the standards, but s/he should not be deciding the standards.

When we talk about standards we're talking about which basic content and skills are taught and learned. Most sixth grade math teachers are not qualified to make that judgment.

Like Anthony, all teachers have carte blanche when it comes to determining how the curriculum is taught but not what skills and content students are required to learn. That is the job of the state and federal education departments.

But isn't the Common Core a mistake? Aren't a number of states having second thoughts and backing out? Every time New York State increased the expectations for students with Basic Competency Tests in the 1970s, Regents Competency Tests in the 1980s, Regents exam passing grades for all high school graduates in the 1990s and finally No Child Left Behind state tests in the 2000s, many teachers and some parents said our students couldn't pass these tests and pressured the state to give up on the new expectations. And every time these teachers and parents were wrong. We should initially expect lower test proficiency rates, but eventually, as students and teachers adjust to these new expectations, the test results will improve.[xx] For once, let's be patient.

COMMON CORE MYTHS

The Common Core standards are not a mistake despite their recent decrease in popularity.[xxi] Myths about the Common Core standards and their failure are prevalent but mostly misguided.[xxii] The standards are tied to a new, more challenging curriculum more in line with the academic expectations for students in countries that outperform the U.S. on international achievement tests and more in line with the expectations of the global workplace and for good citizenship for the future. These standards are "rigorous and traditional" according to Michael Petrelli of the Fordham Institute.[xxiii] Many teachers who initially resisted the Common Core are now proponents.[xxiv] And, when all is said and done, the U.S. student testing system is not all that onerous.[xxv]

Good arguments can be made that changing the standards and increasing test difficulty by themselves won't raise achievement and that we should have just used one of the sets of standards already in place in our most effective states like Massachusetts. Unfortunately, we didn't just duplicate what was working in Massachusetts, and we're now far enough down the road we should continue rather than change directions yet again.

One of the biggest reasons why U.S. efforts at education reform over the past 40 years have failed time and again is unnecessary changes in direction as soon as we encounter reform difficulties. And then there's the excuse that the Common Core is taking all the fun and tradition out of school.[xxvi] Of course, that excuse is probably coming from some folks who would rather waste a couple of weeks getting ready for the holiday pageant.

And then there's the real truth: "There's nothing wrong with teaching to the test if it's a good test." Pearson's tests are far from perfect, but they are better in terms of the content and skills expected of students at each grade level than the tests they're replacing.

Some school districts, schools, teachers and students who normally rank as superior in student achievement (at least in their own minds) are struggling with the implementation of Common Core which has been much too rapid in some states like my home state of New York. But it is also true that these "superior" students and schools could achieve more.[xxvii]

The politically motivated Common Core implementation calendar set by New York State's governor, by the New York State Board of Regents and by our drive-by education commissioners was poorly timed and implemented. But a poor implementation calendar doesn't mean we should abandon a positive, long overdue change in the curriculum.

DO MORE OF THE RIGHT THINGS AT THE RIGHT TIME

This new curriculum asks students to do more of the right things at the right time. For example, in sixth grade math the students being taught Common Core standards are being asked to solve algebraic equations with pictures and graphs and with symbolic variables that create abstract equations. This was previously found in the eighth and ninth grade math curriculum.

Frequently, the equations U.S. students saw in their eighth or ninth grade textbooks prior to Common Core were solved without the pictures or graphs and only with abstract equations with variables. Using these pictures and graphs at the sixth grade level helps students understand more fully what the equations with variables mean and introduces them to algebra at an earlier grade level.

The math skills our sixth grade students are now learning are being taught in Japan, Korea, China and Finland – to the highest scoring math students in the world.

The same can be said for Common Core level expectations in English language arts. Before the "Every Student Succeeds Act" replaced the No Child Left Behind Act in 2015,[xxviii] New York State planned to implement Common Core level science and social studies standards that were designed to mesh with the higher standards in math and ELA. Our students and teachers can and should be achieving at these levels with this more challenging content and skills, but it will take time.

Meanwhile, jumping to firm conclusions about teacher and student performance in the first year of new tests is clearly premature. Unfortunately, in the meantime some of the parents who think their children are math, English, science and social studies stars on the world stage will be finding out otherwise for a while as we get our house in order.

That's no reason to abandon the Common Core. Did parents really think we could increase the challenge level of the curriculum and not have their students bringing home homework problems and assignments the parents didn't recognize? That's nonsensical. [xxix]

Teacher concern about the time required for paper grading and lesson planning for three different levels of students in each class is valid. Most full-time middle school and high school teachers in the U.S. teach students in their classrooms between three-and-a-half and four-and-a-half hours a day, usually in five or six classes of 40 to 50 minutes each.

While some schools have different block schedules with longer periods, the total contact teaching time for middle and high school teachers remains in the three-and-a-half hour to four-and-a-half hour range. Most middle school and high school teachers also have a duty/supervision assignment for lunchroom, bus supervision, study halls, etc., of 30 minutes to one hour each day.

Anthony said he spent two hours a day grading papers and one and a half hours per day doing lesson planning. All told, he and his peers with similar schedules would be putting in about eight to ten hours per day to complete these tasks with some of this preparation and paper grading time done in school and some at home.

Elementary teachers spend an average of 30 to 60 minutes more per day teaching their students (most have no duty/assignment or a shorter duty period) and probably spend 30 to 60 minutes less per day on average committed to paper grading (fewer students) and preparation (much less challenging content and skills).

Note: Anthony has voluntarily extended his work day beyond the hours outlined here by giving his students opportunities to re-test on questions they missed on tests and quizzes. In any case, this is not an excessive, burnout type of schedule for a professional like a doctor, a lawyer, an engineer, an architect, a dentist or a teacher.

As a teacher, assistant principal, principal, assistant superintendent and superintendent throughout my career, I worked ten to 12 hours a day during the school year with seven to eight hour days per day throughout the summer (I worked every summer.), and I had normal vacations and weekends off. All professionals should expect this type of work schedule.

However, some teachers see this issue differently. Some teacher contracts in the strong union states describe "five 42-minute class periods of instruction, one 42-minute supervision period, one 42-minute preparation period and one duty free lunch period of 30 minutes." Some teachers and their union representatives have tried to take this to mean that all the preparation activities and paper grading must be accomplished in that 42-minute preparation period. Not so.

In addition to the three to four hours per day of preparation and paper correcting time, teacher leaders need to work the equivalent of one full month of the present two-month summer break to improve curriculum and testing for their schools. Some other selected teachers with the best skills for re-teaching should be working with the students who are struggling during one month to six weeks of the summer break to help those students catch up.

Those teachers selected to work these extra leadership roles and complete extra summer teaching assignments should be paid extra for their additional time and efforts, creating a new rung on the career ladder for teachers so that all teachers are not paid the same wage based solely on their time in the job and their educational level (masters, doctorate, graduate credit hours, etc.).

THE ELEPHANT IN THE ROOM

As to the "elephant in the room" – tying teacher evaluations to test scores – the answer is both complex and simple. The simple part is that the standardized test scores achieved by any teacher's students must be an integral part of how that teacher's performance is evaluated. When I worked as a high school principal, I always checked high school exit exam performance for students whose teachers I supervised.

Frequently, these exam results produced questions and surprises for me. Why did the students of a social studies teacher I observed using good teaching strategies perform at lower levels than expected on the Regents exam? Why had the students of a math teacher I observed to be a lackluster performer in the classroom outperform others in classes of his colleagues with seemingly better instructional strategies and work ethics? Why had the students of a teacher I considered one of my best teachers and whose students always performed well on the Regents exams taken a sudden dive after five years of exemplary performance?

* It is statistically very difficult to exclusively use high school exit exams and grade three to eight end-of-year bubble sheet math and English language arts tests to develop sound conclusions about teacher effectiveness.

* The student sample sizes are too small and the sample variability is too large to draw immediate conclusions.

A fourth grade teacher with a weak class of 24 students this year will look a lot worse in comparison to her/his much stronger class of 24 last year. The statistical projected growth measurements for students (most frequently called value-added), which take into account each student's prior exam performances, can take the rough edges off of this discrepancy.

However, a few students moving one way or the other in a group of 15 to 30 – due to a variety of student personal issues like a serious student or parent illness, a divorce, a family move, a lost job for a parent – can quickly change students and teachers from "good performers" to "bad performers" on test measurement scales.

Three consecutive years of strong or weak performance in a row for a teacher with math or English language arts tests means much more than one year by itself.

Anthony, like most middle school math and English language arts teachers and some high school teachers, has 120 students taking the test at the end of the year so the initial assumption would be that statistically this is enough of a database to make a solid conclusion about his teaching effectiveness.

However, the variability of one sixth grade group of 120 students to another group of 120 and the variability that came with the new untried Common Core tests with the new curriculum would still leave me hesitant to jump to firm conclusions after just one year.

Two years of consistent strong or weak performance at this level with this number of students is a better base for a principal to use to make decisions about teacher effectiveness and instructional improvement goals and strategies for principals and teachers.

Even after two years I would be looking at the transition time from the old curriculum and tests to the new curriculum and Common Core tests and giving most teachers the benefit of the doubt until I saw a third consecutive year of weak performance. And the fact that the new Common Core tests are not available to teachers and principals makes this transition time longer.

Teachers whose classroom tactics result in poor test scores are usually spending too much time teaching skills and content not on the test and not enough time teaching skills and content that are on the test. There is also frequently an old textbook, curriculum, syllabus or old lesson plan involved.

Conversely, the teacher whose students outperform a principal's expectations based on classroom observations has probably done a good job of teaching the skills and content tested and has allocated her/his time for each skill area properly.

To overcome this problem principals and teachers have to examine the test data, single out specifically where student performance is falling short and create a more effective timeline for instruction throughout the year. The hard part will be getting good teachers to stop teaching topics and units that are not tested and focus in depth on the topics being tested.

Most states and our federal government have spent a lot of money hiring experts to determine what topics should be taught and for how long and at what grade level. If each teacher follows the state level curriculum and their peers at other grade levels do the same, their students will receive the comprehensive preparation they need. Stopping effective teachers from teaching everything in the textbook rather than what's in the curriculum is hard, but it is a critical task for the principal whose role it is to improve instruction and results.

One strategy principals can use to help this process is to get all the teachers at a grade level (all the fourth grade math teachers, all the sixth grade math teachers, etc.) together for a day every semester or every quarter if possible with substitute coverage for the teachers or on a day over the summer or during a school break to do the critical curriculum weeding and share teaching strategies and projects, tests and instructional materials.

These efforts will be more valuable if teacher coaches (trainers who are not the teachers' supervisors, who do not complete teacher evaluations and who understand the elements of good teaching, the new curriculum and the tests) are in the room to help them and if one of the teachers receives a stipend to be a teacher leader for their group.

Principals and department chairpersons should join these groups for a half hour at the beginning and end of their full day's work to offer support and guidance, but the administrators should leave these tasks to the teachers as much as possible.

The "local" testing component used for teacher evaluations in New York State was obviously a compromise negotiated between the state level teacher union, the governor and the state education department to soften the blow of using the Common Core tests as part of teacher evaluations.

The union had an understandable concern that the Common Core tests would be too difficult and, as a result, too many teachers being unfairly evaluated as "ineffective" or "developing" during the early implementation phase.

It turned out to be a bad compromise. Many districts used packaged computerized tests that were designed to mirror the expectations on the end-of-year Common Core tests only to find that these "local" tests, which were supposed to help teachers identify skills for re-teaching their students, produced scores that artificially lowered teacher evaluations.

In the end, a better solution is for principals and the state to use multiple years of student performance for teacher evaluation purposes and to implement an exam process with prep tests and re-testing possibilities to avoid the contamination of the instructionally valid process of re-testing and re-teaching that comes with using these tools for teacher evaluation.

As for the percentage of a teacher's evaluation that should come from these student test results, the jury is still out on that and some experts think this whole idea of teacher evaluations based on student test performance is unfair and misguided. However, my experience tells me 30 to 50 percent of the teacher's evaluation should be based on student test scores once everyone has confidence in the tests and knows the expectations.

What about merit pay for teachers whose students score well on the exams? Until we have some data that says the new Common Core standards are paying off with higher student achievement, and that the new teacher evaluations based on student test scores prove reliable and valid, we should wait with that bonus money for teachers whose students score better on the tests. When the data shows consistent reliability, then we can consider the bonus option, but the option had better take into account student poverty. In truth, I would rather first see any "bonus" money going to teachers who effectively provide leadership for their peers as they implement and adjust to the Common Core or who provide extra "catch-up" instruction to students who struggle.

The present data on the PISA, one of the international tests used to compare U.S. math performance to other countries, with 34 countries and 50 states (84 total), shows Massachusetts ranked number seven in the list of 84 and Mississippi ranked 82 in the same list of 84.[xxx] Interestingly, the variability between poor and wealthy school districts in both states is four to five times as great as their state-to-state comparisons.

In other words, students from poverty in both our highest performing state and our lowest performing state do much worse than students from wealth and advantage in the same states. But surprisingly, U.S. students who come from the most educated homes don't compare well with their peers from other countries.

The teacher concern about cut scores being set by the state at artificially high levels which were designed to produce predictable student failure and teacher embarrassment is inaccurate but understandable. New York State attempted to set the cut scores for proficient levels of student test performance on the new Common Core tests at the same levels as proficient levels on the international tests used for country-to-country comparisons since the 1970s (NAEP, PISA, TIMSS).

Bear in mind: Putting in place new standards and curricula along with more challenging tests will not by itself raise student achievement. Educators – teachers and principals – have to change their practices. Tests and curricula are just the targets.

In the first year of implementation with the Common Core and the new tests it was reasonable to assume that student performance would improve only slightly or not at all. Since mathematical correlations of what had been labeled proficient on the old tests as to compare international tests already existed it wasn't hard to estimate what percentage of New York State students would score at proficient on the new Common Core tests.

The testing "experts" who designed the test knew ahead of time students who performed at 80 percent proficient on the previous standards would only be 40 percent proficient on the new standards. Test developers and the state education department knew only 35 to 40 percent of students would test as proficient or better.[xxxi] And that's exactly what happened.

The students didn't know any less, but the new tests showed 35 to 40 percent were proficient or better statewide and the old tests showed 75 to 80 percent were proficient or better with just about the same level of academic skills being demonstrated by the students on both tests.

It's not hard to understand teachers' concerns about these new tests making students and teachers look bad, but the international comparison data showed for years that only 35 to 40 percent of New York State students were proficient on more difficult tests. We just replaced our old easier exams with a test more in line with the existing international benchmarks. This change was poorly explained by the state education department, the media and the politicians looking for an opportunity to play both sides of this divisive issue.

Both Anthony and Ruth mentioned the value of student project work in their classes. This brings us back to Jim McMahon's play and the use of authentic assessments for student academic work. Is there any role for authentic assessments in our move to a Common Core curriculum and new more challenging tests or are we stuck with "succumbing to test prep all the time?"

CAN AUTHENTIC ASSESSMENTS ACTUALLY WORK?

When I worked as an assistant superintendent in New Rochelle City School District outside of New York City, the New York State Education Department was run by two commissioners with somewhat different mindsets regarding student testing and evaluation.

Tom Sobol brought in some very interesting ideas that included the possibility that authentic assessments of students' academic work like Jim McMahon's play should somehow be integrated into the testing and evaluation process leading to high school graduation.

Commissioner Sobol created an opportunity for school districts to apply for waivers that allowed them to replace a portion of the bubble sheet tests with authentic assessments scored with elaborate and very specific rubrics designed by professionals in the school districts.

Sobol's successor, Richard Mills, started his tenure as a commissioner supportive of authentic assessments. However, Commissioner Mills also oversaw the implementation of new Regents exam graduation standards. The new exams meant a significant increase in the academic skills required for a high school diploma.

With the new reportedly harder tests being phased in, Commissioner Mills came under pressure from politicians, psychometricians, testing companies and lawyers who worked for the New York State Education Department to eliminate the possibility of any type of waivers from any portion of the traditional standardized testing.

The New York State Education Department's lawyers feared lawsuits from parents of students who didn't graduate due to failure on new and tougher required Regents exams and exam reliability was a key to their defense.

Assessing students' work on a play was too unreliable to defend in court, and Commissioner Mills withdrew his support for authentic assessments. In my experience, school district and state education department lawyers seldom lose because they seldom fight. These lawyers seem to me from 40-plus years of watching them too eager to sidestep any conflict even when the fight is difficult but worth the cost.

During the two-year gap in time between Commissioner Sobol's waiver opportunity introduction and Commissioner Mills capitulation to the education department's lawyers, I worked with a large team of teachers, department chair people and principals at New Rochelle and applied for and received approval for 13 waivers to integrate a variety of authentic assessments into the state required student testing and assessment system for the New Rochelle City School District.

One of the most successful authentic assessments was a project at Isaac Young Middle School where eighth grade accelerated Regents Biology students completed research projects with doctors who worked at the Sound Shore Medical Center in New Rochelle. The hospital was within walking distance of the school.

Isaac Young was the city's most diverse middle school with a student population including 30 to 40 percent middle class and upper middle class whites, Hispanics, African Americans and Asians mixed with a larger number of lower income and poverty students of the same racial diversity.

Students substituted an authentic assessment research project in place of 12 multiple choice questions. The switch amounted to 20 out of the total of 100 points on the traditional bubble sheet Biology Regents exams. Each student had a doctor-mentor and the project included lab work, data collection and analysis, a written paper with conclusions and a public oral presentation (sometimes in both English and Spanish).

The rubrics used to evaluate student work were elaborate and time consuming to implement. The effort by the teachers and the principal was enormous. The oral presentations showed off these wonderfully diverse students dressed in white lab coats with ties and business attire and their computer PowerPoints. The applause and beaming students and parents at the end of these presentations brought back the goosebumps and memories of Jim McMahon's students and their play performance.

Over my career I have led many groups of international teachers and principals on tours of our U.S. schools. Since the students from many of the countries that send these visitors outperform U.S. students on international exams, I initially wondered why they were visiting us when we should have been visiting them.

It turned out they wanted to understand why American schools produce so many students who excelled in creative enterprises like entrepreneurship, the arts and scientific research.

Which approach to student academic assessment will maintain and enhance this unique strength of U.S. students? Jim's play and the Biology research projects at Isaac Young Middle School or long lectures followed by drill and practice bubble sheet tests?

I've often wondered how many of those Isaac Young Middle School students are doctors today and would cite this project as the beginning of their pursuit of a medical career. I don't wonder how many remember the experience. I know – they all remember it.

I also believe strongly that whether they chose a career as a doctor, a lawyer, a teacher, an engineer or anything really, participation in this assessment became a formative part of how they saw themselves as learners.

But didn't we sacrifice some of the reliability of the traditional bubble sheet Biology Regents exam? Yes, probably one to three percent, but wasn't it worth the small loss in reliability?

Scaling authentic assessments

So how could we bring these ideas up to scale so that students, parents, teachers and the public are supportive of academic testing and assessment? Our goals need to include using the student assessment process as a way to boost student achievement and motivation to learn, as well as improve the image students have of themselves as learners (like Jim's play). The following should be part of any improvement plan:

- Maintain a base of psychometrically reliable student academic performance measures that allow us to be certain all schools are growing and no populations – not minorities, poor students, special education students or anyone else – is being left behind due to weak or fuzzy standards. If you don't think our student standards and achievement levels are too low for today's global economy, check out what Fareed Zakaria has to say in the Washington Post.[xxxii]

- Dramatically reduce the time and cost of the bubble sheet tests and tell the test makers (and their competitors) the tests must be 60 minutes total for English language arts in grades three through eight and an additional 60 minutes for math once a year. The results of these tests should be made public just as they are now except that the scoring should be completed within two weeks of test administration and the results made public no later than one month after the test's administration so that teachers completing assessment and instructional improvement planning work over the summer have access to the test results. We also need to make all the tests public immediately after the tests are given (minus any field test questions) to help guide instructional improvements.

* Require high school teachers to replace up to 20 percent of their standardized test (Regents exams in New York State) with a project like the one we completed at Isaac Young Middle School with eighth grade biology students. These projects with their detailed scoring rubrics could be drawn from a bank of state education department approved projects or created by classroom teachers and submitted to the state education department project bank for advance approval.

* Encourage elementary and middle school teachers to create their own English language arts, math, science and social studies related projects with the same elaborate scoring rubrics and share approved projects on the state education department website with teacher-authors named and recognized. Adventurous states should include students' scores on these projects in their grade three to eight English language arts and math public test performance reports.

Many teachers (not all) would compete to create and submit to the state education department interesting and educationally valid projects utilizing unique local opportunities and partnerships that create challenging learning opportunities, memorability, goosebumps and beaming smiles from teachers, students and parents.

The teacher concern that more than half of the teachers – physical education, art, music and vocational teachers – have no state tests for their students that will impact their teacher evaluations is actually an advantage for the school, for the students and for their teachers.

For some teachers like high school music and art teachers, vocational teachers and physical education teachers this lack of state testing gives them the freedom to create and implement challenging rigorous authentic assessments throughout the school year and as capstone activities for the courses they teach.

Imagine the learning excitement that could be created with a system of carefully structured rigorous, authentic assessments with well-designed scoring rubrics and public presentations and demonstrations of student academic work. For teachers whose jobs involve preparing students for exit exams to be taken in later years in high school (English 9, Social Studies 9, etc.), authentic assessments throughout the year can be integrated with instructional and exit test scaffolding, which is already a common practice whereby instruction is broken down into smaller increasingly challenging steps that lead logically to exit test levels.

Scaffolding instruction contains exams with questions that lead up to what's required on a final course – or in New York State a Regents – exam. It works by asking students to answer part of a more complicated question that they'll eventually have to answer fully on the final exam, thereby teaching them the structure of a question and the characteristics of the best answers.

The principal's job becomes making certain that all of these measures of student academic performance are rigorous and emphasize essential content and skills (including required math and English language arts skills). The principal should also be checking to ensure these authentic assessments are memorable and achieve student growth on the "soft" skills: motivation, confidence, teamwork, communication and perception of oneself as a self-correcting learner. And, of course, student performance on these measures should count in the teacher's evaluation.

While some educators would abandon the Common Core standards and the push for better standardized tests (See Diane Ravitch's 2010 book *The Death and Life of the Great American School System* and her opinion piece in *The New York Times*.[xxxiii]), I believe we need stronger, simpler, shorter and cheaper standardized tests coupled with world class authentic assessments.

Politicians Need Not Apply

• • •

TODAY, AFTER ALL MY YEARS in leadership positions, I see successful leadership much the same way Steve Jobs saw technology; it's nothing without creativity.

My epiphany came in the late 80s while I was painting watercolors in the evenings, a hobby I'd developed with encouragement, coaching and support from a friend who happened to be a high school art teacher.

Around the same time I started painting, I was grappling with an attendance problem at the high school where I was principal. The teachers complained they couldn't get more students to do better academically unless they showed up for class. If you looked at the data, there was a direct correlation between poor attendance and poor grades on report cards and on test scores. Other schools were having the same problem and responding with attendance policies requiring students to attend class at least 85 percent of the time or lose credit in the course. I pushed hard to put one of these time-in-seat policies in place and after a long discussion the school board and superintendent reluctantly agreed.

At that time I saw all problems like Newtonian physics problems. A projectile is shot from a gun at ground level at an angle of 42 degrees above the horizon with a velocity of 500 meters per second. Ignoring air friction and assuming the terrain is level, how far in meters from the gun will the projectile hit the ground? This perspective helps to solve some problems, is essential at some point in solving most problems but is totally useless in helping to see problems from a different perspective.

The attendance policy accomplished nothing more than added administrative work, time spent tracking student attendance and making legally required complicated arrangements for students to make up classes when they were legitimately sick or otherwise legally absent.

HAPPY ACCIDENTS

When I decided to start painting, the linear side of my brain tried to control the process. I read every book I could find on the subject. But in the end I discovered I made my greatest gains by just letting the paint fly. My best paintings came from "happy accidents," the watercolor painter's term for mistakes that actually make the painting better than anything they could have planned.

I was trying to paint a rural landscape for three hours straight one weekend when, without thinking, my mind shifted gears and I saw the painting in a whole new light. I guess I was training my brain to see things differently because the next week I saw attendance differently.

I asked myself: "What do we need to change in the high school to make the students who skip so many classes and so many days of school feel it was worth being there more often despite the fact that they dislike school?"

At the same time I was painting in the evening, during the day I was working on a project that had been rolling around in my mind for several months – a true alternative program for our high school. The kind of program that approached school like a job, something our most disengaged students might see as more worthy of their time.

ONE GOOD THING LEADS TO ANOTHER

While I was working on the alternative program, two teachers decided to experiment with cooperative learning, which meant fewer lectures and more group work with mixed ability teams of four students working together for the entire school year.

I viewed it as just another bright idea that would create more work rather than produce solutions. Kind of like the attendance policy. And then – happy accident.

Their experiment worked. Toward the end of the year, students were voluntarily coming to school on "non-school" days. Attendance had turned around.

As we looked around the teachers' huge double classroom at the nearly 100 students working together intently in their groups, we were astounded by the level of student motivation and the quality of support the students were offering each other.

Many of these students had been apathetic about school, just going through the motions enough to keep their parents and the teachers off their backs, and many of them had attendance issues that plagued the entire school. Now, they were all voluntarily doing extra review work before the exam and actively helping their peers. We weren't surprised when the failure rate on the exam dropped by 28 percent and the scores of over 90 points on the 100 point test increased by 22 percent compared to the previous school year.

Part of being a good leader is being a good problem solver. And part of being a good problem solver is recognizing the opportunities that present themselves. Not only have we failed to do that in education, we have been on a journey of solving the wrong problems in schools and in many cases by doing so have completely derailed educational improvement. And when someone comes in and tries to identify and solve the right problem, they're much too frequently derailed as well. Debbie Fortunato found that out the hard way.

(Sections in italics are fictional stories made from composites of multiple actual experiences.)

Solving the wrong problem
Tom Galvin and I first met at a sectional finals boys' basketball game when we were both high school principals. He was in his fifth year as principal of Rosemont High School, and I was a principal in year 12 at a high school 30 miles east of Rosemont. Neither of our schools'

basketball teams had made it to the sectionals, but we both knew the rival principals whose schools were playing so we came to the game to see how the contest would turn out for our colleagues' schools.

Tom was the adult version of "big man on campus." With his six foot three inch athletic frame, wavy black hair and good looks, he was a charmer with an Irish sense of humor, a natural born leader, if such a thing exists. He kidded loudly with the other high school principals sitting together in the stands as he made fun of our teams' athletic ineptitudes and coaching disasters that had led to our status as spectators at this game. What made his kidding tolerable was the way he made comments about his own team's missteps with the same gusto that he criticized ours.

The next time I saw Tom was 10 years later at a superintendents' statewide conference. I was heading toward an early retirement from my superintendent duties precipitated by my first heart attack and heart surgery, and Tom was in the middle of his seventh year as a superintendent at Rosemont where he had moved up to the superintendent position at age 39 directly from his position in the district as high school principal. We ended up at dinner together with a bunch of other superintendents with Tom seated next to me. He still showed the same wit, charm and people skills I had seen much earlier in his career, but he seemed more subdued, not as engaged in the conversation as he was 10 years earlier at the basketball game.

He asked if we could meet for lunch on the next and final day of the conference so he could get my thoughts on "some issues in my district," he said. As one of the senior superintendents with one of the largest school districts in the region, such requests were not unusual.

At lunch Tom opened up more than he had in our previous encounters. He had been an excellent high school athlete in football and basketball and captain of both teams his senior year in high school. He had gone to the State University of New York at Cortland and majored in history and social studies education while playing football on their very competitive Division III team. His simple career plan was to become a high school social studies teacher and football coach.

When Tom entered the teaching profession in 1978 his skill set and aspirations lined up nicely with the needs of a number of suburban school systems like Rosemont and he landed his dream job that summer. For 10 years, Tom was a successful football coach. He was also a respected social studies teacher for the first seven of these years and then assistant principal for the last three of these years. In his 10 years of coaching, Tom's football teams had winning records every year, made it to the sectional playoffs eight of the years and won the sectional B class title twice, something that never happened in Rosemont before Tom's arrival.

Football is not that important

Tom loved coaching football but in the end he took the promotions – first to principal and later to superintendent – because he wanted the extra pay and in part because he felt his close friend and trusted assistant coach, Kevin Talbot, was ready to step in and take over the leadership of the football program.

Unfortunately, 10 years into this arrangement Kevin had fewer than 50 percent wins and only one playoff appearance to show for it, which prompted Todd Morgan to run for a seat on the school board.

Todd Morgan's son, starting tailback on the Pop Warner football team, would be on the JV football team next year and Todd wanted to be sure his son received lots of positive publicity as a varsity football player at Rosemont that might lead to a college scholarship.

Tom was clearly torn between his loyalty to his former assistant coach, Kevin, and his disappointment in the team's recent performance, not to mention the conflict it would cause him with this new school board member. Tom's question for me, "What would you do with Kevin and the football coaching position?"

I tried to steer Tom away from his question with some questions of my own about the academic success of the high school, Kevin Talbot's

*teaching skills and the goals of the school board in his district, but Tom
was persistent: "What would you do about Kevin?" he asked again.*

*In the end, I told Tom that football was important but not that
important and it was distracting him and his school board. Kevin had
his chance, time for another coach. See if Kevin will resign so you won't
end up with a public relations mess because he surely has supporters
after all these years with the football program.*

THE BAD NEWS

The bad news for Rosemont High was that Tom Galvin was ever even
considered for the position of superintendent. Tom was one of the good
old boys (and girls as this type of leadership weakness is clearly not gender
specific) that populate too many of the school superintendent positions in
the U.S.[xxxiv] He was endowed with the outward characteristics of wit and
charm – two attributes that serve one well in interviews for superintendent
positions but do little for the school district down the road.

School board members immediately understand superintendent candidates like Tom who make them feel comfortable and secure. Meanwhile,
they're completely unaware that Tom totally lacks the necessary ethics, attention to detail, high expectations for staff, curiosity and the ability to simultaneously maintain both a holistic perspective on the issues facing the district and
a detailed perspective on leadership challenges critical to effective leadership.

The Tom Galvin's of the education system are first and foremost political survivors who can read the political winds and find a way to stay ahead
of them so that they may keep their jobs.

While the School Superintendent was tackling the problem of how to
win more football games, a new high school principal, Debbie Fortunato,
was trying to raise the visibility of academics.

Principal Fortunato and the mysterious dropout rate
*I first met Debbie Fortunato after I had retired. I volunteered as a
panelist reviewing an oral presentation of an educational doctoral*

dissertation by a State University of New York at Albany graduate student. Debbie was a member of the audience for the presentation and a doctoral student herself. When she found out who I was she approached me during a break in the action with a request to meet and discuss her career options?" As with Tom Gavin, I agreed.

We met at a local Starbuck's where she gave me an hour-long earful on life and on education. She seemed to have what it takes to be a great principal and eventually an outstanding superintendent.

When Debbie Fortunato was hired as principal of Rosemont High School, Tom Galvin's school district, a few of the teachers on one of the interview committees and some of the school board members who interviewed principal candidates made it clear they thought Rosemont High School needed an academic shot in the arm. The curriculum, schedule and teaching methods were essentially the same as they had been 30 years earlier when Superintendent Galvin was a social studies teacher. Hiring from outside was rare for this district, but the previous principal had retired suddenly because of a health problem and no one had been groomed for succession.

In her interviews, none of the interview team members mentioned test data, but Debbie had done her homework and she knew the test scores were weaker than she would have anticipated for this mostly high rent suburban district. Also, fewer Rosemont students took AP tests than she would be expected given the district's demographic data.

Furthermore, more Rosemont students failed required end-of-course Regents exams and fewer Rosemont students scored at high levels on these tests, as compared to similar districts. Also, fewer Rosemont students went on from high school to competitive colleges, SAT scores were lower than a trained observer would have expected and the number of graduates didn't match up with the number of dropouts listed. Either some students were missing in action or the dropout rate was worse than reported.

In Debbie's interview, Tom Galvin made it clear he thought academic improvement was important, but he also thought the crux of the problem was poor public relations. The district needed to polish its image.

After she was hired, Debbie analyzed the academic performance data in depth and presented her findings to Superintendent Galvin. Her data showed that the mysterious dropout rate data issue was caused by 15 to 20 students per year who were transferred into a local GED program where they never achieved a diploma. These "transfers" artificially kept the dropout numbers down.

"You can transfer them anywhere you want on paper but they're still dropouts," she said.

Meanwhile, according to the state education department, these transfers should actually be counted as dropouts. Debbie asked Tom Galvin how she should handle it, but she received more of a warning than a response.

"The school board knows about those transfers," Galvin said. "We certainly don't need bad public relations about more dropouts. We need to pass our budget in May and if we don't, you'll take the heat."

When Debbie raised concerns about the AP program with too few students taking the challenging AP tests and Regents and SAT scores that were too low Tom Galvin said: "I'll support any changes you need to make to improve the high school academic results as long as you can do it with the existing budget. Just let me be the one who talks to the school board about it. Don't contact any of the board members, and if one of them calls you or emails you or tries to meet with you just tell them to contact me immediately. Understood?"

Hiding the data

Tom Galvin didn't want to see the real data, and he made sure the school board felt the same way. Superintendent Galvin, fearful of how this performance data would reflect on him personally since he was the principal while this data was turning sour, relied on his political skills to, well, sweep it under the rug.

School superintendents who rely exclusively on their political skills, while ignoring important data, delegating critical leadership tasks and failing to communicate effectively with the school board and the public about these issues, set the stage for chaos among school board members. Think of the most ridiculous day on the floor of the U.S. Congress. You get the idea, in microcosm, multiplied by far too many school districts in the nation.

IGNORING THE TOOLS AT HAND

Making sure the trains run on time and on the best possible schedule for the riders (in the case of schools, students) is one of the essential skills for education leadership, and it requires values such as patience, persistence and attention to detail. For example, the task of building the high school master schedule presents a great leadership opportunity for the high school principal. Unfortunately, it's usually delegated to someone who can be manipulated by adults looking for the easiest schedule possible.

The impact of delegating the high school master schedule is twofold: There's no innovation (not even good management for the benefit of the students), and the staff who know how important the schedule is become disenfranchised by the leadership's unwillingness to recognize its importance.

Meanwhile, a 30 or 50 hour time investment developing a brand new master schedule that assigns the time blocks, rooms and teachers for classes results in fewer students losing courses due to conflicts.

Simply reusing the previous year's master schedule and just making a few tweaks means the schedule moves further and further away from the ideal every year. Most principals just use last year's schedule and assign to another employee – a guidance counselor, an assistant principal, a secretary – the responsibility of making a few minor adjustments to accommodate changes required by new courses, room renovations, teacher retirements, lunch, etc.

And the task of creating the master schedule usually falls to someone who gains an unnatural level of power that can cause problems. And that's a leadership failure.

If the calculus teacher wants to eat lunch every day with the band teacher because they are friends, they will ask the assistant principal creating the master schedule to ensure this is set in the schedule. If the assistant principal completing the master schedule accommodates this request, a careful analysis of the data will probably reveal that this accommodation increases conflicts for students and three or four students will have to choose between calculus or band or some other course in their schedule.

Ditto for the teacher who wants his prep period at the end of the day so he can duck out early to pick up his son at child care, the teacher who wants her prep and lunch periods together so she can help out at her mother's place of business in midday. You know the drill.

I've met many superintendents and principals who struggle with the intricate analysis of complicated operational, academic and financial data required to make critical decisions in their jobs. Most of them were hired for political reasons and survived by delegating complicated tasks to smart employees who would give them easy-to-understand talking points and key conclusions to guide their communication with students, parents, employees, the school board and the public.

These talking points were designed to hide their ignorance about the nuts and bolts of completing the tasks they had delegated.

Relying on staff in schools for essential detail work has exacted a price paid by the students' education. The only thing worse than using staff to do this data work is trying to fake it on important data-laden issues, an act I have sadly witnessed on more than one occasion.

How real educational change happens

Principal Debbie Fortunato gladly agreed to let Superintendent Galvin deal with the school board. It gave her the freedom she needed to move the high school where it needed to go. She enjoyed working with teachers and students, not school board members.

Immediately after meeting with the superintendent, Debbie met with her department chairs and teacher leaders in each subject area who taught a full schedule and received a stipend (in too many schools improvement isn't part of a teacher's usual role) for providing input on plans to improve academics at Rosemont High School.

First, Debbie shared with this group the data she had uncovered regarding student academic performance, the steep decline in honors numbers as students moved from ninth grade to twelfth grade, which led to the low AP exam participation numbers; the weak test scores on Regents exams; and the hidden dropouts.

"This is something we all knew and we understood," the chair of the math department said. "It's also something Superintendent Galvin and the previous high school principal, Tom Meacher, also understood. Everyone just wanted us to paper over it and act like it didn't exist."

"The practice of listing those dropouts as transfers to the local GED program started when Tom Galvin was assistant principal at Rosemont High 20 years ago," the chair of the guidance department said. "We were told all the suburban districts in this area did it, and it was justified by saying we didn't want to make our school look bad when other districts were doing the same thing."

Debbie told the group her personal ethics would not allow her to sign a form to be submitted to the state education department that listed those students as transfers if they were really dropouts. Debbie emphasized that they had about 10 months until that form needed to be completed again, and they had to devise a plan to reduce the dropouts and address the weak test scores in that ten-month period.

"We have Superintendent Galvin's support, but we don't have any additional funding beyond what's already being spent at the high school," she said. She also explained Superintendent Galvin's expectation that the department chairs and Debbie leave the school board communication completely to him.

"If you are contacted by a school board member," she told them, "tell me immediately and I'll inform the superintendent." Debbie suggested they meet again in a week. Meanwhile, everyone at the meeting was tasked with coming up with suggestions for what could be done to improve the academic results at Rosemont High while working within the school's existing budget.

When they met the next week, some of the department chairs were ready to move forward and had some great ideas on how to fund the changes they needed and the specifics of what changes were critical. Others were reluctant soldiers in the reform effort.

The reluctant reformers saw the need and understood the best strategies but were fearful of the political repercussions with the school board, with Superintendent Galvin, with the teachers union and with the parents who had grown accustomed to business as usual.

Debbie told me she left the meeting with her department chairs confused and frustrated. How could she proceed when her staff was so divided?

Then she described to me her own happy accident. She said she went to the gym after the meeting and worked out harder than ever. During the drive home she had an epiphany. Why not make the changes at Rosemont with the eager departments and let the rest sit back and watch.

Debbie formulated improvement plans. "I won't hide the data," she told the department chairs. "If we increase Regents, Honors and AP results in math but science continues to slip that comparison will be obvious to everyone.

"If the dropout rate goes up because we finally start tracking it properly, we'll have to deal with the negative public relations. And I plan to present this data at faculty meetings and parent meetings.

"I won't force you to make changes but you will be responsible for your department's performance. You can expect my support if you make a real effort at improvement even if it doesn't fully succeed. This will be OUR plan; not my plan."

The math department chair said, "Look I'm definitely interested in changing the honors math program. We all know the present honors system is not working right."

Maintaining the status quo
Lois Schafer was the ninth through twelfth grade honors math teacher at Rosemont, where her brand of teaching weeded out all but the most

earnest students. Even with private tutors helping many students, two-thirds of the students selected for honors based on math achievement in middle school ended up dropping out of high school honors math and many completely dropped out of math.

The other math teachers would have loved to have a shot at teaching honors math, but Lois was tight with Superintendent Galvin, and the schedule left her with half as many students as the regular math teachers and no discipline problem students and no special education students.

The plan devised by Debbie and the math department chair was to mix the accelerated honors students into each of the regular math classes with between two and five high achieving ninth graders with 20 to 25 tenth grade students who were performing at average levels.

Honors would become a choice for all the students in the class whether they were in ninth or tenth grade. If you do the extra homework and special weekly math challenge assignments for honors and complete the honors questions on each test and quiz, you're designated honors, with honors designated on your report card and on your high school transcript.

Schools using this approach report that many good math students who were overlooked when the decision of who to accelerate was made (usually in sixth grade or even earlier) take on the honors challenge and become great math students.

Even if they don't have time to take calculus as seniors at Rosemont, these late bloomers are well prepared for calculus at college.

Also, many more students who would have dropped out of the honors program in separate classes with Lois Schafer stay with it in regular classes, and the grading system is not designed to weed them out by being unnecessarily competitive.

They continue to feel like they're math stars rather than math failures. Any system that convinces over half of the best math students in the district they're not good at math is a system in need of change.

In the end, the math and social studies departments decided to move forward with this honors change, while the other departments decided to wait and see how it played out.

How do you pay for improvement?

Most educational improvement plans have financial costs, and leaders frequently end up stymied because they can't identify funding opportunities.

My rule of thumb is never replace a staff retirement or resignation with a simple rehire of the same skill set. Always look for the hidden opportunities in this staff change to put more resources where they'll do more for students. Funding spent on less successful programs, such as expensive special education tuitions and long school bus rides to inferior programs that aren't getting results also present opportunities to improve outcomes for more students.

Finding opportunities to fund alternatives

Debbie's department chair group suggested reallocating savings from unanticipated retirements — one was a home economics teacher and the other a secretary in the guidance office — and a vacant custodial position on the night shift caused by an employee who left for another job. By hiring part-time replacements for these positions with no expensive benefits, they saved enough to hire two certified teachers as teaching assistants at the high school.

Additional savings came by moving high school special education students into a new alternative high school with a work-study component. They were paying to send four special education students ($50,000 each) to other schools. Moving these students back to a new program in the school district saved one bus run and the salary and benefit costs for a bus driver and a school bus aide.

The savings also paid for two more certified teachers working as teaching assistants, a monitor to cover study halls previously covered by teachers and some extra hourly tutoring for academically struggling students.

As Debbie described her new alternative program to me, I recognized the program's structure and details. They were similar to those in a program I had helped design and implement in different school districts as a high school principal, assistant superintendent and superintendent.

Debbie fully understood the chaos in too many students' lives outside of school ultimately caused them to become dropouts.[xxxv] Her alternative program was designed to counteract that chaos. She also understood that while the national dropout rate had declined in recent years[xxxvi] the improvements came to those districts that intervened with new successful approaches to help struggling students before they dropped out.

The alternative program's students attended school for two and a half hours a day in one of three sessions: a.m., p.m. or evening. The students stayed in the same classroom for the entire two and a half hours (as they did in elementary school) and subject specific teachers, who had been relieved of study halls and who were paid a sixth-class stipend to teach an extra class period in the daytime a.m. and p.m. alternative program sessions.

At Rosemont, new subject-specific certified teachers who were hired as teaching assistants (in New York State there are many young candidates with teaching degrees looking for jobs) became regular full-time staff members of the daytime alternative program and received additional pay to work in the evening alternative program. A special education teacher was hired with the savings and served as the core primary teacher for the a.m. and p.m. program sessions.

The other new teaching assistants became regular staff in a daytime tutoring center that served students who were struggling academically. Teachers freed up from study halls by a monitor hired with the remaining savings helped in the daytime tutoring center and the daytime alternative program sessions. The teaching assistants and some district teachers took on extra hourly tutoring assignments after school, at night and on weekends, also paid for by the savings. The tutoring helped students who were struggling in Regents and honors courses.

The students in the three sessions of the alternative program completed an independent study curriculum for the courses required for a high school diploma. Each alternative program session was small (10-12 students) with multiple teachers in the room to provide one-on-one academic support for students. Since the students stayed in their classroom for the entire high school experience and didn't move from classroom to classroom they developed a strong working relationship with the primary teacher in the program who worked with them for the full two and a half hours.

Debbie said the evening classes, which were managed by a certified teacher who needed an administrative internship to complete his school administrator certification, worked well for young mothers, for students who acted out in school (no appreciative audience to react to them) and for students who had to work during the day to help pay the bills. The subject specific teachers and teaching assistants and the administrative intern in the alternative evening session were paid an hourly rate with minimal benefit costs making it an inexpensive and academically effective addition to the school.

In addition to independent study online coursework, the alternative program students completed a 1,000 hour supervised paid work-study internship in a local business. For young mothers, the work-study internship was 700 hours with a 300-hour parenting component. Debbie used one of her newly hired teaching assistants to help these students find internships and supervise the students' work study and parenting experiences.

Debbie emphasized that the elementary school-like structure of the program with one primary adult forming a strong emotional bond with the student helped the potential dropouts in the alternative program overcome the frequent chaos in their lives. She used their vital statistics – poor attendance, failing grades and/or a rash of discipline problems – to identify students who would benefit from a true alternative program.

I wasn't surprised when Debbie told me the dropout rate for her school had been cut in half during the first year the program was in place and that dropouts for her school had been reduced to single digits during the second year of the program's implementation. I had the same experience with similarly structured alternative high school programs in four different school districts. At Averill Park High School where I was the high school principal the dropout rate for the five years prior to the alternative program's implementation was 11.5 percent of the total number of graduates plus dropouts (23 dropouts per year average) and for the three years after the program's implementation the dropout rate was 3 percent (six dropouts per year average).

Debbie found out what I had found out. When students move into middle schools and high schools and begin the endless shuffle every 40-50 minutes from classroom to classroom their working relationships with adults become more tenuous. These students are working with eight or nine adults every day and none for more than 40-50 minutes each.

Secondary school teachers are working with 100-150 students. An elementary teacher knows her students better in October than a high school teacher knows her students in May.

The shift from elementary school to middle school can be very tough for any student, even those with all the advantages. The shift to middle school and high school for kids with problematic home situations and academic failure issues can become overwhelming. These students need to be taught, mentored, supported and monitored much more closely.

School Boards and their personal agendas
I had forgotten about Tom Galvin after my retirement until my work as an educational consultant brought me in contact with a member of the Board of Directors for the New York State School Boards Association. Her name was Cassie Chairmont, and she was a gossipy woman in her 70s whose entire life revolved around the political issues of the 40-plus school districts near her home in upstate New York.

Chairmont let slip to a group of 25 school board members the details of an ongoing political struggle within the leadership team of Rosemont school district.

"Oh that Tom Galvin at Rosemont is so good looking and charming, but he has his hands full with those two school board members of his," she said. "Todd Morgan is gunning for the football coach, and Jessie Thomas is going after the high school principal. If Tom isn't careful, they'll take him out in the process."

She seemed to revel in the conflict and the small ball political intrigue. I just shook my head and wondered what the negative fallout for the district would be.

What not to do

The existing good old boy and old girl networks that are in place around the U.S. now for the selection of superintendents and principals in the pipeline for leadership positions in school districts are woefully inadequate when it comes to selecting the best candidates.

And school board members selecting these superintendents too often operate the same way members of the U.S. Congress operate. They compete for public attention and get it any way they can. Or they come to the job with an ax to grind and they grind it endlessly.

That's what's happening in thousands of school districts all over the U.S. School board members who don't understand the real priorities of their jobs are interfering where shouldn't be and wreaking havoc on the school district leadership team.[xxxvii][xxxviii] School boards are much better at picking political survivors and administrators who fully understand whose ass to kiss than they are at doing the job their legally required to do – setting goals and policy for the school district and supervising one single employee, the superintendent.

Tom Galvin should never have been seen as a potential school or school district leader and the university that trained him shouldn't be in the business of training school administrators.

And so it goes

School board member Todd Morgan played football at Rosemont High School, when they won almost every game with him on the starting team. That's what he told everyone, anyway. The reality is the team won less than half the time, and Todd spent most of that time on the bench.

For years after high school, Todd supported the Rosemont football program coached by Tom Galvin and later Kevin Talbot. He took over Rosemont Pop Warner Pee Wee coaching duties when his son Brian was seven and moved up the age-level brackets in the Pop Warner program each year with his son.

As one of the Pop Warner coaches, Todd met regularly with Kevin Talbot to make sure Todd supported Kevin by running the right offensive and defensive schemes to properly train the youngsters for the Rosemont program.

Despite his ongoing working relationship with Kevin Talbot, Todd had concerns about the Rosemont football program. After Tom Galvin moved up to principal and later superintendent and left coaching, Rosemont wasn't winning as often.

Before he became a school board member Todd tried to share his concerns with Superintendent Galvin, but Galvin brushed him off with his best smile and humorous response and chalked it up to a bad year.

In seventh grade, Todd's son Brian was small for his age but fast and a determined athlete. With Brian two years away from high school, Todd decided to run for the school board and "fix the football program."

He won one of the two vacant seats in the May school board election with 306 votes out of 511 votes cast in a district with a population of 14,000 residents and 6,000 eligible voters, a low level of voter turnout typical for school board elections.

THEY DON'T SHOW UP TO VOTE

Typical voter turnout in a presidential election year is 50 to 60 percent, according to the Center for the Study of the American Electorate.

Not bad, but hardly impressive when compared with other OPEC high wealth countries many of which average over 70 percent turnout.[xxxix]

In New York State and many other states, turnout for school board elections and for school budget votes hovers around 5 to 15 percent of eligible voters. Frequently, the voters select school board members like Todd Morgan who get elected because of single issue concerns. With such low turnout a highly motivated but very small slice of the potential voters can easily sway a school board member election. This can be also true with votes for or against a school budget.

Frequently, a relatively small number of repeat local voters have personal agendas. For example, they hated the new property assessment system, the superintendent who left the district 10 years ago said something that offended them, they like to read the stories in their local newspaper about the latest shouting match at the school board meeting, etc.

And they can send a school district to electoral and management purgatory for decades due to low voter turnout numbers and the weak leadership quality of their school superintendent and school board members to the point where school board meetings becomes a three ring circus.

Is it more than just low turnout? Is the problem more about the quality, qualifications and leadership experience of the candidates running for the school board? Perhaps.

The mythical voter mandate

Many of Todd's votes came from Pop Warner football and Rosemont High School football families and friends, as well as folks who frequented the convenience store he'd inherited when his dad died.

Todd felt he had a mandate to get a new football coach for Rosemont and he set up a meeting with Tom Galvin in July one week after he had been sworn in as a school board member to present his case for a coaching change.

His reasons for the change? The team's losing record, the diminishing numbers of athletes playing football (more playing soccer now), lack of support for the coach among parents and most important Todd's election to the school board on a campaign promise of getting a new coach for the football team. He even had the name of a new coach he thought would be a great choice for the program. His choice was a local guy who had played football for Tom Galvin at Rosemont and later for a Division III college program at St. Lawrence University. He was now a local attorney and a respected coach in the Pop Warner program.

Superintendent Galvin reacted to this proposal with uncharacteristic anger and frustration. "It's not Kevin's fault the team is not winning and the numbers are down. The parents aren't giving him the support he needs to succeed."

Galvin claimed parents were directing their children toward soccer rather than football and tried to turn the blame around. "You really need to look at what you guys have been doing with the Pop Warner football program that's driving parents and students away," he said.

As the meeting ended, Todd acted unsure of himself and mumbled something about getting back to Tom later on the football issue. But it didn't take long for him to rebound with anger.

"The superintendent is blaming me and other Pop Warner parents and coaches for the Rosemont team's poor performance!" he told his football friends and everyone who came into his convenience store. "He's ignoring my election to the school board and my mandate? The superintendent is defending his good old boy buddy, failed Rosemont football coach Kevin Talbot. Meanwhile, students like my son are missing college scholarship opportunities"

Of course, Todd overlooked the fact that his mandate consisted of 306 votes from 14,000 residents in the school district. Todd also overlooked the fact that his experience at the convenience store (the only place he'd ever worked), his years as a student and athlete in Rosemont's schools and his role as a school board member hardly made him qualified to make any kind of personnel decision for the school district.

And maybe most telling: A survey of the residents of the Rosemont School District would have revealed that a significant percentage of the residents could not name one member of the school board.[xlii] *Todd was acting on a mythical mandate, but that didn't not stop him.*

By the following spring, Superintendent Galvin and school board member Todd Morgan were bitter enemies, and Todd did everything in his power to make the superintendent's life miserable including try-ing to make him look foolish at every public meeting of the school board with off-the-wall questions he wouldn't reveal until the meeting was in public session.

He challenged the accuracy of the information supplied by the superintendent and made snide public comments that inevitably made it into the local newspaper.

Todd also convinced his longtime friend and assistant coach in Pop Warner football, Terry Marcus, to run for the school board in the next May election on a platform of changing the football coach and getting a new superintendent, and Terry won a seat on the board with 280 votes, 20 more than the next best candidate.

What passes for leadership?

In too many school districts what passes for leadership is the spectacle on display at every public school board meeting. Local "authorities" like Todd Morgan are elected to the school board because of one issue that's usu-ally irrelevant to the important issues facing the school district. These local school board members generally gain power and are elected because school superintendents are not focusing their time and effort and the time and effort of their school board on the right issues. When multiple school board members with misguided priorities are elected, disaster ensues.

A disaster in the making

Jessie Thomas was a college educated mother of three who took pride in her maternal role and used her psychology degree from Vassar and her competitive instincts to propel her children to great success in school and in the community. Jessie's husband Nate was a local primary care physician and Jessie, a stay-at-home Mom, immersed herself in her three children's lives.

Her oldest son, Ted a sixth grader, was a computer, math and science geek who loved to blow things up and planned on a career designing computer video games. Nate, Jr., in fifth grade, was the family environmentalist, who counted frog larvae in the local streams and joined the Sierra Club at 8 years of age, and Molly, 7, took music and dance lessons and would tell anyone who would listen she was going to be a performer.

Jessie joined and eventually became president of the elementary school PTA and later the middle school PTA. The PTA sponsored science fairs, computer club, and student environmental research in cooperation with a local college and after school dance and music lessons for students. Jessie's children had no desire to participate in sports and Jessie and her husband didn't encourage them in sports.

It was no surprise when Ted, Jessie's oldest, was selected to take accelerated math and science in seventh grade. These select students took a cram course that fit both seventh and eighth grade math and science into the seventh grade. They could then take ninth grade Regents Algebra and Regents Biology in eighth grade and later in high school had the time and preparation to take Advanced Placement (AP) Calculus and AP Biology or AP Chemistry for potential college credit as seniors.

Among Jessie's contacts and friends was Lois Schafer, mother of two and the teacher for all the Honors and Advanced Placement Calculus math classes at Rosemont High School. Lois and Jessie arranged play dates for their children (Lois's son and daughter were in the same grades and elementary school as Nate, Jr., and Molly), and they always sat together at dance or music performances and environmental activities involving their children. So it was fairly natural for Lois to mention to Jessie her concerns about planned changes for the honors math program at Rosemont High School.

Lois's explanation of the planned changes were simple but not necessarily accurate. "The high school principal is dismantling the honors program at Rosemont," she said, "and I doubt we'll have any students ready to take the AP Calculus exam by the time Ted gets to his senior year in high school. Even if we have AP Calculus I won't be able to get the students ready for the AP exam with the diluted program the principal is putting in place. Our best students, like Ted, need the extra challenges of the honors program classes with me for all four years to be ready for that AP exam."

Jessie talked with other PTA parents about this problem and then met with Principal Fortunato to talk about the potential negative impact of the planned changes.

The meeting between the two started cordially until Jessie explained her concern was that honors math was being dismantled and Ted would miss the extra challenges he needed to prepare him for the AP Calculus course.

The principal countered saying the extra honors challenges in the curriculum would be offered to any student who wanted them in every math classroom, including those where Ted would take his math instruction. Rather than segregating the 25 accelerated math students in one separate tenth grade honors section for ninth graders as they came to the high school, they would be mixed into the regular tenth grade math classes with a few in each of the seven sections.

"Honors tenth grade math will be available to any student in these classes (ninth or tenth graders) who was willing to do the extra home-work and weekly math challenges and complete the extra honors test questions," Principal Fortunato said. "All students who do this extra work will receive the honors designation on report cards and high school transcripts with accompanying, appropriate grades."

Principal Fortunato also mentioned the high percentage of students who bailed out on honors math in the present system with 25 students starting the program in ninth grade and only eight making it to the AP exam this past year.

Jessie left the meeting confused and called Lois to get her thoughts on all of this.

"The other teachers don't even want to do the more challenging hon-ors curriculum," Lois said. "They have enough trouble getting the students who are struggling to pass. This looks like it could work on paper but it

will never fly. Ted is an excellent math student. He will have no trouble sticking with the honors math curriculum all the way to calculus."

Jessie considered her options and decided to set up a meeting with the superintendent and the high school principal to see if she could get them to change their minds. The meeting involved Jessie, Principal Fortunato and Superintendent Galvin.

Jessie recited her concerns from the previous meeting with Principal Fortunato and added the input from Lois Schafer (of course without mentioning Lois's name) about the other teachers not wanting to take on the extra work involved in dealing with new curriculum expectations for the honors students.

The superintendent seemed distracted and asked only a few questions. Principal Fortunato was calm and professional and maintained that all the teachers were looking forward to the chance to teach honors students, and that she had no concerns about their reluctance to do the extra work involved.

She also mentioned again the large numbers of honors students who never made it to the AP calculus class and likely should have. The meeting ended with Superintendent Galvin reassuring Jessie and telling her she should give the new system a try. "We can all evaluate the new honors program's success after one year of implementation while your is still in eighth grade where the program changes will have no direct impact on him," Galvin said.

STARS WITH ALL THE ADVANTAGES

In 2013, President Obama's Education Secretary, Arne Duncan characterized opponents of the Common Core as "white suburban moms who — all of a sudden — their child isn't as brilliant as they thought they were, and their school isn't quite as good as they thought they were." (Washington Post, Answer Sheet, Nov. 16, 2013)

Jessie is that mom. Her son is not a prodigy. Yes, he's a good math student but most students with a physician father, a college educated stay-at-home mother and a home with all the books and advantages are likely be a good math students, especially this early in their education.

It's universally understood by educators that many suburban parents think their carefully coached and over-cossetted off spring is the next Einstein. Politics (we need the overwhelming support of those suburban parents to get our budgets approved) prevents educators from being honest about the discrepancy between the little Einstein's actual academic skills and parents' oversized confidence in those skills.

Compare these little Einsteins' academic skills to the academic skills of the students performing at the highest levels in the world and we see we're doing okay but not that great. (Newgeography, 7/25/2013, "High Confidence Not Translating to High Scores for American and European Students").

These perceptions about our little Einsteins make the Jessies of the world an easy mark for the Loises of the world and their willingness to say anything to hold onto their cushy teaching schedules.

What motivates anyone to run for the local school board?

After the meeting, Jessie turned her car around and went to the office of the school district clerk. She asked for and was given a petition which when properly completed allowed her to run for the school board in the upcoming May election. Jessie was elected with 356 votes the same year Todd Morgan was elected. PTA parents who had known her for years during her PTA leadership were her biggest supporters.

Jessie spent much of her first year on the school board, Ted's eighth grade year in school, asking for information and finding out how things worked. It didn't take her long to figure out Todd Morgan, also newly elected, hated the superintendent and wanted a new football coach.

She also discovered Superintendent Galvin was not quite as smart as she'd thought, and he seldom brought real data to the school board regarding Rosemont's academic performance. At a school board member training session in July Jessie received an explanation of her role as a school board member.

Jessie found out that school board members do not make school district personnel decisions other than the single decision of who is superintendent. The school board's role should be limited to the following:

- *Review data about the school district and set performance and procedural goals and policies for the school district.*
- *Monitor and evaluate the performance of the superintendent in achieving the goals and following the policies and procedures.*
- *Monitor data and ongoing work in the school district to ensure the goals are being achieved and policies ae being followed.*

School boards may request data from the superintendent in areas identified as worthy of examination for potential future goals and policies.

In August, during a public school board meeting, Jessie requested a formal evaluation of the academic success of the new honors math program being initiated in September of the year she was elected to the school board (her son's eighth grade year in the Rosemont system). Jessie and the school board agreed the report should be completed by March of the following year so any necessary changes could be implemented the year Ted entered ninth grade.

When March 1 came Jessie asked when they could expect the report she requested the previous August. Superintendent Galvin in the midst of a contentious budget discussion that had to be resolved within two weeks responded with an offhand comment: "We'll get to that at the next meeting."

Superintendent Galvin acted as though he didn't even remember this request and was eager to move forward on the other agenda items. Jessie saw Principal Fortunato raise her hand to get the superintendent's attention after Jessie asked about the honors report during the meeting, but Superintendent Galvin shook his head and they moved forward with the agenda.

When these same stalling tactics played out at the next school board meeting in late March, Jessie called Principal Fortunato and asked for a report on the new honors program directly even though she knew, as a result of school board member training, such requests should go through the superintendent.

Meanwhile, Lois Schafer, who long enjoyed her AP and honors classes with a few select self-motivated students, told Jessie the new honors program was a disaster with teachers openly ignoring the principal's request they provide honors challenges to all students in all classes.

Debbie Fortunato obviously felt trapped between her boss the superintendent who didn't want her to say anything about the honors math program and a new school board member she did not want to anger. Debbie told Jessie she would relay Jessie's request for this report to the superintendent later that same day when they were scheduled to attend a meeting together.

Jessie was fuming. She'd done everything right. She'd tried to talk to these people and they wouldn't even show her enough respect to give her an answer to a very reasonable question, "How well was the new honors math program working?"

Jessie called Lois who gave her some new information she received from the teacher union president. Debbie Fortunato was due to receive tenure in October, but if she was not going to get it the school board had to tell her by July 15.

Tom Galvin's three-year contract ran out the same month, and he required the same 90-day notice if his contract was not going to be renewed. The wheels in Jessie's head started turning. She immediately drove to the home of her longtime friend and PTA colleague Helen Pinkus and proposed Helen run for the school board that May. Helen's petition was properly submitted in April, and with Jessie's support Helen was elected to the school board in May with 304 votes along with Todd Morgan's Pop Warner buddy, Terry Marcus.

Academics become an afterthought of school "leadership"

Rosemont High School, stuck in academic mediocrity for 30 years became a hotbed of educational change in a few short months with Debbie

Fortunato as principal. Debbie met regularly with Superintendent Galvin and told him about the changes. Superintendent Galvin mentioned these changes in brief public comments to the school board at their meetings, but they were clearly low on the priority scale for the school board and Superintendent Galvin. Debbie was fine with that as long as she was left alone to move the high school forward.

By the end of Debbie's first year at Rosemont High, the dropouts were significantly reduced – not in comparison with data that counted the former dropouts as transfers but in real numbers – and the news of the change never made the newspapers.

The honors student count for students enrolling in math for eleventh grade classes, which would include accelerated tenth-graders, as it had during the previous year when the those students were in ninth grade, jumped from an average of 17 students taking honors eleventh grade math to 41 students taking honors eleventh grade math. All the 25 students who had entered ninth grade as accelerated students and an additional 16 students who had not been accelerated students but who had decided to take on the extra challenge of honors math, were included in that number.

By the end of Debbie's second year at Rosemont the English and science departments decided to make the honors program switch. Other high schools were sending teams of visitors to Rosemont to see how these changes worked and how they might adopt them in their own schools.

The following year the honors student count in math for eleventh grade classes was steady at 42 students and the pre-calculus (normally taken by non-accelerated seniors and accelerated juniors) enrollment, which was counted when students signed up for courses in the spring, was up to 65 students and required an additional class to accommodate the extra students.

The tutoring center had doubled in size. The center and the school's new three session alternative program were established using savings from nonteaching and teaching retirements and special education tuitions and transportation reductions.

With the savings the district hired more certified teachers to work as teaching assistants. The failure rate in Regents exams had been cut in half and the percentage of students scoring higher than 90 percent on important required course exit exams had doubled.

As the end of Debbie's third year at Rosemont approached, even the initial reluctant soldiers among the department chairs were bragging to their peers about the positive changes in their school and the important role they had in making these changes.

The rest of the story

Unfortunately, Lois Schafer wasn't happy. The honors program she "owned" for nearly 15 years was now in shared hands. Her classes were bigger and included students who struggled academically and behaviorally, and she didn't know how to deal with them. Many ended up in the principal's office for disciplinary reasons, which reflected poorly on her during her evaluations. She tried to talk to her old friend Tom Galvin about this multiple times but he was having his own problems.

Tom was assistant principal when Lois was hired to run the honors math program and classes 18 years earlier. Tom failed to act when Lois complained. That's when she turned to Jessie Thomas, repeatedly feeding Jessie information she thought would help her cause.

Meanwhile, Kevin Talbot met frequently with Superintendent Galvin. They talked about football strategy and player assignments. They reviewed scouting reports and game films for upcoming opponents. Kevin relied on Tom's expertise and guidance.

Tom told Kevin several times that if the football winning percentage for Rosemont didn't improve eventually Kevin would be out of coaching job. They both knew Todd Morgan was gunning for Kevin.

Kevin tried everything his mentor, Tom Galvin, suggested but it didn't result in wins on the field.

Tom Galvin saw the writing on the wall once Todd Morgan's and Jessie Thomas' friends appeared on the school board ballots.

Engineering elections

In the end, Todd Morgan helped his Pop Warner assistant coach Terry Marcus get elected to the school board and Jessie Thomas followed suit and engineered the election of her PTA colleague Helen Pinkus.

Their successful elections were on the same ballot in May near the end of Debbie's third year as principal. The two new board members were sworn in as required by education law on July 1 at the district's reorganizational meeting. In a surprise vote Jessie Thomas was elected school board president on a 4-3 vote and Todd Morgan vice president by the same 4-3 vote.

Immediately after these votes and the swearing in of the two new board members, Helen Pinkus made a motion seconded by Todd Morgan that they ask the public to leave the room for a brief executive session.

The superintendent had a clear idea what was happening and objected, but Jessie had done her homework well and by a 4-3 vote with "yes" votes from board members Thomas, Morgan, Marcus and Pinkus the public was ushered out of the room and the executive session began.

The beginning of the end

Jessie started by saying Superintendent Galvin's contract would end on October 25th and she wanted to discuss whether it should be extended. She didn't think it should, she said.

Superintendent Galvin reacted angrily and said he had not been informed of any concerns about his performance and the school board's intentions not to extend his contract. Jessie said he failed to provide the report regarding honors math she had formally requested be given in March as agreed the previous August.

Todd Morgan jumped in saying he had raised concerns about the football coaching issue on numerous occasions with no action by the super-intendent. Jessie requested a motion for the school board to direct the school district attorney to draft a formal letter to Superintendent Galvin thanking him for his years of service to the district and informing him that his contract would not be extended and to make certain this letter reached him in time for him to resign, should he choose to do so, before the 90-day limit in his contract became a legal issue for the school district.

The attorney, who was present at the executive session and who had obviously talked with Jessie in advance without telling Superintendent Galvin, said he would proceed as directed if the school board voted in the affirmative on a motion not to renew Galvin's contract. The motion was made by Todd Morgan, seconded by Terry Marcus and passed on a 4-3 vote.

Another one bites the dust

Jessie then expressed concerns about Principal Fortunato's performance and her changes in the honors math program. Helen Pinkus agreed with Jessie and a motion was proposed for the attorney to work out the legal details of denying tenure to Debbie Fortunato, giving her time to resign from the district before the school board formally voted to deny her tenure.

Superintendent Galvin was obviously shaken by the events that had transpired. "Look, I understand you are angry with me, but Debbie Fortunato has done nothing but make Rosemont a better high school," he said. "Test scores have improved. The dropout rate is down. It's a much better school than it was when she arrived. Her evaluations are extremely positive and won't support the action the school board in proposing."

Three board members argued vehemently in Debbie's favor and the "brief executive session" ended up being two hours long. In the end, Todd Morgan called the question on a 4-3 vote and the motion to deny Debbie Fortunato tenure passed by the same 4-3 vote. The attorney said even though Debbie's evaluations were positive and the superintendent was recommending her for tenure the final decision belonged with the school board.

Then Todd Morgan made a motion that the long standing football coach, Kevin Talbot, be informed that he would not be approved as varsity football coach for the upcoming fall season and directing the superintendent to recommend someone else for the position who was not now a member of the existing coaching staff in the district. The three member minority on the school board knew they were outgunned and made no objection and the vote passed 4-3.

The next morning Tom Galvin met with Debbie Fortunato and gave her the bad news. She would not receive tenure as Rosemont High School principal. The new board majority was already running the show and Tom could not control where they were headed.

Jessie Thomas called the school board clerk and told her to advertise for a new superintendent and a new a new high school principal.

Monday night massacre

Rumors immediately flew around the district about the "Monday night massacre" at the school board meeting. Letters drafted by the school attorney to Superintendent Galvin and Principal Fortunato were hand delivered to both administrators later that day.

They requested letters of resignation by both administrators prior to a special meeting of the school board set for the following Monday. The letters made it clear if the school board did not have a letter of resignation to act on they would act to end Superintendent Galvin's contract and deny Principal Fortunato tenure with required public votes at the special meeting.

Facing the negative consequences of such a public decision by the school board, Debbie Fortunato and Tom Galvin both resigned. Tom took a much lower paying job with the state football committee until he reached minimum retirement age and Debbie enrolled in the University at Albany, SUNY doctoral education program.

An unholy alliance

If you think that's the last time that the unholy alliance between Todd Morgan and Jessie Thomas created leadership problems for the Rosemont

School District, think again. Once two or more uninformed egomaniacs realize they can get what they want by not following the rules of good school board member behavior and by making side deals (You give me this; I'll give you that.), they are subject to the whims of whomever misinformed them last.

If a parent doesn't like the basketball coach because his son sits on the bench too much, he can call Todd Morgan and see what kind of misery he can inflict on that coach via a politically savvy superintendent who will do anything to save her/his job. And the parent of a disabled child who wants a one-on-one aide for her son can call Jessie Thomas to be her advocate for that aide.

Before long messy local politics are controlling the school district. School board members succumb to pressures from individuals with an agenda and over time it destroys the leadership culture of their school districts.

Soon individual employees or their unions will be pursuing the school board member "team" route to achieve their goals, and the superintendents and principals will move through the district like a series of revolving doors.

Meanwhile, the district will see the possibilities for real academic growth for students and teachers in the district wither and die. Before long the weakest school districts with this leadership cycle firmly entrenched produce either (1) consistently poor academic performance when compared with similar districts in terms of student demographics, size and financial resources, (2) poor financial health, or (3) both. Many superintendents who survive in these school districts are complicit in this failure of leadership and manage to remain in their positions by hiding poor academic performance and financial data that might end the entire charade.

FROM BAD TO WORSE

Tom Galvin's decision to hide the real dropout data at Rosemont and to continue to hide it for years was a clear ethical message to all the staff members who knew about this deception and who participated in the cover up over the years. The message was: "We can make ourselves look better as a school district than we really are and no one will know."

And it came with a ready justification: Other school districts are hiding their bad data too. Is this really any different from erasing student answers on test bubble sheets in Atlanta, GA, where school administrators went to prison for their errors?[xliii]

Do you think it was easy for Debbie Fortunato, the Rosemont high school principal, to buck this longstanding trend when her boss as much as told her to continue the ruse by telling her the school board already knew about the dropouts who were mislabeled as transfers?

Of course not, but I'm certain one of the reasons her staff supported her is because they knew she was a real education leader. She even found a way to come clean with the data in public and avoid the public relations mess the superintendent feared. The dropouts increased slightly on paper but went down dramatically in actuality and no one made note of it. But her real successes didn't save her when the political house of cards built around Tom Galvin collapsed.

Whenever a school district hires an internal candidate for a promotion there is pressure to hide the data. Tom Galvin didn't want to let the school board and the public know about those false dropout numbers because he would be tied to the poor performance (It happened during his tenure as assistant principal and principal at the high school.) and to the cover-up of poor performance.

Why do you think Tom Galvin's highly developed political skills failed him in the end, when it had saved him from losing his job all these years and even landed him three promotions in the school district?

Multiple reasons: his obsession with high school football wins and losses; his misguided loyalty to his friend, Kevin Talbot; and his refusal to deal with Jessie Thomas when an early and effective communication about the weak honors and AP performance data would have permanently solved the problem?

If Superintendent Galvin had replaced Coach Talbot (which would have been perfectly reasonable given the dwindling number of football participants and the team's dismal record), the problem would never have escalated. But doing this would have meant abandoning his friend and getting entirely out of the coaching role, a role he maintained behind the scenes

If Superintendent Galvin had admitted to Jessie Thomas and Debbie Fortunato at the beginning that he had made a mistake a long time ago with Lois Schafer and the structure of the honors math program, and that he had hidden that error for 18 years, the problem would have ended.

A misguided quest for a winning football team and an ego that refused to admit an 18-year-old error in judgement about an academic program became blind spots. Many times weak superintendents (and sometimes even strong ones) are brought down by their blind spots.

The worst news for Rosemont is that it lost a great high school principal who will have a hard time landing another educational leadership job opportunity. The sting of tenure denial or resignation to avoid a formal public vote for tenure denial can be a career ender for many principals.

Anyone who has any say in hiring principals will know the Rosemont story, and there will be doubts that Debbie Fortunato was guiltless in the "Monday night massacre." This is doubly bad because the teachers and department chairs who had helped to create the positive changes initiated at Rosemont High School while Debbie Fortunato was the principal will be reluctant to make that level of commitment to change in the future, wondering when the new principal who is pushing the change agenda will lose her position or just bolt.

Chapter 11 for schools

So, what strategy has a real chance of helping school districts like Rosemont when they become trapped in this type of leadership crisis whirlpool? Radical surgery.

In fact, this is a good time to dust off the old adage: "Schools should be run like a business." When a business hits bankruptcy there are rules that apply depending on the legal charter for the business. Some of those rules make sense for school districts that are failing miserably academically and/or financially.

The suggestions I make below would work in New York State and other states as well. First, the school board and superintendent must be removed. Usually for businesses in bankruptcy a court appointed receiver takes over the business.

In New York State, historical examples of the state education department intervening in such cases proved they were unable to succeed in this kind of intervention.[xliv]

The New York State Education Department is presently staffed primarily by midcareer teachers who couldn't land administrative positions so they took a job at the state education department. Very few state education department employees have experience as superintendents, school business officials or principals so the idea that they could lead a school district restructuring process is irrational.

But the state education department might be able to develop a cadre of retired school superintendents and assistant superintendents with the expertise and experience to turn around these districts with consistent problems in academic or financial performance.

Care would need to be taken to ensure that the restructuring job was reserved for superintendents and assistant superintendents who created real positive academic and financial change for the districts they served.

Good old boys and girls with political connections who made their names with their charming personalities need not apply. Some states have already moved in this direction with mixed results.[xlv] States would have to avoid the Flint, MI, issue where the interim replacement city manager who had been put in place by the governor of Michigan approved a change in the water supply that resulted in lead poisoning for many children in the city. The people who come in to take over have to know what they are doing and have to be free of undue political pressure.

School administrators who know how to analyze data and determine improvement priorities, initiate successful academic and financial change and evaluate and mentor real education leaders are needed.

The school board would have to be replaced by a team of three retired superintendents or assistant superintendents with expertise in school finances, school academic performance and school operations. Members of the school board at the time of this replacement would not be eligible to run for the school board in the future.

This interim school board would be selected by the state education department and each member of the interim school board would be paid $12,000 per year as consultants for their service (no district contributions for medical insurance or retirement benefits).

The first task of this interim school board would be to select an interim superintendent who would run the district for the next two years and be paid as a consultant with no medical insurance or retirement contributions. This interim superintendent would be paid at the same rate as the outgoing superintendent. This interim superintendent would come from the cadre of experts developed by the state education department.

The cost of the new leadership team should be comparable to the team being replaced given the absence of benefit costs for the newly hired consultants.

To make this plan work, taxpayers would have to get over the concerns about "double dipping" by retirees who collect a pension from their retirement and a salary at the same time. In the end, these are the best candidates to complete the required restructuring. And they're the least expensive way to get the job done effectively.

All existing administrators (academic and civil service) in the district at the time of the restructuring would become probationary employees losing their tenure/permanent status for at least two years and possibly longer while the district is restructured.

Depending on the severity of the student academic performance and financial problems, a percentage of teaching and nonteaching employees with tenure or permanent status as civil service employees (between five percent and 50 percent, a percentage set by state education department guidelines) would lose tenure/permanent status for at least two years with the decision of who loses tenure/permanent status resting with the interim superintendent after s/he had been on the job for 90 days.

The interim superintendent would be provided by the state education department with a separate restructuring budget equal to up to 3 percent of the district's latest annual budget to hire consultants to identify necessary structural changes to improve the district's academic and financial performance and to help evaluate the performance of teachers, administrators and support staff to determine who should stay and who should go and to help retrain those who stay.

If necessary, the interim superintendent could apply to an appropriate court for a waiver to any specific provisions for union contracts which impede restructuring. The law enacted to provide this school district restructuring authority would need to identify the criteria the judge would use to make contract provision nullification decisions.

Done right, a two-year turnaround is possible. In order for these changes to have a real chance for long-term success and to avoid the sand castles on the beach syndrome the interim school board would need to serve two more years while a return to an elected school board is phased in.

During the first of these two years, two newly elected community school board members with three-year terms would be added to the school board in addition to a permanent superintendent hired by those five school board members (three interim members and two newly elected members). During year two, following the departure of the interim superintendent two more newly elected school board members with three-year terms would be added for a total of seven members on the school board.

In year three of the restructuring, following the departure of the interim superintendent, the full complement of elected school members would take their seats (no previous school board members would be allowed to run in future school board elections) with the standard three-year rotation for school board members set in place.

As the last of these newly elected board members take their seats on the school board, the three interim board would members leave the district.

Creating Quality with Tenure

●　●　●

In 2005, I was hired as an interim schools superintendent for a school district living in the aftermath of a financial apocalypse prompted by two things: the school board's refusal to raise property taxes for five years in a row and a misguided effort to improve student performance.

I say misguided because they didn't try anything new and just spent more money on what they were already doing. That was their improvement plan.

Unfortunately, they were spending money they didn't have (a fact that was reported annually by independent auditors), and they eventually had to raise taxes 30 percent and lay off 75 employees to balance the budget. The school board and administration assumed their state legislative representatives would bail them out with extra state aid as they had in the past. That extra aid never came and, when the district's financial train hit the wall, the district became persona non grata in the world of Standard and Poors'. They were bankrupt.

Eventually, legislators passed special legislation that allowed the school district to borrow $10 million to pay off immediate operating expenses. (Normally, New York State school finance law would prohibit a school district from borrowing money for day-to-day operations.)

At the same time that the financial apocalypse was taking place, abysmal academic performance had landed the district's high school and middle school on the New York State Education Department's list of Schools In Need of Improvement (SINI). It was a perfect storm. And it occupied a lot of my time early on in my first year with the district.

Then in May (it gets worse) my security team, led by a retired police officer, an experienced professional I trusted, informed me that eighth grade teacher Terry Bonesteel had been sending inappropriate, sexually explicit social media messages to middle school students.

(Note: Names have been changed even in cases like this where details have been reported in the press or are available through the Freedom of Information Act.)

Terry Bonesteel's salacious social media messages were discovered by a parent who called the school district. A search of the school's computer system files revealed several messages sent. As reported in the newspaper, they included comments like:

Student: "I thought you were gay."

Teacher: "No I told you I love pussy, especially young pussy."

On the advice of our school district attorney the details of the teacher's missives were turned over to the local police to determine if he had committed any crimes.

Unfortunately, by the time the police and prosecutor obtained a warrant (apparently, it takes time) to search Mr. Bonesteel's home computer, any incriminating evidence they may have found was gone. To make matters worse: The police or the parents (not sure which) called the press and the story ended up in multiple local newspapers and in several local TV news reports.

In the meantime, I checked Mr. Bonesteel's personnel file and found an employee counseling memo written to him three years earlier by the former superintendent detailing that Mr. Bonesteel had, on multiple occasions, gone on the Internet and visited pornographic websites while using the school's computer system. The memo warned Mr. Bonesteel his behavior was unprofessional and would not be tolerated and, if repeated, would result in more serious disciplinary action including loss of pay or termination from his job.

Again, I contacted the school district attorney who had written the original memo to Mr. Bonesteel for the previous superintendent and who still worked for the district. "Why didn't you fire this guy when you caught him using the school's computers to go to porn sites?" I asked.

The answer: The New York State education commissioner and a small army of lawyers and independent hearing officers hear all appeals on tenured teacher and principal disciplinary issues in the state, and the commissioner would not support termination on a first offense of this nature for a tenured teacher.

My analysis of previous cases decided by the commissioner which are publicly available revealed that the attorney's analysis was accurate.

Next question: "He's been warned about misuse of school computers, and his actions in this new instance are clearly inappropriate and unprofessional – can we fire him now?"

Unfortunately, that wasn't my decision to make. According to Section 3020-a of New York's Education Law (3020-a Disciplinary procedures and penalties), this was a case for the commissioner to decide after a process that would likely take 12 months.

Typically, the process of what New York's teacher tenure law calls "progressive discipline" takes a year and involves a hearing with an independent hearing officer or a team of three independent hearing officers (based on education law).[xlvi] The commissioner (really his attorneys) and the unions that represent teachers facing disciplinary action mutually agree on the independent hearing officer(s) from a preselected list who then hear the case.

The commissioner's hearing officer is like a judge who may hear oral arguments and possibly testimony from a child or videotaped statements. There also may be a cross examination with lawyers representing both sides. Truthfully, teacher discipline cases like Mr. Bonesteel's frequently fall apart because the witness (usually a child) backs out or buckles under stiff cross examination.

Meanwhile, our lawyer advised us to remove Mr. Bonesteel from the classroom, a tactic we hoped would illustrate the serious nature of the situation and strengthen the case for termination with the commissioner.

So, while lawyers for the school district and NYSUT (New York State United Teachers, the teachers union defending the teacher) worked on briefs, I recommended Mr. Bonesteel work on curriculum tasks in a small room adjacent to the main office at an elementary school where the secretaries and principal could keep an eye on him.

STATISTICALLY ABSOLUTE TENURE

The financial cost of the "progressive discipline" process – and the work it produces for schools – is what ultimately produces "statistically absolute" tenure, zero chance a teacher will be terminated. Simply put: The process of eliminating a teacher (or any other licensed professionals in the education theater) is cost prohibitive and has created an inertia in education as well as in the process of education improvement.[xlvii] [xlviii]

Each school district in New York State (there are 700-plus in the state) has a school attorney on a retainer who provides basic legal advice. The monthly bill includes charges for activities and attorney hours related to typical school district business (contract negotiations, employee discipline issues that don't result in hearings, creating and or reviewing vendor contracts, etc.).

Unfortunately, a teacher discipline appeal to the commissioner is not covered by the standard attorney retainer so an additional cost is charged to the school district for the hours worked to interview witnesses, prepare and submit documents and for the attorney hours at the actual appeal hearing.

Attorney hourly rates vary across New York State with most falling in the $150 to $400 per hour range. A teacher discipline appeal, depending on its complexity and the lawyer's work ethic and billing habits, can involve anywhere from 50 to 200 hours of extra paid time for the attorney ($7,500 - $80,000). In Mr. Bonesteel's case the additional bill for legal services was $24,500.

Meanwhile, the law requires Mr. Bonesteel be paid his full $71,576 annual salary and $31,224 in annual pension, health insurance and employer social security contribution benefit costs even while he sits out the school year. His replacement – a less experienced teacher – cost the district another $61,257 in salary and benefits for the year.

Unlike New York State Civil Service employees, tenured teachers and school administrators cannot be suspended without pay pending the outcome of a disciplinary hearing. So the total cost (salary and benefits plus legal expenses) for this appeal was $127,300.

In the end, the commissioner placed Mr. Bonesteel on unpaid leave for one month. After that he returned to the classroom. The one month dock in pay was about $8,500. This didn't put much of a dent in the $127,300 cost (most tied up in his salary) of removing him from the classroom not to mention the cost to vulnerable eighth graders who might be victimized by putting him back in a classroom.

RUBBER ROOMS

In 2015, the American Enterprise Institute reported 27 cases of conduct unbecoming a professional were brought to the New York City Department of Education commissioner during a 10-year period, and none of them resulted in termination.[xlix]

And those 27 cases that didn't result in termination were a drop in the bucket when compared to the number of cases they never followed through with. Most don't get that far. Many New York City teachers involved in serious misconduct end up in a "rubber room" where they remain until they eventually retire.

Rubber rooms are what teachers called the holding facilities that came to light in the 1970s, where hundreds of New York City teachers accused of misconduct had been infamously paid to do nothing for months or years on end while their cases worked their way through the system. In the 1990s, the rubber rooms took center stage again when New York City Mayor Michael Bloomberg vowed to rid the system of this practice. He was unsuccessful.[l] In fact Joel Klein, Mayor Bloomberg's Education Chancellor, said firing a tenured teacher "took an average of almost two and a half years and cost the city over $300,000."[li]

The decades old fight between the teacher unions, the school districts, the state education department and the legislators who stuck everyone with an unworkable system is a regular source of acrimony among these players and a frequently recycled news story.[lii]

POLITICIANS SEE AN EASY OUT

One has to go back several decades to find out how teacher tenure became an opportunity to protect the perpetrators of unprofessional (and sometimes illegal) behavior.

The history involves many dismissals of teachers in the 19th and early-to-mid 20th centuries initiated by school boards and individual school board members, school principals, superintendents and local politicians, and the reasons for the dismissals were frequently sexist and unreasonable.

Entertaining a male guest after 6 p.m., drinking alcohol in public, inappropriate language in public, failing to attend church every week – it's an excruciatingly long list.

The politics is a little more complicated. When teacher unions formed and began to push for change in the years following World War II, local school boards and the states were, as always, struggling to pay their bills. The increases in teacher pay these unions expected meant higher state taxes and school property taxes (never popular with taxpayers or politicians).

Almost as throw-away items the teacher unions requested better pensions, stronger bargaining rights, and health insurance for their members, as well as stronger job protections in the form of tenure laws. Politicians saw what they perceived as an easy out and took it.

Health insurance, for one, was relatively cheap in the 1950s, '60s, '70s and even the '80s. Strong teacher and principal tenure laws didn't cost anything immediately in terms of increased taxes, and given the history of unfair teacher dismissals in the past they made some sense.

So instead of big teacher salary increases the unions received better pensions, stronger bargaining rights, high quality health insurance and strong tenure protection. Later, with stronger bargaining rights they walked away with big raises, more expensive benefits and bigger pensions, particularly for more experienced teachers in the strong teacher union states. Pensions and stronger bargaining rights for teachers agreed to in the 1950s and '60s would be paid for far into the future.

At the same time, in states with the strongest state level teacher unions (New York, Massachusetts, Illinois, Maryland, Delaware, New Jersey, California, etc.) the unions figured out how to maximize the impact of campaign contributions to politicians from both major parties.

NYSUT (New York State United Teachers) presently has more than 200,000 plus members who pay dues of $400-$1,000 dollars per year per teacher. According to followthemoney.org "NEW YORK STATE UNITED TEACHERS has given $17,383,311 to 509 different filers over 20 years." (http://www.followthemoney.org/entity-details?eid=19234)

This process has been ongoing since the 1960s; teacher unions have received paybacks for their donations in the form of legislation that included even stronger bargaining rights and tenure protections. The majority of these protections survive to this day. While the pendulum has started to swing back it is still strongly tilted to the side of job protection for tenured teachers and principals in the strong public union states.

STORY RINGS TRUE

Unfortunately, Mr. Bonesteel's story rings true for every experienced school district superintendent and school principal. In my time as an administrator, I have personally dealt with or heard from superintendent and principal colleagues who dealt with:

- Several teachers who threatened, swore at, grabbed, pushed, slapped, punched, and even kicked students or parents or colleagues.
- Coaches who failed to supervise students in the locker room resulting in repeated sexually violent hazing and costly parent lawsuit settlements.
- Multiple male and female teachers involved in a variety of sexually suggestive oral and written exchanges with students.
- Male and female teachers involved in sexually inappropriate touching and actual sex acts with female and male students.
- One teacher who repeatedly stole funds from a school account.
- A teacher who used school accounts to purchase personal items on multiple occasions.
- Several teachers with drug and alcohol abuse problems so severe they were taken out of school during the work day on multiple occasions to receive medical attention.
- A sting operation in the restroom of a local department store that resulted in the arrest of a teacher soliciting sex.

Despite the fact that every one of these issues was reported to the appropriate authorities by me and my superintendent and principal colleagues, to my knowledge none of these teachers or coaches lost their teaching licenses or their tenure. A few resigned or retired under pressure from the administration. Some even won lawsuits against the school district for trying to take disciplinary action against them after their actions became public.

WHAT IS PROGRESSIVE DISCIPLINE?

The New York State education commissioner, in cases like Mr. Bonesteel's, is administering tenure laws based on "progressive discipline." Progressive discipline means, except in the most egregious conduct cases, the offending teacher receives a written warning on the first offense. On the second offense the offending teacher receives time off without pay or a fine. Only with the third offense can a teacher be dismissed and lose tenure and possibly their teaching/principal license.

And my experience has been, each case of progressive discipline, during which a teacher receives pay, takes at least one year for the New York State Education Department to process.

In the most severe cases like child sex abuse, testimony from one or more children is required, and many parents, for understandable reasons, won't allow their children to testify. And when children do testify they tend to be unreliable witnesses who are easy for defense attorneys to confuse or intimidate. Sometimes when a criminal charge is filed and successfully prosecuted the school district gets a break and can ask the commissioner to summarily take away the teacher's or coach's license or tenure and have a good chance of being supported. But such breaks are rare.

NOT JUST A CASE OF CRIMINAL BEHAVIOR

The vast majority of New York State's 200,000-plus teachers never engage in misconduct issues of this kind; however, tenure as it presently exists in

New York State – statistically absolute – means all teachers live under a black cloud created by a small minority.

In fact, the absolute statistical nature of teacher tenure also adds to difficulties schools encounter in their efforts to improve student achievement. Many education leaders have given up trying to make educational improvements because they know the odds are not in their favor. The professionals who should be working with teachers – principals, assistant principals, assistant superintendents, superintendents – have become lazy, using the tenure trap as an excuse.[liii] They won't even spend money on teaching coaches, excellent teachers who go into classrooms and provide expert assistance to teachers, in many cases because they view the process as a lost cause. They have concluded their weakest teachers won't make the necessary changes, even with good support and coaching, so why spend the extra money.

So even if the tenure law changes there is work that will have to be done. And that requires willing participants like Sal Bocelli.

(Sections in italics are fictional stories made from composites of multiple actual experiences.)

A true improvement plan

When I began my two-year stint as an interim superintendent in the Candle Central School District, my first meetings were with the five school principals, each one at a different time, in their school buildings.

Academic improvement was one of the school board's key goals for the district, and my review of the data indicated this school board goal was totally on target for this relatively affluent district that underperformed when compared to districts with similar demographics.

Principals are perfectly positioned and empowered to initiate and support radical and subtle change in their schools or to undermine, subvert and sabotage any efforts for academic improvements initiated by superintendents or pushed by school boards, teachers or parents.

Four of Candle's five school principals were experienced, respectful and professional, but clearly overly cautious in their vision and goals for academic improvement. The district's history had been one of flying under the radar, not challenging the status quo and accepting mediocre academic achievement results. I would have to get them to aim higher than they thought possible if I were to succeed at improving academics in those four schools.

At the same time, I would need to value their understanding of their schools, praise them publicly when they made the right moves and achieved success and keep my critical suggestions straightforward, focused and private.

The outlier

Sal Boccelli was the odd man out. He had been a very successful and creative English teacher in Candle Middle School for seven years and then assistant principal before he became principal of the middle school.

He was seen as a good friend and supporter of the teachers in his school so I expected him to be like his colleagues, perfectly content with the status quo.

I expected Sal to defend his school's weak academic performance and provide me with a litany of excuses when we first met. I was wrong. Sal understood the test data and said he was ready to push forward with academic improvements and confront some of the teachers he felt were blocking necessary academic improvement in his school.

Towards the end of our first conversation, I asked Sal how many of his 18 tenured English and math teachers he thought were poor performers and needed "performance improvement" plans in order to create the academic change the school board wanted.

There were six teachers on his list. Sal thought they should all be terminated because of poor performance.

I cautioned Sal that termination for any of his teachers was a long way off (if ever) and a lot of work would need to happen before then.

EFFECTIVE VS. INEFFECTIVE TEACHERS

No doubt: Teachers have an impact on student performance and the research[liv] confirms this as does my experience. Case in point: Rosie Cameron (details altered to preserve confidentiality), was a very effective science teacher in the Averill Park Central School District in upstate New York where I worked as the high school principal.

Rosie taught earth science and worked during summers with a team of teachers that developed the annual required Regents exams. She also helped train other earth science teachers in the region at conferences and workshops.

Rosie's students scored extremely well on the year-end Regents exam. During my years working with Rosie, I saw 85 to 95 percent of her students passing and 35 to 50 percent scoring above 90 percent on the final exam every year. Rosie's classes always featured her students working in teams on interesting lab activities.

Whenever I needed an emotional boost after struggling with student discipline or teacher union issues I stopped by Rosie's room for 10 minutes to soak up the learning going on and the wonderfully supportive classroom atmosphere.

Five years after I started as the school principal, Rosie became pregnant and planned to go on maternity leave in early April, which meant we needed to hire a substitute teacher.

With lots of lead time we advertised in the regional papers and notified all the nearby colleges with earth science certification programs. But late in February we still had only one certified candidate.

New York State had just initiated a program requiring that all teachers hired for all positions (including longer term sub positions such as this one) be certified in their subject area. Uncertified teachers could only be hired if no certified applicants were available.

Violating this rule would have resulted in lots of challenging paperwork to be submitted to the state education department, bad press for the school district since the state education department reported these issues publicly and probably lots of unwanted attention from the nearby state education department for our school district in the future. So we interviewed the single certified applicant, a young man just out of college with good recommendations, and despite our concerns about his laid-back demeanor, we hired him.

Rosie departed for her maternity leave as planned on April 4th after spending a week with her temporary replacement. She left behind detailed plans for the final two major units of instruction and review for the mid-June final exam.

Within one week parents were calling and telling me, my assistant principal and our science department chairperson that the classes were out of control and no learning was taking place. My assistant principal and I conducted several observations of the classroom and while we were in the classroom the students were well behaved, but the replacement teacher's lesson plans were not the lab oriented, hands-on activities Rosie had used but more traditional lecture oriented instruction.

The substitute teacher resorted to lectures because the students were totally out of control and misbehaved badly whenever he tried to complete a more open-ended, hands-on activity. His disorganized, laid-back nature, monotone delivery and inability to recognize or react properly to students not paying attention to his instruction or properly completing the lab activities made the instruction totally ineffective.

We met with the replacement teacher, provided suggestions and gave him an opportunity to view instruction in our other successful Earth Science teacher's classes. But none of this helped and things went downhill quickly. Two students got into a fight in the classroom when Tom, the sub, tried to do a lab activity and more parent calls came every day. We had our science department chairperson take a full day with sub coverage for his own classes to shadow Tom and offer suggestions as well as the same for our other successful earth science teacher, but the problem persisted.

We tried to convince the other earth science teacher to split time with his own classes and Rosie's but he declined our request with a reasonable concern that doing what we requested would negatively impact his own students.

In mid-May with the Regents less than one month away and important review to be completed, I was able to convince our superintendent that we needed an extra sub in these earth science classes with the replacement teacher, one who knew our students and had worked in our school daily for several years. This regular sub could offer classroom control but no certification in earth science.

Sometimes the cause of teacher poor performance is simply not being willing to work hard enough. Sometimes it's not having the skills.

The parent calls stopped with the sub in the classroom. But she told me not to expect much from these students on the earth science Regents exam. "For them earth science ended when Rosie left. They have forgotten everything," she said.

Unfortunately, she was right: Only 48 percent of Rosie's and Tom's students passed the earth science Regents exam given on June 15th. And only two of the 89 students (2 percent) scored higher than 90 percent on the exam. So the research data on the importance of teacher effectiveness in student academic achievement comes as no surprise to me.

How it happens that we never seem to improve

During my next meeting with Sal at Candle Middle School, he identified six teachers he thought would benefit from academic improvement plans. I convinced Sal he would likely only have the time and resources to work with three or a maximum of four teachers with any depth.

My final prescription for Sal: Pick the three you think will move your whole building forward the most if you are successful in your efforts.

When we met the following week Sal had chosen three teachers he would be working with intensively. They were:

(1) Jim Hollister, a 45-year-old seventh grade English teacher and teacher union officer who took every sick and personal day off every year. Jim seldom assigned his students writing assignments that required grading and spent the majority of his class time "discussing" novels most of his students hadn't bothered to read. These discussions frequently veered off topic to Jim's favorite pastimes of major league baseball and movies. Jim's students had poor state test results before the Common Core standards arrived and now with the new standards and tests in place he had the lowest scores in the Candle Middle School English department.

(2) *Ralph McGlaughlin, a 59-year-old eighth grade English teacher, was very likeable but used the same spelling tests, textbooks and lecture notes he had used in 1980 when he started teaching at Candle Middle School. Ralph's classes were boring. His bored students occasionally caused discipline issues and his test results were just one small notch above Jim Hollister's.*

(3) *Karen Thompson, a 36-year-old sixth grade math teacher, conducted traditional lecture oriented classes and had frequent classroom control issues. Karen had an excuse for everything and her excuses boiled down to: "If these parents just sent us better students my classes would do much better on these state tests." Apparently Karen didn't receive the memo: Parents were not keeping their good students at home. Her state test data was the worst in the school's math department.*

Sal's reasoning for selecting these three teachers was sound. He selected one teacher from each of the three grade levels in his school and two from the English department, where test results were the worst, and one from the math department which had only marginally better test scores.

He selected two men and one woman and one senior teacher (Mr. McGlaughlin) and two midcareer teachers (Mr. Hollister and Ms. Thompson). These three teachers were representative of his faculty. Sal said he had not had any major conflicts with any of these staff members that would make his efforts to address their performance weaknesses look like an effort at retaliation or a personal vendetta.

I asked about Mr. Hollister's role in the teachers union, and Sal said he considered this issue and decided Mr. Hollister was a good candidate for an improvement plan because it sent a message that union leaders were not exempt from high expectations.

I cautioned Sal that including Hollister meant that every detail of what we were going to do with performance improvement plans would need to be letter perfect because the union would check every one of those details and call us out on technicalities. Sal agreed to be meticulous with details.

Then I asked Sal which, if any, of the original six he thought should be fired were the closest to being personal friends of his.

He indicated that Tyler Larritan, a seventh grade math teacher about his age (34) and a friend who played basketball with him and several other teachers on Wednesday nights at the school, was the closest to being such a friend.

"Tyler and I play hoops together in the winter," he said, "and we play golf together in the same league in the summer. His wife and mine have been friends since high school. We both attended each other's weddings and his son Matt is the same age as my son Brian and they were on the same Little League team."

"And you want to fire Tyler?" I asked.

"It would be the best thing for the middle school," he said. "Tyler is a very weak teacher. His classes are boring. He doesn't work hard enough. He doesn't offer enough extra help to students who are struggling or any extra challenges to students who are ready for them. Nearly 40 percent of his students fail his class on their report card grades and as a result they don't like him even though he has a decent personality. His students don't do well on state tests. Even the other seventh grade math teachers think he's a stick in the mud."

"So," I said, "if I told you, you can't fire Tyler, and I want you to devise a plan to help him and give him the best chance to improve his teaching, what would you propose?"

Sal thought for a full minute while I waited and finally said: "I'd get him out to see Anthony Tompkins teaching in his classroom. Remember Anthony? He was the guy we saw at the math teacher Common Core training this past summer."

"I remember," I told him. "What else would you do?"

"I'd ask you for money to pay for a math teacher coach to come in and work with Tyler to improve his planning and to observe his classes and coach him," he said. "Oh, and I'd sign him up for that local teacher training on Managing the Classroom for Open-Ended Instruction they talked about at the training this past summer. Tyler struggles with that

and as a result reverts to traditional lecture and worksheet type instruction all the time."

"Good, and what would you do to get this plan started?" I said.

"First, I'd meet with him about the need to improve the test data and suggest more group activities and project-based learning rather than lecturing to see if it might help engage the students more and improve test scores," he said. "I'd share my concerns about his students' failure rates and push the issue of allowing his students to re-test when they didn't succeed the first time they took the test."

Never entertain the thought

Finding the best way to get through challenges without creating conflict, without challenging assumptions and without making employees and school board members feel bad about not doing their jobs properly or effectively is the definition of leadership for far too many school administrators in the U.S.

In my experience, few principals (5 to 10 percent of more than 200 principals I knew quite well) would ever even entertain the thought of firing a tenured teacher because of poor classroom performance.

In addition, teacher performance improvement plans take days, weeks and months to plan and implement properly. Too many principals become overly involved in settling student discipline problems, playing super monitor in the lunchroom and in the parking lot, managing events like proms and graduation and trying to make their employees feel good with social activities and other events that contribute little to student academic success.

Very few principals have the confidence or time management skills required to pull off the task of improving teacher effectiveness. Virtually none would volunteer for this responsibility. I was lucky to have the opportunity to mentor Sal.

Sal naturally exhibited two primary characteristics essential to leadership success: empathy and support for those most in need AND values that reflect high expectations, personal responsibility, hard work and perseverance despite obstacles. And more importantly he understood these two critical leadership elements were not mutually exclusive. Sal understood what I have come to believe. All effective leaders maintain two seemingly mutually exclusive attributes in clear focus simultaneously at all times – empathy and high expectations. This is not my idea. It belongs to Steven Covey (see "The Seven Habits of Highly Effective People").

We all know leaders who are extremely empathetic but who lack a clear vision and who fail to set high expectations for employees, followers or those they serve. These leaders accomplish nothing because all their resources, time and energy go to feeling sorry for those who are suffering and demonstrating caring and concern for these unfortunate folks while nothing goes into improvement plans, honesty about data and implementation of those plans.

We also all know leaders who are full of honesty, facts, figures, plans and goals who have not one tiny bit of empathy or understanding for their employees, followers or those they say they are serving. In short order their leadership falls apart because employees or followers won't follow someone they think does not care about them or the folks they are supposed to serve.

You can't fake either side of this equation and be an effective leader. If you're going to tell people they need to change their ways and that they bear some of the responsibility for their shortcomings, you'd better be sure they believe you care about them and respect them first. Otherwise they will reject your message before you get started. Conversely, if your employees or your citizens know you care about them but you are afraid to tell them the unpleasant truth about their failures and their responsibility to change to make things better you are also going nowhere fast. Great leaders (some like Lincoln, Reagan, Churchill and Thatcher others prefer Teddy Roosevelt, FDR and Clinton) get people to understand that they really cared about them while telling them the truth and setting high expectations without sugar coating the pain required to achieve success.

Sal was the rare rookie who understood this difficult concept and could put it into action.

Uncharted waters

In Sal's school, as far as he knew, no principal had ever checked teacher lesson plans, but if this improvement effort was going to work he would need to know if teachers were planning properly.

"What would you be looking for in those plans?" I asked him.

Sal said he would look to see if Tyler was designing instruction with three levels: For students who were working above grade level, students working at expected grade level and students who were working below grade level.

He also had a bulleted list he'd written for himself. He would check to see if Tyler is:

- *Minimizing lecture time*
- *Eliminating worksheets*
- *Adding more structured student group work and other hands-on activities that increase student engagement*
- *Reviewing and correcting student work daily and sharing feedback with students*
- *Designing and implementing changes in his grading system and his testing process that encouraged retaking of tests to enhance understanding*

"Wouldn't the conversation you're describing be really hard given that you and Tyler are friends?" I asked.

Sal smiled. "Tyler knows I wouldn't lie to him, that I'm not out to get him and that my first interest is in the success of his students and our school. I'd be gentle and honest at the same time. Whatever he requested for his plan, assuming we can afford it, I would find a way to make it happen."

Here was Sal simultaneously exhibiting the necessary empathy for Tyler and high expectations for him. Sal understood that without both of these things he was going nowhere.

Then I asked Sal: "Would you go into the meeting with the improvement plan already written?"

"No, just my notes. I'll write the actual plan once I have Tyler's input,"

Sal also said he'd clarify at the meeting some goals they could both agree on for test score improvement and things he would expect to see in his classroom observations throughout the year that would show him Tyler was on track to make the necessary changes in his approach to instruction.

I asked Sal if he thought he should do a presentation to the entire staff regarding the English language arts and math state test data.

"Yes, but I might need some help with the similar schools comparison data," he said.

I told him I could help with that, and I shared with him a graph I had already created that showed the some of the academic performance comparison he needed to explain to his staff.

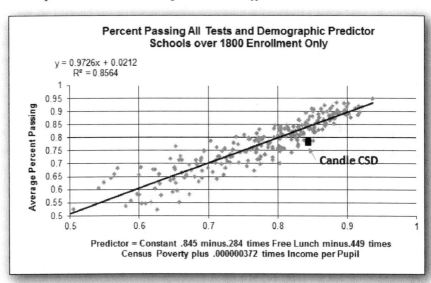

A TRUE MEASURE OF PERFORMANCE

During his career, Charles Winters, a New York State Business Official, St. John's University professor and respected colleague of mine, developed a sophisticated system for measuring school district academic performance based on demographics. It looks like the fictional scatterplot graph above.

His system was based on three criteria: eligibility for free or reduced price school lunch and breakfast, U.S. Census data on poverty and income data from New York State income tax filings.

The straight line on his scatterplot graph represents predicted academic performance using the best fit combination of all three variables. This particular combination produces the most accurate prediction of student performance on the state tests. As the scatterplot graph illustrates, the Candle School District performs below average. The grey marks that fall above the line represent high performing school districts in comparison with those with similar demographics and those below the line are underperforming. Candle, represented by the black rectangle, is well below the line.

As the Business Official for the Newburgh Enlarged City School District and as a consultant for the New York State Association of Small City School Districts, Mr. Winters compiled extensive data sets on student outcomes, demographics, local costs and state financial support. Mr. Winters used the "scatterplot" graph because he found it was an effective visual for displaying multivariable data.

Mr. Winters's school district comparison data became a key element in the Campaign for Fiscal Equity lawsuit and a companion lawsuit filed by several small cities in New York State that ended with a plan to redistribute $5.5 billion in new aid to school districts in the state with the primary focus on those serving the largest poverty populations. Like many states, New York sent too much state aid to wealthy, suburban politically connected school districts and underfunded poverty students' education and this disparity resulted in exacerbating the difficulties children from poverty have in producing acceptable results on standardized tests.[lv][lvi]

I'd come up with a less sophisticated but similar measurement based on free and reduced lunch data while I was an urban schools superintendent and before I met Mr. Winters.

The New York State Education Department, in general, uses test scores exclusively to compare school district performance. It's on par with comparing a struggling inner city hospital to the Mayo Clinic, apples to oranges. They have completely different clientele and resources available to them.

Why does the New York State Education Department improperly compare schools? It's really pretty simple. I my opinion, it wouldn't be politically prudent to compare districts while properly adjusting for demographics. When you start comparing one low poverty (wealthy) suburban district to another similar district, you're guaranteed to piss off some politically powerful suburban parents, teachers, administrators and school board members.

This is a problem because without knowing which *high poverty* schools are actually high performing we can't duplicate what they're doing. The same can be said for low poverty schools.

The plan continues

Sal also wanted to explain to all of the teachers what we saw in the math teacher training that summer: planning on three levels, less lecture and more group work, grading papers every day and allowing his students to re-test on stuff they missed until they answered correctly.

"Good idea," I said. I reminded him we had several days of training to digest what that trainer was selling. "You'll have an hour and a half meeting. Don't expect full buy-in from your teachers."

Then I asked Sal if he thought Tyler would work hard enough to make this plan succeed?

Sal hesitated for most of a minute. "I don't know, but it's worth a try," he said. "He's been a member of our school's staff for more than 10 years, and he's done what was expected of him, no more and no less. I shouldn't write him off before I give him a chance to improve."

I asked Sal to identify a poor performing teacher who was a friend because the strategy he'd create to help the teacher who was his friend is the same one that should be used for every teacher who is not performing up to expectations. In fact, Sal and I both knew it was a good idea to make certain that at least one of identified poor performers who other teachers might see as one of the principal's friends was on the list. That way we could minimize the concerns that this is just a list of teachers the principal was out to get for some personal reason.

"Unless you think the time commitment is too big, I want you to include Tyler in the group of teachers for improvement plans this coming school year," I told him. "Do you think you'll have the time to do all four and get everything else done?"

"Yes," Sal said, sounding only slightly unsure of himself.

"Tell them in writing in advance what you want to talk to them about when you meet with them and encourage them to come to the meeting with a union representative if they want one there," I said. "Make sure they know the union rep is their choice not the choice of the union.

"Meet with these teachers and after the meetings write up the four improvement plans. You'll need to be ready to implement them during the first week of school. But only after you've presented the test data comparison to the entire staff." I said.

INEFFECTIVE OR JUST LAZY

Ineffective teachers, in my opinion, fall into two broad categories: people who don't have the skills to teach and, another much larger group, those who just doesn't want to work that hard. One of the jobs of an administrator is to diagnose which category struggling teachers fall into so they can apply the right pressure and choose the proper incentives and supports required to make the necessary changes.

Even a talented teacher who doesn't want to work hard will fail to succeed, and it's a problem not unique to New York State.

In the 1980s, shortly after California implemented the infamous Proposition 13, limiting school property tax increases thereby reducing funding for schools, Massachusetts implemented its own version of a school property tax increase cap. Just as it had in California, the Massachusetts law resulted in the layoffs of many experienced Massachusetts teachers.[lvii]

The high school where I was principal in New York State was near the Massachusetts border so when we had an opening for a for a one year maternity leave math teacher position, we received several applications for the vacant position from experienced Massachusetts math teachers who had lost their jobs in budget cuts. The reciprocity of the math teaching certifications between the two states made these applicants a potential good fit for our needs.

Math is always a problematic teacher recruiting area, and maternity leaves are always difficult positions to fill with quality applicants. I was happy to include three of these experienced Massachusetts math teachers in the final teacher interview group. The interviews were impressive, and all of the experienced Massachusetts teachers interviewed indicated they could handle the transition to the slightly different New York State math curriculum without a problem.

After a phone recommendation check with principals and department chairs in Massachusetts we offered the vacant job, which included three classes of intermediate algebra and trigonometry with a required end-of-year Regents exam, to one of that state's teachers. He came with excellent recommendations, tenure in a local Massachusetts school district and five years of experience teaching intermediate algebra in Massachusetts. Al, we'll call him, even used the same textbook and a similar end-of-year Massachusetts final exam paperback review book which he brought to the interview to show us.

Al settled into his new job quickly. He was a traditional teacher with lots of lecture time, worksheets and homework. His classroom observations showed his students on task and working on the math and Al in control of the class and explaining the concepts with clarity and a professional approach. After the first 10-week school quarter I was worried about a higher than usual number of student failures on Al's report card grades and encouraged him to do more to provide extra help to students who needed it.

He responded positively to my suggestion and said he'd provide more after school help for students who needed it. The next quarter the failures were down a bit and all seemed to be proceeding according to plan with an experienced and effective teacher at the helm.

In April, after an unexpected retirement in Al's previous Massachusetts district he was notified he would be getting his old job back starting the following September. But Al was with us until the end of the school year and his students took the Regents exam on June 21. Once the exams were corrected and the scores turned in we never saw Al again.

Forty-one percent of Al's students passed the Regents exam. Only two out of 64 (3 percent) in his three classes scored above 80 percent on the test. In previous years our pass rate had been 75 to 90 percent with 40 to 60 percent scoring over 80 percent every year for as long as anyone could remember.

What happened? As a former math teacher I could see from the test data that many of Al's students missed the same questions, basic questions that they should have known. It appeared at first glance Al had not taught the entire curriculum, and, as a result, his students failed.

Our school did not offer summer school opportunities for students so I offered to come in, in the evenings and teach gratis intermediate algebra and trigonometry to prepare them for the Regents retake in August. Several students took me up on the offer.

One incident during these 10 sweltering three-hour-long evening sessions with no air conditioning in the school stuck in my mind. The 100 point intermediate algebra and trigonometry Regents from that era always included two or three questions on Part I worth two points and an optional 10 point question on Part II on the "law of sines" and the "law of cosines."

These are relatively simple problems that require using one of two formulas to find the length of unknown sides and the number of degrees in unknown angles in triangles when you know two angles and one side or two sides and one angle. This topic can be taught in one or two hours and it becomes a gift of 14 to16 points on the 100 point Regents exam.

After I showed my summer review class the formulas for the law of sines and the law of cosines and we solved for the unknown values in a few triangles one of the students said: "Don't you think we should have seen those formulas sooner?"

I mumbled an apology and as soon as the class was over I headed to my office where I pulled out the Massachusetts review book Al left behind. As I skimmed through ten years of Massachusetts final exams in intermediate algebra, I saw no questions on the law of sines or the law of cosines. And traditionally these formulas were dealt with in New York State schools in late April or May.

Al taught the curriculum he was familiar with and didn't do the extra preparation work required for the new topics in the New York State curriculum, especially after he found out in April he was going back to his old job in Massachusetts.

While his old Massachusetts school and our school used the same textbook they selected different chapters and units to teach. Al had stayed in his comfort zone and our students had failed as a result.

Teachers in Need of Improvement

Sal Boccelli and I met to develop the similar schools comparison data he would to present to the faculty of the Candle Middle School. I invited a school data expert from the local education consortium our district worked with to help us in our efforts.

We needed to find 15 to 20 middle schools in New York State in districts with about the same total enrollment as our middle school, roughly the same demographics in terms of percent of students receiving free and reduced lunch and the same incomes and the same U.S. Census poverty statistics, and compare these schools on their performance on the grade three to eight English language arts and math tests.

Within a week we had a scatterplot graph and test results chart showing the comparison, and as expected Candle Middle School was performing well below average in comparison to these similar schools for grades six, seven and eight on both English language arts and math tests.

Candle Middle School's weak performance was no surprise to me or Sal, but it would be for Sal's staff who had only seen comparisons of their district's performance to districts with many more poverty students, the kind of comparison we usually see in the local newspapers.

Once we had the data in hand I quizzed Sal with the kinds of questions he could expect from his teachers when he presented this data to them in his opening day faculty meeting. I asked him:

- *How do you know these schools are a fair comparison for our school?*
- *If the state education department has no problem with our school's performance, why should we be worried?*
- *What are these schools doing that's so different from what we are doing?*
- *What kind of resources will the school board be giving to our school to help us improve scores?*
- *Why are we all of a sudden a low performing school?*

Once we went over those questions – and the answers – Sal gave me the bill for improvement: $50,000 for coaches for all his teachers and $100,000 for his department chairs and a few key teachers to work on curriculum and assessment with the teacher coaches during school vacations and after school during the school year.

I told Sal I would find a way to fund this effort.

Coming up with the funding for academic improvement

In order to produce funds to pay for academic improvement, I dove into the school district budget and pulled out my surgical tools, so to speak. (A hammer will not do the job.)

Our school bus transportation supervisor had retired and instead of just filling the position I planned to hire a retiree as an interim supervisor. I knew that would save $30,000 in benefit costs. The retiree's experience would also help us study how we could make long-term savings in student transportation by consolidating school bus routes, not a popular move in communities where people depend on school bus driver jobs for their health insurance and retirement. However, it's fiscally sound.

Meeting with the district's special education director, we determined we could move three senior special education students out of costly private placements into work-study internships inside the district and save the district more than $120,000 in tuition and student transportation costs.

This kind of change can also be unpopular with parents of special education students even when it reduces the time their children spend on buses to schools in some cases 90 minutes away. In my experience, this kind of move is not only fiscally sound but also educationally beneficial for the students.

Special education students' education experience is more meaningful when they're immersed in their own communities.

Sal left my office ready for his opening day meeting with his teachers and ready to implement a plan that offered the potential to produce improvements for four of his teachers and therefore their students using a model he developed.

He was also ready to set up a plan for his department chairs and teacher leaders to work on curriculum improvement tasks during school breaks and develop a plan to use teacher coaches to help the four teachers targeted for improvement plans and also to provide instructional improvement help to the rest of the math and English departments.

Sal and I also set up a meeting with the local consortium that did teacher training and he called his principal friends for advice on English language arts and math candidates for the teacher coaches we would request from the consortium (BOCES). Sal also decided to involve his teachers in the interview process to select the new teacher coaches.

THE MYTHS SURROUNDING TEACHER OBSERVATIONS

Over the course of the seven years I taught physics, AP Physics, general science, earth science, general math, algebra, geometry, trigonometry and pre-calculus, I was observed by my principal or another school administrator nine times.

This frequency of observation was more or less typical for teachers in the 1970s. Each of these observations consisted of the administrator arriving to my 40 to 45 minute class without warning, staying for 15 to 20 minutes while writing furiously on a set form specified in the teachers union contract and meeting with me for 10 minutes at a later time while we both looked at copies of what he had scribbled on the form.

The forms used in the 1970s started from the basic assumption that I would be lecturing at the front of the classroom and the students would be playing spectator in their neatly ordered desks. The categories on the form led to recommendations related to classroom management (were the students well behaved and attentive), room décor (were posters in vogue), avoiding monotone speech and presenting the instruction in an interesting manner. The only suggestion I remember from these discussions that had any value for me in my teaching was one about a specific student with a hearing problem I had not known about and locating his desk closer to the front of the room so he could hear me better.

One of the reasons I became a school administrator was because I was convinced that I could do a much better job in this area and help my teachers be more effective by providing them with real suggestions that had a positive impact on their students.

I attended every training session I could find on the topic of instruction. I relentlessly quizzed the professors in my school administration courses who taught classes on the topic of instructional improvement for teachers and the classroom observation process. I read every book I could find and always asked my peers for tips and ideas on how to improve my own performance in this key job performance area. And, basically, I came up with a lot of what I can only describe as mumbo jumbo.

Over my years in school administration as fads came and went principals became scribes who recorded every classroom observation detail:

- Student: "Will this be on the test?" Teacher: "Harry, just do it."
- Students chattering in the back of the room while teacher continues to talk about Roman Empire at the board. Teacher: "Quiet down back there." Students quiet for two minutes then back to chattering.
- Students in groups confused about directions for dissection task. Student: "How are supposed to cut the frog's leg?" Teacher: "It's on the board."

It takes about five minutes of playing scribe before you realize you're missing the recording of many valuable details and making all kinds of judgements about what to write down and what to omit.

You are also scribbling illegible extraneous and disconnected details or typing partial or misspelled words and phrases many of which will make no sense to you or the teacher later.

"Scribe observers" also immediately know they're missing the big story of the instructional successes and failures in the classroom because they're too involved in recording details of the action. Time and experience improves this process but not enough to justify the time invested.

Pre-observation conferences became an expectation in the 1990s with administrators meeting with teachers in advance of lessons to be observed. The goal was to ensure the administrators conducting the observation understood the exact plans, the specific needs of the students and all the lesson implementation strategies and contingencies so that s/he could more fairly evaluate the teacher's instruction.

New York's current formal teacher observation technique[lviii][lix] requires the following:

* The principal or other school administrator completing the observation sits with the teacher in a pre-observation conference and together they record their expectations for the lesson to be observed on a state prescribed pre-observation form. (The teacher has completed their portion of this form before the meeting starts.) (30 minutes)

* The principal or other administrator observes the classroom at the previously scheduled date and time, assuming of course that two students don't get into a fight in the lunchroom on that day and totally destroy the administrator's schedule or the teacher's daughter doesn't wake up sick and he has to call in sick to stay at home and take care of her. (45 minutes)

* The principal or administrator "writes up the observation," meaning turns the scribbles or partial sentences and phrases into something

that resembles a reasonable description of the activities that happened in the classroom. (60 minutes)

* The principal or administrator attributes the details of his observation in each of the 60 specific text boxes related to prescribed instructional skills on a computerized form. (45 minutes)

* The principal or administrator adds any recommendations and praise. (30 minutes).

* The principal or administrator sets up a post observation conference with the teacher to discuss the lesson and any specific suggestions or compliments for a job well done and the teacher makes her/his case for or against the administrator's conclusions and recommendations. (45 minutes)

* Total average administrator time per observation = 4 hours and 15 minutes

Note: Times in parentheses are averages and sometimes they are much longer.

Unfortunately, too often the class observed is a typical "dog and pony show."[ix] The teacher feels obligated to orchestrate this "show" based on her/his perceptions of the observer's expectations.

The worst part of this process is that when it is completed the teacher returns to the classroom and the administrator goes back to her/his office and both are, more often than not, left with the feeling that they somehow missed the big picture and that the entire process, despite the enormous amount of time invested, really hasn't helped to improve the teacher's instruction.

Teaching is a difficult, complex process. The differences between good and bad instruction is easily missed by the untrained eye. In addition, if the administrator observing the class notes 50 separate details in her/his 40-minute scribing effort on the observation form and provides six separate suggestions related to the lesson observed, it doesn't mean the teacher, even a teacher who is trying hard, will be able to implement the suggestions and improve her/his practice.

The order of implementation of the suggestions and the supportive skills required to make the six suggested changes may be intertwined. Attempting to implement these suggestions could result in confusion rather than real progress.

So how do you move the teacher forward? Consider how other fields involving complexity train people to improve their performance.

If you are learning to improve your guitar playing skills, any decent music instructor will first ask you about your goals: Do you want to play in a band? What kind of music do you want to learn? Then the guitar instructor will listen to you play some chords and leads for a few minutes and pick a strategy to help you move forward toward your goal with one or two things to practice and one or two songs to work on until your next lesson.

A good guitar instructor would never consider telling you to play the guitar for 40 minutes while he was scribing about what he saw and heard while you played. He might record you while you're playing and have you listen to the sounds you produced, but he would never consider filling in a form with 60 guitar skill-related text boxes the two of you could discuss.

After a few minutes of listening to you play, a good guitar instructor would decide where to start the improvement effort and the specific tasks that would achieve the step to moving you closer to your guitar-playing goal.

And, crucially, the guitar instructor would know which key skill needed attention first, which songs and practice activities would give the biggest, quickest payoff in student improvement and his improvement plan would be sure to guarantee that the student saw some recognizable improvement immediately.

Anyone who has taken lessons in watercolor painting, golf, biking, fitness or tennis (as I have) or any other complicated pursuit would recognize the pattern.

New York State's teacher observation process grew out of heated negotiations between the teacher union lawyers and state education department lawyers. Basically, a group of lawyers with no experience in education adopted a model created by a noted instructional expert named Charlotte Danielson.[lxi]

My take, the Danielson list of essential teaching skills and successful classroom attributes is that it is good, but incomplete. It should actually include a more comprehensive list that teachers and administrators can pull from. Trying to look at too many skills and attributes in one classroom observation, which the present New York State prescribed process virtually requires, is a recipe for failure. Choosing a few key skills from a more comprehensive list would lead to more growth and improvement.

WHERE DO WE GO FROM HERE?

So what approach might work for a principal and teachers trying to improve instruction?

As a principal I found that if I spent five minutes in eight classes, I learned more about the instruction going on in my school than I did with 40 minutes invested in one class. I also found out (like the guitar and golf instructors I used over the years) that one well selected suggestion or question or one crucial specific item of praise directly related to simple goals was more likely to improve performance than several comments jumbled on one long confusing form.

But what about scribing? Tell the teacher to regularly video tape his class and watch the tapes. It's more accurate and less judgmental than the scribing. And believe me if the class is a hot mess or an inspiring success the tape will tell the tale accurately.

How about the long form and all the text boxes and teaching skills? I suggest the teacher and principal pick two or three key skills each from the list of 60 and focus on their combined list of four to six skills for the year. No one should be trying to look at 60 areas of improvement at one time. Imagine trying to hit a golf ball while considering 60 separate swing ideas.

Another way to support teachers in their efforts to produce better results is to set them up to work with their peers in co-teaching activities that build on both the teachers' distinct strengths. They will learn from one another in a non-judgmental environment.

A good principal will know which teachers could pull off a cooperative teaching venture with a peer and will make the necessary arrangements and provide the right kind of encouragement. And if the teachers think inviting the principal or department chairman in to see them co-teach a class is a good idea, let them extend the invitation. But if you want to see real growth and development rather than a dog and pony show, don't require they make the invitation.

Towards the end of my 13 years of being a school principal I tried to visit each of my 70 teachers' classrooms for five minutes five to eight times a year and complete the required (but largely unhelpful) one to three formal observations per year.

At the time, tenured teachers in my school were required to have one formal observation per year and non-tenured teachers three. For teachers with improvement plans, I tried to increase the number of five minute visits to 25 or 30 visits, and I increased the formal observations from one to four.

However, I tried to focus these extra formal observations on three to six skills for each teacher. I selected these skills after discussions at the beginning of the school year with the teachers who had improvement plans.

I used the five minute visits to see if teachers at every level (tenured, non-tenured, improvement plan) were making progress on the following:

- Reducing time wasted on excessive lecturing. (Classrooms can be very boring places.)[lxii]
- Engaging students on appropriate curriculum related tasks.
- Planning at multiple levels with extra help for students who needed it and extra challenges for students who were ready for it.
- Giving students regular feedback on the accuracy of their academic work so they had a chance to improve their grades.
- A grading system that allows students to re-test if they didn't succeed initially.
- Managing classes in a time efficient and respectful manner.

I left a one or two sentence hand written message in the teacher's mailbox after each five minute visit.

The handwritten message I left was usually one statement of very specific praise. For example, "I really liked the way you…" I also asked one question, such as, "Do your students have any opportunity to raise their grades if they do poorly on the unit test you mentioned?"

I saved myself a copy of any hand written messages from five minute classroom visits to integrate into my next formal observation for the teacher. After that formal observation I discarded them so that I didn't get into hot water with the union for trying to circumvent the union approved formal observation process.

Sal executes the teacher improvement plans

Sal selected a few key things to work on with the four teachers: planning and teaching for three levels of students; short, focused, effective lectures; more group work or other hands-on, engaging activities for students (which would require having the classroom management skills needed to run these activities effectively); daily grading of student work and opportunities for students to improve their grades.

These improvement areas are all part of one or more of the 60 required teaching skills and text boxes contained in the formal observation form, and if they are done well, these teachers will move from being very weak performers to decent teachers.

Sal knew the decisions regarding the order of implementation for these improvement areas and the exact details of how they would play out in individual classrooms should involve the teaching coaches and the improvement plan teachers to minimize the feeling of being overwhelmed, create teacher ownership and create some early success that would motivate continued effort toward improvement.

Sal was committed to investing between 12 hours and 22 hours per teacher during the school year on just the formal observation part of the improvement plans. Normally, his commitment for the formal observations of these teachers would have been less than half that time.

Add another 10 to 20 hours to his workload for hiring and super-vising the teaching coaches. On top of that, add the extra five minute classroom visits for the improvement plan teachers (roughly three or four hours per teacher) and all together Sal would be adding about 60 to 100 hours of work to an already very busy school year to work on the improvement plans for these four teachers.

The improvement plans begin

When we met on the second Wednesday of the school year, Sal said the four teachers designated for improvement plans had been respect-ful during their meetings with him. None decided to bring in teacher union representatives to their meetings with Sal. Only Jim Hollister set up a second meeting with the teacher union president and Sal to voice some concerns.

His concerns: "Can you really require me to turn in written lesson plans? What if my style of teaching doesn't agree with the style being pushed by the English language arts teaching coach? Can you really require me to grade papers daily and design lessons on three levels?"

Sal turned back all of these questions with direct answers, "Yes, I can require you to turn in lesson plans. Your teaching style needs to change because too many students are failing the required exams. You need to grade papers daily so that you know what your students know and what they don't understand so that you can make the right adjust-ments to your instruction."

Sal knew this wasn't the last we'd hear from Jim Hollister, but Jim went away without continued objection except for saying on his way out that this whole process might well be grounds for a grievance based on their teacher union contract.

Sal and I had anticipated the threat of a teacher grievance and called our school district attorney ahead of time to be sure we were on the right track with our approach. Our attorney was helpful in supply-ing some additional models of teacher performance improvement plans that had been written in other districts, plans that had successfully survived grievances on appeal to PERB (Public Employment Relations Board, the government oversight division that decides on public union contract disagreements in New York State).

Opening day

On opening day, the faculty raised many of the questions we anticipated and a few we had not. Some of the questions we had not anticipated, included the following:

- *Do you really think our students can do better on these tests? Remember this is Candle Middle School not the wealthiest suburb in the area.*
- *If you're expecting us to design three levels of lesson plans and grade papers every day, are you planning to pay us more?*
- *If you think we should re-test students over and over until they finally get it right, aren't we just lowering our standards and making it too easy for students to just blow off the first test?*

I could tell from the way he explained this exchange to me it was a good one for him and the school faculty. Sal said he maintained his sense of humor and laughed with his teachers when it made sense but he also made it clear that he believed that Candle Middle School students could do better on the state tests. Sal felt at the end of the meeting that the majority of his teachers agreed with him on this point. Sal also said that he emphasized to his teachers:

- *Yes, I am asking you to work harder and smarter and as the principal that is my job.*
- *I'm sure you can see that what I am proposing will require me to work harder and smarter too.*
- *You know me and you know by now after my time as a fellow teacher, an assistant principal and my first year as a principal*

that I will listen to you guys every step of the way and we will work things out as we improve together.

Because we had been late in the summer with our request for teaching coaches BOCES sent rookie teaching coaches for English language arts and math. Sal involved his teachers in the final interviews and they appeared confident the coaches selected would work out fine. Again, by involving the teachers Sal showed his understanding that making the teachers part of his leadership team at every point in the process increased his own effectiveness as an education leader.

In addition to bringing in the BOCES teaching coaches, we posted new teacher leader positions at a salary Sal and I had set in advance using figures from our rough instructional improvement planning budget.

Sal used his department chairs to help select the finalists for English language arts and math teacher leaders for each grade level (six, seven and eight). A schedule was set up for the curriculum work to be done at the end of the summer and over school breaks during the year.

Sal and I set up a formal meeting for October 1st to see how the entire plan was going and to evaluate our next steps and necessary adjustments. In a district the size of Candle School District, I tried to stop by without an appointment and visit with my principals informally in their schools two to three times per week for 15 to 30 minutes. It is not in my nature to wait a month on something as big as these improvement plans.

Frequently, these conversations were held while we walked around the school building. If the principals were tied up in a meeting, I'd just wander around the school by myself and talk to the people who worked there to get a better feel for operations within each school. Sal and I met with each other at least two to three times a week for 15 to 30 minutes to discuss the progress of the overall teacher improvement plan so when the formal meeting arrived there were few surprises.

Sal reported at our meetings that the four teacher improvement plans were being executed as planned. As expected, the teachers were having some problems adjusting. These were big changes and it was not like throwing a light switch. It required real work, daily mistakes and lots of extra time invested during the school day and at night after the students were gone. This extra time investment should be expected when we change the way we've been doing something for several years.

Sal pulled all four of his improvement plan teachers out of their classrooms for a day so they could observe more successful teachers in other schools. The two math teachers observed Anthony. (See "Common Core is Not the Problem" chapter). The two English teachers observed Susan Hammer, a teacher with a reputation similar to Anthony's who taught middle school English. She was identified as a star by our newly hired teaching coaches and was confirmed with star status when I spoke with her superintendent.

The superintendent had nominated Susan for a Teacher of the Year Award the previous year.

All four improvement plan teachers saw Anthony and Susan implementing three-level instruction, giving brief lectures, assigning student group work, doing daily paper grading and providing re-testing for students. They also had a chance to meet with Anthony and Susan privately for an hour after their classroom observations to ask questions. They also saw them handle classroom management and organization of instruction. Both Anthony and Susan worked in districts with a higher level of poverty (more free and reduced lunch students) than Candle School District.

All four of the improvement plan teachers were observed by the teaching coaches multiple times and all four were scheduled to co-teach multiple class period units with the teaching coaches. These co-teaching units provided a good opportunity for teachers to practice with someone who is not their boss. That's how you improve.

The teacher coaches and the four improvement plan teachers jointly developed the co-taught unit instructional plans. Sal said he planned to start collecting the improvement plan teacher lesson plans on October 20th after the co-taught units were completed.

All four teachers successfully completed the co-taught units and Sal said the feedback from the teachers, department chairs and teaching coaches was generally positive except for the teachers' concerns about the new heavy workload and time commitment required to teach with the new approach.

Several times during our conversations about the improvement plan teachers Sal and I would look at each other and shake our heads as one of us said, "How did these four ever get tenure?"

How did these teachers end up receiving tenure? My experience with how people like these four teachers are hired and given tenure is a sad tale with many intersecting threads and dependent parts. There's a lot of blame to go around and fixing this issue is a difficult challenge.

We've all read news stories comparing our teachers with teachers in other advanced countries. It's true the average SAT scores for those enrolled in college as education majors is near the bottom among college academic programs, but it is improving.[lxiii] Given new academic requirements for teacher certification, including national and state level teacher certification tests of math, language arts, pedagogy and subject area expertise, the recently hired teachers in most states (some southern states are still an exception), are generally academically competent enough to succeed.[lxiv]

However, this was less the case in earlier generations when the quality of these skills was more variable for those hired as teachers. There were Harvard educated teachers and some people who should never have been hired to teach, many of whom were given tenure and are still in classrooms. Mind you, the quality of the teacher prep programs is still highly variable.

So, if we have academically competent teaching candidates for most teaching positions, how do we end up with these poor performers? In every school district where I worked during my 45 year career the hiring process included steps that guaranteed a less competent and less diverse teaching workforce.

Any skilled reviewer of the applicant resumes available for 80 to 90 percent of the teaching positions where I helped to select a successful teaching applicant could find five to eight resumes that warranted an interview for the applicant. (That changed some after the economic downturn in 2008, when many teachers were laid off and colleges and universities continued to pump out new teachers. In 2013-14, while I was an interim superintendent in a small school district in upstate New York, we had five elementary school teacher openings and 900 applications. Consequently, we didn't even look at new graduates. New graduates were only considered for teaching assistant positions.)

There were exceptions in hard to recruit positions like physics or math or computer science or earth science. And there were specific high poverty or rural schools or districts where I worked that encountered significant difficulty finding high quality teacher applicants. But in general a qualified and reasonably talented pool of applicants was generally available, a luxury found in New York State but not necessarily in every state.

Unfortunately, more often than not, residents, school board members, teacher union members, principals and other administrators and superintendents intervened in the hiring process. In many cases less qualified applicants were hired despite the fact that they were easily identifiable inferior to other candidates.

Frequently, a surreptitious email or phone call was made to someone who was involved in the decision making process. Inevitably the brother of a friend of the principal, the sister of a teacher union representative on the interview committee or the nephew of a board member (or some similarly connected individual) would call their "insider" contact who was intimate with the hiring process and "put in a good word" for a specific candidate.

In general, the parties involved in these conversations don't see the harm in their actions. They are merely trying to help someone they know (or their brother or friend knows) land a job, and if their actions are successful they assume the candidate they are promoting will perform positively.

It's a culture. The insider receiving the request is just trying to make themselves look powerful and helpful to whoever it was that asked them to perform this subtle hiring manipulation.

Usually, the candidates who are beneficiaries of the surreptitious phone calls and emails are the same ethnicity or attended the same college as the person making the phone call or sending the email. And the insider who then subtly manipulates the hiring process is also of the same ethnicity or in some way connected to the same college or friend or relative or peer group.

The ethnic diversity issue can be as much of a problem for minority dominant districts and staffs as it is for white dominant districts and staffs. Increasing diversity in ethnicity, training and teaching skills in the final teacher employee pool has been shown to improve student achievement.[lxv]

In my experience, these calls are a form racism and classism and serve only to perpetuate a weaker teacher workforce in many school districts.

How did this play out in Candle Middle School?

So it was when Jim Hollister was hired (a friend of a brother of a member of the hiring committee who recommended his hiring); when Ralph McGlaughlin was hired (the nephew of a friend of the assistant principal for the school at that time); when Karen Thompson was hired (the former student who attended all schools in the district K–12 and graduated from the high school and who encouraged several of her former teachers to call interview hiring committee members and the principal before she was hired); and when Tyler Larritan was hired (the graduate of the same college and a close friend of the same college soccer coach as the school district's athletic director who was called by his good friend the college soccer coach and who in turn called the principal of the school to promote Tyler as a candidate when he was hired).

All four of these candidates were white and middle class and attended one of three regional state college teacher preparation programs — the same profile as 74 percent of Candle's other teaching staff members.

WHY DO WE DO IT?

Unless there is a conscious effort to the contrary people tend to gravitate toward hiring people like themselves,[lxvi] frequently making the egocentric inane comment: "Oh, she reminds me of a younger me."

This issue of behind the scenes phone calls and emails on hiring decisions became so troublesome for me when I was a superintendent I adopted a personal policy: If anyone, including a school board member, called me or emailed me to "put in a good word" about any candidate for a vacant position in the district I immediately informed the entire board about this phone call or email. I said I did this to make certain "everyone had the same information."

Of course, I never received any more calls or emails promoting specific candidates, but everyone else in the hiring process still got their calls and emails.

Hiring graduates from the same college programs impedes progress when the teacher preparation program is ranked low in terms of the quality of their teaching graduates.[lxvii] [lxviii]

What are the elements of a good teacher prep program?

* The professors are conversant in the new Common Core standards.
* The SAT scores of the program graduates are higher than average.
* The level of academic challenge in their teacher preparation content classes (history classes for social studies teachers, math classes for math teachers, etc.) is high.
* They teach new and innovative pedagogy.
* The professors actually taught or worked as a principal in public schools recently.
* They teach effective classroom management for classes that have students engaged in open-ended learning activities.
* Their graduates are succeeding as illustrated by the performance of their students on required state exams.

Modern management theory

Sal and I also understood that when these four Candle Middle School teachers were evaluated by their principals for a tenure recommendation, principals were supervising approximately 70 teachers.

Most modern management theory says an effective supervisor should supervise six to 12 employees. Even with the help of an assistant principal the numbers are overwhelming. The principals completing these teacher evaluations had little meaningful training in teacher evaluation or instructional improvement.

Most troublesome of all: The principal knew these teachers had been hired because of their successful behind the scenes phone calls and emails – not because they were the best candidate. They're both beholden to a different party, the party that got them hired.

The principals in charge when these teachers' tenure evaluations were being completed were under political pressure to recommend them for tenure. How could they not recommend a teacher for tenure whose "connections" had gotten them the job in the first place?

These teachers didn't work for the principal who agreed to their hiring. They owed their jobs to their connections and thus couldn't be properly evaluated for job performance.

Sal collects lesson plans

On October 20ᵗʰ, three of the four teachers turned in their lesson plans. Jim Hollister filed a grievance citing what he perceived as a violation of the contract provision that stated "each teacher's schedule must include one 45-minute preparation period per school day."

Jim's grievance contended that it takes more than 45 minutes to plan for the new approach to instruction that had been modeled in the co-taught unit with the teaching coach and had been discussed with Susan Hammer when he observed her classes.

The grievance also contended that the contract between the teachers union and the school district did not specifically give the principal the authority to request Jim's written lesson plans in advance. And since written plans had never been requested by any principal in the Candle School District previously, this request constituted a violation of past practice.

Sal and I were not surprised by this grievance or by the arguments it made. When we contacted the school district attorney about the improvement plans before the start of the school year, she said these were the two most frequent areas of contention that resulted in teacher grievances.

As long as we had data supporting our claim that these teachers' performances had to improve (we had it with their students' test data and the similar schools data) and we had given them instruction and support in how the plans needed to be written and implemented (the work of the teaching coaches and their visits with Anthony and Susan had done this) we should be able to win the expected grievance, according to our school district lawyer.

Sal wrote a response denying the grievance as required. The attorney and I reviewed Sal's draft before he gave it to the president of the teachers union. The union appealed the grievance to me as superintendent and I wrote a similar denial which was also reviewed by the attorney.

These two grievance stages took three weeks. Then the union appealed my denial to the Public Employment Relations Board and a hearing was set for four months later. In the time between the grievance filing and the Public Employment Relations Board hearing the district can require the teacher to continue to do what is being grieved. And we did. Despite loud protestations from Jim Hollister and the teachers union president we told Jim and the other improvement plan teachers they had to turn in written lesson plans.

Ultimately, all four teachers turned in the lesson plans as required. All four demonstrated weaker planning than necessary for successful instruction. Ralph McGlaughlin, Karen Thompson and Tyler Larritan tried to do a good job with this planning task, but they didn't understand the detailed decision making required to plan for three levels of instruction.

They didn't know how to reduce their lecture time and increase student group work. They were uncertain how to break students into different groups for each day's instruction, what student classroom activities they'd need to grade to make instructional adjustment decisions and how to build a re-testing component into planning. Sal met with each of these teachers with the teaching coaches for three to five full 45-minute periods to discuss and refine their planning efforts. Everyone in the meetings worked hard at this task and slowly over a two-month period the teachers' plans improved.

Sal made certain each of these teachers had ownership for their own planning by letting them do it "their way" as long as they hit the key planning goals.

Jim Hollister was a different story. Jim's plans consisted of one or two word entries for each planning activity. As an example, when plans called for mini lecture notes Jim wrote "book discussion" and nothing more. When the plans called for adjustments for less able and more able learners, Jim wrote "oral questions."

When Sal met with Jim Hollister and the English language arts teaching coach as he had with the other improvement plan teachers, Jim used the time to argue that his planning was adequate and anything else expected by Sal and the teaching coach was nothing but busy work.

When the plans called for re-testing Jim said he didn't believe in re-testing and would not be implementing this procedure in his classroom.

When Sal spoke to the teacher union president about this conflict and requested her support, she refused. "Jim has told me to stay out of this issue and I will honor his request," she said. "I have advised Jim and so has the local New York State United Teachers representative that he should do what you have requested until his grievance is decided at the Public Employment Relations Board. He's obviously not listening to us."

Sal started the formal observations of the four improvement plan teachers during the first week in November. In his walk-through classroom visits, which had started for all the middle school teachers at the beginning of the school year, Sal had seen attempts at more group work and multilevel instruction in Ralph's, Karen's and Tyler's classrooms. Their classrooms weren't stellar but the teachers were trying to make the shifts recommended by the teaching coaches.

Sometimes the classes were rowdy as the teachers learned more about how to manage student group work. Sometimes the teachers' plans for three student levels of instruction backfired and they ended up spending all their time with one group or they had to abandon their multilevel plans and resort to whole group instruction. But it was also clear they were trying to do what was expected.

Sal's classroom visits showed Jim Hollister was proceeding as though the improvement plan did not exist. He was always at the front of the room lecturing or talking about movies and baseball. He did nothing to even indicate any effort to change his approach. He was being defiant and apparently planned to stay in that mode at least until the Public Employment Relations Board decision came down.

Sal and I discussed this regularly and we decided after talking with our school district attorney that the best course of action would be to document what Sal was seeing with memos to Jim and copy the teacher union president each time Sal visited the classroom.

The teacher contract described the possibility of a brief classroom visit but didn't have a specific form to record the visits so we resorted to memos, which we saved to be integrated into the long-form observations when they were completed.

Sal and I had another extended meeting in November to discuss his work with the four teachers. Sal had already made his first set of four scheduled formal observations of the teachers. For each of these four observed lessons Sal met with the teachers before his classroom observation and the teachers explained their lesson plans.

In these pre-observation meetings Sal also asked several follow-up questions to see if the teachers were attempting to plan their lessons on three levels, incorporate more student group work, minimize and condense lecture time, implement strategies to provide extra help for students who were struggling and extra challenges for students who were ready for them, grade student work daily while analyzing it to make instructional adjustments and incorporate re-testing procedures so students who wanted to improve their grades had a chance to do so.

He also checked with teachers to get their perspective on their work with the teaching coaches. Was it helping the teachers? Did they need additional supports to be successful in their improvement plan? Each

132

pre-observation meeting with the four teachers took more than an hour and Sal made extensive notes that he incorporated into the final written formal observation document.

Three of the teachers (all except Jim Hollister) indicated they were trying hard to make the changes the teaching coaches recommended. Sal met with the teaching coaches in advance of these pre-observation meetings with the four teachers and they confirmed the teachers were making an effort toward improvement. The teaching coaches reported that all three of those trying to make changes were struggling.

Ralph was disorganized in his planning and had significant trouble with classroom management when students worked in groups or on other open-ended activities.

Karen had trouble getting all the papers corrected each day and getting her lesson plans done in advance. She was also lost in analyzing the data to make instructional adjustments.

Tyler struggled with devising three level plans and his commitment to coaching athletics three sport seasons meant time after school for extra help and re-testing for his students was in short supply.

All three struggled to boil their lectures down to a few minutes per day. The teaching coaches said the teachers tried to get away from the front of the classroom and get students working in groups, but they frequently spent 30 minutes lecturing leaving only 10 minutes for group work and other student directed activities instead of their planned 30 minutes for these activities. But all three were trying and improving slowly.

Jim Hollister presented Sal with his lesson plan for a 40-minute lecture on the book "Where the Red Fern Grows." He was still married to his lecture-heavy style of teaching.

"These students will be going to college in a few years and they will have to learn from lectures," he argued. "I'm getting them ready for that college environment and I see no need for me to change my approach."

When the English language arts teaching coach mentioned his students' test scores as a reason to change, Jim responded with the same line he'd used with Sal: "The students who work pass my class and do well on the test. Those who don't fail. They need to work harder."

Jim was reveling in his status among his teacher peers as the rebel who would not kowtow to this overreaching principal and superintendent. I was a target of Jim's wrath because I had made certain all the teachers knew I supported Sal in his improvement efforts with money for teaching coaches and teacher leaders and encouragement at the school board level.

Sal's formal observations revealed just what the teaching coaches predicted: The three teachers making legitimate efforts to improve were providing better instruction than they had in the previous year when Sal had observed them, but they all had a long way to go.

Ralph's class was just barely under control with students passing notes and sharing semi-silent jokes and laughs while he lectured for 25 minutes on the form and style of sonnets. No students appeared to be taking notes and Ralph provided nothing but a few scribbles on a chalkboard.

The students were better in groups where they were asked to analyze a specific sonnet, but they were confused about the directions. Three times Ralph had to stop the class and again explain his expectations. At the end of the 40-minute period the initial group sonnet analysis was incomplete, and Ralph's plan had been for students to complete two full sonnet analyses in class. He failed to collect their work.

Karen's lesson plan involved a brief lecture on solving simple equations using rudimentary graphic pictures as a way to illustrate the variables and numbers. Karen had planned to talk for 10 minutes and then have students working in pairs on a series of similar and increasingly complex problems for the final 30 minutes of the period with the results of their group work to be collected and graded.

Karen took a full five minutes to get the students started as she had no kickoff activity and her lecture went on for 30 minutes with students complaining they didn't understand and Karen resorting to repeating what she had already said to no positive effect. The group work was haphazard with some groups doing most of the expected tasks and others never even starting.

When the bell rang Karen, who had not watched the time, yelled at students as they rushed out to complete the group tasks as homework. She also failed to collect the group work as she had planned.

Tyler's classroom showed the most growth. Tyler's plan was to lecture for 10 minutes on Expressions and Equations using a model lesson from the EngageNY online curriculum and then to break students into groups of four to complete increasingly complex tasks related to the lecture content.

He started the lesson with a two-minute quiz on rational numbers (the previous unit) that immediately focused the class and moved directly into his lecture emphasizing the notes students would need to take to help them with the group work while writing on an overhead at the front of the room.

Tyler stopped his lecture several times, once to give a quizzical look to two students who were not paying attention (they immediately quieted and came back on task) and on four other occasions to ask open-ended questions. Tyler paused before calling on students at random to answer his questions.

This was a new technique Sal had not seen in previous observations for Tyler and it worked well to keep students attentive and engaged. Tyler also asked for a show of hands twice on questions about his lecture to check for student understanding and made a simple re-explanation when students' hands indicated they hadn't understood him initially. This technique was also new for Tyler.

The lecture lasted 15 minutes instead of the planned 10 but it was a solid explanation of the information students needed. When students broke into their groups they struggled with the expectations and Tyler ended up running around the room to answer their questions and keep them moving forward.

For a few minutes things were chaotic but Tyler and his students stuck with it and kept working. With five minutes left to go in class,

Tyler figured out that students would not be able to finish all of the examples so he had them turn in one paper from each group for grading.

Students could finish the other four examples from the group work for homework. This was far from a perfect lesson but it was a significant improvement from what Sal had seen the previous year in Tyler's classroom.

Tyler had even joined a group of math teachers from several districts organized by Anthony Tompkins ("Common Core is Not the Problem" chapter) that met outside the school day to develop plans for extended student projects that allowed students to apply their math skills in creative situations.

He asked Sal to pay for a water cannon and some other equipment he used for these authentic assessment projects, and he found a partner-teacher in the science department who worked with him. Parents were invited to an evening demonstration of one of these projects presented by their students in the gym.

Jim Hollister's class was a disaster. Jim stood at the front of the room and pontificated for 40 minutes. He asked a total of two questions of the two smartest students in the classroom during the entire class period and responded to the two students who answered his simple questions correctly with sarcasm and a smirk.

Only four of the 22 students in the class even had notebooks out to take notes, and it appeared none of these four students wrote anything down. Jim did not write anything down on the board or the overhead and provided no hand-out materials to the students.

As expected with this approach, students were bored and restless but their fear of Jim who was famous for a short temper and verbal tongue lashings kept them from visibly acting out. So they just sat there and suffered with no visible interest or engagement in Jim's ineffective lecture.

In my weekly visits to Sal's school and our monthly meetings about the improvement plan, Sal and I regularly commiserated about the impervious nature of teacher tenure protections in New York State.

Tenure ensured the Jim Hollisters and Terrance Bonesteels (remem-ber the teacher who sent salacious emails to middle school students) of the world would remain in our classrooms.

Regularly, teacher unions are bashed in the local, regional and national media for perpetuating these harmful barriers. At some level you'd think the teacher unions would relent in their efforts to maintain these protections and listen to reason to improve their image on this issue, but they don't.

WHY DO TEACHERS AND TEACHER UNIONS DEFEND THE PRESENT TENURE PROTECTIONS SO STRONGLY?

Teacher unions work so hard to protect tenure rights for economic reasons. The unions have pushed the bulk of the teacher salary increases to the experienced teachers. These experienced teachers sit on the teacher union negotiating teams and want that money for themselves. The way they see it they have been paying union dues for many years and they deserve the fruits that come with their contributions. They figure the rookie teachers will eventually get their rewards later in their careers.

But this arrangement creates perverse incentives that impact the teacher tenure issue directly. If a superintendent in Mississippi can engineer the dismissal of an end-of-career senior tenured teacher, s/he will save about $28,000 per year in salary because the replacement rookie teacher will be making that much less.

Meanwhile a Long Island superintendent has an $85,000 yearly financial incentive to engineer the dismissal of a highly paid senior tenured teacher. If we let finances distort the process of trying to improve teacher quality, we'll be forever trapped in low performance.

The high salaries for the most senior Long Island teachers have created pushback from taxpayers fed up with onerous and ever-increasing school tax bills. If tenure protections are weakened in New York State, the school districts on Long Island (and elsewhere throughout the state) will be under tremendous pressure to find excuses beyond real classroom perfor-mance weaknesses or actual teacher misconduct to dismiss their most senior teachers.

Any proposed solution that attempts to address teacher tenure issues in New York State and the other strong teacher union states will have to address the "tax factor."

A workable strategy to counteract the economic factor built into teacher tenure/performance decisions is required before we can make any changes to the tenure laws in strong union states. Any effective strategy must elimi-nate the economic reason teacher unions fight all changes in tenure laws. As long as the financial incentive to fire senior teachers exists, it will override performance issues.

Solution: If the school district does NOT save money when under-performing teachers or teachers with serious misconduct are dismissed the problem is solved. Any money saved with the hire of cheaper teachers to replace dismissed tenured teachers should go to the other teachers already working in the district and the economic incentive disappears.

The Improvement plans move toward resolution
I continued my weekly drive-by visits with all of my principals as well as my monthly meetings with Sal about the improvement plan teachers. The teachers with improvement plans continued on the same general path with three making steady but slow progress and one stuck in rebel mode.

When Sal and I met in February he hit me with surprise news: Ralph McGlaughlin had given Sal a letter specifying his intention to retire in June of that school year. Ralph's decision was prompted by a provision in the teacher contract that guaranteed Ralph the health insurance he wanted in retirement as long as the district received this notification prior to February 15.

Ralph had also had a brief conversation with Sal when he delivered the letter.

"I like the ideas we have been working on to improve my classroom effectiveness and I will continue to work on them the rest of this year," Ralph said. *"I think I really am a better teacher now. But the truth is that this is a lot heavier workload than I had before and it's a bit more than I think my health can take. It's time for me to go."*

The conversation ended cordially with both of them smiling and shaking hands. But I could tell Sal was a bit disappointed.

The following week the long awaited Public Employment Relations Board decision arrived. In our hearing with the union in January the Public Employment Relations Board hearing officer asked many questions of both attorneys, of me, of Sal and of Jim Hollister.

His questions were mostly procedural regarding notification dates, documents and contract statements relevant to the issues of this hearing. We all knew these hearing officers dislike making real decisions and prefer compromises that award both sides half of a very ugly baby that neither will love. So, it was no surprise that this decision followed that pattern.

The decision stated that Jim Hollister could be required by the district to submit lesson plans, and that those plans had to meet the standard the district had set with the training completed and that Jim's plans, meaning those submitted to Sal and reviewed by the hearing officer at the time of the hearing, clearly didn't meet that standard.

The hearing officer also concluded that the initial November observation of Jim's class constituted ineffective performance based on poor planning and a failure by Jim to implement the critical expectations the district had identified: three levels of instruction, more group work and less lecture, daily paper grading and an opportunity for students to re-test and raise their grades. (Hurray for the district!)

But the decision also said that Jim should have been given more notice of his performance deficiencies (no later than June 1st of the previous school year) and an opportunity to improve his planning skills over the summer before any negative consequences could result from his poor instructional planning and poor teaching.

Since the district had not notified Jim far enough in advance the instructional improvement plan would have to be extended through June of the following school year before any teacher disciplinary sanctions (letter of counsel followed by time off without pay and eventually dismissal) could be started. And since these sanctions were progressive Jim would be entitled to the full summer's notification and improvement opportunity each time before a stiffer penalty was applied.

We would be looking at a minimum of three more years of hard work for Sal before Jim faced dismissal from his position if he continued in his rebel mode of refusing to even try to improve his instruction.

Sal and I were both frustrated but the lawyer for the district said we had done as well as we could expect, and that if Sal stuck with it and documented everything in another three years (assuming Jim Hollister didn't have a big change of heart and teaching skill) we would be in a position to request his dismissal.

Sal and I both knew he was looking at a long difficult road ahead if he decided to continue with Jim's improvement plan for the next several years. True to form Sal called me at 7:30 a.m. on the Monday after the Friday hearing decision, before I had my winter coat off, with his thoughts on how we should move forward with Jim.

"Look I've invested a lot of time in Jim Hollister and these other three improvement plan teachers," Sal said. "I'm really pissed the hearing officer decided to give Jim a stay of execution that will require a lot more work of me — for three more years. But the gains have gone way beyond these four teachers.

"I have teachers that I didn't even have on my radar as having performance problems telling me they are working hard to implement the changes we want to see and inviting me into their classes to see them first hand. That would not have happened without my initiating these improvement plans. And, while Jim may require more work and time than I should have to invest, letting him off the hook at this point would kill all my efforts to improve academic performance in our school. I started this improvement thing now I have to see it through."

Jim Hollister wasn't happy but the next set of plans he submitted tried to address the issues the Public Employment Relations Board hearing officer said were critical. However, Sal's classroom visits and the next formal observation showed that while Jim's plans had improved, his performance in the classroom had not and the critical changes were not in place in the classroom.

Jim apparently had a preset student group game activity he would bring out whenever Sal came to the room and he would start the game as soon as Sal showed up. Sal and I spoke with the school district attorney who concurred with us that we should document this game as a ruse to hide his lack of real change with memos Sal would send to Jim after each visit.

For his last formal observation of the year Jim tried to complete a lesson according to the plans he had submitted but it was a total failure, even worse than the initial failures of the other three improvement plan teachers. And of course Sal documented this on the formal observation form. The three-year plan for Jim was off to a predictably discouraging start, but I had confidence in Sal's perseverance.

A large time investment to create instructional growth
When Sal and I met in March and April to discuss the teachers with improvement plans, we focused most of our conversation on Karen and Tyler. Ralph would be leaving at the end of the year and he was still improving his practice. Jim was still writing barely acceptable lesson plans and trying to hide his teaching deficiencies with one ruse or another any time Sal stopped by his classroom for a visit.

Sal wrote a short memo after each visit to Jim's classroom documenting Jim's continued resistance and poor teaching and he wrote a strongly worded final formal evaluation documenting Jim's lack of teaching performance improvement. All of these documents were checked by the school district attorney.

Karen Thompson was making steady improvement. In Sal's last surprise formal observation on an unannounced date he had seen the class start with a two-minute quiz with students immediately at their desks and working.

Karen collected the quiz for grading and launched in to a 13-minute lecture on evaluating expressions with whole number exponents. The lecture was much more focused than lectures from previous classes observed by Sal.

Students paid attention and took notes. Karen also asked five well thought out questions using good technique by asking the question, pausing and then calling on students randomly. Then Karen broke the class into groups of four and asked students to use their notes to evaluate a series of increasingly complex expressions like the ones she had just lectured about.

Karen told the class she would collect one paper from each group at random to grade at the end of the class period.

The students were generally on task and helpful to each other in the groups and even though they didn't get every one of the expressions done on the handout Karen collected the sheets and said she would grade them by counting the number of correct answers and giving extra credit to the groups with the best results.

Some of the groups were off task at times and Karen still needed to recognize their problems and intervene early when off-task behavior occurred. But the class was much better than in past years and much better than Sal had seen earlier in this school year.

Tyler was Sal's big success story. Tyler's background in athletics translated to his being more competitive than most people. Once Sal discovered this, he used Tyler's competitiveness to help motivate Tyler to make the necessary changes in his teaching approach.

For instance, Sal knew Tyler was good friends with Mike Morrison, a social studies teacher in the school who was very effective with student group work. Sal arranged for Tyler to observe Mike's classes in action and once Tyler saw the excellent rapport, fast-paced group activity and positive reinforcement Mike provided to his student groups, he adopted Mike's strategies for his own classroom and did his best to enhance them and even outdo Mike at his own game.

When Sal completed his final formal observation in Tyler's classroom it had the best of Anthony's classroom, Mike's classroom and Tyler's best personal adaptations of both on display. He also adopted Mike's re-testing strategies. Tyler had gone from being a candidate for a teacher improvement plan to a model teacher who Sal could use to demonstrate how to run a classroom for other teachers who were struggling. And he had done it all in one year.

And then another surprise arrived in May. Karen Thompson submitted a letter of resignation effective June 30.

"I've really learned a lot this year," she wrote. "Initially I was angry with you for making me complete a teacher improvement plan. I thought it was unfair because I was doing a good job. Now, I understand that I really did need to change how I taught and I know now that I can do what is needed, but I just don't have the time to do it.

"My two sons are two and four years old and my husband travels a lot for work. To do this job right with all the re-testing, paper grading and planning for three levels of instruction I need to put in a minimum of 9 to 10 hours every school day plus time over the school breaks and in the summer to improve my plans and tests.

"My own sons need more time than I can give them right now with me teaching full time. So I'm going to work at the day care center where they have been going for a lot less money until they are older and then I plan to come back to teaching. I hope you'll give me a chance when that time comes."

Sal who was shaken by this news assured her he would give her that chance because of all the improvement he had seen in her performance during the school year. They parted with a heartfelt hug and Sal called me immediately.

I recognized the disappointment in his voice. "C'mon I'll buy you lunch," I said.

We met at the diner and talked privately in our semi-reserved corner booth where we ate lunch together at least once a month.

"I put so much time and effort into these four teachers and two of them are leaving and one dug in his heels and hasn't improved at all. I'm really feeling discouraged, like it was all a waste," Sal said, as soon as he sat down.

"Tyler is a real success story," I told him. "Karen and Ralph found out what good teaching requires and made a choice that teaching right now at the level we expect is not for them. And both significantly improved their teaching skills this year because of what you did for them, which means their students benefitted.

"Jim is a dud but even he is starting to make changes. He's just moving too slowly. What you did with Jim sent a message to the whole staff that poor teaching in your school will not be tolerated. That's very important. And remember when we started you wanted to fire them all."

Sal smiled and sighed. "Okay, who besides Jim Hollister should I put on a teacher improvement plan for next year?"

GET THE BOTTOM FEEDERS OFF THE BOTTOM

My proposed solution would address teachers with misconduct issues like Terrance Bonesteel and recalcitrant poor performers like Jim Hollister. I call it the "2%/5% provision."

I propose that all school districts be allowed to designate for immediate summary dismissal any teacher who has received progressive discipline (letter of counsel or time off without pay) for any type of misconduct that has been properly documented and any teachers who have completed a one-year performance improvement plan and are judged by their administrative supervisor to still be performing ineffectively.

This summary dismissal opportunity comes with restrictions and procedures. The restrictions are: (1) the number of tenured employees for the school district (includes teachers, guidance counselors, principals, librarians, everyone in the school district who gets tenure) eligible in any single year for this type of summary dismissal may not exceed 2 percent of the total population of tenured employees in the district rounded up to the next highest whole number and cannot exceed 5 percent of the average yearly number of tenured employees rounded up to the next whole number in any five-year period.

(2) If any summarily dismissed tenured staff member is replaced by a staff member who receives lower wages, 100 percent of the difference between the regular wages of these two employees at the time of the summary dismissal will be split in equal shares among all the tenured staff members in the bargaining unit of the employee who was summarily dismissed.

For the next ten years the amount of this distribution to the members of the bargaining unit that represents the summarily dismissed tenured employee will be decreased by 10 percent of the original total distribution each year resulting in a distribution of $0 in year 11 and thereafter.

The procedures that come with the "2%/5% provision" are as follows:

(1) The summarily dismissed employee may appeal on procedural grounds only.
(2) The appeal will go to an independent hearing officer (similar to that used in civil service employee discipline cases).
(3) The employee is placed on leave without pay pending the result of the appeal.
(4) The evidentiary rules for the hearing will be similar to those used for a civil service employee discipline hearing.
(5) If the appeal is for a case of misconduct the appeal will determine if the correct procedures according to the district's established contractual rules and the state's laws and PERB decisions were followed by the district in completing its due process, making the disciplinary decision regarding the employee and implementing and documenting the employee discipline. The appeal will not examine the appropriateness or validity of the original employee discipline issue.
(6) If the appeal involves issues of teacher or administrator job performance the only issues examined in the appeal will be: (a) was the nature of the employee's poor performance clearly defined and

provided to the employee in writing on or before June 1st of the year in which an employee improvement plan commenced? (b) Did the improvement plan provide clear direction on performance changes required and non-evaluative support such as paid teacher or administrator coaches who met at least monthly with the employee? (c) Did the district document according to its own established procedures observation and evaluation documents the lack of employee performance growth required by the improvement plan?

If these steps are properly followed, the hearing officer must uphold the summary dismissal. If the hearing officer finds that the procedures were not properly followed the district owes the dismissed employee the unpaid salary from the date of the beginning of the leave without pay up to a maximum of one year after the hearing decision is rendered, but the summary dismissal stands as implemented by the district.

By the way the 2%/5% provision could be negotiated at the state level. That makes what I am proposing more likely to work politically. The percentage may be adjusted for different states and regions with different rules and expectations with regard to tenure.

Also, if a school or district is performing poorly academically in comparison to other schools or districts with similar levels of student poverty and resources (school or district performing below the predictor line like Candle Middle School) these numbers may be adjusted upward by the state education department.

For example, Candle Central School District, a poor performing district compared to similar peer school districts (see graph earlier in this chapter that compares school district academic performance for districts with similar demographics), would be allowed to increase the percentages of tenured employees eligible for summary dismissal from 2%/5% provision to 5%/10% provision.

Underperforming districts like Candle would be eligible for these increased 5%/10% summary dismissal percentages. Another year or two of poor performance and the numbers would increase to 10%/25%, giving the district the possibility of making more rapid changes when persistent poor student academic performance indicates a rapid change is needed.

Note: It is important in making the decisions of which schools and school districts are eligible for an increased percentage of potential summary dismissals of tenured employees that district and school academic performance measures are properly adjusted for student poverty and apples are properly compared with apples. To do this correctly requires a mathematically accurate academic performance predictor line. This data should also include adjustments for potential measurement error by using multiple years of academic test data that prove beyond any doubt that the school or district is clearly underperforming academically.

As I've noted elsewhere in this book changes in leadership should be required in districts with persistently weak academic performance. In addition, districts faced with rapidly declining enrollments or enrollment changes caused by charter school implementation should have expanded opportunity to summarily dismiss additional teachers with misconduct issues and performance problems that resulted in inadequately implemented performance improvement plans. After all, why should districts be forced to lay off effective teachers and keep teachers with documented problems?

At first glance we might assume teachers (or principals and other employees with tenure) would not see this change in the law as beneficial. However, essentially what would happen is that each year a few of the poor performing tenured teachers and teachers with ugly misconduct issues would be leaving the district at a very slow rate (no more than 1 percent a year average in most districts). Meanwhile, the remaining teachers who are doing their jobs well and avoiding misconduct problems would be getting paid more due to the salary redistribution section in this recommendation.

How much more? In the highest paid districts in the country about $2,000 per year per teacher more, in average paying districts $1,300 per year and in the lowest paying districts $750 per year. And this number is negotiable.

If teachers wanted one-and-a-half or two times the salary savings this number could be negotiated. A properly negotiated dollar value would prevent administrators from using this law change to summarily rid themselves of teachers due to personal issues while offering the legitimate opportunity to rid the profession of poor performers who drag down the entire profession.

I realize that what I have proposed will not be satisfactory for those who believe that all the problems in the American education stem from poor teachers who should be fired immediately with no job protections. The truth is that those people are wrong. Many of the teachers seen as poor performers (like Tyler, Karen and Ralph) were never given the direction and support they needed throughout their careers.

Most principals have difficulty diagnosing the causes of poor teacher performance and implementing effective plans to improve teacher performance. Most principals and superintendents are reluctant to take on the legal challenges, the financial risks, the extra workload and the thorny political issues related to improving teacher performance.

I also realize that what I have proposed will not be satisfactory for those who believe that all the problems in American education stem from bad parenting.

Throughout my career I have told the teachers who complained to me about how "bad" their students were the same thing: "The parents are not keeping the good students at home. So suck it up and do what needs to be done with the students who have shown up in your classroom. Those students need a good education. If you need help come to me and I will help you."

Wouldn't I be doing the same thing as those teachers who complained to me about their "bad" students if I said: "Just give me some good teachers and I can make this school great."

These are the teachers we have, and it's our job to work with them and make them better. Yes, we need to push out a few (like Jim Hollister) who won't even try to make the necessary changes. But anyone who thinks we're going to save education in the U.S. solely by firing teachers that person needs to reconsider.

Special Education: All Heart and No Head

● ● ●

SHORTLY AFTER I STARTED MY career as an educator, the federal government enacted Public Law 94-142[lxix], the Education of All Handicapped Children Act, which became widely known as the Individuals with Disabilities Education Act, IDEA for short.

The law was created in response to the deplorable conditions of education programs for disabled children. Before PL 94-142, children with severe disabilities were often relegated to basement classrooms with insufficient lighting and poor ventilation. They suffered from neglect and were frequently forced out of school into group homes or sheltered workshops at a young age. It was despicable to say the least.

It's easy to understand why only 5 percent or fewer of children[lxx] were assigned to these "programs" during that era. No parent would subject their child to these conditions unless the child was severely impaired and parents believed they had no other option. When it passed in 1975, the Individuals with Disabilities Education Act was long overdue.

Unfortunately, PL 94-142 was enacted with no regard for its potential long-term financial impact on schools. Not only that, it became a crutch parents were quick to use for their children at the recommendation of teachers who were only too happy to hand their most challenging students off to Special Ed, a massive shift that has essentially institutionalized low expectations.[lxxi]

(Sections in italics are fictional stories made from composites of multiple actual experiences.)

The sky's the limit

Libby Allison was diagnosed as having cerebral palsy when she was nine months old. The doctor identified her as having very limited muscle movement capabilities and limited mental abilities that couldn't be accurately diagnosed until she was older.

By the time she was three years old, Libby's parents, Alice and Pete Allison, understood their daughter would never walk or talk. She could gesture and grunt in a way that her mother understood, but she could not feed herself, use the toilet without help or take a bath without constant support and supervision.

Libby was very active in her remote controlled wheelchair. By age three she was receiving help from the local school district and the county with speech and physical therapy sessions that helped her communicate and perform daily activities within her limited abilities. A special laptop computer allowed her to communicate with her family through pictures, taps and sounds.

Alice became very knowledgeable and involved with the school district Committee on Special Education and served on a Parent Advisory Committee and as a volunteer parent advocate who attended meetings with other parents of disabled children to help them work through issues with the school district that impacted their children.

Libby's I.Q. was formally measured at less than 70 on multiple tests. However, she had a great sense of people: who she liked, who she didn't like, who she could charm and who she couldn't, who feared her and who could be manipulated. Libby's people reading skills and her mother's militant support created an unhealthy dynamic that gave Libby a kind of carte blanche when dealing with many of the adults working in the school.

When Libby didn't get what she wanted – for her snack, for the music she listened to on the bus, whether she would go outside on cold days for recess – she had temper tantrums, hurling her laptop to the floor, screeching, spitting, hitting and biting.

For several years, Libby was "mainstreamed" in a regular classroom with 20 general education students in her elementary school. Her occasional tantrums and need for assistance with eating and using the bathroom required the support of a dedicated one-on-one classroom aide – a full time school district employee who stayed with Libby all day, every day.

Separately, a special education teacher – another full time school district employee – came to Libby's classroom and helped with Libby's instruction for an hour every day. She modified the curriculum and adjusted the lessons so that Libby with her limited I.Q. and motor skills could succeed at tasks.

When the kindergarten class was sorting blocks into red, green and blue piles and correctly identifying how many blocks were in each pile, Libby was given some blocks to play with while the aide told her the colors and numbers.

In third grade when the other students were writing one paragraph essays Libby used her laptop to communicate to the aide who wrote words on a blank sheet of paper corresponding to Libby's communications with the computer.

The regular education teacher and the special education teacher met weekly for a half an hour to plan out Libby's curriculum modifications. Libby did not take the state tests in English language arts or math required of other students. She had her own set of required tests listed in her state mandated Individualized Educational Plan (IEP).

Libby's elementary school day began with a ride on a special small wheelchair accessible school bus with a driver and a bus aide – two more full-time school district employees – who helped Libby and one other disabled wheelchair-bound student with the ride to and from school daily.

When Libby or the other wheelchair-bound student stayed after school for any special activity, the special bus was used for an extra trip to drop off the student who had stayed late at school.

While working as a parent volunteer with the district's Committee on Special Education, Alice discovered that Libby might benefit from more extensive occupational therapy (training in physical dexterity required for day-to-day tasks like eating, brushing your teeth, going to the bathroom, etc.) and physical therapy (muscle stretching and strengthening exercises that can reduce pain and increase flexibility for some people with cerebral palsy). She requested these services for Libby during the school day, and they were added in first grade and remained a part of her weekly schedule with two hours per week of each support service.

Alice knew all the special education and regular education teachers at the elementary school where she volunteered on a regular basis and each year she requested specific teachers and aides for Libby based on each educator's reputation for being uber-supportive of students with disabilities.

Then a new special education director, Gladys Allan, joined the district. Gladys Allan told Alice she could give Alice the aide she wanted for her daughter, but the special education teacher Alice preferred would not be able to work with Libby in fourth grade. The special education teacher Alice wanted would be co-teaching an inclusive special education class with one of the general education fourth-grade teachers, spending her entire day with eight special education students and 13 regular education students while team teaching in a fourth-grade classroom.

Alice was incensed and very fearful. She knew what was best for Libby and she knew these teachers and the teacher Gladys Allan had selected to work with Libby was an older special education teacher who was nearing retirement and who had a reputation for being lazy and dismissive of parental concerns.

A LEGAL BATTLEGROUND

Alice and parents like her make it nearly impossible for school districts to rein in special education services. These parents want to do everything possible to ease the difficult lives their disabled children lead. And who can blame them?

However, where there is money to be spent, there is money to be made by doctors, lawyers, and private therapy professionals who make money by providing services to special education students, a force too strong for most local PL 94-142 required Committees on Special Education to resist. [lxxii] [lxxiii] Over time and particularly when legal battles over issues related to Special Education have left scars in a school district, the local Committee on Special Education runs out of steam.

When Americans ask what their education tax dollars are being spent on, special education is a big part of the answer. Per pupil spending on general and special education in the U.S., adjusted for inflation, has more than doubled since 1970, and a large part of the increase has gone to Special Education.

The 2015 annual per pupil cost in New York State (the highest cost state for educational services in the country) averages $22,552.[lxxiv] The cost for a regular education slot is roughly $18,000 per year. Libby's additional special education services at $109,000 mean Libby's total annual cost is over six times more than a general education student. Figure in the lawyers involved and the cost is unsustainable.

Special Education Student		General Education Student	
General Education Classroom Slot	$18,000	General Education Classroom Slot $18,000	
Bus aide	$30,000		
Depreciation/Operation (bus)	$10,000		
One-on-One Aide	$35,000		
Special Ed Teacher 45 mins. a day	$18,000		
Occupational Therapy	$8,000		
Physical Therapy	$8,000		
Total:	$127,000	Total:	$18,000

THE "NEXUS"

Once PL94-142 blossomed into a full-fledged law with all the associated moving parts, the lawyers and state education department bureaucrats moved in to help resolve disputes. And there were many disputes that needed to be resolved.[lxxv]

The most frequent dispute involved parents challenging student placements decided by the school district's Committee on Special Education. State education department and state and federal regulatory officials complete reviews of school district performance in the special education arena with micromanagement at its worst. For example, the following is a quote from a recent state education department review in Lake Placid, New York.[lxxvi]

"One area of noncompliance was found in IEP implementation: Two students do not receive the frequency and duration of the recommended program in their IEP. Classroom visitations revealed one student was receiving related service during 12: 1+1 instruction and one student with a recommendation of 8: 1+1 special class for 300 minutes was receiving instruction in general education. The 8: 1+1 was used as a location rather than a service. In addition, special education staff were providing duplication of services at the same time (resource room/special class and consultant teacher/special class)."

In my experience, reviews of this kind are most frequently the result of either special education teachers attempting to use the state education department to protect their jobs (this review is essentially saying the student is not receiving IEP-prescribed services) or the result of complaints by parents, advocacy groups or special education service providers or their attorneys.

Such reviews can result in significant legal bills or special education program additions for many school districts. The local special education committee charged with deciding the program and placement for each disabled child is frequently overrun by these students' many well-armed advocates.

In addition, special rules regarding special education student disciplinary actions (when special education students misbehave) require "nexus" decisions[lxxvii] to determine whether the student's disabling condition caused their bad behavior (i.e. Did this student bring a gun to school because he was emotionally disabled?) and these decisions, of course, require lawyers for the school district, which result in more legal bills for the school district.

Winning the war

When it became apparent in the summer between grades three and four that Alice was not going to get her way on the teacher selection issue for her daughter, Libby, she set up a meeting with the superintendent, the elementary school principal and Gladys, the new special education director, to make her strongest pitch to reverse the decision on which teacher would be working with her daughter.

The district's Committee on Special Education had previously met to make the decision on Libby's placement. Alice had been given a chance to make her pitch to that group as a parent at that time, recusing herself from her regular membership on the committee for this decision involving her daughter as she had in the past.

The school administrators were polite but firm, the decision would stand. The Committee on Special Education had made its decision and by state education department rules they could not overrule the committee without creating legal issues for the school district.

The inclusive class (co-teaching, push-in) model required by the state was appropriate to the new, highly motivated teacher Alice wanted for her daughter. Another experienced, certified teacher was assigned to the special education teacher role for Libby.

Alice left the meeting shocked. She thought all her hard work as a member of the school district's Committee on Special Education, as a parent advocate, as an elementary school volunteer and as a member of the district's parent advisory committee guaranteed her the right to control this decision.

So Alice followed the correct protocol and requested an executive session discussion of this issue with the school board and the administrative team to explain her concerns. The school board was polite and attentive but didn't say much during the 15-minute executive session discussion of the issue. They had been advised that legally they could not overrule the placement determined by the Committee on Special Education. Two weeks after the executive session discussion a letter arrived addressed to Alice and Pete and signed by the superintendent saying that the decision would stand.

WHAT'S REASONABLE?

No one expects students like Libby to go without necessary services, but the public education system is buckling under the weight of a law without limits. Inevitably granting every special education student's parental requests means shortchanging some other students who need the dollars or the specific personnel to meet competing goals. Affordability and practicality have to be considered.

And there are ways to make it more affordable.

Take transportation, for example. If Libby rode to school with three other disabled students instead of just one other disabled student, shared her one-on-one aide with one other disabled student, saw her special education teacher a half hour per day instead of one hour per day and received one hour per week each of occupational therapy and physical therapy instead of two hours of each per week, the total extra cost to the school district beyond that of a regular education student would drop to less than $55,000 per year instead of the present $109,000.

And Libby's educational achievement would not be impacted with these changes. She would still be receiving an education in a regular education classroom with her peers. And that's what we want and the law requires – the least restrictive environment.

Many people including taxpayers, parents, teachers and even administrators misunderstand the funding arrangements for special education and make an assumption that special state aid, federal aid and school transportation aid channeled through the states and their education departments pay for Libby's extra service costs. As we saw, Libby's extra services cost $109,000 per year in New York State and the extra state and federal aid that comes to the school district to support Libby's extra services in New York State would be about $30,000-$45,000 maximum from all categories. The rest of these extra costs are paid by local taxpayers.

Adding insult to injury: School districts receiving federal money (that means virtually every public school district in the country) must precisely follow elaborate rules regarding the education services provided to its disabled students.

Each state also has its own complicated rules to carry out these expectations with state education department regulations and a cadre of "special education" bureaucrats who oversee school district implementation of these rules. Typically, these bureaucrats respond to parental complaints with audits of school districts' special education procedures and provide legal pronouncements from lawyers that work exclusively at taxpayer expense to interpret and implement these rules. More legal fees.

A COTTAGE INDUSTRY

The rules and costs associated with special education have prompted it to become an industry unto itself. Shortly after the initiation of the Individuals with Disabilities in Education Act (IDEA) as principals and teachers struggled to deal with severely disabled children, they found like-minded colleagues in other school districts and rented space together to serve the same type of special education students. These special schools also created a system of support services, such as occupational therapy, physical therapy, and social worker or school psychologist counseling for disabled students.

Some of these special schools were operated privately and others were operated by consortiums of public schools. Before long, speech therapy providers (usually working with preschool children who are slow to develop oral speaking skills) were contacting parents of potential clients, evaluating preschool children and selling their services directly to parents who then requested payment for the evaluations and services from the local county or school district. And most of us who have had children of our own at home or worked with them in schools know many children have minor speech problems from ages three to seven and they gradually disappear without speech therapist intervention.

But again, once the ball is rolling.

Committees on Special Education rely on evaluations by professional speech pathologists to approve or deny services, and the providers who do the evaluations see potential clients.

Again, the special education committee can't say "no" to parent requests, especially when a licensed provider says services are needed, and requesting new expensive evaluations by an independent professional is never popular with parents.

A public relations nightmare

When she realized the special education director's decision would stand, Alice lost it. She engaged an attorney to appeal the decision to a state education department representative who reviewed special education issues for the district. After months of review and thousands of dollars in attorney fees the state education department affirmed the district's decision.

By this time Alice had resigned her positions as a member of the Committee on Special Education, as a parent advocate for the district and as an elementary school volunteer. Alice came to every single school board meeting and spoke in the public comment period about how the district was mistreating special education students and parents. Her comments generated a number of articles and letters to the editor in the local newspaper.

In the summer between Libby's fourth and fifth grade years in school, the special education director, Gladys, resigned from the district and took a higher paying job with the same title in a nearby district.

The reason for her departure? The superintendent told her the school board had concerns about his plan to recommend her for tenure. These school board members blamed Gladys for the bad press Alice had gener- ated for the district and as one board member said, "Gladys should have been able to resolve this issue with Alice without so much friction."

An interim special education director who did not have to face tenure issues served the district for the next two years while the superin- tendent and the school board allowed time for Alice to cool off.

When Gladys' permanent replacement, Ellen Thompson, was hired the superintendent shared the school district's history with Libby and Alice and cautioned Ellen to be sure she checked with him and was careful with regard to any decisions that might upset Alice.

LEGAL COSTS AND BAD PUBLIC RELATIONS

The possibility of expensive legal battles and bad public relations for the school district with local press and with their state education department causes most districts to give parents whatever they want to limit friction.[lxxviii] Once one child has his own one-on-one aide every parent of a special education student expects her/his child will have a one-on-one aide. In short order the special education budget has grown to the point it is squeezing out the resources needed for the students who need extra challenges and for the students who need extra help but lack the special education label.[lxxix]

Take two

Ellen Thompson was my introduction to the tug of war between Alice and the school district. I met Ellen Thompson at a meeting of superintendents and special education directors from small rural districts that were discussing sharing special education services to save money.

Ellen told me her history as a former elementary school teacher who earned a Master's Degree in special education which she taught for five years. She had just completed the additional coursework beyond her Master's degree and was now a certified administrator. The school district Libby attended was her first experience being an administrator.

After the meeting Ellen asked for my phone number: "Just in case I need some advice," she said.

One week later Ellen called me and confided in me about her situation with Libby and Alice. She was careful not to reveal any confidential information that could get her in hot water. She was unsure how to proceed with a new issue that had cropped up with Libby, and she wanted a superintendent's perspective but was afraid to ask her boss.

Libby was about to enter ninth grade and her mother was demanding special education services be provided by Rita Henry, an outstanding special education teacher, who had just received a local award as educator of the year.

Ellen, meanwhile, was planning to make Rita the teacher leader for a new program that provided academic support for all high school students struggling with the new Common Core tests (In New York State, school districts are moving to Common Core level work at the high school level).

Rita would lead a program that provided one-on-one tutoring for every student who was struggling with test expectations – special education and regular education students.

PL 94-142 EXPANDS WITH NEW LABEL

A major expansion of special education services took place post PL 94-142 in the late 1970's with the introduction of a new category of disabilities - learning disabled.

During the late 70s and early 80s, the definition of learning disabled morphed to include students who were performing at lower levels than expected. A general education student entering fourth grade who is performing at average levels reads at a fourth-grade level. A learning disabled child would enter fourth grade reading at a second grade level or lower.

Once learning disabilities became eligible for special education services several unintended consequences developed.

First, if I am a third grade teacher with a very poor reader in my classroom who also happens to be a poorly behaved student, I begin to think: "She must be a special education student."

In the early days of learning disabilities identification, these students were most frequently pooled together in their own separate classrooms like more severely disabled students with a special education teacher and sometimes an aide in groups of 12 to 15 students.

Once the student was tested (usually by a school psychologist) and found to be far enough behind academically to warrant the special education label, they were moved to a separate classroom with the special education teacher. If I am the third grade teacher who was certain one of my poor reading and poor behaving students was a special education student, this solution just made my life a whole lot easier. This solution also protected the job of the special education teacher and the teacher aide and grew the special education turf.

If the student being tested for potential special education services showed insufficiently weak academic performance to warrant a special education label, the regular classroom teacher still had one arrow in her quiver: A call to the parent of the poor reader/behavioral problem student saying: "Your daughter is way behind academically. She should be getting special education services in a smaller class with a special education trained teacher and an aide. You should go to a Committee on Special Education meeting and request these services for your daughter. I can't give her the extra help she needs for success."

INSTITUTIONALIZED LOW EXPECTATIONS

Students classified as special education students due to very weak reading skills resulting in a "learning disability" are in general expected to face less challenging reading expectations in their classes. Sometimes this comes with books on tape. Many times it comes with pull-out special education reading instruction that is completed with learning materials many grade levels below the challenge level students will face on the state exams.

Sometimes it comes with longer time periods for completing the tests or an adult reading the text and/or the questions aloud. And for those learning disabled students where the expectations are not watered down their help primarily comes, as required by extensive regulations, from special education certified teachers for set daily time periods and in special education classrooms with regulation-driven class sizes.

As an alternative to this model, special education teachers can be "pushed into" the regular classroom to assist their special education students. Many of the special education teachers in both the push-in and pull-out models are overwhelmed with the content expectations for students in math, reading, science and social studies and the individual needs of their students. In general, special education teacher training does not provide the extensive content training in science, social studies, math and language arts regular classroom teachers must complete especially in middle schools and high schools.

As a consequence, special education teachers in many cases provide less-than-adequate academic support for their students. Many special and regular education teachers resent the push-in approach, as they feel they've lost their own classroom and taken on someone else's work in addition to their own work.

The special education juggernaut has slowed recently with non-special education interventions prompted by a new federally mandated, state implemented program called Response to Intervention (RTI).[lxxx] Response to Intervention requires special education be only a last resort, after all other interventions have been tried.

However, it will take generations to turn the tide. Special education has become a powerful lobby with its own turf – Committees on Special Education in every school district, school administrators and special education teachers and aides in every district, regulations and heavily funded departments at the federal and state levels, cottage industries of lawyers and service providers, parent advocacy groups and influential politicians who can see where the power and money serve their interests best.

In my view, the enormous waste of educational resources and student academic potential resulting from the present special education morass is one of many anchors dragging down our public education system. And the system we have does little to help the students who truly need special education services. These issues for special education and regular education students have become even more critical with new and more challenging Common Core standards.

Everyone's choice for teacher

Rita Henry graduated from college with a dual degree in biology and special education. She went on to become a celebrated special education teacher at a nearby high school. While she taught she returned to college and earned a Master's Degree in special education. The high school principal where Rita worked recognized her unique talents and looked for ways to take advantage of her exceptional skills to help more students succeed.

Rita understood all of the different tests and standards and could provide any student, special education or not, with academic support.

She provided remarkable service for five years at the high school before the principal came to her with a special request. A popular junior, Ryan Walsh, who was an excellent student in all the advanced classes, and an athlete, had a very serious brain cancer and would not be able to come to school for at least four months during surgery, radiation and chemotherapy and recovery at home. The principal asked Rita to tutor Ryan after the school day and on weekends for a $20 per hour tutoring fee, first, at the hospital and later, at home?

Given Rita's challenging workload the $20 per hour was silly but it's all the district could offer. With college applications coming next fall, SAT's looming and an Advanced Placement Biology class in Ryan's schedule it was a tall order, but Rita, true to form, took on the task cheerfully.

When the four months ended Ryan was cancer free and he had maintained his position as the number two student in his class. He scored a 5 (highest possible grade) in his AP Biology exam and he and Rita had become fast friends for life.

Ryan's mother encouraged the school principal to nominate Rita for recognition as the educator of the year, a local television station honor. The principal sent in the nomination form to the station and to no one's surprise Rita was selected as the teacher of the year in a 50 school district region with a five-minute television spot featuring her work at the high school and a tearful scene with Ryan, Rita and Ryan's parents.

Immediately after this spot aired on television, the principal and the school district's new special education director Ellen Thompson approached Rita with a novel idea: What if Rita ran a school-wide tutoring room staffed by teachers freed up from study hall, lunch room and hall supervision duties by monitors.

Rita went home and thought about it and came back with ideas to improve the concept. Students who came in for tutoring needed motivation. They needed immediate positive impact on their grades in the courses where they were struggling.

In her work tutoring students, Rita discovered that component re-testing (testing students a second time exclusively on concepts they had failed the first time they took a test) and teacher grade book test score adjustments that took their component re-test scores into account made a huge difference in student participation and motivation.

Rita told the principal that he would have to make re-testing a school-wide expectation in order for the tutoring center to really have an impact. Rita also made a strong case that she would need a final say on which teachers, teaching assistants and Honor Society volunteer students (something Rita had done in high school which had led to her career choice) worked in the tutoring center.

The principal brought Rita and Ellen to a meeting of the school's department chairs where they presented these ideas. There were the expected questions and concerns: we don't like re-testing and think it's tantamount to lowering standards; teaching assistants aren't supposed to do that kind of work (it's teaching work); the student tutors can't handle this level of professional expectation; why can't we select which teachers work in the tutoring center?

In the end the group supported the concept, primarily due to their respect for Rita, and the principal put the tutoring center on the agenda for the next faculty meeting for a discussion and presentation.

And then the next week Ellen came to Rita's classroom after school and sat down with her to explain the situation with Libby and Alice.

Best laid plans
Ellen and Rita both intended to make certain the tutorial work these students did with the teachers in the program helped their grades in their regular classes so they could see a payoff on their report cards and be motivated to do the extra academic work required by the tutoring.

This strategy meant Rita and her tutoring team would need to work daily with regular classroom teachers to determine which specific skills students needed help with.

The problem: If Ellen and the principal implemented the plan with Rita in charge, Rita would not be available to take on the responsibility of being Libby's special education teacher. And the teacher who would be assigned to Libby instead of Rita was one of the department's weakest teachers. Ellen explained the district's history with Libby and her mother and her fear of a repeat of the elementary episode that had caused her predecessor to leave the district.

Ellen indicated that the superintendent was noncommittal, and that he only wanted some resolution that didn't result in a school board appeal.

Although the superintendent didn't say it out loud Ellen understood the membership on the school board had changed. One member who had been very supportive of the superintendent did not run for re-election and the replacement board member was a parent who had already made a name for herself as one who championed the requests of parents who expected "more" from the school district.

Politics

I advised Ellen to talk directly with her superintendent and find out exactly what he expected her to do. Ellen told me one month later at our follow-up meeting of superintendents and special education directors that she and the high school principal had selected a different teacher who did not have special education certification to lead their new tutoring support program, and she assigned Libby the special education teacher, Rita Henry, her mother requested.

She smiled and shook her head as if to say: "What are you going to do?"

The teacher chosen to lead the new tutoring program was young and enthusiastic, but she feared he would be overwhelmed and other teachers who would have to help with daily grade adjustments and communications about struggling students would not respect him enough to provide the support this new program needed.

The next time I saw Ellen the school year had ended and we were at a meeting of local school district administrators for training on changes to the state's rules for evaluating teachers.

When Rita realized the tutoring center project would be handed over to a rookie teacher and she would be relegated to a semi babysitting role with Libby due to school board and special education politics, she was at first hurt, then angry and finally looking for an out.

Rita considered her options and applied for several jobs outside the school district where she could put her exceptional skills to work. She was selected for a job as a teacher trainer with a local private consortium that provided services to school districts. Rita's pay increased, her level of responsibility and her influence as an educator increased and she had much more flexibility in her job. Unfortunately, Rita was also no longer working directly with students.

The school principal, special education director and the entire school district lost a valuable employee. Libby ended up with the teacher Alice didn't want anyway, Alice made the superintendent's life miserable with another appeal regarding Libby's teacher, first to the school board and then to the state education department.

Immediately following this second appeal in six years by Alice about the district's special education services for Libby, the state education department's special education division initiated an audit of the district's entire special education program. The audit resulted in a 15-page summary finding of needs for expensive and large scale special education program additions and changes for the district.

Meanwhile, the tutoring center Ellen had started with such high hopes had been abandoned after one year of very bumpy operation.

The rookie teacher who had been assigned the leadership role for the tutoring center ended up irritating regular classroom teachers with requests on grading changes and component re-testing for students from the tutoring center. The principal decided in November of that first *year of implementation that the re-testing idea had to be abandoned completely.*

Once the re-testing option disappeared, student participation in the tutoring center dropped dramatically, and the principal and his assistant principal were forced to assign students with failing grades to the tutoring center.

But that didn't work as the students had to face disciplinary consequences before they would show up and when they finally arrived their effort was minimal. By February the center was mostly a mausoleum where teachers did prep work and an occasional student showed up.

When facing a difficult school budget, caused in part by a state education department audit of the special education program that moved more funds from regular education to special education, the superintendent told the principal he had to cut the tutoring center as a budget savings to close the gap.

The last straw arrived in a letter from the state education department that cited the rookie teacher who had run the tutoring center as uncertified because he had provided tutoring services to some special education students and he was not certified in special education.

Undoubtedly, this citation resulted from a complaint initiated by a district special education department employee with concerns about protecting special education department turf and jobs.

A MATTER OF LIFE AND DEATH

While I was a superintendent in Albany, NY, an emotionally disabled and mentally challenged 14-year-old with a history of fire starting, who had spent two years in a juvenile facility, was placed in a foster home and returned to the school district.

When he arrived school administrative staff members who had known the child prior to his court placement came to me to request that he be placed in our district's 100 student high school alternative program rather than our 2,400 student regular high school. These folks who I knew and trusted were afraid this student would get into trouble in the big high school and probably struggle academically without the extra support our alternative program could offer.

I ended up on the phone with our school district's special education attorney (a specialist with many years of experience in this legal niche area). She told me I had no grounds to force the student into the smaller alternative program, and that we would lose the challenge being initiated by the child's publicly provided lawyer. The student had served his time, and we had to treat him like every other student.

I argued vehemently with the attorney, but in the end relented on my initial decision to place the student in the alternative program based on the attorney's advice which I believe to this day was probably legally correct. Within less than two months, the emotionally disabled student, apparently under pressure from gang members who threatened to harm him if he didn't do what they demanded, stabbed another student with a knife in the hallway at the high school.

The victim recovered fully, but the disabled student ended back in a state residential facility until he reached the age of 21. To this day I wonder if the attorneys feel as badly as I do about the outcome of the situation.

So what are the solutions?

Political turf is hard to reclaim, especially when there are so many well-placed and well-armed advocates pushing in an unproductive direction. The money spent on special education has grown enormously in recent years[lxxxi] and failing to change directions to curb these expenses will harm future academic outcomes for our students. Regaining control is critical if we're to improve our education system and it can be accomplished with four relatively simple changes. They are:

1. Limit the extra expenses that can be spent to meet the needs of a child with disabilities to 0 to 6 times the funding received by a nondisabled child in the same school system. Where a child is

located on this 0 to 6 spectrum should be the decision of an independent evaluator paid for by the state. A residentially placed disabled student (totally blind or deaf, severely emotionally disabled, etc.) would warrant up to 6 times the cost of a regular student in nondisabled classes in the district of regular funding (6 extra + 1 regular = 7 times total average nondisabled student funding).

A student like Libby who has severe disabilities, but can be placed with her nondisabled peers, would warrant 3.0 to 4.0 times that spent on a nondisabled student in additional funding. A student with a minor disability might receive 0, 0.5 or 1.0 in additional funding beyond that of a nondisabled student based on the independent evaluator's results.

The Committee on Special Education's role would go from making the decision of what to spend to working with parents and staff members to determine how best to spend the extra funding available. This restriction would apply to all supplementary services, such as speech therapy, occupational therapy, physical therapy and counseling. Given most states provide additional special education state aid funding to school districts for special education student services on a similar sliding scale depending on the type of student disability, these numbers already exist.

2. Private and public service providers are prohibited from evaluating students they'll potentially serve. All evaluations of special education students and potential special education students must be completed by school district employees or consultants hired by the school districts to perform the evaluations independently.

Any disputes with Committee on Special Education placement decisions will be resolved without the involvement of attorneys in a mediation setting with costs borne by the school district, the parents (with a scale based on their ability to pay) and the state. If parents need support in these appeals, the state will provide the support but it should not include high-priced attorneys. Parents may not challenge which teachers are assigned to serve their children.

3. Eliminate the "learning disability" special education category. School districts may provide support to any student who is struggling academically with any teacher or teaching assistant who possesses a valid teaching or teaching assistant certificate, including a special education teacher.

   Any parent may request the opportunity for their child to achieve a high school completion certificate in place of a regular high school diploma and participate in the graduation ceremony, as long as they have completed the academic requirements agreed to in advance by the parent and the school district. These students will not receive a high school diploma (reserved for students who have passed all the required tests and courses without modifications). They will receive a special high school completion certificate listing any testing modifications or other diploma requirement changes. Once the decision to receive a high school completion certificate is made and the completion certificate is awarded, the school district's obligation ends.

This last recommendation will be a hard sell, but it is fair and reasonable. If my child were struggling mightily to succeed in elementary and middle school, I would first advocate for one to five hours per week of one-on-one tutoring from an appropriately certified teacher outside the classroom at the school district's expense. I would not want my child pulled out of his regular classroom to receive a watered down curriculum from a special education teacher.

Research shows that the best remediation programs for elementary students involve one-on-one tutoring not small groups that deal with less challenging skills and content.[lxxxii] The "push-in" approach (now in place in many schools in the US)[lxxxiii] allows for some of the necessary one-on-one student academic support during student group work activities and student time in learning centers. However, some of special education and regular education students will require additional one-on-one tutoring outside the regular classroom and outside the regular school day.

The students previously taught in separate smaller, less challenging classes are at least now being exposed to the grade level content and skills and receive some one-on-one help to try to master the basics of the grade level curriculum.

If my child continued to struggle and apparently wasn't going to graduate from high school and they had tried hard but couldn't pass one or more of the tests or courses required for a high school diploma, I would want to be the one – with my child's full involvement – to make the decision on when to pull the plug on the quest for a regular high school diploma. This is a good time to trust parents to make the right call.

The Politics of Teaching Reading

● ● ●

DURING MY CAREER, I SAT through many conferences with parents whose high school age children were struggling academically.[lxxxiv] Many were children of parents who were unable to provide the care and support required for academic success, but a sizeable group were from two-parent, two-earner families with college degrees.

Many of these parents thought they had done everything they could to put their children on the path to academic success. They read to them when they were young, took them to museums, bought books as gifts, encouraged them in school and checked their homework. And now their students were failing miserably in high school and frequently not even trying.[lxxxv] They were cutting classes, refusing to do homework or study and were totally unmotivated about school and about the future.

When I looked at the standardized test scores for these students, they usually revealed weak academic skills carried over from elementary school, weak skills that turn average students into potential dropouts and, students who should be dreaming about competitive colleges, into students who are just biding their time.[lxxxvi]

We know what works best for literacy and math instruction in elementary schools[lxxxvii]: short, focused whole group instruction; flexible student grouping; learning centers where students work on activities and projects alone and in small groups; probing questions from teachers as they circulate to offer students help within groups and individually as needed; and, of course, regular assessments and adjustments in instruction based on those assessments.

Unfortunately, what we know and what we do are two different things. And the impact is felt by those high school students who are often accused of not trying.

(Sections in italics are fictional stories made from composites of multiple actual experiences.)

The best of intentions

I first met Rose Diamond while working as a consultant for a national school academic improvement organization. She had just finished a summer of Teach for America training and was teaching middle school science and math in a small rural North Carolina school district.

She had very little experience teaching but quickly recognized that very few of her eighth grade students understood science and math well enough and read and wrote well enough to perform middle school level work.

Eager to make a difference, Rose worked with the teachers in the North Carolina district to design curriculum improvements she hoped would result in better student achievement.

She also started a mentoring and career awareness program that brought African American professionals who worked in careers related to math and science into the school to give students role models for what they could potentially achieve.

Meanwhile, she was going to school herself, working on her Master's degree in reading and math in the content areas.

When Rose's three-year stint with Teach for America ended, she was sure she wanted a career in education, but the pay in the small rural school district where she worked was low and her parents were pressuring her to move back to upstate New York, which she did, landing a job in the rural/suburban Elfin Central School District 25 miles outside of Albany..

Rose quickly became a "star" third grade teacher in Elfin Elementary School, establishing classroom learning centers where students worked independently and in groups while Rose circulated in the classroom coaching them and providing support.

She loved the challenge of turning around students labeled as problems in other classrooms, using her instructional skills as well as humor to break down barriers that were preventing them from opening up to learning.

Elfin's school principal recognized Rose's potential and encouraged her to enroll in a program to earn her Master's in School Administration, which she eventually did.

I ran into Rose again at an education conference in upstate New York, just before she started her new position as principal of Eastlake Elementary School.

Eastlake Central School District's superintendent, Sarah Calloway, also a former Teach for America recruit, hired Rose. Together the two women saw themselves as school reformers trying to change public education in the U.S. to better meet the needs of all students.

Eastlake Elementary School needed academic reform. The school was in the bottom quartile in both math and reading when compared to similar rural school districts with a moderate level of student poverty (35 percent free and reduced price lunch).

With Sarah's help, Rose hoped to turn her elementary school around.

A few months into the job Rose, having only recently seen me again at the education conference, asked me to meet with her at a nearby Starbucks. It turned into a regular get together where she sought my advice on her situation as it unfolded over the next two years. Early on in our talks I recognized what she was dealing with as she described two teachers in particular who played central roles in her reform efforts.

The anatomy of a good teacher
Gail Long taught at Eastlake Elementary school. Though she was not a fan of school growing up, Gail developed a love for teaching elementary-age children after she happened to take a course in early childhood education at the local community college.

While completing her required Master's degree during her first couple of years teaching, Gail was lucky to work alongside a skilled elementary school teacher and mentor who was completing a doctoral thesis. Gail absorbed every bit of knowledge she could from her mentor and all of her colleagues and put it to use in her third grade Eastlake classroom.

Gail's classroom was messy and her students were always noisier than the students in other classrooms. There were student papers stuffed in desks, hanging on the walls and piled on Gail's desk. The remains and artifacts of many completed and ongoing student and teacher projects were scattered throughout the room. Hers was not the classroom the principal showed off to school visitors.

When students from Gail's class attended school-wide activities, they were usually ill-prepared and disruptive, much to the chagrin of more conventional experienced teachers like Emma Catlin, Gail's more senior colleague who also taught third grade.

Gail never taught from the front of the room for more than 10 or 15 minutes at a time. When she taught the third grade concept of writing an essay with a topic sentence, three supporting sentences and a conclusion sentence, she first showed them a good example of a well written essay, pointing out each aspect of the essay.

Once they saw a well written essay, she involved them in writing together a group essay on the overhead projector. The group essay included a one-sentence introduction (the beginning), three supporting sentences (the middle) and a one-sentence conclusion (the end).

She followed that by having them write their own essays which she collected and reviewed that night. Writing instruction did not take place every day of the year but instead came in bursts throughout the year. Each burst consisted of 40 minutes of instruction each day for several days as students were taught a new required writing skill.

Gail knew the concept of a beginning, middle and end would be lost on some of her students, but the exercise would reveal how best to group the students.

Open-ended instruction

On day two of instruction, Gail grouped together seven students she knew understood the beginning, middle, end concept pretty well. She provided these seven with an essay topic and asked them to write an introduction, three supporting sentences and a conclusion and compare their work by reading their essays aloud to one another.

As she moved around the room, Gail emphasized the need to be creative and choose words they used when they themselves spoke. She carefully explained the concept of a writer's voice and how they might find their "writer's voice" by listening to their own and other's thoughts.

Guided practice

Gail pulled aside a second group of six students who understood the concept pretty well but needed more practice before they could work as independently as the first group.

For them, Gail had prepared five different essays, each one at a different stage of completion. One was missing only the conclusion, three were missing one, two or three of the supporting sentences and the conclusion and the last had only the essay topic and needed everything written including the introduction. She instructed students to work backwards, starting with the most complete essay.

Direct instruction

A third group of seven students sat in a circle with Gail who gave them ten sentences and asked them questions until they could identify a topic (beginning) sentence, supporting detail (middle) sentences and a conclusion (end) sentence.

Again, with all the groups Gail emphasized originality and "writer's voice."

Gail sat with the third group and again explained a more concrete method for identifying the topic sentence, detail sentences and conclusion sentence. Once they were working on sentence identification *independently with another set of single sentences provided by Gail, she circulated in the room offering help and encouragement and asking students questions so she better understood who knew what.*

Gail asked challenging questions to probe student understanding and to push student comprehension to a higher level. She also asked questions to determine whether she needed to provide whole group instruction.

When she needed to, she stopped the whole class for a brief two minute lesson to help clarify critical parts of the essential thinking required to complete these academic tasks. Sometimes these brief lessons were directed to one of the small groups.

The students continued working independently on this set of tasks for about 30 minutes with Gail's support. Gail collected all the written work students had completed and carefully reviewed it that evening.

The next day during the 40-minute writing period Gail regrouped the students based on the quality of the previous day's work, moving students from one group to another where necessary and providing a new challenge for the most independent group.

Gail split the most independent group into pairs and gave each pair an introductory sentence. Their job was to write the final four sentences — three with supporting details and one with a conclusion — to produce a final essay.

She again emphasized the importance of creativity and writer's voice.

While they were completing that task, the second group completed the task the independent group had completed the day before and the third group completed the task the second group had completed the day before.

After 40 minutes of circulating in the room to offer help and encouragement, Gail again collected the students' work and graded it that evening.

The third day Gail added a final challenge for the most indepen-dent group: Write a five-sentence essay individually on one of three assigned topics. She asked the middle group to complete the advanced group's task from the previous day and so on and so forth.

When students veered off task she stopped what she was doing and glanced over to that group. That was usually enough for the students, even on their bad days, to return to the task at hand.

Gail may have appeared less organized than some of her colleagues, but she knew the third grade Common Core standards as well as cur-riculum and state tests inside and out.

The doctoral candidate Gail worked with in her Master's program had researched the Common Core standards (then in its infancy) as part of her doctoral thesis and Gail learned from her.

She also participated in a summer session run by the state education department where she helped design the teacher part of the state website https://www.engageny.org/, which was established to help teachers adopt to the Common Core standards by providing lessons tied to the new standards.

Tom McAdams, who was the principal before Rose Diamond was hired, was mostly unaware of what happened in Gail's classroom. In seven years of teaching Tom had observed Gail's classroom twice each year as the teacher contract required but made few suggestions or com-ments and all of his comments related to student behavior and the mess-iness of the classroom.

Tom preferred quiet students who listened passively while teachers lectured in the front of the room. Gail always agreed with Tom when they discussed these observations and then went back to her classroom and ran things her way.

Rose and Gail had discussed educational issues, curriculum and testing more in Rose's first year at Eastlake than Gail and Tom had in the previous seven years.

As part of the academic reform plan, Rose asked Gail to take on the role of third grade team leader for curriculum and test prep. However,

Gail feared the reaction of some of the teachers, particularly Emma Catlin, a longtime third grade teacher.

The anatomy of a bad teacher

Emma Catlin, also an Eastlake Elementary School teacher, was 8 years old when she decided to become a teacher. She loved school and when she played with her dolls she sat them at doll-sized make-believe desks lined up in rows, facing her while she talked to her doll-students and wrote on a small blackboard she'd received as a holiday gift.

Sure enough: Emma graduated with a Bachelor's degree in elementary school teaching and returned to her hometown of Torrance, NY, where she was hired to teach at Eastlake Elementary School in the same building where she had been a student a decade earlier.

Now 50, Emma's teaching was the primary focus of her life with her gardening, tennis and other community activities providing her with many local friendships. Emma had a ready smile and a great deal of respect and support from former students and school employees who had known her their entire lives.

Emma taught third grade and had survived seven different school superintendents. Her elementary school had three principals over the course of her 28-year career. Rose Diamond was the third and youngest principal Emma had ever worked with.

Emma's strengths were her organizational and student management skills. Her students sat in rows, were polite and soft spoken in Emma's classroom and well behaved in the lunchroom, on the playground and in special area classes such as art, music and physical education.

Emma didn't tolerate disobedience or disrespect, especially from children. Her students learned early on it was best not to cross Ms. Catlin less they suffer verbal criticism in front of their classmates or an uncomfortable conference with their parents and the principal.

On more than one occasion, Emma refused to continue teaching students and they were transferred to another classroom.

Like all the other facets of Emma's professional life, her classroom instruction was programmed and with Emma always planted in the front of the classroom.

When she taught her students the required multiple sentence essay – a topic sentence, three supporting detail sentences and a conclusion sentence – she sat them in rows and used the overhead projector.

Emma started with an essay she wrote, one that met all the state standards which she explained to students for the full 40-minute writing instruction period.

The next day Emma projected another essay she had written with the one-sentence paragraphs out of order and asked students to identify the topic sentence, the three supporting detail sentences and the conclusion sentence. Emma repeated this task eight times on that second day of 40 minutes of writing instruction, providing careful and repeated explanations of the correct answers.

On day three Emma presented another essay she had written on the overhead with the topic sentence and the three detail sentences completed and the conclusion sentence started. The students were expected to fill in the remainder of the conclusion sentence using a short list of options. This process was repeated eight times in the 40-minute writing instruction period.

Emma was the only one getting points for meeting the standards.

On day four of writing instruction Emma started at the overhead with a completed topic sentence. The three detail sentences and the conclusion sentence were started with blanks at the end. Students were given options for completing the sentences.

The leaves on the trees could be brown or yellow or red…only one of those three options was acceptable. The weather could be windy, sunny or cloudy. The wind could be strong, moderate or gentle. The conclusion options were similarly limited.

On the last day of writing instruction the students were asked to complete an essay starting with the model on the overhead Emma had created and filling in the remainder of the topic sentence, the three detail sentences and the conclusion sentence using selections from the options Emma had provided.

Emma collected completed essays, graded them and returned them to students to take home and show their parents.

Emma had attended professional development teacher training during her career and these training sessions frequently advocated lessons that required students to work in groups or at learning centers around the classroom. The training emphasized regular testing and quizzes to measure whether students had learned what had been taught. This approach allowed for re-teaching missed concepts to students whose quiz results showed they needed additional instruction.

However, when Emma tried these approaches in her classroom, chaos ensued. Left to their own devices without Emma to control the action from the front of the room students veered off task, misbehaved (once a fistfight broke out while Emma was trying to help another group) and accomplished very little during group work time.

Frequent tests and quizzes required Emma to grade student papers every day, and Emma had little skill or interest in the task of analyzing the quiz results to determine the effectiveness of her teaching.

Emma was uncertain how to proceed with the students who needed extra challenges and those who needed extra support to learn the basics. She preferred to grade one carefully structured activity at the end of a programmed unit of instruction so that all the students could produce the result she wanted.

Like her students Emma's teacher colleagues also understood they should not cross Emma. Three years earlier a rookie second grade teacher who was filling in during a temporary maternity leave made an offhand comment under her breath at a faculty meeting when the principal commended Emma for her students' behavior at recess.

"Goody two shoes," she said under her breath to a colleague.

Emma heard the comment and expressed her displeasure. The rookie teacher was not given the regular second grade teacher opening that developed over the next summer when a teacher retired despite *parent requests and the requests of the other second grade teachers she be given the vacant full-time position.*

The previous principals and superintendents also understood Emma worked best with higher achieving and well behaved students.

More than once, Emma had gone to her friends on the school board to report issues she felt undermined her ability to teach effectively. One of the school board members who had been on the school board for 14 years, Tim Santini, a retired fourth grade teacher from Eastlake, was close friends with Emma and several of the other more senior Eastlake teachers.

Emma knew Tim could be counted on to set things straight if one of the school administrators did anything to disrupt her classroom. In a pinch, Emma also went to the teacher union building representative, Angelica Thompson, with certain issues to ensure administrators and her colleagues left Emma alone so she could teach the way she taught best.

So when Rose, the new principal, announced that classes in grades kindergarten through fifth would be more diversified with special education students, academically weaker students and behavior problem students equally mixed in with regular education students in every classroom, Emma immediately called Tim Santini and two of the other six school board members to explain her concerns.

Over time, in many or even most schools, the same teachers end up with the most challenging students. The principal acquiesces to the wishes of the other teachers because otherwise they end up with a bottleneck of discipline referrals from the same teachers. When all of the struggling students end up in one classroom or in one school or in one school district — as is the case in urban schools — teachers become overwhelmed.

Emma based her pitch to the board members on her concerns that, "Eastlake's most talented students will be held back if they are required to be in classes with the students who are struggling in school and behaving badly. I will not be able to offer Eastlake's best and brightest the

*extra challenges that I have in the past if this change is not reversed,"
she told them.*

Teacher "in need of improvement"
*Late in August, when for the first time the state test results linked to
teacher evaluations arrived, Emma met with Rose. Rose informed
Emma that her students' poor performance on the state tests put her on
the teachers "in need of improvement" list.*

*Emma's students scored only slightly lower on the state tests than
those in the other third grade classrooms, but their calculated predicted
scores were much higher because she had lobbied for and received a
classroom full of high performing students.*

*Many of these "high performing" students showed little or no
academic growth in math or reading after a full year in Emma's
classroom. The negative evaluation of Emma's performance stood in
sharp contrast to years of positive classroom observations from previous principals.*

*Rose's teacher observations during her first year in the building
pointed out the need for Emma to use more group work and less lecture,
to re-teach concepts to students who were struggling, to provide extra
challenges to students who were ready for them and to give students re-
testing opportunities when they initially struggled on tests, but Emma
had disregarded these suggestions.*

*Overcome with emotion and in tears when she was given the evalu-
ation by Rose, Emma quickly channeled her embarrassment and sad-
ness into anger and she set up times for individual lunch meetings with
her friends from the school board.*

And so it goes
*Rose entered the school year in September confident and eager to put her
academic improvement plans into effect with the support of the superintendent and her grade level teacher team leaders. Part of the plan was
a redesign of how to provide help to the weakest students.*

In the past, "remedial" teachers like Karen Carbone had pulled the weakest students out of their regular classrooms for 30 to 45 minute blocks of time in small groups where they received extra reading instruction or math instruction.

The challenge level of this remedial work was one to three grade levels below the regular classroom work and Karen and her special education colleague at grade three, Joe Tasker, who provided the same kind of less challenging instruction, were in Rose's estimation two of the weakest teachers in the entire school.

Both Karen and Joe were supplemental teachers paid for in part by state and federal grants, but they had little positive impact on the education students were receiving or the test scores they produced.

The school had gone through the motions of trying to provide "push-in" remedial and special education services with Karen and Joe working with their students in the regular classrooms four or five years earlier. But that effort had been abandoned because the regular teachers didn't feel comfortable with an additional adult in their classrooms.

The remedial and special education teachers also wanted their own classes and classrooms. They felt they were being treated more like teaching assistants who had to follow a curriculum set by the regular teachers in the regular classrooms.

Initially, when these concerns arose the remedial and special education teachers ended up pulling their students aside in a corner of the classroom or in a nearby hallway to provide their customarily less challenging instruction, and eventually the whole effort was abandoned as a failure by the previous principal.

When the public complains about the dumbing down of the curriculum, this is where it's mostly being done, in separate special education and remedial education classrooms. In my opinion labeling learning disabled students as special education students and saddling them with special education teachers who were previously trained only to teach less demanding (dumbed down) curriculum, has produced generations of unsuccessful students, students who get to high school and just give up on themselves because of weak academic skills.

The "push-in" approach

Now in Rose's restructuring at Eastlake, the "push-in" approach was back with one important detail added: Teacher evaluations for regular classroom teachers like Gail and Emma would be based in part on the state test performance of remedial and special education students as well as general education students.

Superintendent Sarah Calloway showed her support for the plan by making adjustments in the budget for the upcoming school year with cuts in unneeded school bus runs. The funds saved were used to pay two new full-time certified teachers who would work as teaching assistants at Eastlake with grade level teams to provide extra challenges and extra help for students who needed them.

Team leaders also were paid a small stipend for curriculum and assessment work and a teacher coach was brought in to help teachers and Rose implement the plan.

At the same time all of this was being done, Sarah cautioned Rose to be careful not to raise the ire of senior teachers.

"Some of them have friends on the school board and we don't want this plan to create a stir," she told her. "Dot your i's and cross your t's and be very respectful when you discuss with them the fact that performance by remedial and special education students would count toward their end-of-year evaluations."

Unfortunately, it was too late. The plan to include special education and remedial students in teacher evaluations had already sent regular classroom teachers like Emma running to the school board behind the superintendent's back.

Without any notice to Rose, and as it turns out with little communication from school board members to Sarah Calloway, every one of the seven school board members was in private talks with elementary school teachers who were concerned about the rapid pace of change at Eastlake, the impact of the redesign of remedial and special education services, the inclusion of discipline problem students and academically weaker students in all the classes and the less senior grade level team leaders who had been selected for these leadership positions and the impact of these changes on teacher performance evaluations.

And, no this is not the job of a school board, but this dynamic has been going on for decades and in many school districts blocking real reform from taking hold.

The first sign of problems

The first signs of overt problems at Eastlake came in late September as some of the teachers indicated their students were not ready to take the new monthly student assessments that had been created by the teacher team leaders during the summer. At the early October faculty meeting Emma asked Rose a pointed question: "Are these assessments required or are they optional?"

"They're required," Rose said.

After the faculty meeting the teacher union representative, Angelica, met Rose at her office door and handed her two typed union grievance forms.

The first form cited improper labor practices in appointing and paying teacher team leaders for administrative work and for requiring teachers to administer student assessments created by that improper work.

The second cited assigning remedial and special education teachers to teaching assistant work in regular classrooms. Rose told Angelica that she would talk to Superintendent Sarah Calloway about how to proceed and she was certain the school district's attorney would be involved in the discussion as well.

After the union representative left, Rose closed her office door and called Sarah, the superintendent. The superintendent's secretary picked up the phone.

"Superintendent Calloway would like to meet with you at 10 o'clock tomorrow morning," the secretary told her.

Rose was confused. Sarah had always taken her calls and they seldom had formal meetings as their offices were 100 yards apart and both frequently wandered in to each other's office to ask a question or just bounce around ideas.

"What's the meeting for?" Rose asked.

"The teacher union grievances," the secretary said.

Rose was stunned. Sarah knew about the grievances in advance and hadn't said anything. Why?

The morning after

The next morning brought a new Sarah to the table.

"I don't know why you got so far out in front on these issues," she said to Rose. "I told you we had to go slowly to keep the school board in a supportive mode. You knew Emma and several of your teachers had reservations about this plan. You didn't do enough work to bring them along and make these changes piece by piece rather than all at once.

"Maybe if you had worked harder on building a better working relationship with the senior teachers and talked to them in a more respectful manner some of this could have been avoided. The teachers you selected as grade level leaders like Gail Long are too young and inexperienced to be respected by the more senior teachers. And we both know that you can go at this teacher coaching and these assessments at a slower pace to calm things down.

"We also both know that these remedial and special education teachers are very weak performers, and it doesn't make sense to use our political capital with the school board to push them into the classrooms again after that approach already failed in the past.

"They won't help our test scores very much no matter what they're doing with their students. When they meet their students in their own little groups the teachers are more willing to make things work."

Shaken, Rose asked how they would respond to the grievances.

"I'll have the school district's attorney write the response," Sarah said. "We'll be conceding on the points they raised and putting this plan on hold for, at least, a year. You can see how much you can get the teachers to do on a voluntary basis, but it has to be voluntary, not required. You'll need to work hard now to regain their trust and respect. In the future we will need to talk a lot more before you make any major changes."

Rose was devastated. Emma and several of her senior teacher colleagues celebrated by writing a deluge of disciplinary referrals on the difficult students that had been assigned to their classrooms. In the end, at Sarah's direction, Rose was forced to move 14 students from more senior teachers to less senior teachers at Eastlake with four moved from Emma's classroom to Gail's and Molly's (the other third grade teacher) classrooms at grade three.

By the end of December, Rose was buried under four to five hours a day of disciplinary referrals and decided she needed to find a different job. She was certain she could never be a real principal at Eastlake again.

We meet again

By now, Rose was contacting me and asking for my advice. I met with her and tried to cheer her up, reminding her that several of the teachers were using more effective instructional techniques and with the teacher coaching (now optional for teachers), and with the two new teaching assistants now in place test scores were bound to be going up.

I also reminded her that through faculty meeting presentations by Gail Long and others Rose had raised teacher awareness and understanding of the Common Core curriculum and test expectations. She was making progress.

But Rose would have none of what I was selling. "Maybe I made a mistake in getting into education as a career," she said. "I'm still young. I could try something else."

I saw Rose as one of the best real leaders I'd see come to education as a career choice in many years and I told her so. I told her not to be hasty and to think things over carefully. We agreed to meet in January. But when January came Rose had an excuse for not being able to meet. The same for February. Then in March Rose called and asked if we could meet the next day at our usual Starbucks. I was there by 5 o'clock. Rose was already there at a table by the door.

She started talking immediately when I sat down.

"Sarah has put me in a very difficult position and I'm not certain how I should respond," Rose said. "She told me that she can't recommend I continue in my probationary principal's position and she wants me to resign effective May 1."

"Has anything happen since we last spoke? A major issue? More grievances?" I asked.

"No, it's still the same. Lots of student discipline referrals. I've lost all the teachers. I've done my best not to make waves but apparently Sarah is still being pressured by the school board to get me out of there. Sarah has been talking to older retired principals about one of them working as an interim when I'm gone. I know because one of them I know personally called me to ask what was going on."

I could tell that spunky, funny, irreverent, ever enthusiastic Rose was on the edge. That's when she told me Sarah had pulled her into her office and suggested that she resign and say it was because the environment was not gay-friendly. Rose was openly gay and had been since day one.

If anyone called for a reference, Sarah said she would tell them as much as long as Rose agreed not to sue the district.

"Is it a hostile working environment for you?" I asked her.

"Yes, but it has nothing to do with my being a lesbian," she said.

Before the school year ended Rose moved back to North Carolina taking a principal's job in a district adjacent to the one where she had worked previously. Over the next two years she sent me emails that contained four news articles citing outstanding growth in student achievement at the elementary school where she worked.

Meanwhile, when test scores were reported in the local newspaper, it was obvious Eastlake was continuing to underperform as compared to nearby demographically similar school districts.

WHY THE PLAN FAILED

So if the plan was good why did it fail? It failed for multiple reasons. For one: Sarah Calloway did not properly prepare her school board for the changes planned for Eastlake Elementary School. She should have had Rose explain in advance to the school board in executive session how the plan would impact experienced teachers like Emma and what kind of reaction the board members could expect when the plan was fully implemented.

As the more experienced administrator, Sarah was responsible for helping Rose and the school board understand the reaction Emma and other senior teachers would have when they were forced to work with a more diverse group of students.

In every school there are potential leaders and there are blockers. The school district's leadership team – the school board, superintendent and principals – have to have a strategy for working with both and they have to all play a part in developing the strategy to make change happen.

They have to understand the reasons for the change, and anticipate the strategies that will be employed to block meaningful change. And the superintendent has to stand firm when the school board buckles under pressure from reluctant teachers.

Sarah should have explained to the school board in advance the expected impact of including the more challenging students' test scores in teachers' evaluations, the potential friction from working with grade level teacher leaders who were not the senior teachers, the academic need to perform regular student assessments and using these assessments to adjust instruction, the reasons for moving away from lecture-style teaching while incorporating more student group work and learning centers and the impact of having remedial and special education teachers in regular elementary teachers' classrooms.

Sarah should have arranged for Rose and the grade level team leaders to present to the school board in public some of their work during August before the senior teacher/school board insurrection was initiated.

Once the school board understood and bought into what was being done to improve academic performance at Eastlake it would be much harder for them to backtrack when they were pressured by the reluctant senior teachers.

Sarah should have known that grievances and other push back would come and she should have prepared Rose and her school board in advance to expect these tactics. And yes, Sarah, should have supported Rose when the problems arose, although it was probably too late by then for her to turn things around.

The reaction Sarah had to the grievances will bring serious future problems for her and the school district. First, the school board will be emboldened to move further outside its appropriate role and to take greater control of academic improvement efforts, which will weaken Sarah's ability to lead the district.

Second, other administrators in the district who witnessed Rose's fate when Sarah immediately buckled under to school board pressure caused by reluctant senior teachers blocking improvement efforts will hesitate to initiate change.

Third, other groups of employees, such as the school bus drivers who saw their ranks thinned to create funding for the academic improvements will be encouraged to use the same tactics with the school board.

A better response by Sarah when the school board got cold feet on the changes at Eastlake would have been an executive session discussion with the school board with Rose and Sarah explaining the reasons they think the school board should not back off in the face of pressure from Emma and other senior teachers.

There's still a chance the school board would not have supported Sarah and Rose, but at least they would have looked like real leaders to the school board and teachers at Eastlake.

Sometimes the best that can be achieved in these situations is that strong teachers like Gail Long realize the principal and superintendent will not run for cover at the first sign of school board turmoil. And there's a chance those teacher leaders will support their administrators the next time around.

If teachers can go to the school board members directly with their concerns, there is no chance for a principal or superintendent to succeed. The way this played out made it clear that these school board members think it's their job to listen to employee complaints and then make the administrators "fix" them – make them go away.

Training for school board members and education law state clearly that this is not the case.[lxxxviii] School board members are tasked with setting district policy and district goals, monitoring the district's progress in following those policies and achieving those goals. Period. [lxxxix]

There is one – and only one – school district employee school board members should be working with – the superintendent.

Many school board members want to play the role of fixer because they want to be seen as the person running the district. Their ego demands it. Other school board members are sucked into this "fixer" role by friends, neighbors or relatives and have to be reminded on these occasions what their real role is.

When I start work as a school district superintendent I have learned to say in my first public session with all the school board members: "If we are going to work as an effective team we must all share the same information. So my assumption from here on with this school board is that if one of us is given information we will be sharing that information with every school board member and the superintendent. Agreed?"

They always agree. This means if Emma calls board members and complains about Rose Diamond, those board members, who have agreed to this rule in public, are honor bound to share Emma's complaint and its source with the entire school board and the superintendent.

This rule doesn't prevent unethical and incompetent school board members from getting out of line on these types of issues but it does slow them down and it helps to set up a school board dynamic that encourages the other school board members to push back when members step over the line.

I then say: "School board members have difficult jobs. You must set policy and goals for the school district, monitor the district's progress in following those policies and meeting those goals and you can only deal with me, the superintendent, to meet your responsibilities. That's a tall order and I promise to provide you with the information you need as far in advance as possible, to answer your questions in a timely manner and to follow up with issues which are mine and not yours that are brought to you by mistake. I promise to inform you and other school board members as to how those issues are resolved. I also promise you that no employee, parent or student in this district will be coerced, retaliated against or intimidated by a member of our staff and that any employee who violates that expectation will face serious disciplinary consequences.

"In return I expect that all school board members share with me and all the other school board members the specifics of any complaint about our district from parents, students, employees and residents including the identity of those making the complaints. We will of course keep these issues confidential among us and our administrative staff if the board member so wishes and our attorney agrees the issue qualifies for confidentiality."

This is usually followed by a pause, but eventually they realize that there is no other realistic way to proceed unless they choose dysfunction.

Invariably, individual school board members will violate these expectations. The best school boards deal with these violations in private. They send the administrators out of their executive session (including the superintendent!) and make their expectations clear to the offending member and that is the end of the problem.

With more dysfunctional school boards, the school district attorney and the school board president may meet with the offending board member and provide a verbal warning. If the behavior persists, a written warning should be given to the recalcitrant school board member. If the process continues after one to three additional written warnings the proper procedures for removal of a school board member should be initiated.

Sometimes these removal procedures make the "bad" school board member a local celebrity and he is re-elected to the school board. That's a problem. Local communities have to decide if they want a school system that works or a side show at school board meetings.

And if the finances or the test scores in the district are bad (and in the districts with board members who act this way invariably one or both are), removal of the entire school board for financial or academic bankruptcy should be the ultimate consequence.

Those individuals on the school board when the removal occurs should not be allowed to run for the school board in the future after the board removal proccss has ended and regular school board member elections have resumed.

A MODEST PROPOSAL ON TEACHER TENURE

I have thought long and hard about the best potential solution for teachers like Emma in our schools. I fully understand the view that we should just fire them. I also know that many of them were never given the direction and support they needed early in their careers that might have helped them grow into the teachers we really need.

I am an educator and that means I think people can learn, even the Emmas. But Emma needs motivation to learn quickly and our students, who are dropping out due to weak academic skills or scraping by when they should be exceeding expectations, can't wait forever for Emma to get her professional life together.

I propose, in schools like Eastlake where test results have been mired at substandard levels for years, 5 percent of the teaching force or a minimum of two teachers in the building (whichever number is greater) should lose the protection of tenure and be summarily dismissed using the same procedures available for their non-tenured teacher colleagues in the first year of reform.

The principal may choose which tenured teacher or teachers will be summarily dismissed for poor performance based on teacher evaluations that show their performance to be ineffective or in need of improvement. The teachers selected for dismissal must have been given an opportunity to participate in a performance improvement plan before they are dismissed.

Teachers dismissed in this manner should have no legal challenges except procedural challenges. If the district has violated the procedures, the dismissed teacher is not rehired; they receive their salary for one year to compensate for their loss.

Poor test performance for a school in comparison to demographically similar peer schools moves this target up to 10 percent of the teacher workforce in the school or a minimum of four teachers who would lose tenure protection in the second year.

The target in the third year of poor test performance is 25 percent of staff or six employees minimum losing tenure protection including the principal. This last provision means the principal had better choose wisely in years one and two. This process should continue until the entire staff plus principal is replaced, assuming test scores do not improve in comparison to demographically similar peer schools as shown in the graphic for Candle Central School District in the "Common Core is Not the Problem" chapter of this book.

I've also written more about this proposed solution in the chapter of this book "Creating Quality with Tenure." When the process reaches year five of consecutive poor performance the superintendent and the school board should be removed from their positions. Leadership is key to school success and leadership failure should not be allowed to continue forever.

COACHING TEACHERS

Bringing in a teaching coach to work with multiple teachers should be standard procedure in order for continuous improvement in elementary and secondary schools. And that coach should not be a school district employee. Private groups and regional consortiums of public school districts offer teaching coaches on a contract basis.

Why do teachers need coaches?

More than ever teachers need someone knowledgeable they can have candid discussions with about their reservations regarding the changes they're attempting to incorporate into their teaching.

Teaching is a very complex job. The number of children living in poverty has grown, single parent families are becoming the norm and we expect more of students, much more.

Many teachers survive by moving to schools with fewer challenging students. Many just leave the profession. Within five years between 30 and 50 percent of teachers leave the profession.[xc]

This complex job is complicated by the fact that many teachers haven't learned the skills they need to teach effectively, particularly in the high standards environment. Teacher preparation programs have not changed all that much over the years. And even when teachers do come out of college with the skills they need to teach to today's higher standards, they face pressure from their peers to conform to an earlier, easier standard.

And by standard I'm not just referring to the Common Core. The new "standard" in teaching includes the following:

- Teach on multiple levels.
- Going in depth on fewer topics.
- Providing extra challenges for students who are ready for them.
- Providing regular feedback (from one day to the next) so that student understand their errors and make adjustments before the grading is complete.
- Re-teaching.
- Re-testing.
- Rewarding effort and eventual mastery.

We can no longer expect results from a broad curriculum that only skims the surface. In order to teach to a higher standard we to have to focus the curriculum around the critical elements provided by the more challenging Common Core standards.

For example, rather than covering all the topics in a 500-page math textbook, teachers have to analyze the Common Core expectations and find teaching materials that require students to apply fewer concepts at a much higher level than in the past.

It's no longer enough to know how to divide; students have to know when to divide and what the answer means.

In Japan, China, Finland and Korea teachers are constantly revising and improving their curriculum and daily lessons to ensure they're using the best strategies. The most effective teachers share their successful strategies with peers.

Teachers are not just correcting papers. They have to look at the data and see patterns. They have to analyze test scores and figure out strategies for moving forward.

It's not just about memory anymore. It's thinking. It's writing. It's explaining, it's analyzing. Even in elementary school classrooms.

OPPORTUNITY KNOCKS

The economic downturn of 2008 has produced a pool of certified teachers who are looking for a way into the teacher work force, especially elementary school teachers and teachers certified in saturated subjects such as English and social studies.

In the small rural school district of Bern-Knox-Westerlo (BKW), where I recently served as interim superintendent, we had five full-time elementary openings and 900 applications.

We hired teachers with multiple years of teaching experience, who had been laid off, who wanted to teach in our school or who had recently moved to our region to fill the five teaching slots. We also created a new position: teaching assistant with full teacher certification. We set the pay rate for this position at approximately 60 percent of a starting teacher's salary $24,000 vs. $40,000 for a starting teacher with a bachelor's degree.

At BKW, we hired a teaching assistant with teacher certification for each grade level K-6 using money we saved by eliminating unnecessary bus runs (which I guarantee exist in every district) and unnecessary school lunch program expenses.

The new teaching assistants with teacher certification work a longer work day than teachers by an hour and a half which allows them to tutor students or offer extra challenges to students after school.

As you might well imagine these teaching assistants work hard because they want the next available full-time elementary teaching opening that comes open in the district or in another district nearby.

Meanwhile, the district has years to train them and get to know them before a decision is made to hire them as the next elementary school teacher.

Imagine the increased effectiveness of Emma's classroom with an excellent teacher-certified teaching assistant in the room. Imagine Gail's classroom. Imagine the amount and quality of the one-on-one support students in these classrooms would get for extra help or extra challenges with this extra teacher-certified teaching assistant in the classroom.

It also gives rookie teachers opportunity to learn from teachers like Gail Long. These same rookie teachers will also take some of the rough edges off Emma's demeaning approach to discipline.

Emma will also be more willing to try group work and learning centers with extra hands and eyes in the room to help her, and the teaching assistant will see and intervene on off-task behavior before it gets out of hand. Emma's dysfunctional classroom could improve to marginally effective with this kind of help in the room.

Remedial teachers like Karen Carbone and special educations teacher like Joe Tasker, the aforementioned special education teachers, will improve as well. They won't want to look like they're not working hard to help out with a new teacher assistant in the room.

When we operate the way the Emma's of the world operate, we end up with disenfranchised students who never take responsibility for their own educations. Students with no motivation. Students who enter high school with neither the skills nor the ability to succeed. Students who end up in the principal's office with parents who can't understand where they went wrong.

Charter Schools, School Choice and Poverty

● ● ●

I WAS TWO YEARS INTO my position as superintendent of schools for the City School District of Albany in April 1999 when I read a blurb in the local newspaper about plans to establish New York's first charter school – in our district.

It was the first time I'd heard about it. Since my arrival, we'd been busy plugging up financial holes (more than $20 million) in our leaky ship, restructuring academics, identifying the worst performers on the district's shaky administrative team, negotiating with our teachers union and our civil service union and trying to coalesce a solid majority of our school board around some guiding principles.

My inherited business official, who had been an unsuccessful candidate for the superintendent position, told my newly hired Assistant Superintendent for Curriculum and Instruction: "Welcome to the sinking ship." He bailed on the sinking ship shortly thereafter.

Now, just when I thought we were coming out of a storm, the state's first charter school was on its way.

At least we would have a year to plan, or so I thought.

According to the law that established charter schools in New York State, charter schools were to be treated like a private schools when it comes to making requests for transportation, textbooks and school nursing services, all items public schools typically provide to private schools without reimbursement.

The deadline for making those requests is April 1ˢᵗ. The April 1ˢᵗ deadline had been in place for many, many years and survived multiple challenges from private schools wanting to make last minute changes and additions to services and supports – transportation, nursing services, textbooks – they routinely received from their public school district. (Not to confuse the issue but the whole system of reimbursement has created a boatload of administrative work even without charters. Students who attend Albany Academy private school, for example, receive services from the City School District of Albany, which then turns around and bills each and every home school district for services for students attending the private school.)

Time and time again, the April 1ˢᵗ deadline was upheld by the education commissioner in order to ensure the public school district had ample time to plan their budgets, budgets that were approved (or not) by the public in May of each year.

So, imagine my surprise when on June 15, 1999, the SUNY Charter School Institute approved the New Covenant Charter School to open September 1, 1999!ˣᶜⁱ (Original charter school law has since been amended. Charter school applications are supposed to be approved in June for opening in September of the following year.ˣᶜⁱⁱ)

Maybe even more shocking than the start date was that news of the new school came without anyone from the SUNY Charter School Institute contacting anyone in our school district to find out what impact this approval would have on the 10,000-plus students who would remain in our public schools.

Our district had only two-and-a-half months to prepare for this new charter school. On top of that we had to find a way to pay $3.2 million in tuition payments – $8,000 for each student.

We had no provisions in the school district budget for sending the charter school $3.2 million or busing 400-plus students to a new and as yet unknown school site.

The school nursing services for our district had already been established as had remedial services and textbook purchases. All of this would need to be unraveled and reorganized in a nightmare of last minute changes. And worst of all the 400-plus students the charter school would serve had not yet been identified or recruited.

We didn't receive the wildly inaccurate list of 423 New Covenant Charter School students until August 25, 1999, one week before school started. Little did I know, at the time, this was the tip of the iceberg that was about to rip a huge new hole in the hull of our barely floating public school district ship.

A "MARKET" THEORY OF EDUCATION

Charter schools are an idea that emerged in the United States in the early 1990s. The principles behind their growth developed from a "market" theory of education.[xciii] The public schools are a monopoly. They need competition. With competition, especially in the urban areas where standardized test scores show dismal student academic performance, the public schools will be forced to compete and improve or they will lose students and dollars to higher performing charter schools. This theory hasn't played out well.[xciv]

Charter schools arrived on the scene with support from conservatives[xcv] who hated the powerful and selfish teacher unions and the bloated administrative bureaucracy of urban schools and from many urban liberals and leaders in the African American and Hispanic communities who were ready to try anything to improve failing urban schools.[xcvi, xcvii]

Charter schools were given freedom from state regulations and union contracts for teachers and administrators to create entrepreneurial educational ventures designed to put staid, failing urban public schools to shame.

They were also afforded longer school days and longer school years and organized around themes or instructional approaches.

Charter schools and the market principles they are designed to epitomize are reasonable ideas, but like many reasonable ideas in the social science/political/economic arena, charter schools, especially as they were implemented in New York State, had unintended, catastrophic consequences.

Unintended consequence No. 1: charter schools discriminated against students with academic, behavioral and special education challenges and –

in my opinion and according to recent news reports – still do. As a result, the most challenging students are boomeranged back to the regular public schools in what becomes a constant revolving door disrupting education for all.[xcviii] Over time, our remaining students in Albany included an overwhelming percentage of students with academic, behavioral and special education challenges. And that was reflected in the test scores.

Unfortunately, unlike the most challenging students, the tuition payments sent to the charter school did not boomerang back.

While there are some, select charter schools with strong leadership and exemplary programs and some cities with comprehensive charter school systems and programs (i.e. the KIPP network, schools in New Orleans and with some important exceptions in Newark, DC and NYC) that contradict this trend,[xcix] many do not. Overall there has been no magical urban student achievement growth resulting from charter schools and the unintended consequences of charter schools have created serious issues for the public school districts they were supposed to improve.

And there's been very little measurable academic growth at most charter schools or at least a very mixed bag of academic growth for urban students as a whole in the U.S. due to the initiation of charter schools.[c] [ci]

ENTER SCOTT STEFFEY AND AARON DARE

Within hours of the announcement that the SUNY Charter School Institute had approved New Covenant Charter School for a September 1999 start I was on the phone with anyone who would return my calls: the state's governor, education commissioner, comptroller, the school district attorney, etc., explaining the impossibility of this school's arrival on the approved timetable.

My conversations were usually brief and concluded when I was basically told to, "Suck it up and make it happen." Why? "Because Republican Governor George Pataki engineered the charter school approval process as a concession from the state legislators who received a pay raise in return and they are not going to change it now."

One conversation stands out in my mind. It was with Scott Steffey who was, according to articles in the local newspaper, the Chairman of the SUNY Charter School Institute that had approved the New Covenant Charter School and the timetable for its initiation.[cii]

When I explained to Mr. Steffey the impossibility of finding $3.2 million in our already approved and very tight budget and effectively completing all the last minute busing and other changes the new charter school would require he responded, "If it hurts you, that's even better."

The state legislators who voted in favor of the charter schools in order to receive pay raises were not aware of Scott Steffey's attitude toward our district or the 10,000-plus students we worked hard to serve every day. I'm certain the legislators were thinking of a more gentlemanly type of competition where we all did our best to serve the students in our schools without, by design, hurting students, parents, taxpayers and employees.

Unfortunately, the system they designed with rogue charter schools that required no approval from local taxpayers or the local school boards, and a funding formula that sent significantly more money to the charter schools than any savings strategy could create, produced significant fallout for the system as a whole.

By the way, Mr. Steffey's impolitic approach with me and others reflected badly on his politician friends who wanted to make this transition as smooth as possible and soon cost him job. He was replaced by a soft spoken representative who did a much better job of hiding the uglier motivations behind the charter school movement.

In July 1999, soon after the approval of the charter school my assistant superintendents and I met with a few members of the New Covenant Charter School Board including their president Aaron Dare. Aaron was a likeable young African American man whose wife was a teacher in one of our elementary schools. He was an active leader in Albany's largely poor, African American Arbor Hill community.

Aaron was in the process of starting a real estate development business primarily focused in the Arbor Hill area and he played a leadership role in the city's active Urban League. He was well over six feet tall nearly 300 pounds and a former high school basketball player at Albany High School.

Aaron's stepfather, Sam Walton, had left the position I now occupied as superintendent of the City School District of Albany a little over one year earlier after numerous public squabbles with the school board and the mayor.

Our leadership team and I did our best to explain our concerns about the large size and abrupt initiation of the New Covenant Charter School. But Aaron and his board members were adamant, the school would open as planned in September 1999 with a full contingent of students assuming they could successfully recruit these students during the summer.

NEW COVENANT CHARTER OPENS ITS DOORS

New Covenant opened its doors in old used trailers on a dusty lot in the Arbor Hill section of Albany on schedule in September 1999 and operated under a contract with Advantage Schools, a private school management company from Boston, MA. In addition to the $3.2 million that would come from us, there were rumors that New Covenant had undisclosed financial backing from political conservatives who were loyal to Governor Pataki.

As we predicted the busing and other supports were a mess despite our best efforts to reorganize and reschedule everything during the summer. The extremely late and inaccurate student list caused much of the confusion. And our own school district budget was a disaster with the new $3.2 million-plus expense we hadn't planned for.

A reasonable assumption would be that Albany could just close one of its elementary schools and create savings to offset this new charter school expense. But which school would we close?

The students New Covenant recruited came from all over the city. If we closed the existing Arbor Hill Elementary School, which still had over 400 students after New Covenant opened, we would have to bus those existing Arbor Hill students all over the city to the vacant slots in the other elementary schools created by New Covenant's arrival.

A school closure would create another busing nightmare (we already had one busing nightmare with the new bus routes required to get New

Covenant students to their new school site from all over the city), and the parents of the Arbor Hill students, who had not enrolled their children in New Covenant and who had supported the public schools by staying put, would arrive at the next school board meeting with pitchforks in hand.

When the smoke cleared after the list of New Covenant students finally arrived in late August, we considered laying off teachers and consolidating classes. But the savings would have paled in comparison to the tuition payments we were sending to New Covenant. And the last minute chaos of disrupting classes in elementary schools throughout the city to make these few 11th hour teacher cuts did not justify the cost of the disruption.

Besides we would be laying off cheaper, last hired teachers who we had worked hard to recruit to improve the quality of our workforce. This is an important detail often overlooked by reformers. Union contracts require school districts to lay off their newest teachers first, which means that large urban districts competing with charters often have to lay off their youngest, most promising and least expensive teachers first, many of whom end up working for the new charter schools. We decided to wait and look for potential savings from consolidating classes and eliminating teaching slots in the following year's budget.

After several years of New Covenant Charter School's operation we came to understand that, at best, our class consolidation, teacher layoffs and redesigned bus routing (which added a whole new extra expense our district had not faced before) could save about $0.25 (25 cents) for every dollar we sent to the charter school for tuition.

To make up for that, we had to raise taxes more than we should have the next year and the year after that and the year after that, etc. Another unintended consequence.

With students traveling to New Covenant from all over the city, none of our elementary schools lost enough enrollment to make sense to close even when we considered neighborhood school boundary changes. Not only that, New Covenant had a principal, teachers, custodians, secretaries and school monitors that had to be paid. It required heat and lights. It paid a trailer rental fee. All bills paid by tuitions from the City School District of Albany.

The city of Albany had in essence added an expensive new elementary school with no clear way to pay for it. The few teachers we laid off or did not hire due to classroom consolidation in the years after that first year of New Covenant's existence were all at the beginning of the salary scale. Over time our teaching staff just grew older and more expensive per teacher as all the newer and cheaper teaching positions shifted to New Covenant. So charter schools worked out to be a big drain on resources and funding for the communities that had them. Unintended consequence No. 3.

Not to mention: New Covenant's enrollment claims, which the school principal processed for payments, were wildly inflated and based on flawed enrollment and attendance lists. More than 70 students listed in the initial enrollment of 423 turned out to be students who were in the district's regular public schools daily and had never attended New Covenant. Another 80-plus students moved back and forth through the revolving door between the district's public elementary schools and New Covenant Charter School over the first several months.

According to research carefully completed by the school district's attendance personnel, each of the first four bimonthly claims for payment to Advantage Schools from New Covenant was overstated by over $100,000. That's nearly half a million dollars in claimed overpayments.

Of course we appealed this overbilling to the New York State Education Commissioner, Richard Mills, and were denied just as we were denied in our appeal to Mills requesting a delay in New Covenant's implementation schedule due to their late approval date.

The political fix was in. The Governor had made certain this school would start in September 1999 and receive all the funding (even the funding it didn't deserve due to inflated enrollment numbers).

Political statements can't wait (especially this one as it was voted on and passed in the middle of the night sometime after 2 a.m. along with legislative pay raises)[ciii]. This school was a political statement made by Governor George Pataki, the same George Pataki who was a self-proclaimed Republican candidate in the early days of the 2016 Presidential election. He brought a national conservative political idea – charter schools – to New York State in an effort to set himself up for an unsuccessful presidential bid.

Then in early November Aaron Dare phoned me to report that his charter school board had decided to switch to a new management company. He said they should have a new partner identified shortly. However, his next request was a surprise. He said: "Make the December check out to Aaron Dare and send it to me directly."

Now I don't pretend to be the sharpest knife in the drawer but even I could see that this was a bad idea. I called the New York State Education Commissioner's office, the New York State Governor's office, the New York State Comptroller's office and our own school attorney's office to say, "This can't be right. What should I do?" They all had their representatives tell me to do exactly what Aaron had requested. And I did.

We ended up sending out two checks for more than $450,000 each, one in December 1999 and a second in February 2000, made out to Aaron Dare personally. Then the rumors started to fly. Aaron had not spent the $900,000 on the charter school; he had instead invested this money in a failed real estate venture in Arbor Hill. Reports in the newspaper indicated Aaron had built a new business center in Arbor Hill[civ] and he expected to rent this facility to an outside business. But the rental contract evaporated after the construction was completed and the construction bill had to be paid.

Within months the golden boy had become the public goat in a huge political failure for the Governor who had pushed hard to get New Covenant approved. Aaron also was tagged as the goat for a huge financial failure that left the New Covenant Charter School short on funding in its first year of operation. We all expected Aaron Dare to go to jail and for New Covenant to close its doors.

But politicians, especially governors with presidential ambitions, don't "go gentle into that good night." Strings were pulled and Aaron (temporarily) stayed out of jail after resigning from the charter school board and his leadership role in the Albany based Urban League of Northeastern New York. [cv] Local business and community benefactors (likely at Governor Pataki's urging) rushed in to save New Covenant from financial disaster.[cvi]

The Albany mayor, Jerry Jennings, had a running feud with me and several school board members who had disrupted the old ways of pay-to-play in the city. Rumors were rampant about previous school district contracts tied to kickbacks and campaign contributions and school system jobs awarded on the basis of patronage and nepotism with whoever was in the role of superintendent at the time. It was no surprise when Jennings stepped in to take over Dare's business center.[cvii] So the school survived despite its problems.

Today, Aaron's "business center" houses offices of the Albany Police Department. Aaron Dare went to jail a few years later on charges related to another real estate scam. New Covenant limped along with terrible test scores, a series of management companies and repeated financial issues until 2010 when it finally closed its doors for good after its charter was yanked by the SUNY Charter School Committee.[cviii]

The SUNY Charter School Institute changed its name to the SUNY Charter School Committee during this 11-year period and with a Democrat now in the role of governor the new committee finally felt comfortable deciding that New Covenant had been given more than enough time and warnings to improve and ended its charter.

New Covenant ended just as it began on a political note. The local newspaper noticed and reported that during the intervening 11 years the school had moved out of the trailers and into a new home with a $16 million mortgage and that the public (now the City of Albany, not the school district) would be stuck paying off the loan over the next couple of decades despite the school's demise.[cix] Later the school district investigated purchasing the empty school. [cx] New Covenant wasn't the only Albany charter school to close its doors after a history of academic underachievement.[cxi]

The whole thing left a bad taste in my mouth. So when I took a position as an interim superintendent in Sarandon, NY, a medium-sized urban district near Syracuse that had been blessed with two charter schools I was more than a little wary.

(Sections in italics are fictional stories made from composites of multiple actual experiences.)

A complicated school district

Sarandon Central School District was like many of the smaller rustbelt cities in New York State and throughout the United States. During a boom period that extended from WWII up through the mid 1980's manufacturing jobs in shoes, drugs, textiles and electronics parts had been mainstays of the economy. Blue collar union factory jobs for many residents paid decent wages that could support a family.

But then the effects of globalization, technology and outside low wage competition for Sarandon's union wages and benefits began to cause major economic shifts. First, the textile factory closed and moved to Mexico. Then the shoe factory moved to North Carolina and later to someplace in Asia. By the mid-1990s, the drug firm packed up for Texas and the final straw fell into place when the electronics firm was sold to a much bigger company that sent those jobs to China.

By 2010, when I arrived for a one-year stint as the interim school superintendent, Sarandon's population had dropped from a 1984 high of 28,000 to 15,000 with senior citizens on fixed incomes remaining and many families with children gone. The percentage of students in the schools receiving free and reduced price lunches had jumped from 18 percent in 1982 to 66 percent in 2010.

What was once a sleepy little blue collar town was now an unstable community with meth labs, gangs, a huge new sheriff's department sub-station, two food pantries for poor residents and more than a few home-less men and women wheeling around shopping carts filled with empty bottles and cans. More than 600 vacant homes in the city and nearby were owned by the banks. More than half the businesses on Sarandon's Main Street were shuttered and had been that way for several years.

A dwindling tax base due to declining property values from the vacant homes and businesses meant the school district I was now leading had significant fiscal problems, and it showed in the academic results of the district's schools. They were much weaker than schools from other districts with similar levels of student poverty and much weaker than the results the community saw during its economic heyday.

A school board with a penchant for squabbling publicly pushed out my predecessor and decided as a last resort to hire me when the school superintendent candidate pool was too weak to produce someone they could agree was worth hiring. Their decision to hire an interim for one year gave me a limited timeframe to, in the words of one school board member, "straighten out this mess" before they tried again to hire a permanent superintendent. (Note: Most education professionals shy away from such "messes" because the dysfunction tends to derail careers.)

Sarandon's public school teachers and principals were demoralized by this point, struggling to keep their heads above water. Their classes were bigger and the students needier than ever.

The district's image was terrible due to a barrage of bad press. Most of these teachers and principals lived in the city of Sarandon or nearby, and the bad press meant regular doses of barely concealed scorn from many taxpayers and more than a few parents whose children struggled in the schools.

Compared to the community median, teachers received generous salaries and benefits which raised the ire of the downtrodden community, especially when the school district budget vote arrived each May. The budget vote had failed in five of the last seven years resulting in a severe reduction in school services and even larger class sizes.

Immediately after my arrival in the district I toured the five schools with their principals and added to what I already knew about the district from my online search of news articles, financial reports and test data. The principals like their teachers were downtrodden and uninspired.

In 1985, the district had five elementary schools and a large middle school and a large high school and all of these schools were bursting at the seams with too many students, a total enrollment of 4,700. By 2010, the district enrollment had shrunk to 2,100, less than half. Five elementary schools had become three with the two youngest and most dynamic principals being pushed out when their schools closed.

The most recent elementary school closing created significant parental pushback when new elementary attendance boundaries added some poverty children to an elementary school that previously served few poverty children.

Years earlier, budget cuts had eliminated assistant principals from the middle school and high school and the remaining administrative team members including the business official averaged 61 years of age. They were respectful and seasoned. They would not cause me problems, but they would also bring me few new ideas or potential solutions to the issues we faced.

The three elementary school principals were nervous about their jobs and their futures. They'd lost more than 200 students in the last two years to two recently opened charter schools. With just slightly more than 700 students in grades K-5 remaining in the district's schools, the entire elementary school population could now easily fit into two of the three existing elementary school buildings.

Although my school building tours were instructive I actually gained more valuable insight into the school district and community from a high school science teacher named Tonya Harris who made an appointment to see me during my first week in the district.

Tonya was in her mid-50s and short with long straight grey hair, a quick smile and a very direct manner of speech. Her piercing brown eyes never left my face while she spoke and I could tell what she was saying meant a great deal to her.

Tonya knew I only had one year to make lasting change and she'd heard through the grapevine that I would do more than just collect a paycheck. She wanted me to know what I was in for.

I always carry a notebook to meetings. It's a prop I seldom use. In this case I made an exception because of Tonya's earnestness. I looked at my notes later on:

School board – want their names in the paper and praise from public, no real ideas, just want someone to blame, waste money on things outside the classroom, created enemies when they mishandled elementary redistricting three years ago.

Principals – just going through the motions, no new ideas, downtrodden as a result of being beat up by the school board, newspaper and superintendent.

Teachers – unwilling to work hard enough or just don't have the skills, arrive late and leave early, focus too much on salary, benefits and retirement and not enough on students. Blame the newspaper for the bad press, blame the students and their parents, haven't

changed how they teach even with big changes in school population and new tests.

Students — more students on free and reduced lunch than ever before. Need more hands-on activities and one-on-one coaching to learn and opportunities to re-test. Education for these students is critical.

Parents — overwhelmed, many more single parent families, many in trouble with the law, parents frequently out of pocket, an absence of quality child care for younger students, many parents trying to get by cobbling together multiple part-time jobs, doing their best but not enough.

Taxpayers — angry, don't understand why teachers with a four-year college degree and a Master's earn so much more than the rest of the community, angry because state has cut aid and that increased local school property taxes, quick to blame the superintendent, principals and teachers.

Newspaper — has been on the warpath with the school district since editor's daughter was laid off from her teaching job 12 years earlier, little communication from the district with the local newspaper. They write what the district's enemies tell them.

Charter schools — political stepping stone for Kim Neely, vice president of marketing for Sarandon Bank and Trust (SBT), father owns the bank, bank has grown to 200 branches regionally, Kim plans to run for the U.S. Congress, applied for the two charter schools and now applying for a third.

Twenty minutes later my head was spinning.

Much of what Tonya said linked back to an important point we both understood but had not discussed in depth: Teaching children from poverty is hard work and academic success for students of poverty is statistically much more elusive than academic success for middle class or wealthy students.

Many taxpayers and parents, especially those who attended wealthy suburban schools or schools like those found in Sarandon a generation earlier when its economy was much stronger, don't understand the difficulty of creating academic success for disadvantaged children.

When I chose education as a career I, like other teachers, immediately accepted that everyone I knew would think they understood my job because we all went to school. However, not all schools are equal. Increasing poverty rates and economically changing communities mean that the yardsticks used by many parents and taxpayers to measure the success of their local schools are inadequate for the task because their yardsticks are based on a personal school experience that no longer exists for many students, parents, teachers and principals.

WHY IS EDUCATING STUDENTS FROM POVERTY SO DIFFICULT?

When children who grow up living in poverty enter kindergarten they are on average one to two years behind their peers who come from wealthy or middle class homes. If you sit with kindergartners from poverty who have not attended preschool and ask them simple questions, you'll notice the difference immediately.

Ask them to name colors while pointing to a color chart. Ask them to count to ten. Ask them to sing the alphabet song with you. Point to an alphabet of capital letters and ask them to identify multiple random letters. Ask them to open a book for you to read to them and note whether it is right side up or the front is facing you. Accompany them to the playground or the lunch room and watch how they play and interact with their peers.

Do they share toys? How do they handle normal conflicts and disagreements? Listen to their speech patterns. Do they enunciate clearly? Do they use complex sentences? Elaborate vocabulary? Do they know the names of people they have met including you?

Now repeat this process with some first-time kindergartners who did not attend preschool but are from wealthy or middle class families.

Children living in poverty struggle with these tasks. They struggle because they haven't been exposed to the same learning opportunities as children from wealthy or even middle class homes, and they haven't conversed with adults as much or received as much effective adult support as the kids from wealthy and middle class homes.

In academic literature this is known as the "30 million word gap." Basically, children who are raised in two-parent, college educated, financially stable homes receive an enormous amount of additional "verbal engagement" from their parents and preschool teachers who read them books, talk to them regularly and help them become adept at understanding language.

Some of the students from poverty will surprise you with their strong skills and knowledge and some of the students from wealthy and middle class homes will struggle like their peers from poverty. In fact, the number of poverty children who overcome the difficulties in their lives and achieve school success and later life success is remarkable.[cxii] Their stories are instructive and prove they are definitely worth the investment in dollars and professional effort that increases their chances for success. But the odds for success are stacked against the children who live in less affluent homes, where, let's face it, food alone is not abundant.

Despite the views found in racially biased "scholarly" papers this obvious disparity in the skills of poverty kindergartners is not caused by some genetic flaw in their makeup.[cxiii]

For many, their suboptimal development begins in the womb. If their mother's diet is poor; if she doesn't or can't see a doctor regularly; if she smokes or drinks excessively; if she takes drugs or lives in an environment with lead paint, airborne mercury or other harmful chemicals; if she is under constant stress due to financial, environmental or emotional stressors she can't control; if she's in prison or without a steady job or without a partner to help her with her pregnancy; any of these factors will reduce the odds her baby will be born with the optimal chance for later good mental and physical health and success in school. And some studies point to a host of other potential prenatal factors – including a mother's stress levels – that negatively impact children.[cxiv]

And then there are cases like the one in Flint, MI, where an error by state and local government officials resulted in many children – and mothers – being exposed to lead in their drinking water.[cxv] Lead exposure causes developmental delays, long term IQ depression and significant reductions in chances for school success for children who have been exposed to this destructive chemical.

As a result of extensive national press coverage of the Flint problem many in the U.S. have learned about the problems caused by lead and other environmental hazards that all too frequently negatively impact children of poverty. They have also learned that lead in the water is not a problem unique to Flint, MI. In Albany, NY, where I was superintendent a garbage incinerator created a health hazard for residents in a predominantly poor, African-American part of the city for years until it caused a problem at the Governor's mansion across town.[cxvi]

Once a baby is born into that environment a new set of potential problems emerges: Will the child grow up in a single parent home? Will the baby's mother or father be available for childcare on a regular basis or will economic pressures make them less available? Does the primary caregiver/parent suffer from mental or physical health issues that will prevent them from being successful in parenting? Will the baby or one or both parents face environmental issues (like lead, mercury, alcohol, drugs, etc.) that negatively impact the baby's health and well-being? Does the primary caregiver have the training, support and skills to care of the baby effectively? Is the baby seeing a doctor for regular checkups? Are the child's diet, sleep patterns and regular activity schedule appropriate? Does the primary caregiver speak with the child regularly? Do the parents speak English? Do they speak English well? Is the child's home and neighborhood interesting, safe and emotionally supportive or do violence, crime and emotional trauma create an unsupportive stressful environment for the child? Does the child get to experience an enriching home and neighborhood environment that creates questions, context, communication skills and knowledge that helps them progress normally later on in school?

Some individual parents and their children overcome the odds, but on the whole almost no high poverty schools succeed to the degree that average schools serving wealthy or middle class students succeed, and it's not because they haven't spent enough money, tried hard enough or worked hard or smart enough. The reason is that overcoming poverty is nearly impossible.

If you look at New York State Education Department data, you'll see that no high poverty schools performed as well as the lowest performing wealthy schools, putting to rest the assumption that if teachers in high poverty schools just tried harder, students would do better.

Statistically there is very little chance (according to available data on the New York State Education Department website) that even the best performing high poverty school will perform as well as the lowest performing wealthy school. Growing up in poverty is (unfortunately) one of the best predictors of poor educational outcomes.

The best analogy I can come up with to help non-educators understand the "poverty problem" for schools involves those huge backpacks you see on middle school students' backs with about 40 pounds of books making them lean forward from the waist like a football runner going through the line.

Imagine as soon as they are conceived every child, poor, middle class and wealthy alike, is fitted with one of these backpacks and carries it throughout infancy, toddlerhood and their school career. Now imagine the mother is a heavy drinker during her child's pregnancy...add two heavy rocks to the backpack. But the child's grandmother, who is the child's primary caregiver, spends countless hours talking with the baby and reading to her after birth...take out one of those rocks. The baby's home is in a gang infested, crime ridden neighborhood with lots of yelling and conflict in the neighborhood and at home and the baby is sentenced to see and hear all of it...add two rocks to the pack. The grandmother caregiver takes the baby for regular doctor checkups and makes certain she is given a proper diet, plenty of sleep and regular exercise...take out one of those last two rocks.

Is it so hard to understand why some of our children struggle in school when they arrive wearing backpacks with about 100 pounds of rocks on their backs? While a few of those heavily laden backpacks will be worn by children from wealthy and middle class homes, the majority will be on the backs of children from poverty.

So does this mean there is nothing we can do about the "poverty" problem in schools? No, absolutely not. There are many things schools can do to lighten those backpacks for struggling poverty students and for the smaller percentage of students from middle class and wealthy homes who also struggle in school. However, it turns out, we can't completely fix the problems that poverty causes for our students.[cxvii]

But haven't we all heard stories about magical schools and classrooms where students and teachers overcome poverty's ill effects? Yes, but those stories, as it turns out, are nearly always incomplete and to understand why we first need to understand how poverty impacts student performance on standardized tests.

How students from poverty perform on standardized tests?

Let's first look at how 100 students from your typical wealthy/middle class suburban neighborhood school (fewer than 10 percent free and reduced price lunch eligible) perform on a Common Core level standardized test. Let's assume this group of 100 students performs at an average level when compared to similar wealthy/middle class suburban neighborhood schools. The number and percent of students in the wealthy/middle class school who were "proficient" or "advanced" totaled 50 (50 percent of 100 is 34 + 16 = 50)

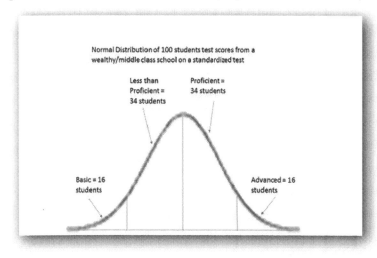

If the same standardized test is given to 100 students from a high poverty school (60 percent or more free and reduced price lunch eligible) that performs at average levels in comparison with schools serving similar populations, the graph and student distribution numbers will change as shown below. The number and percent of students from the poverty school that were proficient or advanced totaled 22 (22 percent of 100 is 20 + 2 = 22).

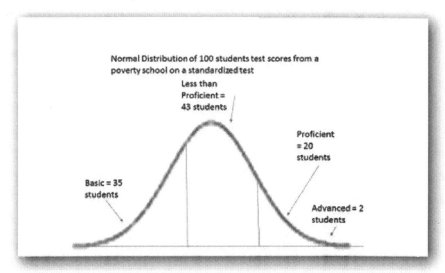

This percent scoring "proficient" and "advanced" is important because in general the new Common Core standards are designed so that the skills required to score at a level of "proficient" or above correlate with expected success in college and the high skill jobs needed for the modern workforce.[cxviii]

The common assumption is that a properly operated high poverty school can overcome all the disadvantages students come in with, but the data tells a different story. Consider the next graph. The dots represent the average test scores for multiple tests for 700 school districts on the older and easier New York State standardized tests. (Those given prior to the 2012-13 school year.)

The vertical axis represents test score passing average. The horizontal axis represents a combination of measures of student poverty and wealth:

free and reduced lunch eligibility percentage, U.S. Census poverty data and student family income, all data readily available through the New York State Education Department, which uses it to determine state aid.

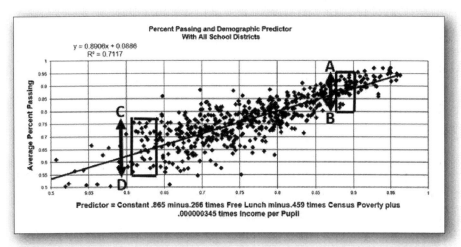

The "predictor line," the diagonal line running across the graph, results from a unique statistical combination of three poverty measures that were the best predictor of student performance: free and reduced lunch eligibility, U.S. Census poverty and household income.

The left hand box (near double arrow CD) illustrates the range in performance between highest performing (C) and lowest performing (D) high poverty schools and the right hand box (near double arrow AB) illustrates the range in performance between highest performing (A) and lowest performing (B) wealthy districts.

What story does the graph tell?

- There's a bigger range of scores among high poverty (CD) school districts than low poverty wealthy (AB) school districts. (See the distance from C to D which is larger compared to the distance from A to B.)
- The highest scoring high poverty schools (C) still score lower than the lowest scoring low poverty wealthy (B) schools.

- If we could get the lowest performing high poverty schools (D) to perform as well as the highest performing high poverty schools (C), the impact on student achievement would be GIGANTIC.

What if an oncologist said s/he could increase her/his patient survival rate from 30 percent to 40 percent? Use the same analogy for financial data. You get the picture.

Can these schools overcome all the ill effects of poverty? No. Can they do a lot to close the gap between the highest performing and lowest performing high poverty school districts? YES!

And the impact would be dramatic.

However, note the range in scores among the low poverty (wealthy) school districts as indicated by the length of the double arrow AB. There is a range. Some wealthy schools perform better than other wealthy schools. We can conclude that better instruction and more effective use of resources could result in significant academic gains for students even in wealthier school districts.

Meanwhile, many of these poorer performing wealthy school districts (B) try to skate by. How? By comparing their performance to high poverty schools (CD) not to their demographically similar peers (A).

The solid slanted "predictor line" on the graph shows the predicted pass rate based on each school's percentage of poverty students. Schools up in the AB region with very few students receiving free or reduced price lunch do quite well on standardized tests, with somewhere between 80 and 95 percent of students passing the older easier tests (this pass rate dropped nearer to 50 percent with the new Common Core tests).

In the CD region, the schools where 60 to 80 percent of the students are eligible for free or reduced price lunch, students generally achieve a lower pass rate (55 to 77 percent on the old, easier tests, 15 to 30 percent on the new harder Common Core tests) that is statistically predictable based on the number of poverty students they're educating.

The passing rate change for high poverty school districts (C to D) from the lowest performers to the highest performers on the older pre-Common

Core tests is 20 percent. For the wealthy/middle class school districts (A to B) the difference is 15 percent.

If all school districts performed at the optimum levels this data indicates is possible, the academic performance gap between our school children who live in wealthy/middle class school districts and those who live in poverty districts would shrink by about 5 percent, our students' total test score performance would rival the best in the world and as many as 20 percent more of our children attending poverty school districts would leave their K-12 education career and college ready.

That's where the real achievement gap exists.

However, consider in the graph below and the meaning of lines GA and FC.

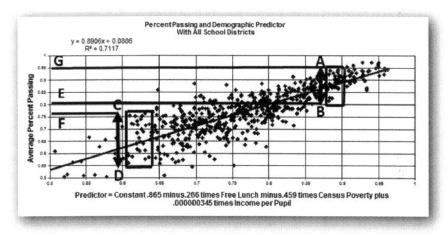

The difference in academic results between the highest performing high poverty schools and the highest performing low poverty schools (the left axis difference between lines FC and GA) is very large. This means even the best run high poverty schools we have right now can't completely overcome the ill effects poverty.

To properly measure the performance of any school district or school you need to compare that school district or school with demographically similar peers. Otherwise you're just blowing smoke. You're either trying to make a school or school district look bad by comparing it with wealthier peers or make a school or school district appear to be better performing than it really is by comparing it to schools or school districts that serve more poverty children.

So the data says three things, all of which are under-reported by the media and misunderstood by parents and many educators:

(1) Schools can make a significant difference in children's lives by increasing the probability for future academic and career success by being more effective.

(2) To accurately evaluate school or school district academic success we need to compare performance to demographically similar peers.

(3) Current school district performance data for 700-plus school districts in New York State indicate that no school districts are overcoming ALL the ill effects of poverty.

A chance meeting that potentially helps the cause

In mid-October, as I strolled through the supermarket Sarandon, I witnessed an encounter between a child about 9 years of age, her mother and a pudgy young man with enormous glasses.

The child ran toward the young man excitedly yelling: "Mr. K, Mr. K." The mother stopped her shopping cart near the young man and started a conversation.

"Mr. Kubiak, Celia obviously misses you. School's not the same without you," the mother said.

"I miss all my students," he said. "They were a great group."

The little girl started pleading with the young man to come back to her school.

"I'm teaching at Tech Charter now and my students are third graders not fifth graders, remember?" he said.

"I wanted to enter Celia in the lottery for Tech Charter for this year, but they're not taking fifth graders yet," the mother said.

Not wanting to be intrusive, I moved on.

When I reached the checkout line 10 minutes later the young man was in front of me in line. I started a conversation while we waited in line.

"You're a teacher at the new Tech Charter School?" I asked.

"Yes, I teach elementary school. I switched over to the charter school last year," he said.

"I heard that mother call you Mr. Kubiak," I said. "I'm Lonnie Palmer. I'm the new interim superintendent for the Sarandon City School District."

"Uh- oh, I better be careful," he said, smiling. "I'm Harry Kubiak."

We shook hands. "I'd like to meet with you for coffee some time to discuss the charter schools and get your take on the school district I'm running now. I'm thinking your perspective might be helpful to me," I said.

"That's a refreshing outlook. I tried to meet with the former super-intendent after I decided to move to the charter school but he said 'no thanks.' I guess he was angry at me for leaving," he said.

We ended our conversation in the parking lot with another hand-shake. I told him I'd be in touch to set up a convenient time for us to meet.

The next morning, I approached my secretary, Betty, who had been an invaluable resource on school district history and people. "What's the deal with Harry Kubiak?" I asked.

Harry was "the" star elementary teacher in the district. He did great stuff with science and technology with his students who loved him, but he had an ongoing feud with the principal at Eastside Elementary so he left for the charter school.

I had met Eastside's principal, Tim O'Grady, and toured his building with him. Tim presented himself as a by-the-book, low-key, don't-upset-the-applecart leader with a very serious demeanor. He ran a tight ship and would be slow to adopt new ideas, creating a difficult environment for Harry's entrepreneurial approach. I could easily see where these two personalities would clash.

I asked Betty to set up a time when I could meet with Harry Kubiak at the charter school in his classroom. Whatever worked best for him, I told her.

A great teacher in action

The following Thursday I arrived at the Sarandon Technical Charter Elementary School. The office secretary buzzed me in after speaking to me on the video screen.

"Well that's a first," she said, as I came through the door. "One of the Sarandon City School District administrators visiting a charter school."

I smiled in return. "Hey, you guys are just the competition. Not the enemy. Besides maybe I can learn a few trade secrets," I said.

She chuckled and escorted me to Harry Kubiak's classroom.

Harry's classroom was a beehive of activity with third graders working in groups on a science activity. Harry stopped the class to introduce me to the students. The students looked at me briefly and then went back to their animated conversations about some science activity.

Harry's challenge for his students was in four parts and showed up on a screen at the front of the room. After Harry pointed it out he suggested I circulate to see what the students were doing.

The challenge was: 1. Find the name and the geologic history of the long skinny hills that line up north to south near Syracuse. 2. Find an example of these hills on a topographical map, draw a scale model side view and provide the coordinates of the northern tip of the hill. 3. Determine what kinds of rocks and dirt should be found in those hills. 4. Design an experimental activity the class can do to test your assumptions.

As Harry circulated in the room, students rushed up to him with questions and he always responded with questions of his own. If the students were unable to answer his questions, he simplified the question and led them to the answer for the original question.

He gave them excellent nonverbal hints: pointing to the map, opening the book and pointing to a page in the book, pointing to a student he thought could answer the question. He looked for every opportunity that would prompt them to answer the question themselves (i.e. think for themselves).

I asked one tall girl in a group of five students what kind of hills they were studying.

"Drumlins," she said.

"How do you know that?" I asked.

"Cary," she said, pointing to a girl sitting at a laptop computer at the desk beside her. "Cary's our computer expert for this project," she said.

As I leaned in to ask Cary a question, Harry clapped his hands twice and the room immediately fell silent.

"Twenty minutes till clean up and submit papers," Harry said. "Is everyone going to be done? Red group leader?"

A student standing at a cluster of desks across the room responded first: "Yes Mr. K.," he said.

"Green group?" Harry asked.

"All set Mr. K.," said a second student to my left.

Groups yellow, purple and my blue group were also ready and within moments all were back working in their groups.

I returned my attention to Cary. "How did you find out about drumlins," I asked.

"A Google search and some articles about drumlins," Cary said. "I took notes on the articles and shared them with everyone in my group. I did my research while they were working on the topographical map. Tim (she pointed to a light-haired boy in her group) showed me what they learned from the map."

Are you always the computer expert?" I asked.

"No, we take turns," she said.

I turned to Tim. "Can you show me how you figured out the coordinates for a drumlin?" I asked.

"Sure, come with me," he said.

Tim took me to the back of the room where several topographical maps of the region were hung in a row on the wall.

"The hills are where the lines run in circles inside of circles and we wanted long skinny circles that pointed up and down. And we found this one," he said, pointing to the map. "The northern point is at the top and the coordinates mean the numbers on the edge of the map that go with this point. That's 43 degrees north and 76 degrees west."

"Who taught you to do that?" I asked.

"We worked on this while Cary was finding out about drumlins on the computer. Mr. K gave all the groups some hints, and we looked it up on the computer. We also figured out that when the circular lines are close the hills are steeper and that helped us draw the side view of the hill."

Tim focused his attention to his group. I moved on to the purple group.

"How did you figure out the geological history and the rocks and dirt you'd expect for these drumlins?" I asked one of the boys in the purple group.

"We did some online research and read some pages in the earth science books over there," he said, pointing to books on a nearby shelf.

"We found out they came from glaciers that melted somewhere between 20,000 and 200,000 years ago. They are mostly sand, clay, gravel and some boulders pushed here by the glaciers," he said.

"What experiment have you devised to test your guess on the hill's composition?" I asked, turning to a girl in the group.

She looked me straight in the eye while she flipped open her notebook to a side view picture of the drumlin. "We'll go to the drumlin and drill some cores of dirt and rocks and the teachers at Syracuse University will tell us what we dug up.

"Sally's father (she pointed across the room to another group) has a coring tool that's like an electric drill with a pipe on the end and

Tim's father (she pointed at the Tim who had helped me with the topographical map) works at Syracuse where we'll have the samples tested."

That's when Harry clapped twice again. "Okay, clean-up time and papers in. One from each group and today student four will be the lucky student," he said.

The students moved their desks back into rows and put the computers back at their charging stations and sat down. On cue Harry clapped twice again and the group went silent.

"Tonight I'll review your papers and select one. We'll use that group's experiment," he said. "Math test tomorrow," he added. "Study your notes and make a 5" X 8" card with notes you can use during the test. If you need a blank card pick one up on the way out. See you tomorrow."

The bell rang and the students disappeared out into the crowded hallway.

Harry smiled with obvious pride in what I had seen. Then he motioned for me to sit down to a chair next to his desk. I sat down and he sat on top of a desk facing me.

I asked Harry why he left the regular public school.

He hesitated before he admitted he and the principal didn't see eye to eye. "He wanted me to run a traditional classroom with lots of lecture and drill and practice to prepare students for the state tests. You saw my class. That's not how I teach. And my students always do well on the state tests.

"Then Kim Neely approached me and suggested I come to the charter school. She offered me more money and a chance to be the head teacher. She said I could hire the teachers and promised me a raise every year if the test scores were good."

"So you're happy here?" I asked already knowing the answer.

"It's like I died and went to heaven. The teachers are great. The students are great. Once in a while I have to deal with some student discipline issues that I don't like but mostly it's been perfect for me."

"In your shoes I probably would have made the same decision. But I'm certain there is also a part of you that feels a bit guilty about bailing on the school district," I said.

"Yeah," he said, "especially when I see my old friends I taught with around town. I know the charter schools have made things even more difficult financially for the district's elementary schools, but I keep coming back to the fact that this was the right decision for me."

We toured the school building and I shook hands and exchanged pleasantries with the three other teachers, the custodian and the woman who buzzed me in. Everyone seemed happy and glad to see me except for the second grade teacher who looked a little frazzled.

"Harry we have to talk about Allan," she whispered. "He disrupted class again; I've told you before I can't teach when he's having one of his tantrums."

Harry sighed. "I'll stop back after I see Mr. Palmer out," he said.

I thanked Harry and asked him to keep an open mind about how we could work together in some ways that might build on the charter schools and help the district schools in the process.

He'd try to keep an open mind, he said.

An idea takes form

By the time my principals arrived the following Tuesday in Tim O'Grady's office for our monthly principal's meeting I had some data in my hand relating to the two charter schools. I set up these meetings on a rotating basis in each of the schools with the host principal assigned with the task of showing off to me and the other principals something new that was happening in the school. Tim had decided to show us the reconditioned furniture in his cafeteria. Not quite what I had in mind.

I handed out enrollment sheets that showed student flow back and forth between the elementary charter schools and the district elementary schools on a monthly basis for the previous school year and so far, for the current year.

The charter school started with grades K-2 and now were serving K-3 and planned to grow to include K-4 and K-5.

The plan for each of the two charters was to remain small, one section of students at each grade level.

I asked the principals to study the enrollment sheet for a few minutes and then asked if anyone saw a pattern.

Cora Jenkins, the Westside Elementary Principal and my best principal, spoke up first.

"I assume you already know the charter schools don't take any special education students," she said. "And they are sending us back about one student per month from each of the two charters and taking one new student off the waiting list every month."

"That's right," I told her. "And what can you tell me about the students they're sending back."

"Well, none of them will be winning Nobel prizes," Tim O'Grady said.

The principals laughed. "That's right, Tim. They're sending back students who have behavioral issues, attendance problems and academic problems," I told them.

"What will be the impact of this over five years?" I asked.

"The test scores in our schools will drop and theirs will go up," Cora said.

"And my job in dealing with student discipline issues will become harder as we have a higher concentration of students with discipline problems in each class," Tim said.

"And our class sizes will move all over the lot," said John Schroeder, an elementary principal from Northside, a third elementary school in the district. "I know Tim already has a big problem at grade two with the students who have come back to him this year.

"The district cut a teaching slot in Tim's building at grade two when the charters opened, but several of the students who came back were from Tim's school, and the ones who took their place were mostly from Cora's school with a few from mine. It's a mess."

The principals asked if there was funding available for a new teacher slot at second grade in Tim's school to address the problem.

I asked about the present second grade class sizes. It depended on the school. One had 29 and 30 students per class. Another had 23 and 24 and the other 21 and 22.

I asked if the district ever considered changing the boundaries for the elementary schools.

"Yes, several years ago when the enrollment was shrinking. We changed the boundaries and it was a disaster," John said. "Parents were at school board meetings for months yelling at the superintendent and the school board. When the smoke settled I had 15 percent more free lunch students in our school and the parents were not happy about that."

I wasn't surprised. That's usually a sensitive issue. I explained that we all knew the district didn't have the money to add a teacher without some major cuts. Plus, adding a teacher in October was a band aid approach to a problem that will be increasing over the next several years. The charters will continue to grow. Even after they reach maximum capacity, they'll continue to sort out the highest performing students and send the rest back to us.

"We need a long-term strategy. I'll work on identifying some potential budget cuts, but I want everyone to come up with some better long-term solutions to solve this class size issue AND provide the district with a proactive strategy to compete effectively with the charter schools.

"If we don't compete in the end they'll take all the students who are easier and cheaper to teach, the ones who will pass the tests, and leave us with the more expensive ones who will struggle on the tests," I told them.

We all knew we couldn't save enough to cover the tuition costs for the students in the charter schools without even more serious and painful cuts on our end. The budget cuts would go beyond what we'd already done and impair our ability to compete even more.

The teaching slot the district had eliminated to help pay for the charter schools was already a problem so that strategy wouldn't work in the long run. I set up a special administrators meeting for the next week that included principals, the transportation supervisor, special education director, school facilities supervisor, food services director, technology director and business official to discuss potential budget cuts and a long-term strategy to compete effectively with charter schools.

"Do you really think Sarandon can be proactive?" Cora asked.

"Yes, and I think that's why they hired me to help us figure out how," I said smiling.

Sarandon's school principals were just figuring out what I had already learned in my time in Albany: New York State's poorly crafted charter school law encouraged charter schools to sort students so the regular public school ended up with the most challenging and expensive students to educate.

HOW DO NEW YORK'S CHARTER SCHOOLS SORT STUDENTS?

Most charter schools select their students by what appears to be an open and fair lottery. However, frequently the lottery is rigged. They turn away special education students and English language learners.

When I worked in Albany, the charter school's answer to questions about special education student enrollment was: "I'm sorry but we don't offer a program appropriate to the needs of special education students."

It was blatant discrimination against students with disabilities and nobody called them on it. It also created unfair test score comparisons and disguised big discrepancies with per-pupil operating expenses.

At that time in Albany, NY, the cost per pupil was about $10,000 and $3,000 of that came from the state. For every special education student, the district received another $2,000 in state aid, but the actual additional cost for a special education student was much higher.

On average, special education students cost a school district $5,000 to $50,000 more per student each school year than general education students. Some are even higher. Some of the individual special education students I have dealt with in my career had expensive program placements that cost the school district more than $200,000 a year for a single student when you figure in special school bus transportation, school nursing services and counseling services and private placement tuition.

While the charter school would have received the additional $2,000 in state aid for each special education student on top of their regular tuition of $8,000 per student, they knew special education was a money losing proposition, so they opted out.

As I write this book in 2016, the Albany charter school tuition per student each year has increased to $14,000 per year from the $8,000 per year we saw in 1999.[cxix] The district's yearly cost per pupil in 2015 is $19,000 per pupil.

On the surface it looks like the charter schools are being shortchanged, receiving only $14,000 of the $19,000. But when you factor in the exclusion of special education students and the fact that the vast majority of charter school students in Albany and across the nation come from elementary schools, which cost 25 percent less per student to operate than middle schools or high schools, $5,000 per student per year is a windfall.

And the inequality doesn't end there.

THE RETURN RATE

In my experience as superintendent of schools in Albany, 10 percent of charter school students returned to our district schools each year. The return rate for regular public schools competing with Success Academies in New York City and the KIPP Academies (one of the largest national charter school chains) is similar.[cxx]

Why do 10 percent of students leave charter schools each year? There are multiple reasons: students misbehave, don't work hard in class, attend irregularly, regularly fail tests or get failing grades on report cards and are all too frequently are treated harshly with repeated school suspensions or other punishments or they receive regular demeaning verbal comments from adults in front of their student peers. Eventually (if they have an option), they'll leave.

Some charter schools also run longer school days and longer school years. Some assign more homework and use a more rigorous curriculum. For many students and some parents these longer school days and years, the extra homework and the rigorous curriculum represent a level of commitment they are not ready to accept.

Furthermore, some charter schools require significant parental participation in school activities and events that are difficult for parents to accommodate.

Charter schools – whether inadvertently or by design – are sorting students. Some charter schools are blatant about removing "troublemakers." Others just let the process play out naturally.

Over time that sorting process gives charter schools the appearance of superiority and leaves an even higher concentration of disadvantaged students in regular public schools.

The end result is the same. Over time the charter schools end up with more of the students who score well on the required tests. And the impact is far reaching.

The deck is stacked

For the benefit of simplicity, let's assume all 900 elementary school students in the fictional Sarandon School District take state tests and 22 percent (198 students) score at proficient and advanced levels on the new Common Core level tests before the arrival of the charter schools.

Of those 900 students, 20 percent (180 students) are labeled special education students, 5 percent of whom score at proficient or advanced levels. Five percent of 180 is nine, which means nine special education students would pass the test.

If 198 students passed the test (22 percent of 900), and nine are special education students, then 189 (198 – 9 = 189) of those who pass are general education students.

Then the charter schools open and show a passing rate of 26.5 percent. It looks like the charter schools are doing a better job, right?

The fact is the charter schools don't offer a special education program thereby excluding the 20 percent of students who are special education students, students whose lower test scores pull down the district schools' passing rate from 26.5 percent to 22 percent.

Meanwhile, the higher concentration of special education students left behind in the district schools (that now have only 700 students remaining) pull down the passing rate for the district's remaining students even more from 22 percent to 21 percent. (180 X .05 plus 520 X .265) / 700 = .21 or 21 percent).

TAKE IT ONE STEP FURTHER

Factor in the annual 10 percent "return rate" (students going back to the district school) for each charter school, and 20 students who don't score at proficient or advanced levels leave the charter schools and return to the district. As part of the sorting process, the two charters schools in the district take in a different 20 students each year, five of whom will score at proficient or advanced levels.

Do that five years in a row and the 10 percent return rate will culminate with the charter schools together taking in 25 additional high performing students, taking the passing rate from 26.5 percent to 39 percent.

Do the math:

- .265 (26.5 percent) X 200 (two charter schools with 100 students each) = 53 charter school students out of 200 passing
- 53 + 25 additional high performing students = 78 high performing students scoring at proficient or advanced levels out of a student enrollment of 200, which equals 39 percent of students scoring at proficient or advanced levels.

Meanwhile, the "return rate" artificially depresses the test scores for Sarandon's regular public schools and at the end of five years only 16.7 percent of the district schools' students score at proficient or advanced levels.

Do the math:

* Before these 25 students who scored at proficient or advanced levels left, 21 percent of the district's 700 non charter elementary students scored at proficient or advanced levels (700 X 0.21 = 142) or 142 students who passed the tests.
* After the charter school return rate shifted 25 high scoring students to the charter schools and replaced them with 25 who were failing the tests, the district had only 117 passing students in its schools (142 − 25 = 117) or 16.7 percent passing (117/700 = 0.167).

Now, let's assume the charter schools are able to attract an excellent, dynamic teaching staff that implements sound instruction (like Mr. K). It's not hard to believe they could increase the number of students scoring at proficient or advanced levels by 10 percent.

Remember the difference from poor performance to good performance in high poverty school districts was 20 percent. From poor to good is 20 percent and from average to good is 10 percent.

It's not hard to imagine a 10 percent improvement in the percentage of passing students in charter schools due to excellent instruction from teachers like Harry Kubiak in the fictitious charter school.

THE OVERALL RESULT

The total net effect of the sorting process (keep out the special education students, eject 20 poor performers a year and take in 20 average students a year), and the 10 percent improvement caused by better instruction, moves the charter school's level of academic performance from the district's original level of performance (22 percent at proficient or advanced) to 49 percent at proficient or advanced levels.

With 49 percent of the students at proficient or advanced levels on the new Common Core tests the charter school is (on paper) performing at nearly the same academic performance level as middle class and wealthy districts as we can see from the bell curve distribution of scores for a middle class/wealthy school district earlier in this chapter. So the charter schools have a nice little business model that serves them very well.

Niche marketing in education

Almost every business has the same kind of business plan. They don't try to sell to every customer, only to the customers where they can hit their "sweet spot" so they can make the best kind of profits. They go after the clients where they can make the most money. In fact, businesses that don't clearly identify their niche and make products that best fit the needs of their niche clientele or don't market effectively to their niche clientele are the businesses that fail.

We shouldn't be surprised that charter schools have become a niche market business. They're selling their services to the students who cost the least amount to educate and the students who are most likely to succeed on the required state tests. They pick their clients by excluding special education and English language learners and by returning students who do not thrive in their schools. They were designed to operate this way.

Before the Affordable Care Act, who did health insurance companies exclude? People with preexisting conditions who would surely have a negative impact on the bottom line.

The New York State model for charter schools sets these schools up to be a rogue, invasive species implanted in a host school district that is most likely already struggling to keep its head above water. And, as it turns out, the invasive species does real harm to the host.

How do charter schools harm school districts and in the end students who attend public schools?

Charter schools place a financial burden on local public schools that can't be overcome by simply closing a school. Teacher layoffs come in a pattern prescribed by seniority laws (laws the same legislators who voted for charter schools are very reluctant to change because they are strongly supported by the teacher unions that contribute to their campaigns).[cxxi]

The more senior and more expensive teachers' jobs are protected and the least senior and less expensive teachers are the ones who lose their jobs. And finding teacher reduction opportunities is difficult for the school district because the enrollments for the charter schools don't come from any single school in the district schools. The charter enrollments come from all the district schools.

More frequently than not (as we can see in the fictitious Sarandon's enrollment numbers) the numbers don't line up and in the end public schools cannot make up for every dollar lost to charter schools the way a business can make up for money lost to a competitor.

The charter school financial burden results in significant local property tax increases or larger class sizes and a reduction of supports for students remaining in the local public school district. In the end the district is faced with larger classes, fewer supports and an older and generally, but not always, less dynamic teaching staff.

This downward trend in test scores for the students remaining in the district schools is exacerbated by the fact that the teachers in the district elementary schools are facing a significantly more difficult and needy student population due to the concentration of special education, behavioral problem and academically underperforming students.

A 3.5 percent decline in the percentage of district elementary school students achieving at "proficient" or "advanced" levels on the state test (moving along the arrow from C toward D in the aforementioned graph) is a reasonable assumption given the 20 percent range in scores seen in figure (CD). This means the percentage of students in the district's schools scoring at "proficient" or "advanced" levels has slipped from 22 percent to 13 percent as a result of the special education student exclusion, the "return rate" issue and the extra financial and academic burden placed on the district by the charter schools' implementation.

So after five years of operation the charter school is boasting about the 49 percent of its students who are scoring at "proficient" or "advanced" levels on the new state tests, comparable to the scores of nearby high rent suburban districts. And the school district is licking its wounds with now only 13 percent of its students scoring at proficient or advanced levels.

If things run true to form the reporter from the local newspaper who covers the school district won't understand any of the complicated issues behind these two simple numbers and neither will the paper's readers. This newspaper problem is almost always caused by the fact that no one from the school district took the time to build a good working relationship with that reporter to provide accurate information in a timely manner and to explain these issues clearly.

Educators have been trained by misguided PR professionals not to answer the question asked but rather tell them what you want them to hear. That's not a workable plan.

The truth is: Before the charter schools came into existence in the fictitious Sarandon City School District, 22 percent of the 900 students in the district's elementary schools or 198 students were scoring at "proficient" or "advanced levels." After five years, the charter school has 49 percent of its 200 students (98 students) scoring at "proficient" or "advanced" levels, and the school district's elementary schools have 13 percent of their total of 700 elementary students (91 students) scoring at "proficient" or "advanced" levels.

So after all this disruption the total number of students scoring at proficient and advanced levels in the combined charter/district pool of 900 students is nine students lower (91 + 98 = 189) than it was when the charter school started.

And we're full circle back to Scott Steffey, the SUNY Charter School Institute Director who told me in 1999 when the New Covenant Charter School was approved in Albany, "If it hurts you that's even better."

Yes, the charter schools can claim academic success. But at what cost when their success causes the district's scores to drop. It's true that most of the drop in district test scores (and most of the increase in charter school test scores) is artificial and the result of sorting students. But some of this drop in district test scores is real (and largely due to teachers now dealing with even higher concentrations of disadvantaged students). It's a bit like casino gambling where there are few highly publicized big winners, but most people walk away with less than they started with.

The public's lack of understanding of these issues means less and less respect for the public school district that has been forced to host this rogue, invasive species.

It turns out Mr. Steffey is wrong. If the charter school's implementation hurts the local public schools, it's not better, especially not for the students who remain in the public schools.

A QUESTION OF ETHICS

Three times in the last ten years of my career I was approached by charter school management companies interested in my considering an opportunity to work for them. In each conversation I asked about their exclusions of special education students and student return rate. They were blunt: Educating special education students and students with academic, discipline or attendance problems is expensive and would pull down test scores. Their programs weren't for every student. If I couldn't accept that I shouldn't consider working for them.

I said "no" three times. Each time it was for more money than I was earning at the time. One of those times was when I was unemployed and really needed a paycheck. I know many of my public school colleagues faced this same decision.

I have never regretted my decision. The way charter schools are set up in New York State and many other states hurts more students than they help. For me it was an ethical question. Is a bigger paycheck (or even any paycheck) worth more than something that in the end produces more low achievement?

How does this all play out in the fictitious Sarandon School District?

Kim Neely and Art Cameron

Before the next meeting of the Sarandon administrative team I wanted to meet with two key people. One was Kim Neely, the Sarandon Bank and Trust Vice President who started the two charter schools. I was told she was ambitious, smart and hoping to use her charter school success in Sarandon as a springboard for a run for the U.S. Congress.

I wanted to meet her to see if we could work collaboratively to help her achieve her goals, while I implemented some strategies designed to help the Sarandon City School District work its way out of its present mess.

Given the acrimonious history between the school district and Ms. Neely visible in the online archives for the local newspaper, I knew this would be an uphill battle.

I hoped that by meeting on her turf we would have a better chance at building a positive relationship.

Kim Neely did her best within a few short minutes of our meeting to make sure I understood she saw her mission as one of destruction. She wanted to destroy the local public schools.

When I tried to explain to her that the present New York State funding formula for charter schools created a huge financial issue for the school district that we could not readily resolve, she laughed.

"That same tired argument? In business when we are faced with cost issues we cut costs. You need to do the same," she said.

"The decline in enrollment caused by the two charter schools came from all the district elementary schools," I told her, "making teacher reductions nearly impossible. Teacher tenure and seniority laws mean we are forced to keep the most expensive teachers."

Her response: "That's not my problem."

I pointed out that her 10 percent student return rate made it impossible to stabilize class size and enrollment in the district's elementary schools.

She smiled. "Their parents have decided to withdraw them and re-enroll them in the district schools," she said. "We never said our program was right for every child."

I told her that the charter student return rate would result in arti-ficially inflated test scores for the charter schools and depressed scores for the district schools.

Again, she smiled.

"Do you have any proof of that?" she asked.

"Your program is not accepting any special education students. Has the state education department reviewed that aspect of your operation?" I asked.

"Unfortunately, our charter schools don't offer any of the programs the special education students need," she said.

I replied, smiling myself now at her brazen approach.

"So you understand the impact of not offering special education programs has a negative impact on the school district's finances and academic performance," I said.

She smiled again: "Looks like you have a lot of work to do and I'm afraid I have another appointment."

"Before I go," I said, "I'd like to suggest that we both look for ways to work collaboratively to help out the district schools and the charter schools. Would you be interested in that?"

"At present I can't see any way that could happen. Now, I really have to go," she said, standing up from her chair.

And with that she strode purposefully out of her office leaving me by myself.

As usual at 2:30 p.m. on a Friday afternoon I was ready for a cup of coffee, especially after my encounter with Ms. Neely at the bank. Sarandon was a bit too downtrodden to support my favorite Starbucks but the local diner served a decent cup of coffee and I'd already been there enough that the wait staff welcomed me by name.

Before I had my first sip of coffee a tall man in a business suit about my age pushed through the front door, leaned on the coun-ter next to me and said in a booming voice, "Coffee and a jelly doughnut."

The waitress smiled at him. "Hey Art, how's the newspaper business?"

He groaned. "You don't want to know," he said.

I immediately recognized his name and the newspaper connection. He was Art Cameron the newspaper editor. I introduced myself.

He shook his head. "I'm having a tough week, but you're having a tough year," he said.

"They didn't tell me about all these problems when they recruited me for this job," I told him smiling.

I told him I'd just left a meeting with Kim Neely and she was curt to say the least.

"She hates the school district and she's using her charter schools to get even and for good reason."

"What reason?" I asked.

"Well, after she graduated from Cornell and came back to Sarandon she wasn't sure what she wanted to do with herself. She applied for a maternity leave teaching vacancy at the high school in the English department. She thought her Cum Laude grades from an Ivy League college and her father being president of the bank made her a shoo-in for the job. But she wasn't certified to teach so they hired Amy Schroeder, daughter of John Schroeder, one of your principals. Kim has never forgiven them for that."

"But if she wasn't certified and Amy was certified how could she be upset?" I asked.

Art chuckled. "You're new here aren't you? Amy wasn't certified either. She got the job because her Dad was a principal who had more pull with the school board than the bank president."

I put two and two together. "Is that what happened with your daughter?" I asked.

Art's jovial demeanor disappeared instantly. "My daughter was a tenured and very effective elementary school teacher in this district. When the enrollment dropped and the job cuts came she lost her position. But that year the district had a temporary vacancy because one of the senior elementary teachers had cancer and had to take a leave.

"Rather than hire my daughter they hired another less senior teacher from the recall list whose uncle was on the school board. With that temporary year of teaching that woman moved past my daughter on the seniority list and was ultimately hired permanently when the teacher with cancer had to retire due to her illness. My daughter was unemployed for three years."

I had seen this mix before with layoffs, re-call lists, temporary jobs and local school board politics; invariably, it's always a disaster.

"I'm sorry it worked out the way it did. How is your daughter doing now?" I asked.

"She had a tough time." he said, "But she found a job at an elementary school in a wealthy suburb in the Rochester area and she loves it."

I told him I now understood why there had been bad blood between his family and the school district. I also explained that I had discovered that the district had not done anything to develop a decent working relationship with the newspaper.

"I'm certain you've been fed misinformation in the past, but I could use your help to develop a respectful and honest working relationship now between the newspaper and the school district."

I asked if he would meet me for an hour the following week to talk about the direction of the school district.

"I won't be a public relations piece for the school district. I'll be more than a little suspicious of what you tell me," he warned.

Guaranteed bad press

Most of the school administrators I've come in contact with during my career hate the press. School employees whine endlessly about bad press, unfair reporters who misquote them and the failure of the local press to report on "all the good things our students and teachers do."

Reporters (especially today when the media's business model is crumbling) can't waste their time on items that just aren't news stories. Lining up a bunch of students (or more frequently adults who want their pictures in the paper) for an inane photo of the same canned food drive the same teachers have organized for the past 14 years is not a news story.

Real local news stories from schools are linked to regional, state level or national level issues that are being reported on in big time newspapers or on national television news programs. Once in a great while something newsworthy happens in a local school district, but usually it's bad news. Then the reporters call the school district, not the other way around.

And when reporters do call most of my superintendent colleagues run for cover. The reporters call most frequently when bad things happen (a student brings a gun to school, a parent says bad things about his son's principal at a school board meeting, there's a bomb scare at the high school that empties the building and brings in the police, etc.).

In actuality, this is a chance for the superintendent to look "presidential" with a professional, courteous and prompt response that shows s/he is being honest, is not hiding anything and has a plan to fix things if the school district has made mistakes.

But my superintendent colleagues know that if they blow the television or newspaper interview they and possibly their school board members will look like turkeys and in the end it could cost them their jobs.

So what do they do? They duck, issue a vaguely worded press release, ignore the call or do the interview but limit comments to banalities like, "The issue is under investigation and our policy is to not comment until the investigation is completed."

If the superintendent calls the school district's attorney for advice on what to say to the press in these difficult situations they're always told: "Say nothing, issue a press release that is legal mumbo jumbo or stick to our previously approved interview banalities."

Then when the bad press is printed in the newspaper or broadcast on the TV news it's worse than anyone could have imagined (primarily because the reporter has no other side of the story to report) and everyone who works for the school district whines (again!) about the press being unfair to the school district.

In the absence of real information misinformation, by necessity, becomes the news. The newspaper will come out on the same days every week. The 5 o'clock newscast will air at 5 o'clock.

If schools want their good news to be aired and an honest view of their bad news to be part of these communications, they need to do four things all the time. They are:

(1) When bad news events happen in the school district that will become news stories immediately (same day before the evening press deadlines) set up a press conference and invite all the news reporters (newspaper, TV, radio) who regularly cover the district.

When they enter the press conference hand each reporter a press release that clearly explains the district's position on the issues at hand, admits any district errors and outlines the plans in place to fix those errors. No subterfuge, no obfuscation, no weasel words. Just the truth. The superintendent stands in front of the reporters, makes a brief statement summarizing the press release (Don't read the press release out loud. These folks can read.), and answers every single question on the record.

"It's under investigation and I can't comment" is unacceptable. Directness and honesty is required regardless of what the school district's attorneys advise. If the attorneys won't help you figure out what to say, hire new attorneys.

(2) Learn what is meant by news. If charter school "return rates" are a national news issue (which they are) and you can find examples of this issue being discussed in national newspapers and TV spots, you can tie what you want to say about this issue to the national news story and you have a legitimate local news story. This approach should work with most issues that are important issues.

(3) Develop a working relationship with local reporters who cover the school district so that if they had a question related to education they'll think: "I'll call Ms. X over at the school district. She's

honest, knowledgeable and willing to level with me. She'll give me what I need quickly and professionally." If you are a superintendent and you don't have that kind of relationship with the reporters who cover your school district, you have work to do.

(4) Once you've done this for several years in a row you are then in a position to bring unique ideas from your district to the newspaper and expect them to consider writing stories about these ideas. Just don't bring them the 14th year of the same canned food drive with a picture of adults in a row with their names underneath and expect to get anywhere. Make sure what you bring to them is real news.

The cost of doing business

On Monday, I met with the school district's transportation supervisor to discuss ways to save money by reducing bus runs. I also stopped by to see the district's special education director to discuss options for high school junior and senior special education students who were placed in expensive out-of-district placements that could save the district some money and benefit students with some valuable hands-on job experience before they walked across the stage at graduation.

That night at home I finished my academic performance data analysis for the district that compared Sarandon's performance with 25 similar school districts in the state. These districts had the same levels of student poverty and they were spending the same regionally adjusted amount per student.

This regional cost adjustment properly leveled the financial playing field when comparing costs and academic performance for high operating cost Long Island school districts with the same percentage of poverty students with lower operating cost Sarandon in the upstate region.

On Tuesday I met with the school board president. She agreed we should arrange for two Saturday full-day planning workshops on the

first and third Saturdays in November with me and the board mem-
bers at both sessions and the district administrators joining us on the
second Saturday.

It wasn't that hard for me to convince school board president
Mitzy Holland, whose children attended Northside Elementary
School where she had been the PTA President before joining the
school board, that the district needed major restructuring if we were
to improve academic performance as the school board wanted and
survive the changes we'd have to make to deal effectively with the
charter school challenge.

On Wednesday, I met with Cora Jenkins, my best elementary
principal and the one I'd need on my side. My experience had taught
me that support from solid principal performers like Cora is the best
antidote to resistance from less capable peer principals. The less effec-
tive principals would listen to her and I would need her help if we
were going to make any real change. We met in her office at Westside
Elementary and I showed her the comparison of Sarandon's academic
performance with the 25 similar school districts.

"What do you think?" I asked.

"We look awful," she said. "I know we can do better but we've just
been trying to keep our head above water for so many years. Every time
we start to move forward something like these charter schools knocks us
down again."

"I understand and that's why I'm here. I have a somewhat radi-
cal idea that, if implemented properly, could really turn this district
around. But I need your advice as someone who knows the political
situation better than me on how best to proceed to get buy-in from
everyone before we move ahead."

"Well I'm not much of a radical but if there was ever a time to be
radical, it's now," she said.

I laid out my rough "plan." There were too many holes and ques-
tions for it to be a real plan yet but the essence was:

1. *Convert the three existing district elementary schools to parental choice magnet schools giving first priority to students who live in the existing attendance zone for that elementary school.*
2. *Use the magnet school parent choices to balance enrollments so that the class size bulges we were seeing at Eastside didn't continue and grow as the charter schools grew.*
3. *Select a theme and instructional approach that emphasized special characteristics for each of the schools, like Social Justice; Math, Science and Technology; Character Education or Arts and Humanities.*
4. *Give each school a pot of money to help them find creative ways to implement their chosen theme including additional funding for technology, teacher training and curriculum development time, student field trips and books and materials for classrooms.*
5. *Give each elementary principal the help of a paid lead teacher to organize all the essential curriculum restructuring. This teacher would teach a regular class and be paid extra for taking on the extra duties associated with a leadership role.*
6. *Allow teachers to request transfers to different elementary magnet schools in the district and make these changes by lottery.*

"Who will the lead teachers be?" Cora asked.

"Who would be good in your school?" I asked.

"Karen Allington will be an excellent principal someday. She really understands curriculum and instruction. She's a great teacher and she's really respected by the other teachers. They'd listen to her."

"Where will you find the money to pay for this?" she asked.

"I'm working on that right now and hope to have some firm ideas in place when we meet with administrators tomorrow," I said.

"You know the real problem with this plan will be buy-in from the school board, from John Schroeder and from the parents and teachers at Northside," she said.

I asked why she thought that was.

"Well you know the district percentage for free and reduced price lunch is 66 percent. But it's not spread equally between the schools. Tim at Eastside is at 82 percent and I'm at 79 percent here at Westside. John at Northside is at 30 percent.

"When they had to close the last elementary school they had a plan that would have evened out the poverty percentages, but the Northside parents made the superintendent and school board back off their plan to our present numbers. Before they closed that elementary school, Northside had fewer than 15 percent free and reduced price lunch students.

"Four of the five school board members come from the Northside area of town, and they won't like this plan because it means more poverty and minority students attending Northside."

When the district tried to re-draw elementary school attendance boundary lines three years ago to balance enrollments, the Northside parents became very angry because the proposed change meant their school's attendance zone would have gained two large parts of town with many poor and minority students, Cora told me. They didn't want that despite the fact that they have plenty of room in that school building.

"And that's why we now have four Northside attendance zone parents on the school board — to make sure that question doesn't come up again," she said.

Racism rears its ugly head

"You may or may not know it but Northside has smaller class sizes and more teaching help in art, music, physical education, library and computers than they should have given their enrollment in comparison to Eastside and Westside," according to Cora.

"They also have after school clubs, sports and busses that Tim and I don't have," she said. "That is not an accident. It's the way the district politics play."

This was typical.

"What was John Schroeder's role in that school attendance boundary conversation?" I asked her.

Cora hesitated. *"Well, don't throw me under the bus with John,"* she said. *"He and I will be here long after you are gone. Publicly John was very professional and supportive of the plan to change attendance boundaries,"* she said, *"but behind the scenes he was fanning the flames. He told me he didn't want his school to become as bad as Eastside and Westside, and he was sure the proposed change would have resulted in Northside's demise.*

"That elementary school attendance boundary change idea was doomed before it was ever brought to the public," Cora said.

"Okay, so if you were in my shoes," I said, *"what would you do to make sure my magnet school idea gets a fair hearing and doesn't suffer the same fate?"*

Cora shook her head. *"I'm not really sure. It's great you're talking to me, but you'll need to talk to parents, teachers, the unions, and especially the school board, as well. Believe me they will all have questions and suggestions. And even then I'm not certain this school board will let you do what you've suggested.*

"But it's a great idea and it would be a real shot in the arm for our school district. You've got me thinking in a way I haven't thought for several years. Creative ideas are swirling around in my head already."

I ended our meeting with a request: *"Please keep this confidential until we all discuss it in the administrators meeting tomorrow."*

Cora nodded and our meeting ended.

Administrators meet

At the administrators meeting I outlined the rough plan to convert the district's three elementary schools to lottery-based magnet schools with a preference for students from each school's attendance zone.

I sent an email to the school board members in advance of this administrative meeting explaining that I was *"investigating the feasibility and funding possibilities for a magnet school option for the school district."*

I also told the school board we would all be discussing this option in depth at the two upcoming November Saturday sessions and I asked them to *"keep this issue confidential until we know for sure what option if any we might pursue."*

True to form, the school board members were immediately on their phones and computers emailing, texting and talking to anyone who would listen about this crazy superintendent's ideas.

After I presented the magnet school concept at the administrators meeting the room was eerily quiet

"Okay, time for questions, comments and suggestions. Ask me anything you want," I said.

After some initial hesitation Tim O'Grady spoke up. *"Does the school board know about this idea?"*

"Yes," I said. *"I emailed them and I plan to have two full-day executive sessions in November for them to discuss the concept in detail."*

"How would you pay for this plan and how much do you anticipate it will cost?" Cora asked.

"I'm anticipating each lead teacher will require an additional stipend of between $15,000 and $20,000 a year. Each of the three schools would need $30,000-$40,000 of extra curriculum development and staff training funds every year. And the extra computers, books, field trips and learning materials would cost another $20,000-$25,000 per year per school. So altogether roughly $80,000 per elementary school per year or $240,000 per year for the district."

"Where are you going to get that kind of money? This district is strapped in case you hadn't noticed," Tim barked back.

"We have some tricks up our sleeve to help with cost," I said. I motioned to the transportation director. *"Tammy,"* I said, *"what can you tell us about busing costs where we might save?"*

Tammy Collins, the district's young transportation supervisor who only three years earlier had been hired as a part-time school bus driver, was promoted by my predecessor. While he'd made his share of mistakes Tammy was clearly one of his successes.

Tammy handed out a one-page document that she and I had reviewed at our meeting on Monday of that week. Tammy had *contacted all of the nearby school districts who were busing special education students to the 14 sites outside the school district where we had placed our district's most severely disabled special education students. She found four school sites where we could team with one other district and share the cost of busing these students to their school without making the ride any longer than our longest in-district ride for students, which was 55 minutes.*

This allowed her to eliminate two bus runs and reduce the cost on two other's where we would be receiving payments from a partner school district to cut our costs and theirs. All told Tammy's efforts would save the district $180,000 per year if we made these changes. If we implemented Tammy's proposed changes during the present school year we could put aside some initial funding to help us launch the magnet school concept with some summer training and curriculum work with our teachers the following summer.

I then turned to Gail Robinson, the district's special education director, who, like Tammy had a one-page hand out she and I had discussed earlier in the week that she sent around the table to all of her administrator peers.

Gail was another success story from my predecessor. She taught special education full time at the district's high school and for an additional stipend of $15,000 she ran the district's Committee on Special Education with help from an excellent secretary.

She and I had discussed the placements of four of the district's more severely disabled students who were 19 and 20 years old. The state had new requirements for all special education students that they gain a real vocational skill before they graduate.

While these students' severe disabilities meant they couldn't pass the state required academic tests and they would not be achieving a regular high school diploma, they could get an appropriate special certificate in lieu of a diploma if they completed the vocational experience expected of them.

Tammy had some ideas for this vocational experience that would save the district money and give these students a great learning experience. I had teamed up with Tammy before the meeting about four vacant non-instructional jobs the district was in the process of recruiting for at that time that might work as vocational experiences.

When Gail mentioned the students' names all of the administrators smiled because they've known these students since pre-kindergarten.

"I've found an internship here on the high school custodial team for Tom Jackson," Gail said. He'll be working the 4 to 11:30 shift and cleaning the B wing every night. Thanks to Roger for agreeing to take Tom on as an intern."

Roger Hornung was our custodial and maintenance services supervisor. Gail and I had met with him two weeks earlier. Roger was a reluctant convert, but I was sure he would do his best to help Tom Jackson succeed.

"Judy Applegate will be interning in the food services department. Thanks to Georgia for taking on Judy."

Georgia Thomas, our food services director smiled at this comment. Georgia had been a more enthusiastic participant in this process when Judy and I approached her.

"Alex has agreed to take on Samantha Orzo, who will be interning as a clerical assistant at the high school," Gail said.

Alex Casale, our high school principal nodded. "Gail can be very convincing when she puts her mind to it," he said. "Besides we have copy room and telephone answering tasks that would be good for Samantha's skill level."

Gail finished with Cory Salisman. "Cory Salisman will be interning as a mechanic's helper in the bus garage. Thanks to Tammy for finding us this opportunity and agreeing to take on Cory."

Tammy's mechanics were a little reluctant to go along with this until they met Cory, she said. The changes in these special education students' placements to sites here in the school district allowed her to reduce one more bus run and save another $75,000 per year. In addition, the district would save in special education tuitions even after accounting for a new employee who would be hired to monitor these work-study intern placements.

"Mr. Palmer and I met with the civil service union president last week and he agreed we could employ these students in these intern jobs at $10 per hour with no benefits until the end of the next school year, as long as these jobs reverted to their former permanent position status with union wages and benefits at that time," Gail told the group.

"When we figure in the additional new cost of hiring a full-time work-study coordinator for the district, the cost of these students $10 per hour salaries in place of the more expensive salaries and benefits we previously paid for these vacant positions, and the tuition savings from not sending these four students out to private vocational placements, we will be saving more than $200,000 next year.

"And because we can go ahead with these changes right now we can save more than $100,000 in this year's budget. On top of that the students and their parents are thrilled that they will finally be able to stay in the district schools for their education after years of school placements outside the school district," Gail said.

"Will these interns move into regular union wage jobs at the end of next school year?" Alex asked.

"Yes, if they are successful," I said. "It wouldn't be fair to ask them to do these jobs and not pay them the regular rate once they've had a chance to learn the ropes and prove they can do the job. That means we need to stay on top of their performance with their supervisors and the work-study coordinator. We'll also have to be sure the jobs don't require them to pass civil service exams they would struggle to pass."

The total savings from these changes would be somewhere between $150,000 and $300,000 in this year's budget depending on how soon we can get everything started and $455,000 in next year's budget. So money would not be the reason that this magnet school plan does not fly.

Then Cora Jenkins asked a question we had discussed the previous day when we met.

"Mr. Palmer, I'm really glad these special education students will be coming back to the district and this money for school improvements in the magnet plan is great. But I'm afraid John's Northside parents, the Northside teachers and the four school board members from the Northside area will not let your magnet school plan get off the ground.

"Unless I'm not reading them right, I think they will resist anything that puts more poor and minority students at Northside Elementary School and a lottery-based magnet school plan for the district would mean more poor students at Northside. Isn't that correct?"

"That's correct," I said. "Over time all three elementary schools will move toward the district average on free lunch and minority student enrollment percentages. I anticipate the change will be gradual and we can control the rate at which the numbers change. In addition, if we can coordinate our lottery with the charter school lottery, we can deal more effectively with the class size imbalance question the elementary principals brought up last week."

Then I turned to John Schroeder. "John," I said, "I am the rookie in this district and you lived through the elementary boundary discussion here a few years ago. Do you think Cora is correct in her assessment of your parents, your teachers and the school board?"

John cleared his throat. "I will support whatever plan for improvement you decide is best for the district. I also know my parents won't be happy with this plan. Cora is right. Unfortunately, they see adding any poor or minority kids to our school as a loss for them and their kids and they will fight it."

Those parents were successful in their previous fight about the elementary school attendance boundary lines and forced the school board to back off significantly from their proposed lines.

"Remember: Four school board members are parents from Northside who ran for office promising they would not allow the district to place more poor and minority students at Northside. It will be a very difficult

fight to win. And even if you win it will be very divisive for the school district," John said.

"Well, there we have it," I said. "But we also have to consider what will happen if we don't move forward with the magnet school plan. A third charter school is in the works, and they're doing their best to take our strongest students and make the district look bad in the process.

"Pretty soon we'll be forced to close one of our elementary schools, and when that happens the percentages of poor and minority students will shift anyway," I said, perhaps naively. "Northside won't be able to survive as a protected island. Besides all three elementary schools have significant numbers of poverty and minority students already."

The silence in the room told me I'd pushed too hard. Tim O'Grady, who had been quiet for the entire meeting, broke the silence.

"We're just trying to hold on to the little bit of dignity and tradition we have left," Tim said. "What you are proposing makes logical sense but I'm afraid we'll do a lot of work to get it going and then after you are gone it will all go back to where we are right now."

The meeting ended but not before I asked John Schroeder to stay after for a chat.

"John you are a key to whether this magnet school idea has an opportunity to work or whether it's shelved before the conversation starts," I said. "How can I help move your teachers, your parents and with them my board members to our side?"

"I don't know if what you are proposing is possible," John said. "The Northside parents are just trying to hold on to what they see as their final little bit of advantage in this school system. They won't give up what they have without a fight. They're the ones who show up to vote for the school budget and school board."

"I understand what you're saying," I told him, "but let's think ahead a bit. If we can't improve our performance, slow down the charter schools and do something to balance our classes better we'll be forced

to close a school. The logical candidate for that closure is Northside. It has the fewest students and it needs the most facility work."

"That won't ever happen with this school board," he said.

He was probably right but, as the least senior principal, he would be out of a job and that four member Northside majority on the school board could evaporate in the election next May if the other parts of the city finally showed up to vote.

"John, you need to think ahead a couple of moves here. Please consider what I am saying carefully. The only way to preserve three elementary schools in this district is with an aggressive magnet school plan or some similar type of change. Please think this over carefully before you talk to anyone about this plan?"

John said he understood and would think it over.

"John if you have any options I should consider I'm more than willing to listen to them," I said.

John managed a slightly rueful smile as he exited. But I still knew I had a lot of work to do with him if this plan was ever going to have a chance for success.

THE DANCE OF THE LEMONS

Frequently, superintendents are under pressure to ensure that schools serving the wealthiest families – even in high poverty school districts – benefit from resource distribution, which includes the distribution of teachers.

In Albany, NY, where I was the superintendent, the teachers perceived to be weakest were pushed from school to school somehow always ending up in the schools with the greatest numbers of poverty and minority students. The administrators even had a name for it – the "dance of the lemons." It's not unique to Albany.[cxxii]

When I arrived in Albany and witnessed this shameful display of brazen discriminatory behavior, I reversed course and immediately transferred several teachers one of my principals identified as her weakest performers out of the school serving the poorest and highest minority student population to schools with a higher percentage of middle class white students.

Reaction was swift. Everyone from the city mayor to the receiving principals to the teacher union president argued against my decision despite the fact that I did this in an effort to give our most needy elementary school a chance to reboot its program with new young teachers.

After being criticized privately and publicly in the newspaper the teacher union president criticized me for these teacher transfers during the school year-opening welcome-back-to-school event in the high school gym, with more than 1,000 teachers, administrators and support staff in attendance.

I understand why many of my superintendent colleagues chose a less controversial route and continued their district's "dance of the lemons." But that less controversial route is guaranteed to leave the students who most need the best educational opportunity with the least educational opportunity.

In every school district the powers that run the school district and control the purse strings are almost always tied closely to the wealthiest parents and include their chosen representatives who more frequently than not sit on the town or city councils and on the school boards that hire and fire the superintendents. Many parents, teachers, school board members and superintendents think this is just "how things work" and it should be accepted as a given. The best teachers and the best resources go to the "best schools" period.

Btw, most of those teachers I transferred into the less needy schools did very well and later more than one of them thanked me for shifting her teaching assignment to a new school.

"I was stuck in the mud and hating my job and now I love it," one teacher told me.

I've also seen a backlash against the wealthy white parents who frequently "run the urban school districts" by poor minority parents who get themselves elected to the school board and try to steer advantages to schools attended by their children, creating a similar mess but just with different children as victims.

So in Sarandon, the Northside parents were trying to hang on their advantages, if you can call them that. Fewer poverty and minority students in their school, more resources for their children and their school's teachers and more extra supports and programs. They saw Northside as the only "good" school in the district and they wanted to keep that advantage.

Charter Schools, School Choice and Poverty

● ● ●

PART II - THE DEFINITION OF A "GOOD SCHOOL"

REAL ESTATE AGENTS – AND anyone in the Albany, NY, area -- will tell you Lawrence Elementary School is one of the best schools in the Capital Region, superior to the rest.

But the data tells a different story. It shows how the mostly white affluent suburban K-5 Lawrence Elementary School is no more effective than the nearby mostly black K-5 inner city Cameron Park Elementary School. (Not the schools' real names.)

Lawrence's state test scores are higher than Cameron Park's but both are within close range of their predicted scores based on their levels of student poverty. (See graph.) Both schools are performing very close to their predicted line performance and at about an average level in comparison to comparable peer schools.

It's an important distinction to make: Test scores that don't take into account poverty can't accurately gauge the success of a school. I suspected as much while I was superintendent of the Albany City School District. I found that by factoring in the percentage of free and reduced lunch eligible students we could more accurately measure just how well our elementary schools were doing.

Later on, I discovered another school administrator had developed a more sophisticated and accurate version of the same thing. As the Business Official for the Newburgh Enlarged City School District and consultant for the New York State Association of Small City School Districts, Charles Winters compiled extensive data sets on student outcomes, demographics, local costs and state support. He developed a system of measurement based on three criteria: school lunch eligibility, U.S. Census data on poverty and income data based on state income tax filings.

He found the combination of all three that identified the best predictor of student performance on state tests and used the "scatterplot" graph, an effective visual for displaying multivariable data, to illustrate his findings.

Mr. Winters's school district comparison data became a key element in the Campaign for Fiscal Equity lawsuit and a companion lawsuit filed by several small cities in New York State that ended with a plan to redistribute $5.5 billion in new aid to school districts in the state with the primary focus on those serving the largest poverty populations. (The plan was never carried out.)

Mr. Winters's data appears in other sections of this book, but it bears repeating because the commonly accepted definition of a "good" school is flawed. Despite what we read in the newspaper: Test performance alone is not sophisticated enough to evaluate a school's performance.

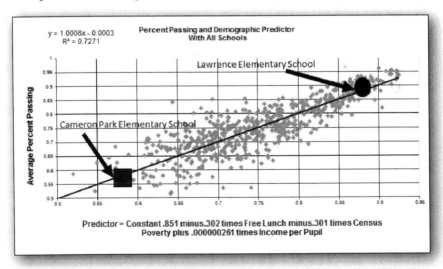

Education entrepreneurs

When I arrived in my Sarandon School District office Monday morning I wasn't thrilled to see three unfamiliar women in the waiting area next to Betty's desk. I hate to start the day with an unplanned meeting, especially a Monday. I'm a creature of habit (like all of us) and I like to lay out a plan for my day and week before I start.

Apparently, that would not be happening this particular Monday morning as Betty ushered me into my office and closed the door after.

Betty, by now, well knew my habits.

"Look, I know it is not what you wanted but these three showed up and said Tonya Harris told them they should talk to you," Betty said. "Given the rapport you have with Tonya I told them to wait. Get your coffee and I'll bring them in here. I gave them 15 minutes."

I sighed and, as always, did as I was told.

When I returned with my coffee the three women introduced themselves. Sandra Talent was short, had reddish hair and a broad smile. Delia Hammond was tall with dark hair pulled back in a ponytail, slender and more reserved. Alice Cummings was a medium height African American woman with a large Afro hair style and looked more serious than the other two woman.

I asked how I could help them. Alice did the talking.

Alice explained that she ran a pre-school for 75 three and four year olds with a before school, after school and summer daycare option. Parents were billed on a sliding scale. She housed her program in one of the district's abandoned elementary schools and paid a minimal rent to the district, but the building had fallen into disrepair with a leaky roof and a heating system that failed regularly.

I interrupted her. "Are you asking me to get the roof and the heating system fixed?"

Alice smiled as did the other two women. "Actually we are asking for a lot more than that," she said.

"What do you want me to do?" I said, cutting to the chase.

"Sandra is a social worker and Delia is a nurse. Both have been taking care of their own young children at home. They're ready to go back to work now and have approached me with an idea," Alice said.

"Delia and I have been researching pre-school home visitation programs like Parents as Teachers, Nurse Home Visitation Program and

Healthy Families America," Sandra said. *"We visited the home visita-tion program in Binghamton and we'd like to bring one of these three programs to Sarandon."*

Then Alice chimed in. "And I would like to expand our pre-school program to all three of the remaining elementary schools and serve more pre-school students with certified teachers. If the programs were housed in the schools, we wouldn't have to worry about the leaky roof and the heat problem and our pre-school students could receive more support from the district."

What I call a "happy accident" was unfolding in front of my eyes. These three women understood the Heckman Curve.[cxxiii] This educa-tional research finding confirmed that earlier investments in helping poverty students had much greater positive long-term impact. Fixing issues in adolescents and adults is very expensive and not very effective. Helping out infants, toddlers and pre-school age children has much more impact for the same amount of public expense.

Now it was my turn. "I have visited the Parents as Teachers pro-gram in Binghamton. It's impressive," I said. "All of what you are pro-posing sounds like a great idea but it will require lots of long-term funding and sustained effort. It is also an excellent opportunity to study the long-term impacts of home visits and preschool participation on student outcomes in the future."

"So will you help?" Alice asked.

I smiled. "Are you three available for lunch this Friday? I'm buying and we'll be talking to the Rotarians who invited me to speak to them about improvement plans I have for the school district."

That Friday we met with the Rotarians. After my 15-minute pre-sentation to the Rotary I met a Syracuse University professor who intro-duced me to a colleague who agreed to help us prepare an application for a $12 million Pew Charitable Trust grant to implement the idea these three education entrepreneurs had brought to me. The $12 mil-lion would be paid out over 20 years.

The money would pay for home visits from trained social workers and nurses for half the children who lived in Sarandon from the first time the pregnant mothers spoke to a doctor about their pregnancy until their children started school.

It would also reduce the sliding scale payment rate for Alice's pre-school so that more poor families could participate. And it would pay for the university to study the long-term impact of the home visits and the pre-school with a natural control group of children that didn't receive the benefit of these services from the waiting lists for both programs.

While $12 million over 20 years sounds like a lot of money, the grant would amount to less than 1.5 percent of the district's annual operating expense over that 20-year period, and it could potentially create a huge long-term positive impact for that 1.5 percent investment.

For my part I would have to convince the school board and the district staff that expanding and moving Alice's pre-school program into our three open elementary schools, eliminating her rent and utility payments and providing supports like school nursing services, bus transportation and a moderate level of administrative oversight was in the best interest of the school district.

Alice agreed her program would hire only certified teachers and she would adjust the pre-school curriculum to coordinate with the district curriculum.

Now we had to wait seven months to see whether the grant application would result in funding. In the meantime I had a host of other pressing issues to keep me busy.

Bringing the school board along

Now that we had the pre-school plan underway, I had another plan and it included Harry Kubiak, the charter school teacher.

I met with Harry and shared with him the data on the charter school's practice of "sorting" students.

"Harry, I know you don't feel comfortable with the idea that Kim Neely is pushing you to send challenging students back to the district," I told him.

"I've checked the grade levels for the students coming back to the district and I know that those students aren't coming from your classroom. I'm guessing your instinct would be to keep them and find a way to make them successful. But that's not what's happening."

Harry looked sheepish. "Yes," he said, "but I don't have control over that."

"What if I offered you the job of lead teacher at Westside Elementary school in our magnet school plan," I asked him. "You'd work with Cora Jenkins, and we'd pay you just what you're making now? We'd make Westside Elementary into a parent and student choice magnet school with a math, science and technology theme, a special budget for computers, field trips and teacher training and curriculum development."

Harry waited a full 30 seconds before he responded.

"That's a good idea," he said. "Would the other elementary schools also become magnet schools? Does the school board know about this? How will you pay for it?"

Fighting fire with fire

I explained to Harry that the proposed district magnet schools would be parental choice schools with waiting lists. "For us to succeed — or even compete — we need to offer parents better choices. Plus, we need strong instructional leadership to create academic improvement.

"And yes we've found a way to fund the restructuring/magnet plan," I told him. "I'm meeting with the school board this weekend to hopefully get them to agree to move in this direction."

Harry hesitated before he spoke again. "First, I'm honored you would think to ask me to do this, but I need to think it over. I like the idea, and I know what you're saying about the return rate."

"Think it over," I told him, "but just keep it between the two of us until I have time to get my school board's input."

We parted ways and I hopped into my car and drove to Westside Elementary School. As Cora Jenkins and I toured her school and stopped in several classrooms, I hit her with my idea to change lead teachers."

"Cora, you've told me that Karen Allington would be a great lead teacher for our magnet program and I think your analysis is correct. Everything I've heard about her is positive. But I have another idea for you to consider."

Cora looked at me like I was crazy. "What?!" she said.

"Cora, what if Karen Allington became the head teacher at Eastside. I saw her with Tim O'Grady at the recent staff luncheon and she has a way with him that might be helpful to everyone involved," I said.

"You're right about Karen and Tim. There is nothing inappropriate there, but he'll do whatever she asks. Tim won't give me the time of day, but I know exactly what you're talking about.

"And creating instructional change in Tim's building will be hard after all these years of Tim's blocking change. It's a great idea. But who will be my lead teacher?" she asked.

I smiled. "How about Harry Kubiak?"

Her face lit up. "He won't leave the charter school and come back here," she said.

"He's thinking it over," I said, "and I'm meeting with the school board this Saturday to see if they will support the whole magnet school idea so let's keep it confidential for now."

Cora smiled again. "I'll keep it quiet but what you're talking about will really shake things up in this district," she said. "You have my support, though. I'll do my best to help."

I liked Cora a lot. She wasn't just willing to go along with my ideas; she added to them with good questions and suggestions of her own. I left our conversation feeling good about the magnet school plan.

The newspaper man

The first time I met with Art and reporter Ellen Casale I brought all the data comparing Sarandon's schools with similar schools and school districts around the state. I explained the comparison data.

I showed them Sarandon's position on the academic performance graph today, where Sarandon had been on a similar graph in its heyday and where it could be now with better performance.

I showed them both the charter school return data (with student names blacked out to avoid any confidentiality issues) and projected what the academic performance data would show if Harry Kubiak's teachers had the freedom and skills to teach the same way he did at the charter school. I explained how the charter school return rate pulled down the district schools' test scores and how the charter school financially impacted the public school district. I gave them two national news articles about "return rate" issues in New York City and Buffalo.

Harry's present third grade class would provide the first state test data for the charter schools. I was sure that would be a news article and I was doing my best to make certain that Art and Ellen understood that Harry's third grade students would probably show 40 to 50 percent scoring at proficient or advanced levels, while Sarandon regular elementary schools were more likely to show scores with 15 to 20 percent of students at proficient or advanced Levels.

I wanted to be sure they also understood that most of that gain in charter school test performance was artificial and came from excluding special education students and the "return rate." I also credited part of this anticipated gain to Harry Kubiak and his charter school teacher colleagues who were doing a great job teaching their students.

Art and Ellen asked lots of questions and listened carefully. Both took lots of notes and as our meeting was ending, Art spoke up.

"Rumor has it you're planning to convert the school district's three elementary schools to magnet schools. Is that true?" he asked.

"Art, you're way ahead of me. I'm meeting with the school board this weekend to discuss our improvement options. With the charter school lottery and this return rate problem we have class size imbalances at the elementary level.

"We don't have enough elementary enrollment, especially if a third elementary charter school comes on line next year, to justify keeping three elementary schools open. And as I just showed you, our test scores need improvement," I said.

"All options are on the table, and you can quote me on that," I told him, trying not to get ahead of myself and the school board. "No

decisions have been made yet and none will be made before we've had input from everyone including the public."

Art smiled. *"You didn't say 'no comment' once,"* he said. *"That's more than we've spoken with anyone from the school district in 10 years."*

A plan gets better by listening

As I jumped in my car in the parking lot after my meeting with Art and Ellen, I called my secretary, Betty, and told her I was heading to Northside Elementary to talk to John Schroeder. I told her to call ahead and see if John could free up 15 minutes for me when I arrived. Fifteen minutes later John met me at the door with a smile, which was unusual for him.

We went to John's office and he gestured for me to sit at his small conference table.

"So you've had some time to think over my ideas about magnet schools and our district's future. What are your thoughts?" I asked.

He responded again with an uncharacteristic smile. "Well I think that the idea might work, but I have a couple of ideas that might make it work even better," he said.

"I clearly don't own all the good ideas," I told him. "What are you thinking?"

John took a deep breath. "What if Northside had a lead teacher for each grade level rather than one for the whole school? We'd split the same total pay six ways. I know it's not the plan you envisioned but it would have distinct advantages in this building," he said.

"What advantages?" I asked. "What would your role be?"

John spoke without taking a breath.

"In my school there is no single teacher the other teachers would see as 'the lead teacher,'" John said. "One lead teacher would be divisive among my teachers. Plus, everything else we do in this building is organized by grade level."

John understood a team of lead teachers would mean more work for him. "I'll have to coordinate everything and manage the individual leaders so they don't go off in their own direction," he said.

"I'll also need some regular after school meeting times with the lead teachers and probably two full days of substitute teacher time each year for these six teachers to get together and plan with me as a group.

"But I think the gains would exceed the losses overall and more teachers would have ownership for this plan. And more teachers would be helping us sell this plan to the Northside parents and the school board. You know I have been reluctant about this idea of Northside as a magnet school, but this might make it work."

"John," I said, "you used the key word – ownership. If you think this approach will give us buy-in from teachers and parents, you have my support. It might even work districtwide. We'll have more teachers to support the restructuring."

We finished our meeting and I headed for my car. I made another call to Betty to tell her I wouldn't return to the office until after 5 p.m. I was headed to the middle school and high school to talk to the principals and then meet with the food services director, the custodial and maintenance supervisor, the transportation supervisor and our special education coordinator in their offices.

When my flurry of drive-by meetings ended, I plopped down in my chair in my own office. It was close to 6 p.m. It had been a whirlwind day, but I accomplished a lot.

I first met with Alex Casale, the high school principal. I suggested we use John Schroeder's lead teacher team idea in the high school and establish a new and expanded high school department lead teacher position that paid a greater stipend than the existing minimal department chairperson role. We could offer teachers who were selected for the position one less teaching assignment so that they would teach four instead of five classes and would take on a greater academic leadership role in the high school.

Alex, who tended to be entrepreneurial in his approach to his job, immediately said that he could see some real opportunities to make this idea fly with good teachers who could provide real and effective academic leadership in his school.

He also (as expected) immediately requested the logical follow up to this leadership structural change.

"This change would have much more impact with another $60,000 per year for high school teacher training and curriculum development," he said. "With the extra money for our lead teachers and the teachers working on curriculum and training it would give my school more buy-in on the restructuring plan."

I knew he was right but realized this meant I'd have to go back to work looking for savings elsewhere in the budget to offset the additional cost.

Next, I met with the middle school principal, Sheila Macgregor, who, as it turned out, had an undeserved reputation for not being very creative. Sheila added another new idea to the mix: A summer school enrichment program for 60 students.

The enrichment summer school program for 60 of Sheila's students who were struggling academically would emphasize painting and drawing, robotics, theatre performance, astronomy and agriculture. No drill and kill workbooks.

Every teacher knows there are three differences between a weak student who makes it through to at least minimal academic competence and a weak student who fails: attitude, motivation and study skills. Yet, traditional academic remedial programs tend to offer nothing but more of the same drill-and-practice activities that have already failed to motivate students.

Our rough budgeting in Sheila's office that day showed that her good idea, including transportation and teacher salaries, would cost the district $115,000 per year. In addition, Sheila's school would need $45,000 each year for teacher curriculum work and teacher training to support the new summer school and curriculum work and training to improve the lackluster school-year program, work and training that would be completed primarily in the summer.

My meeting with our food services director netted some savings as we discussed her plan to consolidate three kitchens into one central kitchen that would prepare food for all three elementary schools and save the district upwards of $95,000 per year in labor costs.

This reduction would mean layoffs in a department that was adding a student worker (also at my request) which would surely create *union issues. But these were issues Sarandon would eventually have to face. And my role as the change agent interim superintendent meant the best time to face the reality of the situation was now.*

My conversation with Roger Hornung, the custodial and maintenance supervisor, was less positive. I asked Roger if he had any ideas for the operation of his department that would save the district the $70,000-$100,000 needed for academic improvements.

"No, we're already stretched too thin and we agreed to take on that student intern which will stretch us even further," he said.

I told him I had an idea and outlined a plan to reduce two nighttime custodial positions in the district (savings with salaries and benefits $94,000) and use a more efficient cleaning team that moved from school to school each night with a higher paid night time supervisor (additional cost $5,000).

The cleaning team would need more high-tech floor cleaning equipment that would use up $10,000 of the savings and the new student intern would become part of this cleaning team. The net savings to the district for this change would be $94,000 minus $15,000 = $79,000.

Roger was upset but professional. I told him I was open to any alternative ideas he might come up with and that I knew we'd need to discuss these proposed changes with the support staff union before moving forward.

I was certain Roger, who had previously been a president of this union before taking over his present leadership role in the district's administration, would be on the phone with to the current president of the support staff union before I started my car in the parking lot.

On another front, the transportation supervisor gave me good news: Our efforts to consolidate special education bus runs with several neighboring districts had resulted in another $105,000 in savings for the next school year.

Our creative special education director provided the last piece of good news: Her plan was to bring seven Sarandon elementary special education students back to the district for their education in a 12:1:2 *classroom to be housed in one of district elementary schools would save $48,000 per student in tuition payments annually. Some of this savings would be offset by the salary and benefit costs for a teacher and two assistants for these students in their new class.*

Her plan also involved selling the remaining five vacant slots in this new special education class of 12 students, one teacher and two teaching assistants to neighboring school districts (at a tuition rate of $35,000 per student per year creating significant savings for the other districts and helping our district's bottom line).

Even with the salary and benefit costs of a new special education teacher and two teaching assistants the Sarandon school district would save $166,000 by adding this class We could potentially generate additional revenue of $35,000 per student in tuition for up to five students ($175,000 in potential new revenue) coming from neighboring districts once this class was up and running.

We decided not to count on that money until the slots were filled later in the year. This change would also allow the district to save an additional bus run ($89,000). We had the savings dollars the district-wide restructuring/magnet plan required. Now for the hard part – getting the school board to support the plan.

I knew the plan could be even better with support and suggestions from the school board. I also knew that without the school board's support this plan had no chance of success. Bitter experience had taught me that if I took ideas to the school board before I had some of the key details worked out and administrative support in crucial areas those ideas could easily be shot down or manipulated out of existence politically, either by individual board members or key administrators.

Take care or your best plans will end up in the idea trash heap before they are even discussed.

Too often I had seen school board members upset that they had not been brought in at the first hint of discussion about any new idea so that their input could guide the idea's birth. I had debated in my own mind the best process to bring this semi-radical magnet school idea to fruition and as we approached the first of the two board retreat Saturday meetings I was still unsure I had done this properly.

In individual goal setting meetings with each school board member and multiple public meeting discussions with the whole school board over the summer after I arrived in the school district a consensus was reached on the most important goals for the school district: improve academic performance for all district students, reduce the hemorrhaging of student enrollment to the charter schools, find the money for the necessary academic improvements without raising property taxes, improve the district's image and improve the academic leadership team in the district.

With the rough draft plans I had been creating with the help of the district's administrative team, we now had enough detail to discuss the plan realistically. I just hoped I hadn't gone too far with the planning before significantly involving the school board.

I also knew from my conversations with school board members individually and as a group that if I had just asked them up front whether they would consider three elementary magnet schools in the district they would have said "no." They would have had many reasons (financial, political and programmatic) as to why this idea was unworkable. At least with the approach I was taking they would be able to see a reasonably fleshed out plan before they made a decision on how to proceed.

The first Saturday session

Sarandon's school board was pretty good, as school boards go. They knew enough not to dial up the verbal volume and exchanges to a point where disagreements turned into long-term hostilities. And when I asked them to keep something confidential they generally kept it quiet, though not always as the newspaper's Art Cameron's question about magnet schools proved.

I realized the two Saturday workshops I planned with the school board skirted the edge of the Sunshine Laws requiring public discussion of school district business. I also knew if we didn't conduct these initial discussions privately the Magnet school idea would never get off the ground because of parental pressure.

Mitzy Holland, short and bubbly, was the school board president. She was a stay-at-home Mom in her early thirties and a Northside parent of two elementary age students.

Mitzy was serving her second three-year term on the school board.

Terry Hansen, a soft spoken local attorney, was also a thirty something Northside parent of a kindergartner. He was in the second year of his first three-year term on the school board.

Melissa Grignon, another Northside resident, was an architect with a great sense of humor. She worked for a large Syracuse architectural firm. She was in her second term on the school board. She had a son in the middle school and a daughter in the high school and both were excellent students and athletes.

Laura Ashton, another Northside thirty-something parent, had a daughter in second grade. She was quiet and studious and worked as a secretary for the county. Laura was in her first year as a school board member.

All four of these board members were white, married and middle class. The lone board member, not from Northside, was Molly Gaston. Molly lived in an older home immediately adjacent to Eastside Elementary School. She was a matronly, good natured, unmarried African American woman in her 60s, serving her fourth term on the school board.

After our coffee Mitzy reviewed the goals the school board had developed over the summer and fall, which my secretary Betty had written with a black marker on a large poster stapled to the cork bulletin board for all to see:

School Board Goals

1. *Improve district academic performance in all schools.*
2. *Reduce student enrollment flow to the charter schools.*
3. *Find a way to fund academic improvements without raising taxes.*
4. *Improve the district's image.*
5. *Enhance the district's academic leadership team with training and teacher involvement.*

This last goal was the school board's way to politely say publicly they had concerns about the principals' leadership skills that needed to be addressed while facing the fact that the tenure laws meant their principals couldn't be fired.

Just as Mitzy and I had planned before this session I presented the comparison data that showed each of the five schools in Sarandon was underperforming. This data brought some questions from the Northside parents on the school board. They all thought that Northside was performing better than Eastside and Westside. When I explained that in comparison to similar schools with the same percentage of poverty students Northside was in fact underperforming despite the fact that Northside had higher test scores than the other two schools. They were initially baffled.

Terry Hansen, who appeared to have more natural understanding of mathematics said it best and brought along his confused fellow school board members, when he said: "Northside isn't doing better; it just has a much easier job and is actually doing worse at that easier job even though it still has better test scores. You can tell that from the graph because Northside is further below the predicted performance line than Eastside or Westside."

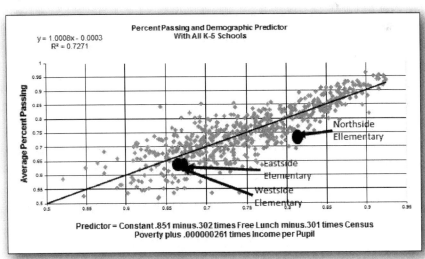

Scatterplot graph courtesy of Charles Winters.

Perception isn't everything

"We have to be careful whatever we do we don't destroy our one single ray of sunshine," Melissa Grignon said, referring to the community's perception that Northside is the star performer in the district.

I didn't respond to Melissa's comment, deciding instead to wait until they saw the full picture.

Once the school board members understood the meaning of the elementary school academic performance graph, I shared return rate data from the charter schools and the class size imbalance data the principals had discussed with me a week earlier.

I also explained how the comparison between charter schools and the district schools would play out over the next few years, as the charter school accumulated more of the academically higher performing students and continued to exclude special education students.

Once they under understood the data and had all their questions answered the school board took a brief break. We decided ahead of time that we'd end at 1:30 p.m. without a real lunch break so that the board members could attend their children's afternoon basketball games, music recitals, scouting events and other family commitments.

During the break I was approached by three board members. "So when do we hear about this magnet school idea?" they asked.

"Right after the break is over," I told them.

Five minutes later all five board members were seated expectantly waiting to hear about magnet schools.

For 10 minutes I outlined the magnet school idea including the concept of an annual lottery that attempted to better balance the percentages of poverty students in the three elementary schools by filling vacant slots in classes.

I explained how the lottery could help the district deal with the class size bubble in Eastside's second grade by taking a handful of applicant lottery students from grade two at Eastside and moving them into grade two at Northside where there was space.

This helped them understand how the district could address the class size imbalances and charter school return rate issue permanently.

When students returned from the magnet schools during the school year the district could look at names on the magnet school lottery waiting list for the right grade level and if possible move students mid-year so that the classes remained balanced or use the lottery the next summer to achieve better class size balance.

"The only way to handle the back and forth of the charter school is to evenly distribute students in our own schools, and Northside had the smallest class sizes. Northside would have to take students from the other schools that had more students who were eligible for free and reduced price lunch," I said.

Then Mitzy posed the obvious question: "If we were to implement this magnet school concept and Northside became one of the magnet schools, wouldn't that increase the percentage of poor students at Northside?"

"Yes it would," I told her.

"But we don't want that," said Laura who'd been quiet all morning. "The Northside parents were very upset when the district tried to redraw the elementary school boundaries two years ago and send more poor students to Northside."

"I understand how the Northside parents feel," I said, "but how do we deal with the class size imbalance and charter school return rate problems and address the school board's goals of improving academic performance, reducing the flow of enrollment to the charter schools and improving the image of our schools?

"We all know this won't be easy, but it's our job to create a long-term plan that achieves all those goals." I reminded them. "What if Northside only had to pick up an average of five poverty students per grade level? Just two or three more poor students per classroom. Would that be too much?" I asked.

I stopped talking and the school board members fell silent for a full thirty seconds.

"How would you do that?" said Terry.

I pulled out a poster I had prepared in advance and tacked it up on the bulletin board. It read:

* *The school board designates all three elementary schools as magnet schools.*
* *Children who are residents of any of the three elementary attendance zone are guaranteed slots in the elementary school where they reside.*
* *Any other classroom slots up to a maximum of 24 students per class are assigned on a lottery basis so that all schools move closer to 40 percent free and reduced price lunch eligibility.*

"So Northside would never exceed 40 percent free or reduced price lunch students with that rule, correct?" Terry asked.

"Correct, Northside is presently at 30 percent free or reduced price lunch enrollment. Unless the Northside attendance area became more than 40 percent free or reduced price lunch students it couldn't exceed 40 percent with this rule in place."

"Lonnie, you're like my husband. Great big ideas and no way to pay for them. How would we ever pay for these magnet schools?" Melissa asked.

I told them that was the subject of next Saturday's meeting and the school principals and other administrators would be on hand to answer specific questions about funding and implementation.

I left the meeting feeling good about the progress we had made, but I had lingering doubts over the concern that Laura had raised.

The Northside school board members feared that sending more poverty students to Northside would move it closer to being a "bad" school. My experience as an educator told me this was not the case. "Good" schools exist at every point on the poverty, middle class and wealthy spectrum, but that was not the perception in the community.

So what makes a "good school" good?

When my oldest son Jason graduated from high school as his class's valedictorian a local charity sponsored a recognition dinner for all the regional high school valedictorians and salutatorians. The students were asked to bring their parents and the single teacher who they saw as the most influential in their school success.

The teachers' spouses were also invited to attend the dinner which attracted a lot of media coverage.

While most of the students invited teachers from their high school years, my son invited his second grade teacher from Krieger Elementary School in Poughkeepsie, NY, Ms. Virginia James.

In 1977, Krieger Elementary School's free and reduced price lunch numbers were on the rise as a result of a new nearby housing project that was home to a lower income, primarily minority population.

Ms. James, an experienced and very effective teacher, immediately diagnosed my son as having every educational advantage a second grader could possibly have. He learned to read before he arrived in elementary school, he loved to do his own "science research" and he was able to work independently.

She provided him with all the right independent learning opportunities in a corner of her classroom for the entire year. She encouraged him, provided the right level of criticism and challenge and rewarded him with enough time and attention that he flourished.

She also knew when and how to involve him in whole group activities with the rest of his second grade class to help him develop his social skills. And while she was doing this for my son she was doing the same kind of high quality teaching with 20-plus other students with skills, attitudes and motivations that ran the gamut.

My son understood after 13 years in K-12 schools that Ms. James was an exceptional teacher.

I'm aware that such teachers exist but it's unrealistic to think that we can put an exceptional teacher like Ms. James in every classroom. It's just not going to happen. It's not a real solution.

Mrs. James was exceptional and that exceptionalism is what gave me pause with the Sarandon issues relating to putting more poverty students at Northside Elementary. I was asking Northside's teachers to become better at their jobs while simultaneously making their jobs more difficult.

Educational improvements that rely on having exceptional teachers in every classroom to carry them out will probably fail. We should not and cannot tolerate incompetent or weak teachers. But even if we do our very best and remove every single incompetent teacher from our classrooms, and we improve the performance of every single weak teacher, we'll still have exceptional teachers in only a few classrooms.

All teachers and principals have tough jobs and all do those impossibly challenging jobs imperfectly. Teachers who teach mostly children from poverty have a much harder job than those who see only a few poverty students in their classrooms.[cxxiv] And as the poverty student numbers increase the challenging job of teaching will become more challenging in a predictable rapidly expanding geometric progression, not unlike the failure rate.

Ms. James was an exceptional teacher because she could diagnose the entire range of student needs in her classroom, plan instruction appropriately and successfully implement her complicated, many faceted instructional plans with sound classroom management, good student rapport and a dash of creativity that my son remembered.

Good and very good teachers struggle with this tall order, no matter how many disadvantaged students they have in their classroom. As poverty numbers increase, teachers face even more daily instructional planning and implementation decisions. They have to work more hours to be as effective. Their planning becomes more complex and the odds of their being able to effectively implement their complex plans become lower regardless of their skill level.

Putting more poor students in teachers' classrooms would make those teachers more likely to fail. And by many international measures a growing segment of U.S. children grow up in less than ideal economic circumstances.[cxxv]

In high poverty classrooms there are more students who need one-on-one tutoring and encouragement,[cxxvi] while there also are a number of students in these same poverty classrooms, like my son, who need more challenging tasks and encouragement. Is it hard to understand why many teachers and principals in high poverty schools end their work days feeling overwhelmed? Why so many quit the profession after a few years?[cxxvii]

Is it also hard to understand why so many effective teachers escape urban and rural high poverty schools as soon as they can get hired for a teaching job in a less diverse suburban school?[cxxviii]

No matter how hard they work and how effective these teachers and principals are in their efforts they must accept the fact that statistically far too many of their students will not succeed on standardized tests or attend college or even graduate from high school.[cxxix] It's discouraging and difficult work.

Further complicating this issue is some alarming data. In 1989, 32 percent of the students in U.S. schools qualified for free or reduced price lunches. In 2013, 51 percent qualified. While some of this increase was attributable to the recession of 2008-10 and will hopefully decline over time, increasing income inequality in the U.S., globalization of our economy and advances in technology will continue to provide a push toward greater student poverty in our schools.[cxxx]

An expanded safety net put in place in the U.S. since the 1960s has helped reduce the impacts of poverty on children,[cxxxi] but these offsets are insufficient to help those schools and classrooms overwhelmed with children from poverty.

In 1960, 9 percent of families with children under age 18 were headed by a single parent. In 2008, the number was 32 percent and the projections are that by 2030 this number will be more than 40 percent. [cxxxii cxxxiii cxxxiv]

While many single parents do a great job with their children, they are facing an uphill battle and long odds.

And the segregation of our schools by ethnicity and poverty also has increased. Today, 40 percent of African American students attend a school where less than 10 percent of the population is white.[cxxxv]

Real estate agents and banks have encouraged segregated housing patterns with red-lining and mortgage underwriting procedures that have reinforced economic and ethnic segregation for most urban and many nearby diverse suburban school districts.[cxxxvi]

The result: More and more teachers are facing very diverse classrooms and many teach only poverty and minority children.[cxxxvii]

Meanwhile, as these demographic changes happened, we raised student learning standards and made the required tests more difficult. And adding insult to injury, some states linked teacher performance evaluations to their students' performance on these harder tests before we had any kind of track record on the new curriculum and the tests and before we had fully trained our teachers.

And finally, for a select few mainly high poverty school districts we brought in "competition" in the form of charter schools, charter schools established with no regard for the impact they would have on the students remaining in district schools.

The school administrators, employees and their unions and school board members in high poverty school districts in many cases contributed significantly to the mess they find themselves in now. For decades they resisted the real changes that might have produced academic improvement.

They protected underperforming teachers and administrators who should have been fired. They wasted money on ever increasing teacher, support staff and administrator salaries and benefit costs while ignoring many common sense financial savings opportunities available to them (See Chapter 7, "Where has all the money gone?") And they whined incessantly about the difficulty of their jobs in the process adding immeasurably to their rapidly declining public image.

A legitimate concern

I knew Sarandon's school board members' concerns about placing more poverty students in Northside were legitimate. The Northside teachers' jobs would become more difficult with the addition of these students in their larger classes.

If the Northside teachers didn't improve their performance (which was already weak when compared to similar schools), the school board members with students in Northside and their Northside parent colleagues would be sending their children to a less effective school because the teachers would be more overwhelmed.

I knew I was asking a lot by asking for all three elementary schools to become magnet schools. I also knew that if the district didn't make this change to three elementary magnet schools we were giving the charter schools the advantage of having our most successful students while leaving our demoralized teachers with only the most difficult and expensive students to educate in more and more challenging classrooms.

The second Saturday school board session

When the school board and administrative team members arrived for the second Saturday session I had already put up on the bulletin board for all to see a poster with a summary of the savings we had found to pay for our magnet schools/restructuring. It was printed neatly in Betty's beautiful handwriting, and I passed out paper copies with the same information.

Projected Savings to Fund Magnet Schools/Restructuring Project

1.	*Initial Out of District Special Education Bus Run Consolidation*	*$180,000*
2.	*Special Education Student Interns filling vacant support staff jobs in the district*	*$200,000*
3.	*Additional Bus run savings from student interns*	*$75,000*
4.	*Food Services kitchen consolidation*	*$95,000*
5.	*Operations and Maintenance Night Cleaning Team*	*$79,000*
6.	*Additional Special Education Bus run consolidation*	*$105,000*
7.	*New In-District grade 3,4 and 5 Special Education class in lieu of BOCES*	*$166,000**
	TOTAL	*$900,000*

As expected, the school board members were skeptical of the numbers so I asked each of the department leaders to explain how the plan would generate the savings. Then came the anticipated questions and the prepared answers I had department leaders rehearse prior to the meeting:

- Yes, the bus run consolidations would work and the rides would not be too long for our students.
- Yes, the student interns would be paid as regular employees in the future if they were successful at the jobs during their internship year.
- Yes, the kitchen consolidation would be safe and effective. We visited neighboring districts already doing this and it was working for them.
- Yes, the custodians could do an effective job and save the district money by eliminating two positions.

Even the reluctant head of the custodial and maintenance department handled the board's questions professionally.

Of course, I couldn't guarantee what he would say when I was out of earshot.

We clarified the meaning of the asterisk next to the $166,000. If we received $35,000 in tuition for each of the students from local school districts who filled five vacant slots in our new in-district special education class, we could use that additional revenue to enhance the financing of our improvement plan. But as yet the revenue did not exist in the school district budget and was not part of this plan. The school board members' biggest concern came in a question I didn't anticipate.

"Which elementary school will house the new in-district special education class with the seven students coming back from BOCES?" Mitzy asked. "If you are asking Northside parents to take more poor students in their classrooms with the magnet lottery you can't also ask them to also take in a class of up to 12 challenging special education students."

I understood and agreed that if the magnet school concept became part of our improvement plan Northside would not be the home for this new special education class. In the back of my mind I wondered if Northside principal John Schroeder hadn't suggested Mitzy ask that question.

When the discussion died down, Terry Hansen asked the obvious question.

"So what will this savings buy us in an improvement plan?" he asked.

This was a question I had anticipated. That's when I put up another of Betty's newsprint posters.

Improvement Plan Expenses

1. *Elementary Magnet School Lead Teachers*
    $20,000 per school   *$60,000*
2. *Elementary Teacher Curriculum Work $45,000*
    per school   *$135,000*
3. *Elementary School Field Trips, books, computers*
    $50,000 per school   *$150,000*
4. *Expanded MS/HS Department Chair role*   *$75,000*
5. *High School Curriculum work*   *$60,000*
6. *Middle School Enrichment Summer School*   *$115,000*
7. *Middle School Curriculum work*   *$45,000*

                                              TOTAL   *$640,000*

Immediately, Melissa Grignon pointed out that the projected savings exceeded the total projected expenses by $260,000 and the fact that the new special education class could possibly create $175,000 more in revenue.

"What are you suggesting we do with that $435,000?" she asked.

"We have a budget that has to pass in May. The savings could go toward other increases in next year's budget and result in a zero percent tax increase." I said. That's important because with all these changes

we're proposing some support staff unions might try to get the budget voted down." I added.

"Will $260,000 or even $435,000 be enough to give us a 0 percent tax increase?" Terry asked.

"I don't know yet and we still have to find those tuition paying special education students, but if the school board asks me to try to hit that zero percent tax increase to make this plan fly we'll sure try," I assured them.

During the break after this presentation/discussion I overheard many good conversations about operational and financial issues related to the plan. Aside from Laura Ashton, who was still obviously reluctant about the idea of more poor and minority students at Northside, the school board members and administrators were discussing implementation ideas and financial issues.

After the break I used board member questions overheard during the break as a springboard for an hour-long discussion about implementation. We discussed costs, the middle school summer school, the curriculum work teachers would be doing at all levels, how we'd pay for the employer's share of social security and retirement contributions related to the extra teacher curriculum work, the unique teacher leadership structure we envisioned for the middle school and the high school with an expanded department chairman role and at Northside with a team of grade-level lead teachers.

As expected the school board members had some great ideas about how to best fit these rough ideas into the special mix that made Sarandon a unique community.

"You'll need to have evening parent meetings at all five schools to explain this concept and the funding ideas behind it. And you'd better be ready for a lot of questions and concerns, especially at Northside," Melissa said.

"Yes, the parent meetings are a great idea, but first we need to meet with the faculties at each school to explain these concepts and answer their questions. They'll have a lot of questions," the high school principal said.

Having recognized the change in tone of articles in the newspaper, he also suggested sharing the plan with the newspaper.

Molly Gaston, who was usually quiet, broke her silence. "This is the first time in all my years on the school board we have some ideas on the table that could actually help disadvantaged students. We have to find a way to make sure this plan succeeds," she said.

When Molly stopped talking you could hear a pin drop. Then Laura Ashton spoke up: "Yes, but the parents at Northside will never accept taking in more students from Eastside and Westside."

Then Terry posed a question I had anticipated. "We understand that John Schroeder will be using a team of grade-level lead teachers at Northside to help with the leadership transition to a magnet school but have you made any decisions on who might fill these roles of lead teacher at Eastside and Westside?"

I answered carefully because I knew the walls had ears and if the teachers union thought I'd overstepped my boundaries, a grievance saying it had not been an open and fair search would follow.

"Well, we have to post and interview for the positions as our teacher contract requires and as we would with any new position," I told them. "But among the candidates we should have a couple that make me confident we will be adding some great talent to our district leadership team.

"Karen Alington, for one, has told Cora she would be interested in being a lead teacher," I added.

Murmurs of approval rose up around the room confirming Cora's initial read that Karen had an excellent reputation.

Terry followed up. "Well that takes care of Westside but what about Eastside?" he said.

"I was thinking Karen might be a great candidate for Eastside," I said.

"Why would you move Karen?" Mitzy said.

"Karen and Tim work very well together and have already talked about some great possibilities at Eastside. And besides Cora and I have a great candidate for Westside."

Then Terry spoke up. "C'mon, don't keep us in suspense. Who are you thinking of for Westside?"

"Harry Kubiak has indicated he might be interested," I said.

They were stunned. "That could make this whole plan work," Melissa said. "Harry's great with students, parents and teachers. Getting him back from the charter schools would be a real boost for this plan. We never should have lost him." Melissa added.

Tim O'Grady grimaced, but we all knew she was right.

We ended our meeting with me sketching out a timetable for how we'd proceed with this rudimentary plan on the bulletin board:

1. *December - School board discusses the restructuring/magnet plan in public at the December school board meeting. Superintendent meets with the newspaper editor and reporter in advance of the meeting to explain the plan and timetable fully. Emphasize that we are discussing all potential improvement plan options and no decision will be made until all of the steps are completed.*

2. *January - Lonnie meets with all five school faculties to discuss the plan and receives input from teachers and principals. This input comes back to the school board with a summary for each school written by Lonnie and Betty. Lonnie shares the five school summaries at each of the two January school board meetings. The five school summaries are shared with Art Cameron.*

3. *February - Lonnie and each school principal meets with parents and residents at each of the five schools and presents a rough draft of the improvement plan that incorporates faculty suggestions that Lonnie sees as workable and valuable and the school board has agreed should be part of the ongoing discussion. Lonnie and Betty produce a written summary of the input from each school meeting and share the summaries with the school board. Lonnie reports to the school board at the next public school board meeting after each parent/resident meeting and they discuss and agree on elements to be included in the discussion moving forward. Lonnie provides the newspaper with regular updates.*

4. *March - Early in the month the school board holds a public hearing related to the improvement/magnet plan to receive input from the community, during which time Lonnie presents the plan as it has evolved with input from teachers, parents and residents. Then the school board will hear from members of the community who want to share their views. At the second school board meeting in March the school board discusses input received and works with Lonnie to produce a final version of the improvement/magnet plan to be voted on by the school board in April.*

5. *April 7 - At the regularly scheduled meeting, the school board will adopt or adopt with amendments an improvement/magnet plan which may or may not include all the elements discussed today and will adopt a proposed school budget for the next school year that includes the elements of an improvement/magnet plan that have survived after all the public and employee input and after any final school board amendments.*

As the school board retreat came to a close, I could tell all the school board members except Laura Ashton felt good about where the meeting had taken us.

I found her in the parking lot. "I know you're not happy about this plan. What can we do to make it work for you?" I asked.

"Look I don't want to be difficult," she said, "but I ran for this school board to make sure the district didn't change the elementary school boundaries and send more poor students to Northside. My family is not wealthy. It's a real stretch for us to pay the rent for our place in Northside.

"We pay the extra to make certain our daughter is going to a good school. I'm not racist and I don't dislike poor people or anything; I just want my daughter to get the best education possible. If Northside ends up with the same kind of poverty numbers as Eastside and Westside I don't think that it can be a good school anymore. If you want me to support this plan you have to exclude Northside from magnet school planning."

I could have responded by telling her the plan would only add two or three poor students per classroom, only 30 total more poor students in K-5 at Northside. I could have said the plan would only change the percentage of students getting free or reduced price lunch from 30 percent to 40 percent not the 80 percent at Eastside and Westside, but she wasn't ready to listen.

I also knew that she wasn't even considering the long-term cost to the district caused by the class size imbalances from the charter school lottery and return rate. I needed a better strategy to convince her and the other Northside parents, so I decided to wait and have that conversation later.

WHEN DATA IS NOT ENOUGH

All school superintendents are sales professionals. They sell ideas.

First, they sell those ideas to their staff members and school board members, then to their students and their parents and finally to their school district communities.

With each sales pitch comes the need for the superintendent to listen carefully to the suggestions, concerns and perceptions of each group and to modify the original idea and sales pitch to incorporate the good suggestions, to include better solutions for the real concerns and to provide information that changes and accommodates the special perceptions that each group brings to the issues being discussed. It's an excruciating, time consuming process that requires the political skills of Machiavelli and the patience of Job.

Sometimes concerns are legitimate and too many to overcome even with the most creative adjustments, but it's the only way meaningful change can happen.

The only reason I could bring my innovative ideas to Sarandon was because I was an interim superintendent. I was there for one year and then gone. I didn't have a future to worry about and if the school board, the unions, the newspaper, the community made it impossible for me to do my job, I could just go home.

A midcareer superintendent with a family in tow doesn't have that luxury. They most frequently end up trapped in a position where they are afraid to propose the best improvement ideas for fear of rejection, and ultimately they get blamed for mediocre results.

Frequently, the resistance to necessary change a superintendent faces comes from seemingly irrational fears based on misinformation. Initially, when I saw this problem as a young school administrator I thought the answer was simply more and better data.

Early in my career as a principal I ran into a series of stumbling blocks when I tried to change the viewpoint of people who blocked change in areas I saw as critically important. I thought better data presented in a more convincing way would change their viewpoint. It didn't.

Eventually, I realized all of us (myself included) make important decisions in part based on data and logic and in part based on firmly held beliefs and assumptions that have nothing to do with data.

For instance, probably because of my work with children from poverty I have a strong set of beliefs relating to what we must do as a nation to reduce the numbers of children living in poverty. It is one of my core beliefs. Too many U.S. children grow up in poverty and despite our best efforts, in the end, poverty stunts their growth potential.

Any idea or proposal that contains even a whiff of disdain for poor people cannot even be considered as an option among the solutions I would consider viable. When someone says to me that wealth and income inequality is not really a big deal in the U.S. my blood boils.

Their logic about markets and incentives, their arguments about globalization and technology and their assurances about Gross Domestic Product and the benefits of our capitalist economy make me want to scream. I realize this is not logical. But it is my belief system and it directly impacts how I evaluate information and how I make decisions.

Laura Ashton's views about the potential arrival of 30 more poverty students at Northside Elementary were based on a similar set of beliefs. My experience tells me that the only way to change the mind of someone with a strongly held belief that contradicts what you know from data and experience requires three steps.

1) Show them it's possible. In this case by taking them to successful schools with higher numbers of poor students.

2) Show them how the change you are proposing reflects another important belief they share with you.

3) Find a way to compromise those two conflicting beliefs.

Applying the principles of the possible and compromise

In Laura Ashton's case the "possible" was actually quite easy. I found three K-5 elementary schools in the nearby Syracuse area with 40 to 45 percent free and reduced lunch eligible students that academically outperformed Northside and arranged parent and teacher visits to these three schools.

We went in four cars to each of the three sites. Fifteen different Northside teachers and parents went to at least one of these schools. John Schroeder and I went to all three schools.

Laura Ashton also went to all three schools and the other school board members went to at least one of these schools.

We saw classrooms in action, we met with the principals, we talked to parents and we met with a group of teachers at each school. We all carried a common list of questions we asked each group of teachers and parents and each principal. Every visit participant made notes and Betty and I collated the notes into a document we shared with the Northside teachers and PTA, as well as with the newspaper and the school board.

Everyone heard and saw the same thing: These were viable, successful elementary schools that any parent or teacher would see as a good place for students to go to school.

I thought long and hard about the beliefs that motivated Laura Ashton and the other parents from Northside. From what Betty told me, I understood a contingent of the old guard teachers from Northside believed that 30 more poor students at Northside would tip the balance and change Northside from a "good" school to a "bad" school.

They were not totally irrational beliefs. The housing values in Northside could decline. Student test scores could get even worse. The teachers, already struggling as the test scores showed, could become overwhelmed as the poverty numbers climbed that extra 10 percent.

So I decided that my appeal to their beliefs had to come in the form of an appeal to fairness, a principle everyone, especially teachers, values highly.

Setting the stage

We discussed the plan in public at the December school board meeting. I met with Art Cameron and his reporter to explain everything immediately before that school board meeting.

A great article summarizing the plan and the decision-making timetable appeared in the press two weeks before Christmas and precipitated a large number of letters to the editor, some positive and some negative. Obviously, the biggest sticking points with the public were the increase in poor student numbers at Northside and how we would pay for these potential changes.

I began my presentations and discussions with the school staffs immediately after the Christmas break. The teachers had many excellent questions and several good suggestions. They asked about pay rates and time schedules for curriculum work. They asked about student selection procedures for middle school summer school. They suggested two different department chair positions one for the middle school and one for the high school.

They also suggested using some of the curriculum money for teacher training and when and how that training would be scheduled. They asked if they would have input on the teacher trainer selections.

Before I tackled the hard sell at Northside I sharpened my selling skills at the other four schools, meeting the faculty at each. I presented district test data, charter school numbers and return rate data and a basic explanation of the rough improvement/magnet school plan.

I made sure everyone had a one-page, front and back, take home document detailing the basic elements of the plan and the test data. I detailed our visits to other elementary schools with 40 percent free and reduced price lunch eligible students and the successes we saw. I told them the names of the schools and their principals and encouraged them to set up their own visits.

Their questions, comments and concerns helped me prepare for the tougher sell at Northside. The overall reaction of the teachers throughout the district was positive and supportive. But they all let me know that even though they supported the plan and looked forward to working to make it a success, I could expect a lot of push back at Northside.

I met with the Northside faculty on January 25th and started by showing them the scatterplot graph that showed they were an underperforming school. According to the test data, Northside's academic performance was below that of schools with similar demographics. Yes, they performed better than Eastside and Westside – the other two schools in their district – but they performed worse than demographically similar schools.

I carefully explained the charter school return rate problem and answered several questions about why just adding a second grade teacher at Eastside wouldn't solve the problem and would leave us with other class size gaps and bulges over the years unless we started to use a parental choice system in the district schools to help balance the classes.

I also spent a greater amount of time than I had with the other faculty groups describing our visits to other successful elementary schools with greater poverty than Northside, mentioning the names of parents and teachers who had gone on the visit. I explained the improvement/magnet school plan as it had evolved and included the suggestions made by the other teachers.

As we reached then end of the discussion, one of the more senior teachers posed a question I had, thankfully, anticipated.

"If our school already has lower test scores than we should," she asked, "how can we possibly improve by taking in more poor students? They will only add to our class sizes and make our jobs even more difficult."

"Good question," I said. "Let me ask all of you a question. How many of you started your career in Eastside, Westside or one of the other elementary schools with more poverty children that the district has already closed?"

There were 16 K-5 Northside teachers in the room and I knew that nine had started their careers in one of the other two elementary schools. Nine teachers raised their hands.

Over the years these teachers had requested a transfer to the "easier" jobs when openings came up at Northside. Like many school districts Sarandon had a teacher transfer policy that favored senior teachers and rewarded them with the most coveted teaching slots.

"Right now Eastside and Westside have about 80 percent free and reduced lunch eligible students in their schools. Northside has 30 percent free and reduced lunch eligible students. Northside's classes average 21.5 students per class, and Eastside and Westside average 24.2 students per class.

The change we're proposing would increase the number of poverty students in each of your classes by two or three free and reduced lunch eligible students per class and increase your class sizes by the same number so that your classes would be closer to the same size as those classes at Eastside and Westside.

"The percentage of free or reduced price lunch students at Northside would increase from 30 percent to 40 percent and Eastside's and Westside's free and reduced lunch percentages would decrease from 80 percent to about 76 percent.

"I realize I am asking you to take on more work and more challenges in an already difficult job. I'm certain you can understand that without this change the whole magnet school idea and parental school choice in Sarandon's public schools will fail.

"Northside is not a country club. At least 30 percent of your students come from homes where they don't have all the advantages. However, all of you, and particularly those of you who started your careers in schools with even more poverty students than you have right now at Northside – you understand how difficult teaching is for your colleagues at Eastside and Westside.

And the return rate problem caused by the charter schools has made some of their classes even larger and more difficult. I'm asking you to think about fairness here. Can you take two or three more poor students in your classes to balance the class size numbers and move the demo-graphics a little bit to help out those teachers. Many of you have friends who teach in those two schools. I'm asking you to think of them and to think about what is fair."

So there was my pitch for what was I hoped would be an equally important value: fairness. I was asking them to subordinate their value relating to fear that Northside, now seen as a "good" school, would be perceived as a "bad" school with this change. We all want to believe we are fair people and we all dislike it when someone is treated unfairly. I had no idea if my value question would work but then I took two gambles, knowing that if either failed this plan was dead in the water.

First, I had warned John in advance that I was going to put him on the spot during the meeting and I told the teachers as much.

"John, do you think Northside can effectively handle two or three more poor students in each classroom?"

John and I had discussed this issue several times and I knew what he had told me privately was, "Yes this can work and I'm ready to help make it happen."

Now, I had to see if he would say this to his staff. John was a star.

"Folks, you know me and you know I won't just say things to please the boss," he said. "I think we can do this and I think we can do a great job at it. This is a chance for us to shift gears and move our school to a new level. Our test scores aren't as high as they should be and our teacher and principal colleagues at Eastside and Westside need our help. We can do this."

Then I took my second gamble. "Okay," I said, "and to prove that I do care what you think about this issue I want you to vote anonymously right now to let me know your thoughts about this important question."

I handed out a simple document to each teacher and asked each one to fill it out, fold it once and stuff it in an envelope I passed out to a teacher in the front row. The form asked a simple question: Do you believe Northside can effectively handle two or three more poverty children in each classroom? Place an "X" next to the appropriate box for Yes, No or Unsure. A comments section was available at the bottom of the form.

"Please fill out this form and don't ask your colleagues their opinions before you fill it out. We want to hear from you on this important question. John and I will count these forms with your teacher union representative. Feel free to write any comments you want on the form. But don't use any identification or any handwriting you think would be identifiable. I'll be sharing a typed summary of these results with the school board."

One teacher asked if the teachers from the other schools voted on this issue.

"No, I don't think it's fair for other teachers to add to your workload and to the difficulties of your job. I'm pretty certain they were all ready to say yes but that would not be fair," I told her.

And then I held my breath.

When we counted the 23 votes (music, art, physical education, special education, librarian, computer teachers also voted in addition to the 16 K-5 classroom teachers) 15 minutes later in John's office, 16 were "yes," six "no" and 1 "unsure."

We were over the first hurdle. There were several excellent teacher comments about the need for high quality training for teachers and patience from the school board and community as they adjusted to the new students and the new expectations.

The parent meetings

When I met with parents, I used the same strategy I used with teachers. First, I met with high school parents followed by middle school parents, Eastside parents, Westside parents and finally Northside parents.

The 20 to 30 parents I met with in each of the first four schools were positive about the improvement program and the magnet school/ parental choice ideas in the plan. They liked the fact that the funding came from within the existing school budget.

Some of the middle school and high school parents who were also Northside parents raised questions about increasing the number of students on free and reduced price lunch at Northside. I encouraged them *to come to that parent meeting and I gave the date, February 25 at Northside Elementary.*

The newspaper reporter attended every one of these meetings and wrote a reasonable and balanced report on the conversations after each meeting including the plan elements, parent concerns and the answers I provided to parents with concerns.

These reports generated multiple letters to the editor from parents around the city including from Northside parents. All but a few of the Northside parent letters were negative and some were very inflammatory.

Letters from parents from other areas of the city contained statements of support and suggestions. The most common suggestion was to somehow implement the improvement/magnet school plan but to exclude Northside from the plan.

This, of course, was not a workable suggestion. The school board members would inevitably send out a blitz of emails after each incendiary Northside parent letter to the editor, and I would do my best to calm them down.

A few parents and a smattering of residents who attended these meetings mentioned concerns about losing bus driver, custodian and food service employee jobs and concerns about the length of the bus rides for special education students.

These comments were primarily expressed by friends and relatives of those who would lose their jobs and appeared to be made so that the commenter could say they tried to help out the person losing their job. In the end these opinions changed few minds.

Several parents had good suggestions. One suggestion from a parent who taught in another school district sounded like I had planted him in the middle school parent group: "Make certain teachers receive training about planning for multiple levels of instruction, about classroom management for students involved in open-ended activities and about how to allow for re-teaching and re-testing so students can improve their grades," he said.

The inevitable question about why we couldn't just add a second grade teacher at Eastside came up in every parent group. After I carefully

*explained the charter school return rate issues four times I was well prac-
ticed with this answer and I could see the parents were getting it.*

*Hiring another teacher would be an expensive solution and we
would be solving this problem with another new teacher we couldn't
afford every fall as the students moved in and out of the charter schools
creating gaps and bubbles in our own classes.*

*Changing elementary school boundaries also wouldn't work as the
charter schools drew students from all over the city and we couldn't
identify in advance the students they'd be accepting or the students
who would boomerang back. The only long-term solution that worked
involved some element of parental choice in the district schools.*

*I knew when I arrived for my meeting with the Northside par-
ents and a few Northside property owners who had no children in
school that it would be a tough meeting. No one said "hello" to me
on the way in, and they sat quietly and attentively as I presented
the information about student achievement, the charter school return
rate issue and the specifics of the improvement/magnet school plan as
it had evolved.*

*Since the information had been in the newspaper several times
starting in mid-January and had generated several negative letters to
the editor from Northside parents and residents I wasn't surprised these
parents were well informed.*

*I spent extra time explaining the school visit process and carefully
identified the parents and teachers who had gone on the visits and what
we had all seen. I ended my presentation with an explanation of the
Northside teacher vote in support of the plan and John Schroeder's comments in support of it.*

When I was finished the comments and questions started.

*School board member Laura Ashton started with a prepared state-
ment: "We agree our schools need to improve their academic performance.
We agree that reducing costs in non-teaching areas, in busing and in special education to provide the funding for the academic improvements we
need makes sense. We agree with all of those parts of this plan but we do
not agree that Northside should become a magnet school.*

"You have said that Northside's test scores are lower than they should be and this plan will make our teachers' jobs even more difficult. We all spent extra to buy or rent homes in this part of Sarandon so our children could attend the best elementary school and what you are proposing will reduce the values of our property, make those extra mortgage and rent payments a waste of money and reduce the quality of our children's education. We will not agree to this part of the plan you have presented."

When Laura finished speaking there was a standing ovation from the parents and residents present. I waited for them to calm down.

"I fully understand the impact of what I am proposing," I said. "However, I also expect Northside to become a great school like the schools we visited. In a great school the best students and the students who are struggling the most are both challenged to the maximum of their potential and encouraged and supported to succeed.

"I am not proposing Northside increase the percentage of students eligible for free or reduced price lunch from 30 percent to 80 percent like it is at Eastside and Westside. I am proposing that your school add two or three students who are eligible for free or reduced price lunch in each classroom. That's five students per grade level or 30 more students for the whole school."

I also asked them to think about what will happen if we didn't do this. The class sizes at Eastside require that we add another second grade teacher immediately. Next year the problem will in all likelihood be at another grade level plus we'll need that extra section at Eastside as those students move up to third grade. When the third charter school comes on line the problem will only worsen.

"If we don't improve our academic results to compete more effectively with the charter schools eventually we will have to close one of our three elementary schools. Right now, we barely have enough total enrollment to justify three elementary schools," I told them. "And what will happen to the class sizes and the poverty student numbers for the two remaining elementary schools?"

The room was quiet until one of the Northside teachers spoke up. "Which school would you close?" she asked.

"We won't be closing any schools this year but another elementary school closure is inevitable in the next few years if we just keep doing what we are doing now," I said. "The school needing the most repairs is Northside, and Northside is not large enough to handle three classes at every grade level. The logical choice for closure would be Northside."

A burly man in his thirties jumped up. "You're not closing this school," he shouted. "This school board will never close this school. Don't you know that four out of the five school board members live in this part of town? We'd tar and feather them if they ever tried to close this school."

I could see the school board members in the crowd looking frightened and nervous. I responded with my most disarming smile.

"Look," I said, "I'm a one-year, interim superintendent doing my best to give you folks your money's worth. If you keep moving down the path you are on you're going to hit a brick wall. It's my job to make you think ahead before the brick wall arrives in your headlights.

"I'm giving you an option that has a chance to work and keep this school open for the long term, to stem the financial tide with the charter schools and to improve your schools' academic performance. You need to think about what I'm proposing because I don't see any other long-term options with a chance to accomplish all of those objectives."

Melissa Grignon tried to help me out: "Mr. Palmer is providing us with an option to improve our schools," she said. "His ideas make sense if you aren't from Sarandon."

Everyone laughed.

"I understand everyone's fears," she said. "But my fear is that if we don't do something dramatic now it will be too late in a couple of years. I know we all don't want to jeopardize Northside.

"For years, Northside has been the only school with a positive reputation. My children went to Northside. I was the PTA president at Northside. But I really believe we have to consider what Mr. Palmer is proposing carefully. If we don't implement this magnet school plan now, I don't see where we go to improve the district down the road."

It was obvious after Melissa finished speaking that she commanded respect in this group. Respect that I as a newcomer couldn't possibly have.

I promised to do my best to listen to everything they said and wrote it down to discuss with the school board the next time we met. The parents and residents stayed for another hour voicing their concerns. I wrote everything down on one of the posters and I saw the reporter in the back of the room scribbling furiously.

At one point one parent became very aggressive. "I don't want my kids in a classroom that's filled with poor students," he said. "The school board has already added too many poor students to our school when they redrew the elementary school boundaries. "

Molly Gaston spoke up. "The students who attend Eastside and Westside are good students," Molly said. "They are not problems and I don't like it when someone speaks about them the way you just did. It's just that we have too many students for the number of teachers and we have too many poor students so that our teachers' jobs are just too difficult. And this charter school return rate problem has just added more of the students who are struggling back into their classes. We need help, and we are asking you folks to help us and ultimately help yourselves."

Molly's respectful demeanor and reputation and her long standing service on the school board ended the overly aggressive comments but failed to win the argument with these parents.

When the smoke cleared it was apparent that Melissa, Molly and I had not convinced any of the most strongly opinionated parents and residents that Northside as a magnet school was a good idea. But I think we had convinced them that if the district didn't do something fairly radical, we were definitely looking at a serious problem in the near future, one that would probably result in an elementary school closing.

They also understood that hiring another second grade teacher at Eastside or implementing a magnet school plan with just Eastside and Westside Elementary schools could not work to solve the swells in enrollment caused by the charter schools' lottery and return rate.

They also understood without some type of successful intervention an elementary school closing would, one way or another, eventually end the "protected demographics" of Northside even if it stayed open. It also became apparent that two of the district's school board members had decided to sit on the sidelines and not take a stand yet in this important discussion despite their previous apparent commitment to the plan.

I called both Mitzy and Terry the next day to see how they saw this issue now that parents' concerns were out in the open publicly.

Mitzy was torn. "I know the magnet school idea is a good idea and I understand it can't work unless Northside becomes a magnet school," she said. "But I was elected to the school board by Northside parents who came out and voted for me in two elections. I promised I wouldn't let the district change Northside by adding more poor students to the school and I don't want to break my promise to those voters."

I told her I understood but that she needed to consider two things. First, the circumstances had changed from when she was elected because of the charter schools. If we didn't do something and the district had to close an elementary school, the demographics for Northside students would be changing dramatically regardless of which school is closed.

"You might be doing more to protect those demographics that parents are concerned about and to keep your promise to those voters by supporting the magnet school plan," I said.

Second, I reminded her that she felt a special allegiance to the Northside parents but that she was now the President of the Sarandon City School District Board of Education and represented all the students, all the parents and all the taxpayers in this city.

"You have to do what's right for the entire school system not just for Northside," I said.

By the time our conversation ended, Mitzy said she would at least think it over, but her lukewarm responses to my encouragement was not a positive sign.

My conversation with Terry was similar but even more discouraging.

"Look, I live in Northside," he said. "These people are my friends. I can't just ignore them and they want no part of Northside being a magnet school. I can't vote for this plan."

I tried to remind him of the values in the plan he had supported for nearly four months from the time of our early November Saturday meetings until this parent meeting in late February.

"I know I am letting you down on this issue, and initially I thought I could support you," he said. "I know you're right, but I can't vote for this plan."

The following Monday I wasn't surprised when I saw that Tonya Harris had made an appointment with me in my office at the end of the day.

After we exchanged greetings, Tonya zeroed in on her reason for being there. "You know the school board is going to split two to three and vote down the magnet school plan unless we do something dramatic to save it," she said. "I have an idea that might get us the support we need for them to approve the plan."

Tonya's plan was simple. The entire city except for the Northside enclave supported the plan. Tonya understood that I had been trying to sell the plan without dividing the city into armed camps that created long lasting bad feelings. I feared those bad feelings would inevitably lead to a crippled leadership team that would for years into the future snipe with each other while their already struggling school district circled the toilet bowl.

Tonya suggested we get all the local powers that supported the magnet school plan to attend the public hearing scheduled in two weeks and have them make the phone calls to school board members in advance saying: "You better support this plan or you won't be re-elected to the school board."

She came with a list of support groups we would need to contact: the active local branch of the NAACP, the local chapter of La Raza, the Chamber of Commerce, my friends at the Rotary Club, the respected local clergy group, the PTA's at four of the district's schools and surprisingly the teachers union.

"You must be kidding," I said. "The teachers union is taking sides on this issue?"

"Well, it took a little arm twisting, but that stunt with the Northside teachers voting in favor of the magnet school plan carried a lot of weight," she said. "That vote means the faculty in all five schools supports the plan. That makes it hard for even the teacher union president to ignore."

I suggested Tonya talk to the folks at the newspaper about her plan and the reasoning for the plan. A meeting with Art Cameron and his education reporter in advance of the public hearing with some leaders from as many of these groups as we could muster would be the best tactic.

Ethically, because I was working for a split school board as I presented this option to the school district, I had to stay out of the advocacy campaign.

"And I will have to tell my school board members that we have met and what you are going to be doing," I told Tonya. "I'll tell them I agree with what you're doing, but I won't step over the line and advocate for the plan's approval with these outside groups unless a majority of them tell me to."

The final piece of the puzzle

Every school district I've ever worked in had employees who were intelligent, had great ideas about how to improve performance or save the school district money and who were totally overlooked by the administrators. Sarandon was no exception.

I had told the school board that our school improvement/magnet school plan would be much more attractive to the public if we could tie it into a school district budget with a zero percent tax increase.

The job cuts for non-teaching jobs was an issue. I had seen this dynamic before. Those job cuts would bring a rash of angry non-teaching union members and their friends and relatives to the polls to vote down the district budget in May.

The only palatable option to overcome this negative energy was a zero percent tax increase. The problem was, according to my math, we were about $350,000 short of that zero percent increase. Our identified budget cuts and expected expenditures from the improvement plan left us needing to find additional cuts to make up that $350,000.

In Sarandon, the school district budget was $40 million. Half of this $40 million came from state aid and the other half ($20 million) *came from local property taxes. This means that to raise an additional $200,000 in property taxes the school board would have to raise the property tax rate one percent. To get $350,000 we needed we'd have to raise property taxes 1.75 percent.*

In a normal year 1.75 percent is a good number. With all the changes planned for the school programs and the non-teaching job losses we'd be fighting this year a 1.75 percent school tax increase wouldn't work.

I had solved several small problems with our business official Marty Garrison throughout my year in Sarandon. He had always impressed me with his quick wit, his ability to soften the atmosphere and generate smiles with intelligent and thoughtful puns and his clean easily explained budget numbers.

In early December when we met to discuss our improvement plan, we identified the $350,000 gap in question. Marty had computed the rollover cost of keeping our existing budget with the new contractual required salaries and best estimates on benefit costs and all other known adjustments.

On a separate single page summary, so it would be easier to explain to the school board and the public, Marty had then added the new costs and savings from our plan with all the details about benefit costs and revenue expectations.

At school board meetings Marty kept his head down and said very little. He played the survivor role in a politically charged environment and who could blame him. I felt Marty was potentially one of those employees who had some great ideas and who unfortunately all too often was overlooked.

"Look Marty, you've been in this district eight years," I said as our meeting ended. "You're obviously smart and you know where the money goes. What's the easiest way for the district to come up with $350,000 to get us to a zero percent tax increase this year? And, don't worry, I won't throw you under the bus and blame it on you. I'm the interim here. I'll take any heat that comes our way."

Marty hesitated. "I told your predecessor that we had significant savings potential in employee health insurance, but he was afraid to make a change given the political climate so the idea went nowhere," he said.

"Tell me more," I said.

Marty continued. "Our district is part of a consortium that buys health insurance with a consulting group and we have been part of that group for 10-plus years. A few years ago some members of the group found out that the consultants were taking fees from the insurance companies in addition to the fees we paid them to negotiate for us."

I was incredulous. "The consultants were taking fees from both sides in the negotiations?" I said.

Marty shook his head. "I know it sounds crazy but yes that's what they are doing," he said.

It was my turn to shake my head. "The district is still using those consultants?" I asked, incredulously.

Marty nodded, yes. "The school board talked about switching to a new consultant group after I spoke to the superintendent two years ago, but when the school board discussed the issue in public the present consultant group sent a representative to talk with them and he turned out to be a personal friend of school board member Terry Hansen.

"The superintendent didn't want to push the issue given the fact that Terry already had concerns about his job performance and they had argued publicly over other issues.

"We also decided not to join a new group of school districts that's doing better with drug prices by pursuing discounts with the drug companies," he said.

"Why didn't we join that group? That sounds like a no brainer," I said.

"At the time the new drug purchasing group was looking for members the superintendent was just trying to keep his job, and we weren't really doing anything new. We were all just doing our best to survive."

"Are these two programs both creating savings as they predicted?" I asked.

"If our district changes health insurance consultants and drug purchasing groups as the other school districts have, these two items together could save the district more than the $350,000 we need."

I asked him to gather the information together in a single page handout we could give the school board at the next meeting and discuss *in public. "Be sure to list by name the districts that are involved in each program and their projected savings at this time," I said.*

We discussed this at the next school board meeting and the school board approved this last piece of savings to get our budget to a zero percent tax increase.

Publicly, I made a point of taking the "blame" for promoting the switch in health insurance consultants. Privately, I told the school board in executive session that Marty should receive a pay raise and a new title or they would probably lose him to another school district. I made this recommendation without telling the school board that Marty had given me the key information about the health insurance consultant.

But Terry Hansen was having none of it. "These administrators already make too much. We can replace Marty if we need to," Terry said. He was obviously upset at the change in health insurance consultants and blamed Marty despite my best efforts to protect him.

I did my best to smooth things over with Terry, but I could tell he was not pleased with me or with Marty despite the critical cost savings.

The public hearing

The public hearing was raucous. More than 450 parents, residents and community leaders showed up for the meeting along with three Syracuse's television news crews, our local newspaper and reporters from two bigger newspapers from Syracuse.

After I did my well-rehearsed PowerPoint presentation and answered the same set of questions from the floor about just adding a teacher at Eastside and how we were going to pay for all these academic improvements, the school board opened the meeting up for public comments, two minutes maximum per speaker. We'd alternate between the two microphones placed in the aisles of the auditorium. These guidelines had been published in advance in the newspaper when the hearing was announced.

As soon as this public input process began lines of ten to 15 speakers formed at each microphone and the school board's timekeeper was charged with ringing a two-minute bell.

Some of the speakers were professional and read carefully written notes and shared copies with school board members. Others were parents who were very nervous first time public speakers who told heartfelt stories about their children. Some were employees of the school district and others former employees who had retired from the school district.

Representatives from all the groups Tonya Harris had contacted made strong statements in support of the plan including the teacher union president who said (unhelpfully) that the community had not listened to the teachers about their needs in the past and had better listen now and approve this plan.

He was, of course, booed. The television cameras recorded lots of great video and they completed several follow-up interviews with speakers in the hall outside the auditorium.

The Northside parents were not intimidated by the news crews or by the community groups that favored the plan. They had planned well for the meeting by picking 24 well prepared parents and residents each with slightly different arguments to make in their two minutes at the microphone.

The Northside parents had also recruited three retired teachers from the school to support their position and remind the people present that they had taught many of them in their classrooms. The three retired teachers spoke as a trio and said the approval of this plan would be the end of Northside Elementary School as they knew it.

The public comments went on for two hours and twenty minutes while the school board and I faced the audience and the speakers. The television cameras panned back and forth from the speakers to us as the reporters furiously scribbled notes. Many of the speaker comments were personal and critical and the majority of the criticisms were directed at me.

These critical comments came despite repeated admonitions from Mitzy to refrain from making personally critical comments about individuals.

Some of the comments were:

- *"Mr. Palmer, how could you, an outsider, come to our city and propose this divisive idea? Why didn't you respect the wishes of the community, the parents and the school board and drop this plan months ago?"*
- *"Mr. Palmer, why do you insist on eliminating all these jobs? Don't you know these people have families to take care of?"*
- *"Mr. Palmer, why can't you see that the simple solution is just to add another teacher at Eastside?"*

Some of the personal negative comments were more like threats and were directed at the school board members.

- *"Melissa, you are a Northside parent. How can you possibly support this plan?"*
- *"Terry, you promised us you'd make certain this school board didn't put more students from Eastside and Westside into our school. You better keep your promise."*
- *"Mitzy you told me before you ran for the school board that you'd pull your son Ryan out of Northside and put him in a private school if the poverty numbers continued to grow. What are you doing now?"*

When the public comments ended, each of five school board members made public statements. They thanked the public for coming out to voice their views on this important topic.

Laura Ashton reviewed and supported the arguments made by her Northside parent friends. "Northside should remain a neighborhood school and not become a magnet school, but the other aspects of this plan should be approved," Laura said.

Melissa Grignon gave an impassioned plea to support the plan and reminded Northside parents that good people who want similar things can disagree about the best way to achieve those goals without becoming enemies.

Molly Gaston also supported the plan and said she was proud to see all the groups coming together to support it at this crucial time, and she thanked each group individually.

"You folks know me and you know I would never do anything to hurt ANY child," she said. "I strongly believe that if we implement this plan properly it will help all the children in Sarandon, including the children now at Northside Elementary."

When Molly finished speaking there was a notable pause...who would speak next? It was easy to see that Mitzy Holland and Terry Hansen were reluctant to speak. Neither wanted to offend groups of people who had spoken passionately on both sides of this question. I was certain both were not thinking kind thoughts about me as they sat there pondering what they would say. After all, I was the person who had put this bullseye on their backs and forced them make a difficult decision.

Finally, Terry spoke up. "I understand the importance of what we are discussing tonight. I've thought about it long and hard. All of the speakers' comments tonight made me think even more. But in the end I am going to keep my promise to the voters who put me on the school board. I can support all aspects of this plan except making Northside a magnet school. I'm with Laura. Northside should remain a neighborhood school."

Mitzy was sitting next to me. I could see her hands were shaking. It was 10:30 p.m. and when she spoke her voice cracked.

"There are great points made by all the speakers here tonight and I want to consider them carefully before I make up my mind how to vote," she said. "The school board has set a date of April 7 to adopt a budget and vote on the school improvement/magnet school plan. I'll use the next three weeks to make up my mind which way I'll vote. Thank you again to everyone for their input here tonight. Meeting is adjourned."

The school board vote

Of course, Mitzy had set herself up as a target for the three weeks between the public hearing and the school board vote on the plan. Every group that had spoken at the hearing had representatives meet with Mitzy to lobby their views privately and request her vote.

She also received phone calls every day from Northside neighbors and parents lobbying against the plan and reminding her of her promises to them when she ran for the school board. Some school board members would have reveled in this much attention, but I knew Mitzy well enough to know she did not.

I was part of the school district email group that included the school board so I saw the exchanges between school board members about the plan. The lobbying grew more heated with every passing day.

I thought more than once that I had been wrong to acquiesce to Tanya Harris' strategy of bringing in the community groups to pressure the school board for the plan's passage. We might win the battle to gain the plan's approval and lose the long-term school district leadership struggle by creating a permanently divided school board.

Tough decisions don't necessarily split a school board permanently, but persistent acrimonious communication that becomes disrespectful will create a long-term split and I could see that pattern developing in the emails.

When the day of the vote came, Mitzy looked tired. I could tell she was straining not to lose her composure with a public meltdown. Terry Hansen, who had always been a positive factor on the school board with his humor and his insight, had become aggressively negative toward Mitzy, pushing her closer to the edge.

His email comments and the comments under his breath at the school board table made it clear he would see Mitzy's voting in support of the plan as an unforgivable act of disloyalty to the Northside parents they both represented.

The school board met in the high school auditorium with a smaller crowd of about 200 residents and parents. I saw Harry Kubiak in the back of the room sitting with Kim Neely. Karen Allington sat next to Cora Jenkins and Tim O'Grady. Tanya Harris sat in the front row next to the president of the local NAACP. The television cameras and reporters who had covered the public hearing were all in attendance.

The vote on the improvement plan was the first item on the agenda. Once the vote on the improvement/magnet school plan was made as motion, which was read aloud by the school board clerk, Laura Ashton immediately moved, as expected, to amend the plan so that Northside Elementary School would remain a neighborhood school and not become a magnet school.

After a one or two sentence comment from the four committed school board members on this amendment with Laura and Terry supporting the amendment and Molly and Melissa opposing it, it was apparent that they would split their votes, two to two. Mitzy, as expected, would be the tie breaking vote.

Mitzy, as always, sat next to me at the school board table. She slowly took out a sheet of paper from a folder with some carefully printed notes and read a statement.

"For the past several months since the school board began discussing the magnet school plan I have wrestled with two important values I hold very dear and two competing visions about what is best for the school district," she said. "The details of this plan require that Northside become a magnet school or the plan won't work.

"Eastside and Westside are overcrowded and both have high percentages of poor students. A magnet school plan that excludes Northside isn't a magnet school plan. A magnet school plan would fill Northside's vacant classroom slots and move us a little closer to balancing the number of poverty students in each classroom and school.

"The plan Mr. Palmer has created with input from parents, teachers and community members is an excellent compromise that is widely supported by the community. I believe this plan would improve the results for all the students in Sarandon's schools, including the students at Northside.

"I'm also convinced," she said, "that the charter schools have made it imperative that we act now or our district's future opportunities for improvement will be lost forever.

"However, if Northside becomes a magnet school and accepts the 30 additional disadvantaged students the plan requires, I will be breaking a promise I made to the Northside parents who helped elect me to the school board. I told them I would never support moving more disadvantaged students into their school.

"So, there are the competing values: What I believe is best for the whole school district and all the children in our schools and keeping my promise to the Northside parents who elected me to the school board. Both are important values.

"In the end I have decided to keep my promise to my friends and neighbors and vote against the plan as it stands and for the proposed amendment to the plan that excludes Northside Elementary School."

The crowd erupted with cheers and applause. The television cameras panned to the crowd and back to Mitzy. I saw looks of consternation from the administrators and head shaking from Tanya Harris and the NAACP President in the first row. It was only then that I realized Mitzy had more to say and was waiting for the crowd noise to abate.

"Do I hear a motion to call a vote on the amendment proposed by Laura Ashton?" she said.

"I so move," Terry said.

Mitzy called the vote and it passed three to two with Melissa and Molly voting against the amendment.

"The amendment passes," Mitzy said.

"Do I hear a motion to call the question?" Mitzy asked.

"I move we call the question," Terry said.

"The question: Should we approve the plan as amended has been called," Mitzy said. "All those in favor of implementing the school improvement/magnet school plan with magnet schools at Eastside and Westside Elementary and a neighborhood school at Northside Elementary say aye."

Three board members, Ashton, Hansen and Holland in unison said, "Aye."

"And those opposed?" Mitzy said.

"Nay," said Grignon and Gaston.

"The ayes have it and the plan is approved as amended," Mitzy said.

The board's work was again interrupted by loud cheers, whistles and applause from the Northside parents and their supporters. Then I again noticed Mitzy was waiting for quiet so she could speak and, *despite my feelings, I couldn't help but see Mitzy was feeling awful about what had just happened.*

Then she spoke up again. "I am keeping my promise with this vote but I am giving Mr. Palmer a letter resigning my position on the school board at the end of the meeting tonight," she said.

The room was still.

"I am resigning because I believe that by keeping my promise to the Northside parents I am not doing my job as a school board member, and this school board needs five members who do their jobs," she said.

By the time she finished Mitzy was barely speaking above a whisper and tears were pouring down her face. I felt bad for her despite the fact that I was disappointed with the way the vote had gone. I don't think any of us saw how difficult this choice had been for her.

Terry Hansen, who I suspected was feeling guilty for his barbed comments over the previous few weeks, immediately made a motion that the school board take a recess for 15 minutes, and it was approved in seconds.

The school board members scattered and Tonya Harris cornered me immediately to ask what Mitzy's actions meant. Was the plan dead? Would Mitzy be replaced immediately? Could we potentially get someone to take Mitzy's place who would support the plan?

As I was telling her I didn't know what would happen, three television reporters approached me with microphones in hand and cameramen behind them. They wanted a comment and since Mitzy had ducked into the women's bathroom, they approached me.

I have learned from difficult experiences that ducking news reporters' tough questions always leads to bad news so I did my best to answer.

"No, I don't know what Mitzy's resignation meant for the plan," I told them. "Yes, the school board had decided that Northside would remain a neighborhood school and would not become a magnet school. No, I did not know how the school board expects to implement a magnet school plan without Northside in the mix."

I told them clarification would come following the break.

As I expected the television news reporters and their camera crews left the scene before the break ended to dash back to Syracuse and put what they had recorded into the clips that would be on the 11 o'clock news.

When the break ended, Mitzy was not in her seat and her purse was gone. She had left the scene. About two-thirds of the crowd had also left. The four remaining school board members and I would have to sort out the mess that remained.

Melissa Grignon, the school board vice president, turned to me.

"Okay, Lonnie, what do we do now?" she asked.

"I need the school board members who approved the amendment to our plan to clarify for me their intent with this change," I said. "We've been talking about a lottery to give parents a choice among the elementary schools. The lottery was supposed to come only after all of the students in each school's neighborhood had made their school choices.

"Lottery students would only be accepted if their acceptance moved the schoolwide percentage of free and reduced price lunch students closer to 40 percent and their addition to the school they picked in the lottery did not exceed the class size goals of 24 students per class." I explained.

"How will that work if Eastside and Westside are the only ones in the plan? They have similar poverty numbers and class sizes?"

"First, it means that Sarandon students get to go to their neighborhood school if they want to," Terry said.

This comment brought applause from the remaining Northside parent audience members.

"For the students who enter the lottery, which tells us those parents want their children to change schools, if moving those students from Eastside to Westside helps to balance classes we grant their request. Simple as that," he said.

"What will make them want to make that request?" I asked.

"Under this improvement plan all three elementary schools are going to offer unique themes like Math, Science and Technology or the Visual and Performing Arts. These differences will provide the incentives required," Terry said.

"I know the intent here; I'm just not certain it will work. What if Eastside has second grade classes of 29 and 30 and Westside has classes of 24, 24 and 25"" Do we move students from Eastside to Westside until we have a balance?"

"Yes," Terry said.

"We can certainly try it to see if we get the lottery applicants we need to deal with the charter school return rate and class size bubbles the charter school program has created in our schools." I said. "But I don't think this will do what we need from a class size balancing perspective. There is not enough room in this equation with Northside removed from the mix," I said.

I asked the school district's attorney who had joined us for this important meeting how we should go about filling Mitzy's spot on the school board. She replied using the microphone so everyone in the auditorium could hear.

"Petitions signed by at least 100 eligible voters supporting the candidacy of prospective school board members are due in the school board clerk's office by April 26," she said. "Given the number of reporters in the room this vacancy will be publicized, but the district will also need to run a formal advertisement in the newspaper."

The school board finished the meeting with an approval of the school district budget for a May public vote. The budget included the projected zero percent tax increase, all the savings and expenses in our improvement plan plus extra savings from employee health insurance and employee drug coverage.

I could see groups of meeting attendees collecting in areas of the auditorium, discussing how to proceed given the school board's actions and Mitzy's resignation.

The magnet school portion of the improvement plan had failed to include Northside, and I knew what was next.

The following morning when I arrived in my office at 7:30 a.m. the phone was ringing and with Betty not yet at her desk, I answered. It was Harry Kubiak.

"Tough loss last night," he said. "As you probably expected I've decided to withdraw my name as an applicant for the lead teacher job at Westside with Cora Jenkins. I'm sorry but I was expecting you'd have a true magnet school program.

"Without Northside in the mix it's not a real magnet program. And as you probably also expected. Kim Neely offered me a raise of $15,000 to stay where I am. I know you can't give me that kind of salary. I'm sorry. It was a great idea; it just didn't work out."

"Harry you're a great teacher and you have a wonderful little school. Kim Neely is lucky to have you as a lead teacher. I understand completely. Good luck to you in the future," I said and hung up the phone.

Within three minutes the phone rang again and it was Cora Jenkins.

"Lonnie, I'm sorry this didn't work out the way we planned. I still think we had some great ideas. As you probably anticipated Karen Allington has decided she wants to stay here and be my lead teacher. Tim O'Grady was so negative when we talked after the school board vote last night that he scared her off. I have no idea who will be willing to work with him as a lead teacher. He's such a bear to work with.

"I'm certain you understand that forcing Karen to work with Tim would create a mess. I have no suggestions for you only bad news which you don't need right now."

I thanked Cora for the information and made a note to stop by Eastside to talk with Tim O'Grady. I had no idea how to patch this mess. When I left the district at the end of June there was still no solution.

During the next two weeks, three unknown school board candidates emerged who had hopes of either claiming Mitzy's vacant seat or unseating Melissa Grignon who was running for re-election.

Two of the four candidates were Northside parents who were running to protect the victory Mitzy had given them and to try to unseat Melissa. Melissa and a member of the NAACP who had the backing by the groups that had come out to speak in support of the magnet school plan before the school board vote were the other two candidates.

My worst nightmare had come true. I would finish my work in the school district in June and leave a school board with a true long-term split.

The budget vote passed in May and Melissa Grignon was re-elected to the school board along with one of the two Northside parents who had tried to unseat her and claim Mitzy's spot on the board.

This didn't surprise me. While the magnet school plan with Northside as a magnet school had support throughout the community, the Northside parent turnout for the vote was very high and turnout elsewhere in the city was too low.

The new school board would have a true three to two split and the email exchanges I saw in May and June and the public and private comments I heard at my two remaining school board meetings after the budget vote indicated it would be a very contentious school board.

With my term in the district ending June 30th the school board decided to hire another interim superintendent because the pool of applicants was still weak. The board selected as their new interim superintendent an experienced colleague I knew who had a reputation from four previous interim school superintendent positions as someone who minds the store and keeps things moving smoothly but creates little change or improvement. They call them babysitters.

When a letter arrived from the New York State Education Department during the first week in June saying that a third elementary charter school had been approved for Sarandon, I was not surprised. I discussed the letter with the school board and the newspaper ran an editorial saying Sarandon had more than its share of charter schools. But the editorial would do little to change the situation now or in the future.

The only good news from this time was notification to the school district that our collaborative grant application to the Pew Charitable Trust for $12 million to fund an expanded pre-school program for half of Sarandon's three- and four-year-old children and a home visit *program for half of the pre-school children from birth to age 3 had been approved.*

Our partners from Syracuse University came to my last school board meeting in June to celebrate the program's kickoff with the three women who came to me with this idea earlier in the school year.

Of course, the article in the newspaper prominently mentioned the Northside parents' comments that this program would require the district to house 150 three- and four-year-old children at the three existing elementary schools in the district and in the process put 10 more classrooms to use, thus justifying keeping Northside and the other two elementary schools open for several more years. They were right to a degree. But once the newest charter opened and was at full enrollment their argument would no longer be valid.

I called Mitzy Holland's home five times during my last three months in Sarandon and left a message each time. She never returned my call.

When I called the third time I left a message. "I'm sorry this didn't work out," I said, "and that you were caught in the middle. I fully understand the decision you had to make and I'll always remember you as a dedicated and insightful school board member. Good luck to you, Mitzy."

Marty Garrison came to me in late May to say that he had applied for the position of Assistant Superintendent for Business in the nearby and much larger school district in Liverpool, NY. I gave him a very positive recommendation in a letter and in a phone conversation with the Liverpool superintendent. On June 10 he accepted the Liverpool district's offer which included an $18,000 yearly pay increase.

His last day in Sarandon coincided with mine on June 30th. I helped the district find a retiree who agreed to work as an interim business official until a real search for Marty's replacement was completed.

My last official act in Sarandon was to attend a final Rotary Club luncheon meeting where I was given an award for my service to the community in my one year as interim superintendent. The award mentioned the Pew Charitable Trust grant.

As I sipped on my club soda and made small talk, the Syracuse University education department professor who became one of the district's partners for the Pew Charitable trust grant found me.

"I thought for a minute that you might actually pull that magnet school idea off, but those Northside parents were just too tough," he said.

I grimaced and nodded.

"Of course John Schroeder didn't do you any favors. He was out there telling everyone to make certain that plan failed. I heard him right here in this restaurant say, 'I only have three more years to retirement; I'll never let them make Northside a magnet school or let them send me a special education class of students that will make my job more difficult. Forget it. This plan will never fly.' I was going to call you and tell you about him but I just didn't feel that was my job."

I ducked out of the luncheon as soon as I could and during my final two-hour ride home to Albany, I thought about the strange events of this past year in Sarandon. Maybe I never should have pushed the magnet school idea.

Maybe I shouldn't have gotten into a conflict with Terry Hansen with Marty's suggestions to reduce health insurance costs. If I had anticipated John Schroeder's deception, I could have headed off the worst of his influence in the final decision. Maybe I shouldn't have pushed any of the school choice part of the improvement plan on these folks. It was just too much for this community to handle given its history.

I believed the idea of using teacher leaders to supplement the weak principal group was a good improvement strategy. I also believed in my heart that I had helped them create a plan that used their money more wisely in ways that had the best chance to improve instruction, test results and future opportunities for the children of Sarandon.

I was certain I had done all I could to involve people in the decision-making process during the year, but in the end the plan had come up short. The Northside parents' resistance to having more disadvantaged students in their school was too strong. I wish I could say it wasn't race related.

The plan as it was finally approved would be insufficient to meet Sarandon's needs for the long term. It was a sad end to a long year.

SO IS SCHOOL CHOICE A GOOD IDEA OR A BAD IDEA?

School choice, in my experience, is a good idea that can be easily hijacked and turned into a bad idea. Anyone who visits Harry Kubiak's school in Sarandon, any effective KIPP charter school or any of the many very "successful" charter schools in New York City, New Orleans, Houston, Newark or Washington, D.C., and many other urban settings can see that the children in these schools are motivated and working hard.

The test scores for stellar choice programs also indicate academic success that apparently outshines students in regular public school districts where the choice and charter schools exist. Of course, a primary part of their test result success is in many cases due to their exclusion of special education students and their return to district schools of students with disciplinary, attendance and academic problems.

The magnet school program in Albany where I was the school superintendent when New York State's first charter school opened and other magnet school programs in cities around the U.S. offer an excellent non-invasive parental choice option for parents.

Effective magnet schools (or properly structured district run charter schools) select students by lottery, emphasize an instructional theme or approach (math, science, technology, Montessori education, social justice, visual arts, etc.), take their share of special education students, spend roughly the same amount per pupil except for additional grant funding that is outside the regular school budget, run on the same school day and school year schedules as the district's neighborhood schools and in general provide the same level of services as the regular neighborhood schools.

Parents and students who are committed and feel a special allegiance to a magnet (or district run charter) school by choice will do more to succeed in that school. School choice works well when implemented properly. Up until now, that has not been the case.

STUDENT TRANSIENCY AND SCHOOL CHOICE

Choice schools also have a built-in educational advantage that is often overlooked – reduced student transiency. When poverty strikes its body blows – a father loses his job, a mother goes to jail a grandmother gets sick – children frequently end up moving from a low rent apartment to a lower rent apartment elsewhere in the city.

Too frequently with neighborhood schools this necessitates a change of schools. Regardless of where a student lives in the city students, who attend magnet schools or district run charter schools keep attending that school; they just travel on a different bus.

Neighborhood schools in general don't work that way. In Albany, we offered to bus neighborhood children who had been forced to move back to their old neighborhood school, but their families seldom took us up on our offer. Student transiency has notable negative impacts on student achievement in school.[cxxxviii]

A district-wide charter/magnet/school choice system like that envisioned and partially implemented in New Orleans has the potential to capture the benefits of parental school choice without the negative impacts of the rogue, invasive species charter school choice.

But it costs more to operate choice schools: increased student transportation costs; extra supplies, materials and curriculum development; extra planning time and training for teachers and more administrative oversight.

To be a true school choice program, a school has to be special in some meaningful way and special costs money for field trips, extra computers and all the other extras, but the cost can be more than the investment is worth.

Many, but not all, of the strong charter school programs also have problems with high return rates for students who struggle with their more challenging academic, behavioral or school attendance expectations. Many charters, but not all, do not accept special education students and English language learners. Most of the academic performance comparisons between charter schools and traditional public schools fail to accurately take these facts into account.[cxxxix]

None of the comparisons of student academic performance between charter schools and district schools that I could view online took into account the fact that students who spent some of their school time in both the charter schools and the district schools should be counted as partial students in the academic results of both sets of schools.

And the districts that are home to charter schools are in many states facing undue financial pressures because the costs of adding a charter school in most cases can't be fully offset by closing a regular public school in the host district. The state funding formulas for charter schools in general do not take into account the fact that the vast majority of the high cost students and high cost teachers remain in the regular public schools and the low cost students and low cost teachers go to the charter schools.

Even with these built in advantages, the failure rate for charter schools nationally is high.[cxl]

In the region near Albany, NY, where I was superintendent, five of 12 approved charter schools failed for academic or financial reasons within ten years of opening.[cxli] That's a lot of academic failure, wasted public money and unnecessary disruption to children's lives that can have permanent negative consequences.

Many people who have talked to me about charter schools assume they're seen positively by the local school district's taxpayers. In Albany we had our taxpayers vote on whether they wanted more charter schools. Our attorney advised us not to do this because the vote would be 'advisory' since these taxpayers had no control over whether the New York State Education Department or the SUNY Charter School Institute (CSI) approved additional charter schools for our community, but we put it up to vote anyway.

The taxpayers voted overwhelmingly – "NO." They knew their tax bills were increasing at an alarming rate and one of the primary causes was charter schools. They also knew all about the educational and financial failures at New Covenant and other Albany charter schools and they wanted no more. But that did not stop the New York State Education Department and Charter School Institute from approving more Albany charter schools. And in Albany and nationally the charter school failures and problems are mounting.[cxlii]

How to make school choice work.

So how can school choice work to take advantage of its obvious strengths and successes and how can we use school competition to help all the students in the district and the charter and magnet schools? I see two viable options. Viable option No. 1 requires adopting a medical axiom for education: primum non nocere, first do no harm.

I understand why charter school supporters want to punish the public educators who refuse to change, who block and stifle innovation, who have produced abysmal academic results for their students and who make charter school or magnet school initiation a complicated mess. I want to punish these folks, too. But punishment is a bad business plan and a bad reason to start a charter or magnet school. It is also guaranteed to violate the axiom primum non nocere.

Elon Musk, the creator of the innovative Tesla electric car, did not develop Tesla to punish the GM executives who allowed GM to become a charity case for the federal government.

To my knowledge he never said: "If Tesla hurts Ford, that's even better."

Put aside your desire to use school choice as a way to punish the public schools that resist necessary and important change. Instead, let's collaborate to create the best set of school choice options. We can punish these folks in other ways and, as you'll see below, I have some good ideas on tactics that might work better for this necessary punishment and actually advance our mutual school choice principles.

When charter schools are thrust upon public school districts without the district's input or involvement, it skews the "competition." The incentives for the charter schools favor niche marketing, excluding special education and English language learners and produces high student return rates and skewed test data.

These strategies also tend to create a financial windfall for the charter schools, which is worse in states where the sharing of resources puts undo pressures on public school district budgets. With many for profit charter school programs now marketing their wares the latter issue is not a small one.

Using the corporate analogy, would Honda spinoff a new product line as an independent company that would "compete" with Honda by taking away customers, reducing profits and creating public relations issues for Honda? Would we expect Honda's spin off to take the "sweet spot" customers away from Honda leaving Honda with fewer high end more profitable customers?

Probably not. But Honda might spin off a new product line that remained a part of the corporate structure with enough independence to ensure innovation and creativity without doing harm to the parent company (see Acura).

Knowing when and how to create spinoffs that foster innovation without damaging the parent corporation is critical to corporate leadership success. We would never think of telling Honda (or the local hospital or fire department or the U.S. Army) that we're going to introduce a competitor that they would fund so that we could create "competition" that would make them improve. And we shouldn't be taking this approach with our schools.

The belief behind charter schools is that urban public school districts, their superintendents and their school boards are not innovative enough or entrepreneurial enough to initiate truly creative and successful school choice options for parents and students. In truth some urban public school district's leadership teams fully deserve that characterization, as they work assiduously to protect their own power and their existing failed systems.

However, other public school leadership teams would welcome the opportunity to create charter schools and magnet schools and implement a wide range of creative and successful parental school choice options. The school choice successes in New Orleans, Washington D.C.[cxliii], Houston and Newark clearly reflect this possibility.

These school choice options initiated by the school district's leadership team have none of the incentives for niche marketing: excluding special education or English language learners, creating high return rates or massaging the test data for public relations purposes. They also have no incentives to steer additional unwarranted monies away from the local neighborhood schools to the choice schools.

A vital school choice program run by the host urban school district is an essential part of any effective educational improvement plan. However, my experience has taught me that to work effectively, school choice plans would require a significant change in educator tenure and seniority laws in most states in order to be effective.

When charter schools started popping up in Albany, NY, where I was superintendent, I investigated the possibility of a charter school run by the district. We already had a successful magnet school parent choice plan in place. The charter school idea provided additional options for parent choices.

However, we never initiated any charter schools for two reasons:

1. The New York State law that created charter schools required the charter schools to have a separate school board and administration. They could not be part of our school system – unlike Honda's spinoff.

2. The first choice the independent charter school board would have is which teachers and principals from the school district they would take and which ones would they would hire new from outside the district?

This means if our school district initiated charter schools, we would have faced all the problems that come with an invasive species.

If a charter took over one of our schools and the leadership of the new charter school told me, "We don't want these 25 teachers or this principal. We'll hire our own." what would I do with the 25 teachers and the principal?

The attorneys who worked for our school district told me that seniority rules and laws would require us to lay off the 25 least senior teachers and the least senior principal in the district. Those 25 teachers and that principal were some of our best employees. The idea of creating district charter schools won't work with existing tenure and seniority laws, and this problem is not unique to Albany or New York State. (Read all about it in Dale Russakoff's excellent book "The Prize: Who's in Charge of America's Schools?")

When it comes to school choice, the only way to make it work is to give the regular public school district the same exceptions to regulations and laws that have been offered to the rogue invasive-species charter schools.

Any school established by an organization outside the school district is not going to work – whether it's a private company or a group of individuals – because the incentive is to exclude students who are difficult or expensive to educate.

The charter school law changes required to make charter school choice work for school districts in New York State are relatively simple to explain and politically difficult to achieve.

- Charter schools initiated by the school district need to be run by the school district's administration and school board.
- Any district initiating one or more charter schools should be able to lay off underperforming teachers who have failed to fully and effectively complete performance improvement plans. (The number of layoffs can only equal the number of teachers displaced due to the initiation of a charter school with any remaining required layoffs coming from seniority lists.)

The political situation is difficult because the changes I propose will take power away from those who want to use school choice to punish failing urban public school districts (mostly conservatives and Republicans) and because the teacher unions (mostly liberals and Democrats) won't support any plan that allows school districts to lay off more senior teachers even those with performance problems.

But there might be a way to achieve a political compromise. Since what I am proposing has elements that are disliked by folks at both ends of the political spectrum it might be acceptable if it also contained multiple elements both sides desire.

By increasing school choice opportunities my proposal would be something both liberals and conservatives would support. In addition, if this change were limited to those school districts with abysmal academic performance and came with numerical limits on the percentages of teachers who could be negatively impacted based on how bad the test scores were, it might find a way to obtain legislative approval.

I can hear the charter school proponents, "Yeah, sure, allow the monopoly of public school districts to remain undisturbed. What you're talking about is not going to change public education. Where's the punishment you talked about in this idea?"

Here's how the negative incentives I envision would work. A district performing well below the projected performance line (see School District A below) would be given three years to show marked improvement (above or near the projected performance line) or the school board, superintendent and any assistant superintendents in the district would be replaced by a team appointed by the state education department.

This team would run the school district for three years. The projected performance line gives school districts a realistic and achievable performance target similar school districts are already achieving.

(Note: Data in scatterplot graph modified by adding mythical school district A to illustrate the point.

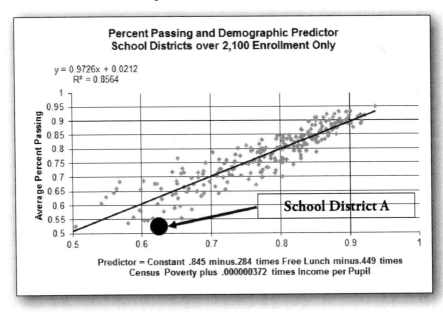

Percent Passing and Demographic Predictor
School Districts over 2,100 Enrollment Only

$y = 0.9726x + 0.0212$
$R^2 = 0.8564$

Predictor = Constant .845 minus.284 times Free Lunch minus.449 times Census Poverty plus .000000372 times Income per Pupil

In the corporate world when a business underperforms the CEO, top management and the Board of Directors is replaced. When a corporation hits rock bottom it is placed in receivership and run by a court appointee.

To my knowledge no one with recognized business leadership training or skills has ever advocated that struggling businesses give some of their revenue to start-up competitors so the business that is struggling will be forced to improve its performance.

But what about the monopoly of public education? Don't we have to do something to break it up?

Public education provides education to ALL children. Siphoning off a few children for some exclusive educational treatment can't be done without creating incentives to siphon off the "right" kids. Creating financial and public relations incentives that might help a few children at the expense of many more students is not the answer.

* The second viable option for school choice is also relatively simple to explain but politically hard to accomplish. We all understand that poverty makes teachers' jobs more difficult. The more disadvantaged children in a classroom the more difficult the teacher's job becomes. The vast majority of the existing charter schools in the U.S. continue the growing pattern of school segregation we see today.[cxliv]

The problems children in poverty face don't stop when they exit the school's doors. Most urban and many rural children in poverty leave school and return to chaotic homes in high crime neighborhoods with inadequate local support services.

Their schools are significantly overburdened and so are their community mental health resources, medical support services, low cost effective child care services, city and village government employees and their police and fire fighter support.

These children and their parents and caregivers are struggling daily to survive. Meanwhile in suburban neighborhoods a few miles away the biggest problems are higher tax bills, late snow removal and street lights that need repair.

Instead of giving poverty parents the choice of an unproven rogue, invasive-species charter school or a failing neighborhood school, why don't we let them choose a successful suburban school nearby?[cxlv] How? By giving them a check that subsidizes part of their rent (beyond present Section 8 housing rental subsidies) from the time the children's mother/primary caregiver is pregnant until the last child has graduated from high school.

A $600 per month payment made out to a rental agency to reduce potential misuse of funds would be enough to give many poverty families the help they need to afford an apartment in the suburbs while their children are infants or are just starting in school.

A $600 per month rental subsidy is $7,200 per year per child (obviously families with multiple children would need $200 or $300 more per month).

If we look realistically at the cost of an effective school choice program (charters or lottery magnet schools) with specialized curriculums, student transportation inefficiencies, extra computers and field trips, extra teacher training and greater administrative costs the total yearly per pupil costs are in the same ball park.

And the rent subsidies have the advantage of placing the children in safer more stable neighborhoods where they are less likely to face peer pressures that might push them towards drugs, crime or early pregnancy. True these problems exist in suburban neighborhoods but on a much smaller scale.[cxlvi]

School districts that have fewer than 30 percent free or reduced price lunch eligible students and average or above average test scores when compared to similar peer school districts could serve as a home for some of our disadvantaged urban and rural children. I have selected the 30 percent free and reduced price lunch eligible target to avoid the possibility of reaching a "tipping point" that might cause middle class/white parents to abandon the school district. Research indicates that the 30 percent target would not cause white flight and can improve outcomes for poverty children.[cxlvii clxviii]

The rental subsidies I am proposing for these disadvantaged students' families would continue to be added until the district reaches 30 percent free and reduced price lunch eligible (FRPLE).

School districts that already have more than 30 percent FRPLE would not be expected to participate in the program. These districts are already doing their share by helping the children in poverty. Similarly, academically low performing school districts would not be asked to take on greater responsibilities with children in poverty until their test scores improve (unlike the plan for Northside in Sarandon).

Teachers in the suburban school districts who took in these new students would be facing classrooms with higher levels of poverty. But they would not be facing larger classes as these students would be residents of their community living in apartments and homes that are already in the community. These teachers would also not be facing the overwhelming numbers of poverty children their urban colleagues now face.

Why not just build more low income housing in the suburbs instead of using rent subsidies?

Low income housing in the suburbs creates significant, focused political backlash that's difficult (maybe impossible) to overcome. This political backlash would be ameliorated with rent subsidies that provide rental support at multiple geographic sites in the school district.

In addition, low income housing in the suburbs is usually concentrated in cheaply constructed apartments which never endure, create an eyesore and become a school problem for the children who live in them: "Oh you live in *those* apartments."

All parents of free and reduced lunch eligible students in underperforming high poverty districts would be eligible for this rental subsidy as long as they moved to an address in one of the approved school districts.

However, many urban and rural parents in poverty could not take advantage of this opportunity because of job, home, neighborhood or family responsibilities or transportation complications. Better regional mass transit could help but a $600 per month rental subsidy (beyond the present Section 8 subsides available in many places in the country) can't overcome a two-hour bus ride to and from a minimum wage job.

This is a good alternative, but it's far from a perfect option for all children in poverty, especially with the U.S. now exceeding 50 percent of children who are free and reduced lunch eligible.[cxlix] And it's important to note that a rental subsidy approach to ameliorating poverty's negative impact on children's success has a proven track record for academic and later life outcomes.[cl cli clii]

A rental subsidy option for improving school choice for poverty parents is also the right thing to do because it fosters socioeconomic and ethnic integration of our schools. Desegregation (despite the disagreement from the political right in the U.S.) actually works to improve academic outcomes for all children.[cliii] Besides, it is the right thing to do for our children and for our communities despite the fact that there will be expected resistance.[cliv]

Right now, we're basically moving the chairs on the Titanic. As long as we remain stuck with only poverty education solutions that foster ever increasing segregation of poverty students, we will continue to see alarming academic results for far too many of our urban and rural poverty students.

Our children need to learn to work together and live together (obviously!). And the adults need to model that kind of cooperative behavior by supporting a solution like rent subsidies that move more poor urban and rural students to academically successful wealthier suburban schools.

Children from the rental subsidy families will have a slot in a proven successful school where their chances of high school and college graduation will be greater. And given what the data say about upward mobility opportunities for African American children in the U.S. today,[clv] we should not waste time in implementing this change.

Not all suburban school districts will become target districts for rental-subsidy families. Many of these school districts do not perform better than expected and some suburban school districts already have too many poverty students to be asked to take on more.

What about Lawrence Elementary School?

The goal is not to make our schools perform worse, which is what charter schools have done in many communities where they have been established. Schools like Lawrence Elementary School would not be able to enroll more free and reduced lunch eligible students until the school's performance was above the predictor line. And when that happens they cannot exceed 30 percent free lunch eligible and their performance would have to be monitored to ensure they did not fall below the predictor line.

The first place to start is with schools that fall below the predictor line and carefully monitor the impact on the school receiving the students.

Remember: primum non nocere.

Where has all the money gone?

● ● ●

(Like herding bees, Part I)

Almost every time I told someone I was writing a solutions-based book called "Why We Failed: 40 Years of Education Reform" they asked the same question: Where has all the money gone?

The American public knows we're spending more on education than we have in the past. They also know we're not seeing results.[clvi] They want to know why.[clvii] One reason change has been so hard is that the same public that believes our education system is failing thinks their local school is a success and doesn't need to be changed.[clviii]

They're right about the fact that we're spending more – way more.

In 1970, the average annual cost per pupil in New York State was $1,327, according to the National Center for Education Statistics.[clix] Factor in simple (Cost Price Index - CPI) inflation (6.46) and that number today should be $8,572. But the actual median expenditure per pupil in New York State in 2014-15 was $22,552[clx]; that's 163 percent or $13,980 more than inflation can explain (1,327 X 6.46 = 8,572, 22,552 – 8,572 = 13,980).

And New York and other big spenders like Massachusetts, Illinois, Maryland, Delaware, New Jersey and California are not the only ones spending more. The five lowest education spenders in the nation – Utah, Idaho, Arizona, Oklahoma and Mississippi – also have consistently spent more than inflation. In 1970, they were spending $610 per pupil per year. [clxi] In 2015, they spent an average of $7,490 per pupil; that's 89 percent or $3,549 more than inflation can explain (610 X 6.46 = 3,941, 7,490 – 3,941 = 3,549).[clxii]

We've reached a cost-per-pupil crescendo that started gaining steam in the 1990's, one that has risen steadily since I started teaching in 1970.[clxiii clxiv]

So where has all the money gone?

(Sections in italics are fictional stories made from composites of multiple actual experiences.)

Like herding bees

In 2013, I was interviewing with the Mt. Mason School District school board for a one-year position as interim superintendent. Before heading out to meet them, I read several online news reports and viewed TV clips about the bitter feud between the school district and its three unions (teachers, support staff and administrators) over long, unsettled labor contracts.

As I drove into Mt. Mason I was greeted by a "Welcome to Mt. Mason, NY State's Friendliest Small Town" sign that belied the news reports I had read about and seen on television which featured picket signs and angry, yelling townsfolk.

As I drove around the town in the hour I had to kill before my interview the word that came to my mind was "sleepy." A few small shops, a diner, two gas stations, a car wash, two liquor stores and a large grocery store dominated the "downtown" area. There were very few cars on the road at 7 p.m. Several suburban housing developments directly off the two main roads on the way into town had well-kept lawns and homes. Most of the residents apparently commuted to work in Albany or Schenectady.

I spotted the three elementary schools and the nearby middle school and high school that served the 2,100 students in Mt. Mason. The 1960s and 70s era school buildings looked good from the outside and there were no ongoing major construction projects.

My online check of Mt. Mason's schools and their test scores showed them as average performers in comparison to other school districts with similar demographics. This was interesting only because the bitterness generated by extended union contract talks, now stalled for five years, can frequently push student test scores down over a period of time.

When I arrived to the interview room I was greeted by Mt. Mason's five school board members and the BOCES (Board of Cooperative Educational Services) regional school district superintendent, Paul Johnson, a colleague I had known for more than 20 years. Everyone was cordial and positive in demeanor and tone.

Again, this contradicted what I had seen on television and read about in the newspaper. I knew from other superintendents this board had two bitter factions and that the BOCES superintendent, Paul Johnson, had weathered several contentious arguments with them over previous superintendents who the board thought were unsuccessful. They blamed Paul who, as BOCES superintendent, had helped recruit those superintendents.

One group, the apparent board majority with three members, feared a contract settlement that "gave away the store" with higher salaries for employees and inadequate give backs from the unions on benefit costs and work rules.

The second group, the board minority with two members, feared that continuing strife from the unsettled contracts would tear the district apart, damaging academic results and exacerbating a negative climate in the schools for students, teachers, parents and administrators.

I based my answers to their questions on my previous experience in districts with difficult employee contract negotiations where I had to repair damage caused by long-standing contract negotiations.

I was pretty sure all involved feared being viewed as the "losers" in the never-ending negotiations battle. Saving face and pride are the two biggest impediments to settling long-expired contracts.

My answers to their questions emphasized three key points:

1. *The school board needed a simple set of negotiation goals for each unsettled contract.*
2. *The best way to identify compromises we could all live with was with data showing how Mt. Mason compared with the other school districts in the area.*

3.   *The school board members needed to get out of the way so the
     interim superintendent could settle the contracts.*

Mt. Mason was too small to drive the local employee labor market.
Bigger districts do that and then only to a limited degree. The best Mt.
Mason could do was make certain their settlement reflected or at least
moved the district closer to the norms in the region.

The interview was brief and I assumed when it ended quickly that
I somehow missed showing those present the key ingredient they were
searching for so I was surprised when the next day the Paul Johnson
called me to offer me the position.

The offer came with a warning.

"I'm not supposed to tell you this but you and I have worked together
for many years and I want to be honest with you so you know what you
are getting into," Paul said. "They are still bitterly feuding and they are
exhausted. In your case, the majority ruled."

I had worked with split school boards before and it was very difficult. In time this one would prove even more difficult.

"Okay," I said, "let me meet with them and discuss what I want to
do. If they still want to hire me when we're done, I'll take the job. If not
I'll tell you 'no thanks' and we'll go our separate ways."

My next meeting was set for the following Monday night at 7 p.m.

I was prepared with some large poster-sized sheets of paper and
some magic markers, some blank sheets of 8 ½" by 11" copier paper,
some pens and six copies of the existing teacher contract the superintendent's secretary had graciously provided to me.

"I know this school board has a long-standing disagreement about
the unsettled contracts," I told them, once we settled in. "I also know
your board is split on the issue of whether I can successfully help you
settle the contracts and run your district effectively for the next year.

"I also have some doubts about whether I can do this successfully
given the level of friction I've read about in the newspaper and seen on

television. And given the disagreement you have about whether I'm the right person for the job."

I then proposed a 90-minute session that would help both of us decide whether or not to move forward.

At first there was silence. Then three of the school board members said they would be willing to work with me for 90 minutes. One of the two reluctant board members, a big grey-haired man in a red plaid flannel shirt, wanted to know what we'd do for 90 minutes.

"I don't want to waste an hour and a half if you're not going to be our superintendent," he said.

I responded. "I'm going to try to get all of you to agree on some goals for the teacher negotiations. Whether I am here or not those goals will be helpful moving forward," I said.

The other reluctant member, a thirty-something woman with long black hair and large tortoise shell eyeglasses, spoke up.

"We already know what we want from those negotiations and we haven't been able to agree for several years. How are you going to get us to agree in an hour and a half?" she wanted to know.

"Whether we can come to an agreement on these goals in a reasonable amount of time will reveal if an effort to resolve these unsettled contracts makes sense for you and for me."

"Okay, let's get this over with," the man in the plaid shirt said. The woman followed with a nod.

I asked the board majority (three members), who shared concerns about the financial costs and work rules for teachers, to sit together in one corner of the room and the board minority (two members) with concerns about the negative climate in the district to sit together in the opposite corner of the room.

When the chairs and tables were rearranged I handed each of the five board members paper and a pen and each group a marker and poster-sized paper. I also gave each school board member a copy of the existing teachers' contract, which expired five years earlier but still remained in force due to New York State laws and supporting court decisions.

"It's 7:15 p.m.," I told them. "For the next 10 minutes I want you to individually write down your three most important goals for teacher negotiations.

"Feel free to write more than three as you're making up your mind, but when 10 minutes are up I want three in priority order with No. 1 being most important and No. 3 being least important.

"Don't confer with your fellow school board members. I want these to be YOUR teacher negotiations priorities not someone else's."

While they completed the task I wandered around like a high school math teacher checking my students' classwork.

A pattern began to emerge.

The majority members had more specific numerical goals about salary increases and benefit costs and about prep period times and class loads for high school teachers. The minority group had more goals about getting the contract settled quickly to repair the damage that had been done by protracted negotiations.

Neither group had any goals about saving face or looking like they were winning and not losing the negotiations, but I could read between the lines.

By getting the board members to write down their goals I was forcing them to put their cards on the table. Like most, this group did not want to appear shallow so they skipped writing down the goal of winning. But I knew we'd have to face this issue head on before a final agreement on the contract could be ratified by the school board.

Every negotiations I've participated in included personal animosity and issues related to ego. Many school board members and superintendents try to make themselves look important by verbally promising unrealistic unachievable negotiations goals. But they hesitate to put unrealistic goals in writing.

When ten minutes were up I asked one member of each group to record the three goals of each board member while the others took a short break. Five minutes later the majority group had nine goals and the minority group had six goals.

I asked the groups to edit, combine and simplify their goals as concisely as possible and write down the most comprehensive list possible that included every board member's priority goals.

The room was instantly buzzing with what any teacher would call "good talk" about the key issues and their importance. When I stopped the conversations I asked one member from each group to print in large letters their final goals so everyone could see them. The group of three had consolidated their nine goals into six. The group of two board members had consolidated their six goals to four.

I gave them the next 15 minutes to discuss these goals and advocate for their own point of view within their group regarding which goals were most important and why. When the 15 minutes of discussion ended I had them tack their lists of six and four goals to the bulletin board at the front of the room and prioritize the goals on their group's list by using six small stickers.

They were to affix three stars next to their first priority goal, two stars next to their second priority goal and one star next to their third priority goal.

I made certain the goals that didn't make the cut in the final priority list for both groups were visible to members of the other group. I wanted everyone to know that sacrifices had been made by their "opponents" to reach this shorter priority list. Goals that didn't make the cut included those about repairing damage that had been done to the school district's reputation as a result of protracted negotiations, teacher class loads and work schedules and the school year and day length.

I asked them to move their desks and chairs back into a rough class-like formation. When the desks were back in order I moved the two completed goal sheets up side by side on the bulletin board at the front of the room and I told them to read the two sheets for the next three minutes and identify the surprises and the anticipated items they saw in the list created by the other group. This is what they were looking at (excluding the goals that didn't make the final priority list).

Board majority group's priority goals for teacher negotiations:

1. Teacher raises of less than 1 percent new money in total per year including incremental steps; no more than inflation; and no retroactive raises.
2. Teacher contributions for health insurance increase from zero percent to 40 percent.
3. Retirement incentive to clean out some of the deadwood teachers at the top of the salary schedule.

Board minority group's priority goals for teacher negotiations:

1. Settle teacher contract negotiations this year.
2. Give teachers a fair salary increase to reduce negative climate in the district.
3. Teachers should contribute something toward health insurance.

All five school board members understood that the cost of "increment" (teachers moving up the salary schedule from one step to the next) meant most teachers would receive a built-in raise at each step.

These amounts varied due to the anomalies of one or more previously negotiated contracts. (Which steps received raises is usually based on who's on the negotiating team. A zero percent raise is likely due to the fact that the teachers on the negotiating committee were not on those steps. And once something like that is established it becomes an anomaly that creates bulges in the annual budget.)

Increments cost Mt. Mason district an additional 1.2 to 1.8 percent of the total teacher salary cost each year. Step raises ended for individual Mt. Mason teachers after 30 years. Teachers received these step raises even while the contract was expired, a requirement based on New York State labor law and supporting court decisions.

Mt. Mason teachers received no raises beyond step raises over this five-year period of stalled negotiations, and I knew the majority board members would never ever agree to retroactive raises.

However, both groups of school board members had goals of giving some level of salary increase beyond the increment raises as we moved forward.

I asked the five school board members what surprised them about the list created by the board members in the group they were not part of.

"I'm surprised they listed health insurance contributions as a priority goal. They never said that before," said the grey-haired man.

"We have always supported health insurance contributions just not at 40 percent," said the young woman with the tortoise shell glasses.

I jumped in immediately. "Okay, let's stay on task. What about the other group of board members? What surprised you about the board majority's goals?" I asked.

"Both groups have goals about salary and health insurance," said a quieter man in his thirties, who I later learned was Mike Testa.

"That's right," I said. "Let me see if I can get both groups on the same page on those two goals."

I realized later that Mike Testa could be helpful to me. He was thoughtful and his soft spoken manner was less antagonistic than that of the grey-haired man in the plaid shirt. Mike could also get the black-haired woman in the tortoise shell glasses to soften her approach so that better communication took place.

I turned to the board majority seated to my right. "You have set 1 percent total new money and no retroactive raises as your salary goal. Do you know what your teachers are paid relative to other districts in the area?"

The grey-haired man I now recognized as the school board president, Harold Smith, spoke. "Our teachers are paid too much already," he said. "They only work ten months and they get all those school vacations. We shouldn't give them any raise at all."

When he finished speaking an older grey-haired woman seated to his right, who I later learned was Helen Anderson, spoke up. "To answer your question, we have heard our teachers make more than those in Amsterdam and Gloversville. They're nearby and comparable to our district." she said.

"But have you seen an actual salary comparison on paper of all the local school districts?" I asked.

"No." she responded.

"Have any of you seen a written summary of all the local district's health insurance costs per teacher and contribution rates teachers make for their health insurance?" I asked the entire school board.

"We have heard that the teachers in the same two districts contribute 20 percent toward the cost of their health insurance, but we have not seen a written summary of all the local districts," Helen Anderson said.

"If the other districts paid their teachers more or paid less for their health insurance with teachers paying a higher percentage of their health insurance costs, would that alter how you see these issues?" I asked the three members of the school board majority.

"Yes, we don't want to be taken advantage of by the teachers union, but we want to be reasonable," Helen said. "We should look at that data and make sure we're headed toward the average for the area, no more and no less on salary and health insurance."

During this entire conversation the third member of the school board majority, a big man dressed in blue jeans and a rumpled black sweatshirt, who I later found out was named Doug Allen, said nothing.

"What do you think about the teacher salary question?" I asked him in an effort to involve him in the discussion so I could better gauge his viewpoint. Doug looked confused.

Harold jumped in to protect his friend. "He thinks our teachers are paid too much and should contribute more for their health insurance; same as me." Harold said.

Doug smiled and pointed to Harold. "What he said."

I found it amusing the first time Doug said "what he said" after Harold said something. About the tenth time I found it annoying. It was pretty much all I heard Doug say the entire year I worked in Mt. Mason except when he talked about his pride and joy, a red pick-up truck.

344

I turned to the two member board minority group. "Your group said you want a fair salary increase for the teachers. How would you measure whether the salary is fair?" I asked.

"I see where you are going with this," said the woman with the tortoise shell glasses I later learned was Tabitha Conner. "We'd have to look at our district's salary in comparison to other local districts, and I think we can live with that on both salary and health insurance."

"I think a compromise you can both live with can be made. Give me a minute to write it down." I grabbed a Sharpie pen and wrote out:

1. *Teacher total new money salary increases (step plus raises) and health insurance savings in comparison to projected health insurance costs and salary costs without a new teacher contract settlement when combined (a) should not exceed one percent of the 2015-16 salary base per year for the period of the contract. And, (b) should move the district to within 2 percent of the average salary and health insurance costs per teacher for local school districts.*

I placed my newly minted goal on the bulletin board beside the other lists of three priority goals and asked if everyone could live with it.

They studied the proposed negotiations goal and then asked several questions. Who do we compare ourselves with? How would we determine the salary base? Who will put together the comparison data? How soon would we have this data? How would the teachers' expectation for retroactive raises figure into this goal? I answered each question carefully, explaining what I knew and what it would take more time for me to figure out. After ten minutes of questions, they were silent.

"Can you live with this?" I asked. They all nodded, in a few cases looking very surprised.

"What about our other goals?" Tabitha asked.

"I have no problem with them. We should make them goals two and three," I said.

Our final list of three goals was:

1. *Teacher total new money salary increases (step plus raises) and health insurance savings in comparison to projected health insurance costs and salary costs without a new teacher contract settlement when combined (a) should not exceed one percent of the 2015-16 salary base per year for the period of the contract. And, (b) should move the district to within two percent of the average salary and health insurance costs per teacher for similar school districts.*
2. *Retirement incentive for teachers.*
3. *Settle the contract this year.*

I looked at the clock. "It's been 90 minutes. I think we're done here," I said and smiled.

They all smiled and began to chat with one another while I packed up. Harold Smith approached me.

"Look, you did what you promised and we all want you to stay on as our interim superintendent if that's okay with you?" he asked, almost apologetically.

"I believe I can settle these contracts and achieve these goals, but you have to let me do the negotiations my way without the school board directly involved and without making inflammatory public statements," I said.

I knew from my conversations with the BOCES superintendent, Paul Johnson, that Harold Smith had inserted himself directly into the negotiations in previous years. His yelling and rants at board meetings and in the press had added immeasurably to an already acrimonious relationship between the teacher union leadership and bargaining team. If he stayed out of the way I could get this done. If he stuck his nose in as he had in the past, nothing good could happen.

Harold looked sheepish. "I'll leave it to you. The other approach hasn't worked. I'll trust you. I promise," he said. We shook hands and both smiled.

"I'll work out the salary and start date details with Paul Johnson and your outgoing superintendent and I'll be back in touch once we have a signed contract," I told him.

"I know you think I'm the problem here based on what you've seen in the news but you haven't dealt with Sally Anselm, the teacher union president. She's a bitch on wheels and she'll make your life more miserable than you can imagine," Harold said.

"Harold, I have a bit of experience dealing with unions. I'm certain Sally and her negotiating team will be tough, but I feel confident we can find a way to make things work out." I said.

This was not my first rodeo.

FDR WAS MOSTLY RIGHT

Soon after becoming a teacher in 1970 I remember reading that Franklin Delano Roosevelt, the famous Democrat and depression era and WWII president, did not believe in public union negotiations for salary and benefits.[clxv]

This confused me. Weren't the Democrats supporters of unions? Didn't FDR help to establish the National Labor Relations Board and support private unions? Why this stance on public unions?

FDR apparently concluded that the city, county and village legislators, state legislatures or Congress should set wages and benefits for public employees and that while the public sector employees should be free to join unions their involvement in negotiations with their government employers made no sense.

After 40-plus years working with public unions I've come to the conclusion that FDR was mostly right. The situation in Mt. Mason is typical of the teacher and public employee negotiations that distract us from the critical task of making our public institutions more responsive and effective while wasting enormous amounts of precious leadership time and public tax dollars on local negotiations.

Frequently, these negotiations in the strong public union states pit David, played by the local public employer, against Goliath, played by the local public union and its state level partner. And it's not just the teachers union, it's the bus drivers union, the administrators union, the support staff union.

As a result of laws and court decisions, public union employees are guaranteed annual raises based on seniority steps, continuing high cost health insurance sans teacher contributions and high employer contributions to state controlled pension plans.

Guarantees produced by laws and supporting court decisions apply to state, local government and school district employees in strong public union states.[clxvi] Public unions in these states also have an unfair advantage because they provide campaign contributions and endorsements to members of both Democratic and Republican parties.[clxvii clxviii]

The public unions received paybacks in the form of a ratcheting up of negotiations advantages over the decades of the 1960s through the 1990s. In New York State, Democrats received the majority of this largesse, but the Republicans took their share as well. The union contributed millions to their campaigns and continue to contribute to this day.[clixix]

To make these negotiation contests less lopsided, school districts, towns, villages and cities try to arm themselves with the best slingshots available (expensive labor attorneys),[clxx] who have developed an extremely well-funded cottage industry that grows into a more expensive and debilitating barnacle on the public school district ship every year.

While private worker union influence has shrunk over the past five decades due to the impact of globalization and technology,[clxxi] public unions have become even more pernicious, particularly in states that made strategic errors by passing laws that tilted negotiations toward unions.

Public employee unions gained negotiating power primarily in blue states like New York, Rhode Island, Massachusetts and California. States like Ohio and Wisconsin, where Republicans have recently taken control, have tried to create a more equitable balance.[clxxii] The U.S. Supreme Court in 2016, short one member due to the death of Justice Antonin Scalia, tied 4-4 on a crucial case that could have had negative impacts on public union finances.clxxiii But entrenched power seldom slinks away quietly, especially when serious money is on the table.

In Albany, NY, where I served as a school superintendent for six years, extended and acrimonious negotiations with our teachers union, our support staff union and our school administrators union included several incidents that illustrated the bitterness that can come from these public union conflicts.

* My mailbox was destroyed by early morning explosions on three separate occasions during negotiations.

* Someone banged on my door at 2 a.m. waking and frightening my teenage daughter and my ex-wife while I was working at an extended night time negotiations session with the teachers union.

* My car was "parked in" by a vehicle belonging to one of the district's teachers who parked his car one inch from my vehicle in an attempt to make it impossible for me to drive home after a negotiating session that didn't end until 4 a.m. (It took me an hour, but I got out of the spot.)

* At the height of the same negotiations a disgruntled and ineffective payroll employee who was also a member of the support staff union leadership was involved in several conflicts in the office and had repeatedly been uncooperative with her supervisor. This employee was transferred to a different job in a different building at the same rate of pay. I had investigated the possibility of terminating this employee, but the school district's attorney told us that given her union leadership status firing her would probably result in a reinstatement by the Public Employee Relations Board (PERB) that oversees challenges on such issues.

  The day she left for her new work assignment the entire payroll file for our district was deleted from our computer system. This delayed paychecks for 1,200 employees and required several employees to work overtime on the weekend to hand write checks for the impacted employees who received their paychecks one to three days late.

Despite the fact that we could trace the payroll file deletion back to the specific computer used by this employee our attorney strongly advised us not to take further disciplinary action against her due to her union leadership status and PERB rules and decisions regarding union animus (retaliatory actions by public employers toward public union leaders).

* A confidential negotiations document I had given to the school board describing my plan to begin to replace through attrition the existing high school educated teacher aide staff with lower paid and more highly qualified teacher assistants with teaching certification or at least a bachelor's degree was pilfered from my desk and altered to say my plan was to immediately lay off all these employees (over 100).

The altered version (I had no plans to lay off anyone during this process.) was distributed to all the members of the district's support staff union. Imagine my surprise when over 150 members of this union showed up at our next school board meeting with no warning.

These employees, who attended the meeting as a result of theft and deception, were armed with picket signs calling for my firing and they chanted repeatedly "Palmer must go" for the benefit of the television and newspaper reporters they had called in advance of the meeting.

* During the acrimonious negotiations with our support staff union I visited one of the district's elementary schools to check on the progress of summer cleaning and maintenance work. When I returned to my car I found I had a flat tire. I pulled into the adjacent gas station and asked them to fix the tire while I grabbed lunch in the diner across the street.

When I returned from lunch the mechanic said, "Well, I can fix the two holes in the tire tread but the 14 holes in the sidewall are another matter. You'll need a new tire."

＊ When I was the interim superintendent in Troy, NY, I made decisions that reduced unnecessary overtime for custodians. Several of those custodians were making more in yearly wages than my newer school principals due to "boiler" time where they "watched" the steam boilers in the high school and the middle school at night, supposedly for safety reasons. No safety issues had ever been noted during these overtime shifts and I had previously worked in other school districts with steam boilers like those in Troy that did not pay overtime for steam boiler supervision.

Shortly after I ended "boiler babysitting" a bullet hole mysteriously appeared in a window in my office, the air conditioning in my office did not work and wasn't fixed for several months (this resulted in severe allergies I struggle with to this day) and a key supervisory custodial employee took a leave of absence of more than one year in duration for an unspecified illness creating significant operational issues for the district and for me.

I don't need to be convinced that public unions are a menace, but I had to put aside my distaste for public unions and find a way to work out the contracts that had expired in Mt. Mason. Fortunately, I knew where to find the money needed to resolve these long standing disputes given my experience in the intricacies of teacher salary and benefit costs.

It's a simple salary schedule, right?

When public union contracts expire the assumption is, moving forward, that teachers, support staff and administrators won't receive raises. That's just not the case. Most teachers (and support staff to a lesser extent) are paid according to a salary schedule with yearly steps. Here's a simple example: First year teachers (step 1) are paid $40,000; second year teachers (step 2) $41,000; third year teachers (step 3) $42,000; until the 25th or 30th year of service.

If the contract expires and negotiations have not yet produced a new agreed upon contract, existing law and court decisions (in New York State this is called the Triborough Decision[clxxiv] because the original decision that impacted public workers on the Triborough Bridge in NYC) require step raises to continue even without a new contract.

Every teacher contract has a built-in "cost for step" that will increase the wages paid to teachers even if no contract is settled. Generally, depending on the distribution of teachers along the seniority steps on the salary schedule, this "cost of step" is between 1 percent and 2 percent of the total wages paid to teachers (the teacher salary base).

The Triborough Decision removes much of the incentive for public unions for fear of losing something.

The state legislature in New York could tilt the negotiating field back toward public employers by passing a law that said unions negotiating expired contracts will not receive any step raises nor will they receive retroactive raises, but the New York State Assembly and Senate are too much under the thumb of the public unions for that to happen.

When a teacher contract is settled the percent raises teachers receive are most frequently, but not always, applied to all the steps on the salary schedule equally. For example, if teachers received a 2 percent raise on top of their step increases, the $40,000 starting (step 1) salary would increase to $40,800 with the $800 added to the original starting salary (0.02 X 40,000 = 800). Similarly step 2 salaries would increase by $820 to $41,820 and step 3 salaries would increase from $42,000 to $42,840.

And advocating for more pay for teachers hasn't attracted new people to education as a career because of the way the money is divvied up by the union negotiating committee.

When the same 2 percent raise is applied to the larger salaries for the later steps, the dollar value increases. A teacher moving from step 24 to step 25 with this same contract settlement would see a salary increase from $63,000 to $65,280 or a gain of $2,280. In other words, the highest paid teachers receive the biggest raises.

Over many years and multiple contract settlements this effect widens the salary schedule so that now on Long Island and in other high-cost areas near New York City there are multiple school districts where teachers start their careers at about $60,000 per year and 30-year teachers are earning $120,000 to $140,000. This effect is much less notable in the states with weak or non-existent public unions, where many teachers presently start their careers at or near $30,000 to 35,000 and end their careers with salaries of roughly $60,000.

The increment raises in states with stronger unions are part of what I refer to as the "union premium." It's one of the places where the money has gone, and it directs most of the money to older, more experienced teachers rather than directing it to new teachers to attract new talent.

Rather than setting up the raises so that everybody gets a $1,000 raise, the veteran teachers who are most frequently the leaders in the teachers union and the representatives on the teachers union negotiating team, push for a percentage. Two percent of $80,000 is more than 2 percent of $40,000.

Many teacher union negotiating teams also "play games with the salary schedule."

The teachers on the committee will create bigger step raises for steps 12, 13 and 14 because they're on those steps and make smaller step raises for steps 8, 9 and 10 because those teachers are not on the negotiating committee. It's all the same to the school district; that is until they hire a bunch of new teachers in the same year.

They've built into their salary schedule that teachers at step 12 receive a huge raise and sure enough 12 years later they have to make a kindergarten class 26 students instead of 20 because they're have a big unplanned payout. It makes it very difficult to plan.

While we may deplore the ethics of this action, few school districts fight hard to stop it from happening because it will make reaching a settlement that much harder to achieve and fighting it will not create any immediate savings for the district. A shortsighted mistake.

If the district leaves the setting of step values to the teachers union to decide they will inevitably give the smallest raises to the brand new starting teachers because they are not yet on the staff to defend themselves. This is why starting teacher pay has not gone up more than inflation in New York State or across the country.[clxxv]

The extra raises go to the most experienced teachers who have paid union dues the longest. The next largest raises go to mid-career and later career teachers. Not surprisingly, the biggest raises go to the top end teachers and those on the negotiating team.

How do I know new teacher salaries haven't gone up?

When I signed my first teaching contract as an uncertified junior high school science teacher in Albany, NY, in August of 1970, I couldn't believe my good luck. My annual salary was $8,200.

With an inflation factor of 6.46, my $8,200 1970 teacher salary would translate to an expected salary for a starting teacher with a bachelor's degree in 2015 of $52,972 (6.46 X 8,200 = 52,152). The latest data (2012-13) I could find for the City School District of Albany showed beginning teachers were paid $51,146.[clxxvi]

Starting salaries are still at the same place as they were in 1970.

Meanwhile, senior teachers are receiving big raises that add significantly to the district's cost per pupil while creating only marginal or non-existent improvements in teaching quality.

Multiple successive contract settlements that give in to these tactics produce salary schedules with step raises all over the map (some years $3,000 and some years $0).

This adds to school districts' long-term financial problems as invariably a year arrives when a large number of teachers are due to receive that $3,000 increment and this blows an enormous hole in an already stressed school district budget.

Management 101 for school districts

Shortly after I started the interim superintendent position at Mt. Mason, I met with Tom Garrigus, the district's long-time business official. Tom was tall and gangly and given to fits of nervous laughter. He had a great sense of humor that made my time in Mt. Mason almost bearable. Tom made it clear he would do whatever he could to help me, but he wanted nothing to do with dealing with the school board.

I asked Tom for a graph summary of the salary schedules of Mt. Mason and 10 nearby school districts that showed their teacher salaries from when they started with the district until they reached the district's top step on respective salary schedules. I wanted to compare what those ten districts paid their teachers at each step and what Mt. Mason paid its teachers at each step to two things:

1. The average step-by-step pay for teachers for the 11 districts.
2. The average of the districts' step-by-step pay for teachers plus four percent.

I picked four percent because I was thinking the other districts in the area would probably raise their salaries by about one percent per year for each of the next four years. Regional salary settlement data told me my 1 percent estimate was a good guess based on the most recent teacher salary settlements in our part of the state.

So our "target" four years out would be the present teacher salary average plus 4 percent.

Since Mt. Mason's salaries overall were in general slightly less than the area average this would translate to roughly a 1 percent mid-year raise for Mt. Mason teachers during our present year and roughly one percent per year raises over the next four years of a five-year contract.

I knew the contract would have to include a one-time, off-schedule payment to the teachers, a "signing bonus," that wouldn't increase the salary schedule. This signing bonus was the norm for the state on long expired contracts. It was not a retroactive raise that changed the salary schedule just a one-time payment to the teachers. I knew this one-time payment would have to be explained carefully to the school board and would also have to fit within the 1 percent total salary schedule cost goal the school board had agreed to.

The Mt. Mason school board struggled for years to settle the teacher contract. They needed a longer term settlement – five years – to bring stability to the district.

I knew recent contract settlements in the region included incremental raises plus 1 percent per year. So if the contract we settled with the teachers union gave them a 1 percent raise during the present school year and went out for four additional years, a settlement with 1 percent "new money" each year on top of the district's 1.4 percent average incremental raises would keep the total salary cost (excluding any savings we could create with health insurance) at around 2.4 percent per year (1.4 percent increment plus 1 percent raise equals 2.4 percent total salary cost to the district). If we could create some health insurance savings to offset the new salary costs, we could meet the school board's goal of 1 percent new money each year for the four future years of the contract.

For this plan to work and to meet the school board's agreed upon goal of no more than 1 percent of new money each year of the contract, the health insurance savings would have to more than offset these salary increases. We had some work to do.

When Tom, the business official, came to me with the Excel spreadsheet graphic in less than a week, I was very pleased by what I saw.

Mt. Mason Teacher Salary Comparison with
10 Neighboring School Districts

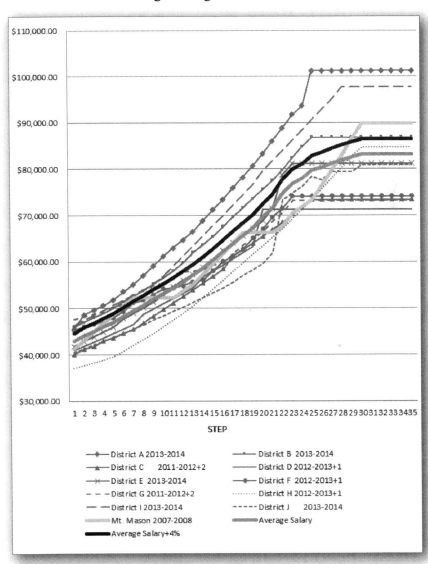

THE GOAL: A SALARY AGREEMENT NEAR THE BLACK LINE WOULD ACHIEVE THE GOALS OF SMOOTHING OUT THE SALARY SCHEDULE AND ADDING ONLY 1 PERCENT NEW MONEY BEYOND INCREMENT EACH YEAR.

Mt. Mason's teacher salaries (represented by the wide light gray line on the graph) tracked mostly below the wide darker gray line, which is the average of the 11 districts and further below the wide black line which is the average of 11 districts plus four percent, our end-of-contract target.

Overall, Mt. Mason's teachers were not overpaid in comparison to other teachers in surrounding districts, despite the contrary opinions of some school board members.

Yes, there were some expected anomalies (the wide light gray line moves up and down and does not increase steadily) due to the teachers union steering higher step raises to teachers on the negotiating team who, again, tend to be higher on the pay scale. The anomalies showed up as the horizontal flat places on the light gray line graph – the places where the step raises were $0.

Typically, there are between 20 and 35 incremental steps in a teacher salary schedule. The most noticeable anomalies in Mt. Mason's salary schedule were:

- *At step eight the present salary was more than the average for the region plus 4 percent. Light gray higher than black.*
- *There were no increment raises between steps eight and 11 and again between steps 18 and 21. Wide light gray line is horizontal.*
- *Between steps 22 to 27 Mt. Mason's teacher salaries are well below the average for the region. Light gray well below the darker gray line.*
- *The Mt. Mason teachers at the top of the pay scale were being paid significantly more than the average top end teachers regionally. Light gray higher than dark gray.*

I knew I'd have to address the facts that teachers on step eight were overpaid, based on the average in the region, that teachers well into their careers (steps 22 to 27) are underpaid and that teachers at the top of the scale were overpaid based on the regional average.

And who will I be sitting with at the negotiating table? Teachers who were already at that overpaid top end and wanted more. That's one area where too much of the money many school districts spend is going.

Meanwhile, Harold, like the public, thinks teachers make too much money and has some grandiose idea that he is going to rein in these teacher salaries, but you're not going to do that as a school board member in tiny Mt. Mason, New York.

A Mt. Mason teacher who stayed in the district for an entire career would end up making about the same or a little less in total career wages as an average counterpart in other nearby districts. If we gave the teachers 1 percent new money per year for the next five years, counting the present year, and worked on reducing the anomalies in Mt. Mason's salary schedule, we could smooth out the jagged Mt. Mason salary line and move teacher pay closer to the average for our particular region of New York State.

It's hard for the teachers union or school board to argue with a new contractually agreed upon salary schedule that moves the district closer to the norm for the region.

Ultimately, this was a math problem with a solution. But egos and turf wars usually supersede mathematics and experience has taught me that I am much better at math than I am with egos and turf wars.

At the executive session preceding our next school board meeting I showed this complex graph to the school board. I was proud of what we'd created. I explained what the lines and data behind the graphs meant and waited for questions. It didn't take long before Harold Smith erupted.

"What are you trying to do? Confuse us? What are all these lines? We can't offer the teachers increment plus 1 percent per year. That's our maximum amount. Don't you have any idea how to negotiate?" he bellowed.

I sighed. This was going to be a long year. "I'm sorry Harold. I think I made this graph too complex," I said. "Give it back to me and I'll simplify it. This is not for the teachers. It's just for us. I'm just trying to get our goals straight and to show what we'll need to do to achieve those goals."

I said this as calmly as I could to avoid a pointless confrontation. Harold realized he'd stepped over the line we had agreed to both honor about his leaving the negotiations to me and he nodded. I collected the graphs and acted as if nothing had happened.

The next day in my office I simplified the graph to three lines and stapled three pages together with the three-line graph on top, the 13-line original graph next and the salary data for all the districts on the third page. This is what the simplified three-line graph looked like.

Mt. Mason teacher salary comparison with
average of ten districts and average of ten districts plus 4 percent

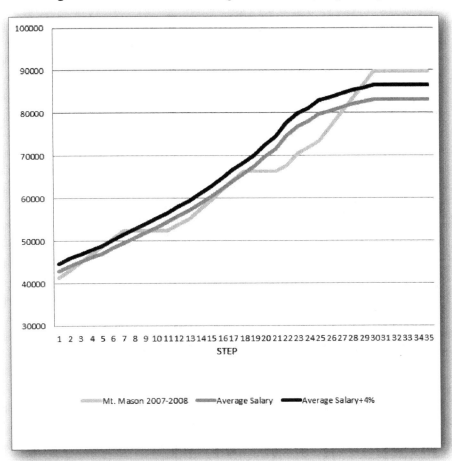

I called Harold Smith as soon as I had two versions of the new graph printed. I left a message on his cell phone requesting he stop by my office so we could review negotiations data at his convenience. Harold arrived in my office within 45 minutes and, after I closed the door, I sat next to him at my conference table just as I'd sat next to struggling math and physics students in my high school teaching days. I showed him my new three-page creation starting with the simplified three-line graph.

The fact is he didn't understand the graphs and his fears prompted his executive session outburst. He was afraid I was going to try to trick him with some kind of scam. I was going to have to individually coach him through every bit of math required by the negotiations to keep him on my side. And I would have to do this coaching before I presented it to the whole school board to avoid having him railroad the process because he didn't understand the math.

This individual coaching strategy should be part of a required course on being a school administrator because it trips up many a fledgling superintendent.

I knew my best bet was to invest this enormous amount of time to get Harold on my side. Also, Harold's questions and misconceptions about the graphs were helpful to me as they gave me insights that honed my explanation skills for the next executive session when I had to explain it to the whole school board.

Within a half an hour Harold was relaxed and claiming credit for simplifying the graphs so that everyone could better understand them.

At the next school board executive session the simpler graph became part of a co-presentation to the rest of the school board with Harold and me sharing the explaining of the graph and answering the other board members questions. All the school board members indicated a willingness to use these graphs as a guide to a potential salary agreement with the teachers that achieved our target of 1 percent new money plus increment for the settlement.

The 1 percent total new money raises beyond increment each year for five years, if applied correctly to smooth out the anomalies in Mt. Mason's salary schedule, would allow our salary schedule to line up with the average plus 4 percent line on the graph in five years, which is where we expected the other local districts' average to be in five years.

Now, we had to work on the more difficult issue of health insurance. We had to identify our specific goal for health insurance and we had to do it before I met with the teacher union bargaining team. The legal restrictions on bargaining with employee unions prevent adding new issues or "changing the goalposts" with adjustments to financial or other targets after the negotiations have commenced.

"How much will the 1 percent in additional salary costs total each year? Is it more than we'll save with health insurance?" Helen Anderson wanted to know. I picked my words carefully because I did not want to offend anyone. I knew the district was wasting far more on health insurance than they were saving on salary increases by not settling this contract.

"The total annual teacher salaries for the district were about $12 million. One percent of $12 million is $120,000 so for us to come out even we have to save at least $120,000 a year on health insurance plus the cost of this year's mid-year raise and any one-time, off-schedule payment, and I'm certain we can do that," I replied.

As we ended our executive session conversation on salaries for teachers I knew it was a good time for a discussion about another key aspect of our negotiations strategy.

"We need to settle salary and health insurance with the teachers first; then we can work out the same basic things with the support staff and the administrators. Their unions are the tail to the teacher union dog. They won't hold out for larger raises or a better deal on health insurance once they see the teachers' settlement," I said.

Setting realistic goals for teacher contract provisions on health insurance would require research on the costs and teacher contributions for health insurance from the same 10 neighboring school districts we were using to measure teacher salaries.

It's the health insurance, stupid

When I started my first job as school superintendent in Albany, NY, in 1997, I, like many rookies who gained their primary educational leadership experience as principals, knew next to nothing about school district budgets, school labor contracts and employee health insurance costs and options.

I had lots of experience in all of the intricacies of academic requirements and improving student test scores, developing teacher classroom effectiveness, school schedules and school building budgets. Unfortunately, I had to learn a whole new set of financial skills in short order and in the hardest way of all, while under the gun in multiple difficult labor negotiations with entrenched and politically powerful unions. Any mistakes in my journey along this tricky path would potentially result in financial catastrophe or major labor unrest for our school district.

One thing that helped me immensely as I moved along this precipitous and dangerous learning curve was an outstanding (and expensive) school attorney named Jeff Honeywell.

As we stumbled our way through a complicated and confusing thicket of information, we became as much good friends as we were work colleagues. I sought and valued Jeff's advice for 20 years after our initial time together in Albany.

Jeff Honeywell is one in an army of high-priced attorneys specializing in school district law located all over New York State and in the other high cost-per-pupil states.[clxxvii] These attorneys and their firms are frequently organized into groups of super specialists: one who handles complicated special education issues; another who handles environmental issues; another who deals with charter schools; another who handles school construction; another who handles school district bonds.

Every one of these specialists charges several hundred dollars per hour for their services. In a district the size of Albany in 2016 with a school district budget of roughly $200 million, the total legal fees approach $400,000 - $600,000 or more annually.

So when we think of the extra costs for school districts that deal with public unions we should not forget the money we pay to lawyers who give superintendents essential help in resolving labor contract issues and other thorny legal issues that are much more complicated in states with strong public unions. It's part of the "union premium."

To my knowledge gains in student learning have never been shown by research to be positively linked to increased legal expenses for school districts.

When I arrived in Albany in 1997, the teacher union negotiations had broken down and there was a total lack of trust on both sides. Our school district negotiating team consisted of myself, Jeff Honeywell; our excellent school business official, John Paolino; and two very effective school board members, Theresa Swidorski and Barbara Gaffuri.

They were all honest to a fault and professional in all their interactions as members of our bargaining team. However, every time our school district team provided carefully researched salary and health insurance data to the teachers union negotiating team the teachers challenged the data as inaccurate and inflated.

Despite the fact that our data was based on actual payroll data and verifiable health insurance bills, the teachers union representatives on the negotiating team or their NYSUT (New York State United Teachers, state level union) labor relations specialist challenged the data and called it untrustworthy.

After extended arguments we were able to resolve our concerns about salaries, but we could not find a strategy whereby the union team would accept our data regarding health insurance without a challenge.

The stumbling block was the existing and expired teacher contract that continued in force at that time due to the Triborough Decision. The existing teacher contract required that the teachers make zero percent contributions toward their health insurance and provided teachers with a very expensive "Cadillac" Blue Cross Blue Shield Matrix plan. The Triborough Decision meant the teachers' zero percent contributions for their expensive Blue Cross health insurance would continue until a new contract was settled.

The annual health insurance price tag for members of the teachers union at that time was $10.2 million per year and was expected to go up by more than $1 million for the next school year. With more than three quarters of the teachers getting step raises and all teachers contributing zero percent for the expensive health insurance, the teacher union had little incentive to settle a new contract.

The teacher union bargaining team had drawn a line in the sand at zero percent contributions on Blue Cross Blue Shield for teachers and refused to believe it was really costing us $10.2 million a year.

They wouldn't back down and we couldn't afford to continue without contributions by teachers given the annual expected health insurance inflation rate of 5 to 10 percent a year at that time. We were requesting teacher contributions of 5 to 10 percent on these premiums, but we couldn't even hold a realistic discussion about contributions until we agreed on the actual cost of health insurance.

For many months in our negotiating sessions the teachers union claimed they didn't believe our health insurance numbers no matter what we did to reassure them at the negotiating table.

In New York State, public unions and their employers are required to negotiate in good faith which means lying, stalling and changing your demands during the negotiating process are verboten.

Of course PERB (Public Employees Relations Board), the government unit charged with implementing this cumbersome system, is in my view, a toothless tiger. The worst I've seen them do is issue a judgment that becomes a bad public relations piece in the newspaper and then goes away.

So they could do nothing to make the teachers union stop saying our numbers were wrong.

In any case, we decided on a new strategy. We called their bluff. We would give the teachers union the $10.2 million we were spending that year on teacher health insurance and they could buy their own insurance with a bid by local health insurance providers.

If our health insurance numbers were inflated, they should be able to buy the Blue Cross and Blue Shield Matrix Plan and still not have to require a health insurance contribution from the teachers. If we were right (and we knew we were), we could pocket the inflationary savings in lieu of a teacher contribution toward the cost of their health insurance.

Finally, the contract settled with this provision in place. A few months later we held the bid for teacher union member health insurance. Two local providers, Blue Cross Blue Shield and a local network called MVP submitted bids. Blue Cross Blue Shield bid $11.4 million, $1.2 million more than MVP's $10.2 million. To keep their zero percent contributions by teachers for their health insurance the teachers union would have to switch all their members to the less expensive and less desirable MVP plan. I was feeling good about the fact that our cost numbers had been proven honest, that we had saved $1.2 million and that the teachers union would be eating some well-deserved crow when they told their members about this difficult choice.

Then I received a surprise call from Blue Cross Blue Shield. They were reducing their bid amount by $1.2 million to $10.2 million. My reaction: "Can they even do that?"

I immediately called Jeff Honeywell who explained to me that yes they could reduce their bid and that I should accept this lower bid because not accepting it would just make all of our teachers change health insurance plans with no financial gain for the district.

It was then that I realized Blue Cross Blue Shield had always been charging our school district far more than the fair market price for our teachers' health insurance. Later I received a call from the MVP representative who said she expected things would go this way all the time. I was the only one in the dark on how this bid would play out.

Blue Cross Blue Shield knew our teachers didn't want to switch plans. They understood the difficulty of the school district's negotiating position with the teachers union. To this day, I believe they padded the insurance bills for years because of our weak bargaining position.

This pattern exists in all school districts and particularly school districts in states with strong public unions. Union premium school districts pay top dollar for almost everything from health insurance to bank services (local politics requires the selection of a local bank), school construction (better work out a project labor agreement with the construction unions, which will mean higher construction labor costs and construction bid prices to avoid costly delays) and fire and liability insurance (better give the bid to a local firm). Local politics, legal fees and union pressures come to bear on almost every item in the school budget.

Lesson learned: It's just as important to look at the specific health insurance plan and what you're paying for it as it is to focus on the percentage employees are contributing toward the plan. That was true in Mt. Mason as well.

An above average school district
When Tom Garrigus came to me with a summary of the health insurance costs for 10 surrounding school districts, I had already received

some data from the local BOCES (Board of Cooperative Education Services) that made me suspicious. Our real problem, I realized, came from the district's very high health insurance cost per employee and not teacher salaries, which were close to the regional average.

The 25 school districts in the local BOCES consortium included some smaller urban districts with 3,000 to 5,000 students, some smaller suburban school districts with 1,500 to 3,000 students and some very small rural school districts with between 500 and 1,500 students. In this 25 school district mix, the highest per-pupil cost for health insurance belonged to Mt. Mason at $3,924 per pupil.

Mt. Mason was 43 percent above the average of the 25 school districts. The average per-pupil spending on health insurance for these 25 school districts was $2,750 per pupil, which meant $2,750 of the cost per pupil went to district's health insurance bill. If Mt. Mason was spending the average amount per pupil on health insurance, the overall budget savings would be $2.5 million per year (15 percent less on the local property tax rate).

In fact, my paper copy of old state level figures from two years earlier had Mt. Mason listed at the 99th percentile in health insurance expenses per pupil among school districts in the state. Tom's summary illustrated the same.

Teacher Health Insurance Costs for Mt. Mason and 10 Neighboring School Districts based on 2015 numbers

District	Total Cost for Family Plan	Total Cost for Individual Plan	Cost per Teacher Including mix of Individual, 2 person and family plans	Teacher/Employer Health Insurance Cost share split	Health Insurance Cost per pupil including retiree health insurance
District A	18896	7369	15595	20/80	2611
District B	16448	6415	13576	15/85	2461
District C	17755	6924	14680	15/85	2611
District D	16448	6415	13576	20/80	2317
District E	16257	6340	13441	15/85	2437
District F	17755	6924	14679	12/88	2754
District G	18211	7102	15056	20/80	2568
District H	19224	7497	15894	18/82	2780
District I	20156	7860	16665	15/85	3020
District J	17405	6787	14390	10/90	2762
Mt. Mason	22179	8649	18338	0/100	3924
Average for 11 Districts	18248	7116	15087	14.5/85.5	2750

Doing the math on the figures in Tom's chart I found out that if we could get just the 200 teachers to shift to a new health insurance plan that cost the region's average of $15,087 per employee from the very rich plan they had now, which cost the district an average of $18,338 per employee, we would save the district $650,200 annually (18,338 − 15,087 = 3251, 200 X 3,251 = 650,200).

If the teachers moved to this new health insurance plan and contributed 15 percent of the cost of their health insurance, the district would additionally save $452,610 annually (200 X 15,087 X .15 = $452,610).

That meant we needed to move the teachers into a cheaper plan and get them to contribute toward their health insurance. Both would be important to the long-term financial health of the school district and would create an annual savings of $1.1 million ($650,200 + $452,610 = $1,102,810), money that could be invested into a results-oriented academic program and offset the increase in salaries we had to offer to get the health insurance change we needed.

If we could get the support staff and administrators to make these same changes with their 100 employees, we could save another $551,405. And if we could get future retirees to also switch to the cheaper plan and contribute toward their health insurance, we could recover the entire $2.5 million.

Existing retirees will eventually die and be replaced by new retirees who will have the less expensive plan, projecting more savings for the district. The economics of actuarial science apply to public employee contracts.

Anyone who has dealt with these issues realizes that convincing employees to shift to a new and less expensive health insurance plan is not easy. Employees (especially those who will soon retire with health insurance fully paid for by the school district) are understandably concerned that in an effort to save money the school district leadership team will push them into a poor quality health insurance plan that won't provide the coverage they need.

In the strong public union states, most employees who retire from the school system — teachers, support staff and administrators — are guaranteed health insurance in retirement (this health insurance becomes a supplement to Medicare when the retirees reach age 65), and the cost for this retiree group is a significant factor in the district's health insurance cost equation.

By law in New York State the quality of the health insurance for retirees cannot be unilaterally changed by their employer once they have retired. And the contribution rates for retirees toward their health insurance cannot be unilaterally changed. A different health insurance plan can be provided to retirees, but it must be substantially the same as the plan it replaces.

In Mt. Mason the two other groups of individuals who received their health insurance from the school district besides the members of the teachers union included 150 retirees and 100 support staff and administrative employees. We would have to consider their concerns and involve them in the discussion.

By law we could not force the retirees who had retired with zero percent health insurance contributions to contribute. That horse had left the barn and would not be back.

I knew I'd need help with negotiations so I made three phone calls.
First, I called a labor attorney I knew I'd need to help me with negotia-
tions. I had already mentioned the need for this attorney in executive
session with the school board, and they knew I'd be making this call.
The attorney I called, Alice Donnelly, was a school district attorney I
worked with multiple times in the past. She was professional, reason-
ably priced and lived near Mt. Mason. I asked her if she was interested
in helping me with the union negotiations in Mt. Mason.

"With any other superintendent, no way. I read the papers and I know
Mt. Mason is a mess. But with you there, how can I say no." she said.

I told her Mt. Mason was receiving bad advice on health insurance.
I asked her to recommend two or three health insurance consultants who
could help us broker the best deal on health insurance for the school district.

"We need a health insurance consultant who can talk to retirees and
the support staff and administrator unions, plus the teachers," I said. "I
know the law says we can't change the retiree health insurance quality
even if we decide to change the provider so I want your advice on how to
proceed and avoid becoming embroiled in contracted legal issues," I said.

She paused, thinking. "I'll email you contact information for three
consultant groups that have multiple experiences at making this kind of
change with unions and retirees," she said. "They're groups serving big
enough numbers of participants to command good prices from the insur-
ance companies and providers. Who are you presently working with?"

"Alex Karrel from Summit Insurance Consulting." I replied.

Alice informed me that Summit had a reputation for taking consult-
ing payments from both the school districts and the insurance companies
they're supposed to be negotiating with on behalf of the school districts.
They have lost clients. "As their group size has shrunk, their health insur-
ance prices for their clients have increased dramatically," she said.

I had heard this from other sources. Because the contracts hadn't
settled for five-plus years the situation just grew worse over time. The
amount Mt. Mason spent on health insurance added up to more per
pupil than any other district within 100 miles.

With what we could save in health insurance we could more than pay for a reasonable teacher salary increase and still have money left over for some necessary academic improvements.

"We'll have questions about pricing and options for community-rated insurance (a rating based on a community's usage of health insurance) products and pricing rated on our specific group so we'll need someone who fully understands that part of the business as well," I said.

"Our group including the retirees is probably younger and healthier than the average school district so pricing rated on our specific group might be the way to go. I'll send you the school board negotiations goals and the data we have on health insurance and salaries. I'll also set up a time for us to talk with the school board in executive session as soon as possible. The school board has decided to let me handle the negotiations, but you might have to convince them to add you."

Every school district in New York State (733) is doing these kinds of negotiations all the time. Imagine every individual Starbucks negotiating its own health insurance contract. Rest assured your cup of coffee would cost a lot more than it does now.

After Alice and I hung up, I called Sally Anselm the teacher union president and set up a time for the two of us to meet to discuss negotiations. She wanted to bring her entire negotiating team.

"Let's just the two of us meet so we can set a date for a formal negotiations session with everyone including all of our team. I want to give you some data we've assembled that will hopefully be helpful for us as we move toward a settlement," I said.

She paused. I knew this wasn't what she wanted or had expected to hear. "Alright, but no surprises. I'll set it up with your secretary," she said.

Then I phoned Harold Smith and asked him to come to my office so we could review the health insurance data.

"You want me to clean up the data again before you give it out to whole school board?" he asked.

"That's right," I told him. "That way we won't have to do it twice and I'll get it right the first time."

Harold came to my office within the hour. After he and I reviewed the health insurance data, I made two small adjustments he suggested and put aside copies for our next executive session.

I also explained to him my thoughts regarding the need to change the school district's health insurance consultant and my suggestion for an attorney to help us with negotiations. Harold hesitated and I could see the wheels turning. He had run the school district negotiations for the past five years. They had accomplished nothing. Now he was relinquishing control of this process to me, a new lawyer he hadn't met and a health insurance consultant we had yet to hire.

"What if I invite Alice Donnelly to an executive session with you and the other board members where we can discuss the health insurance data and you can get her recommendations. When she leaves, we can discuss whether we should hire her and follow her advice?" I said, sensing his concern.

Harold smiled. "That sounds good as long as we get to meet her first before we decide to proceed," he said.

When Sally Anselm, the teacher union president, arrived in my office I thanked her for coming and handed her the three-page salary summary sheet and the health insurance summary data. She looked surprised. Sally was a high school English teacher in her fifties with short grey hair and glasses that hung on a lanyard around her neck.

"It's two summaries. One on salaries and one on health insurance for neighboring districts. Tom Garrigus assembled it," I told her. "Feel free to ask Tom any questions you have about it. Also, feel free to check Tom's data by calling your teacher union colleagues in any of the neighboring school districts.

"You should share this with your negotiating team in advance," I said, "so they understand it. I'd like to get started with negotiations sessions as soon as possible. We should all be working off the same data. I'm only here one year and I want to settle a reasonable contract both the school board and the union can support."

I handed her a separate page identifying Districts A-J. "These districts agreed to give us all this data on the condition that we not release their names publicly as some of them are also in negotiations," I added. "I'll have my secretary get to work on setting up a few negotiations dates." I said, expecting Sally to leave.

But she had a question. "Who will be on your negotiating team? If Harold Smith is on your team it will not work. We've been down that road too many times before," she said emphatically.

"Harold will not be part of our negotiating team and there will be no school board members on our team," I said. "We hope to have our team set by next week and have our first negotiating session by October 1st. I am meeting with the school board next week to share this data with them and finalize our plans."

Sally smiled. "Look, I know we need to make some kind of health insurance change and we're willing to be reasonable. That health insurance is our only bargaining chip in these negotiations. All we're asking for is that we're treated with respect. We're willing to give these negotiations another try, but I have no patience for Mr. Smith or his loud-mouthed, nasty public attacks on teachers," she said and turned and left my office.

Health insurance 101

Every school superintendent (and mayor, and town manager, and public university president, etc.) is forced to complete a brand new crash course about health insurance purchasing every few years. Failure to completely digest all the essential assignments in this crash course in a timely manner results in the school district (or city, village, university, etc.) paying much more than is necessary for health insurance for employees and retirees. As the complexity rises, a few principles re-emerge with every re-teaching of the health insurance course.

* First, if you try to do this as one small school district, city, village or university you will have little bargaining power due to your small numbers of employees and retirees. You will need to be part of larger group.
* Second, you cannot navigate these choices without professional help in the form of a health insurance consultant who represents a large insurance purchasing group of employees and retirees, knows

the players, has their respect and has successfully negotiated recent agreements for clients like you.

* Third, these consultants make their living by negotiating the best rates with professional negotiators who represent the insurance companies and providers. The health insurance consultants can just as easily turn their negotiations prowess into a big gain for themselves and a small gain, no gain or even a big loss for the school district. Or the initial big gain for the client can turn, over time if not monitored and adjusted, into a big gain for the consultant and no gain or a loss for the client. The health insurance consultants need careful monitoring and regular audits and checks.

* Fourth, because of changing laws, prices and contracts the target of the best health insurance at the lowest cost is always moving. Sitting still means health insurance consultants, health insurers and health providers will take advantage by raising rates more than health insurance purchase prices and actual health provider price inflation requires. Any school district like Mt. Mason that stuck with one health insurance provider and consultant arrangement long past its expiration date is certain to be paying top dollar for a defective product. The providers, insurance companies and health insurance consultants know this and make a lot of their money off of unknowing school districts.

* Fifth, the employees and especially the retirees will not want to change their health insurance to follow the moving target. Changing health insurance is guaranteed to be a huge hassle for employees and retirees and always brings the understandable and all too frequently reasonable fear that quality will decline and doctors and other providers and essential drugs will disappear from approved lists or become too pricey to purchase. Making the necessary changes in health insurance will require lots of education for all the participants and sound selections regarding health insurance consultants and health insurance plans. And it will take enormous amounts of patience and school district leadership time.

* Last, a key to getting this education to work effectively with employees and retirees is to have them share substantially in paying

for health insurance. If they have "skin in the game" they will be more interested in learning all the intricacies and be willing to shift insurance companies when necessary.

So the superintendent who decides to do the right thing and look at the options for a new health insurance arrangement is stepping into a gator-filled pond. But s/he has no choice unless s/he is willing to let her school district pay more and more and more for lower and lower quality health insurance.

The lawyer sets the stage

When we met with the school board, I started handing out the health insurance data and explaining it with the help of Harold, doing my best to keep his ego in check by sharing the stage with him. I had created a small packet that included the school board's final goals for the teacher negotiations, the three-page salary comparison graphs and data and the health insurance comparison data.

When I explained the health insurance data, Harold jumped in to note his preferences. "See those districts with 20 percent contributions by their employees. That's where we should be." Harold said.

"The average for these 11 districts is 14.5 percent contributions," I told them. "Remember, our goal is that we get a health insurance contribution close enough to the area average that our total cost for teacher salaries and health insurance, including the teacher salary increment cost of 1.4 percent average, increases by no more than 1 percent of the salary base cost per year."

Immediately after this I introduced Attorney Alice Donnelly to the school board, but before I could describe the key role I foresaw for Alice, Harold interrupted.

"Alice, why do we need to spend $200 an hour for you to get involved in negotiations? Why can't Lonnie do this himself with the help of our local attorney who costs half as much?" Harold barked, as his sycophant supporter Doug sat smirking beside him.

I had forewarned Alice over a sub shop dinner in advance of our school board session of the obstacles she could expect to encounter when she met the school board.

Alice smiled at the obvious attempted provocation. "Lonnie is very experienced and will lead your district to a successful negotiations conclusion. I'm a contracts expert, and if someone with my skill set is not there at the negotiations table the final agreement will probably miss some of the critical details in the actual contract writing. Grievances and labor strife will follow. Also, I have a lot of experience settling contracts in districts with a history similar to Mt. Mason's. I'm certain that experience will be helpful."

Harold stopped and considered this new information.

Harold's pause gave Helen Andersen, the grey-haired woman on the board majority, time to jump into the conversation. "Why can't our regular attorney, Jack Bulloch, complete this as part of what we are already paying him to do?" Helen asked.

"Excellent question. I know Jack. He's a great guy and good attorney, but he has never settled a teacher contract like this and he has tried to help you do that repeatedly over the past five years. I spoke to Jack before this meeting and he thinks, as do Lonnie and I, that a new face for the district at the negotiations table would help get a fresh start and move toward a conclusion faster and more amicably."

"Given your experience do you think we can achieve our goals?" asked Tabitha Conners, the obvious leader of the school board minority.

"I think your goals can be achieved, but it may take several months." Alice answered.

Then came a question Alice and I had rehearsed during our sub shop dinner.

"After looking at the health insurance data and getting our history on health insurance how do you think we should proceed so that we can get a better price on health insurance for our employees and retirees?" I asked.

Alice looked around the room. "When we had a similar problem in Allenville we created a formal Request for Proposals from health insurance consulting firms to manage the health insurance purchases of the school district.

"We invited all the unions and the retirees to a session with the school board to participate in interviews of all the responding firms.

Then, after interviewing all the participants and discussing the inter-views with all the unions and retirees the school board selected one firm from the group.

"The firm met separately with the school board and superintendent and also separately with each union and separately with the retirees to understand the concerns of each stakeholder group. Then they made recommendations to the school board at a public meeting regarding changes in health insurance for the school district," she explained.

Harold Smith pounced immediately. "So, you're recommending we hire another high-priced consultant for health insurance?" he asked, shaking his head.

Alice, remained calm and her voice showed no emotion. "Your school district is already paying a health insurance consultant. The company is Summit Insurance Consulting, and I believe you've met their representative, Alex Karrel," she said.

Harold was not taken aback by his obvious error. "Yeah, we met him. Another empty suit as I recall and you and Lonnie are telling us he hasn't been doing his job, right? How do we know another one will do any better?" he asked, obviously frustrated and just as obviously play acting his Grumpy Old Man routine to impress Alice and the other school board members.

"You'll get to interview all the RFP respondents and listen to all the input from the unions and retirees and hear my recommendation and Lonnie's before you decide who to choose from among the firms. Summit Insurance will most likely submit a proposal so if keeping them makes the most sense you can do so at that time." Alice answered.

"Well, we better not do anything to hurt those retirees. They're important people in our community," Harold said.

Many of Harold's votes in the school board election came from senior citizens, including retired school district employees. Harold like many school board members railed about both health insurance com-pany rip-offs and high school property taxes AND about not hurting retired employees who enjoyed their expensive health insurance benefits. The same retirees voted for Harold to protect their over-priced benefits.

Harold decided he needed to be on stage again. "How much will this cost us? We know that you're expensive at $200 an hour. Jack only charges us $100 an hour. How many hours of your time will this take?" he asked.

Alice anticipated this question. "In Gloversville, we settled in six months and it cost the district 60 hours of my time or $12,000. In Rome, it took two years and 125 hours of my time or $25,000.

"Your situation has been difficult, but Lonnie is only here one year. We need to get this done promptly. Both sides are motivated to settle and this data on salaries and health insurance plus the school board's goals which are reasonable give us a good chance for a relatively quick settlement," Alice said.

Alice left and immediately after she was gone Tabitha Conners turned to the other school board members. "She's a professional who knows what she's doing," she said. "She'll help us get this done properly and quickly. I told you it was a mistake to hire Jack Bulloch. He's a real estate attorney."

Harold rose to the bait instantly. "Jack Bulloch is an excellent attorney and he's saved the district money every year with his lower fees. These school district attorneys charge way more than they're worth," he said with equal contempt.

I jumped in hoping to return to the task at hand before we had an explosion of egos. "We can talk about long-term attorneys some other time. For now, let's agree to hire Alice for negotiations at $200 per hour?" I asked.

The board members all nodded with Harold glowering and Tabitha chuckling.

"I'll put it on the agenda for our next public meeting," I said. "Let's move on to the health insurance data discussion and how we should proceed with that issue."

Tabitha Conners held up the health insurance summary sheet. "If I'm reading this right, we would save even more if we could convince the teachers union to agree to a cheaper plan than we would by increasing employee contributions for health insurance," she said.

"If the 200 members of the teachers union switched to an average cost plan, the district would save about $650,000 per year. If we can convince the 100 support staff and administrators to make the same switch, we could save another $325,000 a year," I said.

Tabitha hesitated while doing some quick math in her head and Helen Anderson jumped in. "What about the retirees; can they switch plans?" she asked.

"The retirees must be allowed to keep the same insurance or be offered an equivalent insurance plan at the same price. We can't force them to switch. Offering them a different but equivalent plan would require legal advice and help from the health insurance consultant Alice mentioned earlier. It's tricky but doable. If we work all that out and the retirees switch to an average cost health insurance plan, we would save another $487,000 per year. So, the answer to your question is — yes!" I said.

Harold couldn't stay out of the conversation for long. "Yeah, but what about contributions for health insurance from the employees? That's what we really want," he barked.

"If the teachers contributed at the average rate in our region, 14.5 percent, the district would save an additional $550,000 per year. The support staff and administrators contributing at this rate would save the district an additional $225,000 per year. We can't ask the present retirees to contribute because by law their contribution is set at the rate it was when they retired which is zero percent. But we should work at getting future retirees to contribute at these same rates," I said.

Tabitha's calculations were complete in her head. "So, if we get the unions to agree to all these health insurance changes and we get them to agree to the salary raises of one percent plus increment, we'll save $1.5 to $2 million a year on health insurance and we'll be spending $150,000 more each year for teacher salaries? Nice work Harold. Why'd we wait five years to do this? That was really stupid," she said with glee.

Harold immediately went on the offensive. "Those damn teachers wouldn't agree to change their health insurance or accept reasonable wage increases," he barked. "We offered and they said – no! I told this board and three different superintendents these unions were killing us with their health insurance and nobody did anything. So don't blame me," he bellowed.

I tried to cool things down by speaking softly. "Listen, we can't let these issues or the unions divide us. We have our goals and if we stick to them we can be successful with these negotiations. There will be no gains made by trying to blame each other for problems in the past. We need to move forward."

The room was silent. Tabitha was smirking. Helen was trying to suppress a smile and Harold was scowling. The other school board members didn't make eye contact with me or with each other.

I wrapped it up. "I will let you know when we've scheduled our first negotiating sessions, and you'll see our contract with Alice and the dates for the health insurance consultant RFP interviews in your next school board packets for action at our next public meeting," I said. And we adjourned.

This would be a challenging group to keep together all the way to the finish line.

"Working with a school board is like herding cats," a school super-intendent colleague of mine once told me.

"More like herding bees," I told him. "And eventually one of them will sting you." I had multiple stingers at the ready in Mt. Mason.

As I drove home that night I couldn't help but think of all the money wasted on health insurance providers and health insurance consultants by Mt. Mason and many other smaller and larger school districts across the state and the country. And it wasn't just health insur-ance that gobbled up the critical funding that should be going toward improving educational outcomes for students.

Part II - So, where has all the money gone?

● ● ●

THE UNITED STATES HAS INCREASED the amount we spend on K-12 education exponentially[clxxviii] and yet we're bombarded daily with news articles and opinion pieces highlighting the fact that almost all academic testing and other school performance data (National Assessment of Educational Progress, SAT, high school graduation rates, state Common Core test results, etc.) has remained flat.[clxxix]

So, where has all the money gone?

It's gone to teaching employees and more important to their health insurance and pension benefits, especially in high-cost, union-strong states.[clxxx]

The U.S. average (that's the national average) ratio of pupils to teachers has increased 40 percent since I started my career in 1970 from 22.3 pupils per teacher then to 15.9 pupils per teacher now, according to the National Center for Education Statistics.[clxxxi]

In 1970, there were almost four-and-a-half (4.483) teachers or other professional educators for every 100 students. In 2013, there were more than six (6.289) teachers or other education professionals for every 100 students. ((6.289-4.483)/4.483 = .403 (40 percent)).

- States with stronger unions (NY, NJ, MA, IL, CT, RI, NH, DC, and VT) – high-cost states – have the lowest pupil-to-teacher ratios, with 12.0 pupils for every teacher.[clxxx]
- States with weaker unions (UT, SC, AZ, ID, NV, OR, TX, and AL) – low-cost states – have higher pupil-to-teacher ratios, with 18.4 pupils per teacher.[clxxxiii]

The teaching staff increased 84 percent between 1970 and 2013 in strong public union, high-cost states – going from 4.5 teachers or other professionals per 100 pupils in 1970 to 8.3 teachers or other professionals per 100 pupil in 2013 ((8.3-4.5/4.5) =.84).

In weak public union, low-cost states, school districts only experienced a 20 percent increase in the teacher population – going from 4.5 teachers per 100 pupils to 5.4 teachers per 100 pupils during the same 1970 to 2013 time frame ((5.4-4.5/4.5) =.20).

If you're wondering why the strong public union states increased the number of teachers so dramatically, remember union budgets grow or shrink based on the number of teachers paying union dues. More teachers means more dues, which is why unions always lobby for more teachers.

One might assume more teachers were added due to increasing enrollments in the schools, but the total K-12 enrollment (46 million K-12 students at the height of the baby boom) dropped significantly in the 1980s. It's rebounded today but isn't much higher than it was in 1970 (48 million).[clxxxiv]

The reason for the lower pupil-to-teacher ratio is we've added teachers in special education; English as a second language; the arts; remedial education; and vocational education. We've also added teachers to reduce class sizes.

In low-costs states most of the 20 percent increase in new teachers went to special education. In high-cost states about half of the 84 percent increase in new teachers went to special education.

Special education expenses for teachers, teacher aides and teacher assistant salaries and for tuitions for special education students placed in programs outside the school districts grew from 4 percent to 17 percent of a typical school budget between 1967 and 1991, according to the Economic Policy Institute.[clxxxv] And, the cost per pupil was much higher in 1991 than it was in 1967.[clxxxvi]

And special education expenses didn't stop growing in 1991. I estimate special education costs account for 25 percent of school districts' much larger budgets in 2015.

In the three districts where I served as a schools superintendent, anywhere from 40 percent to 60 percent of teachers, aides and assistants who work with special education students were not accounted for in the special education category of the school district budget for a variety of reasons mostly related to accounting rules. Also not included was their health insurance and pension costs. The same is true of transportation (school bus purchases or maintenance and operations expenses related to special education) and clerical staff who worked for special education.

In the small school district of BKW (1,000 students in all), we had a secretary who only worked on special education. Her salary and benefits were not within the special education category of the school district budget; she was in the clerical category. When people say special education is only 10 percent of the school district budget, they're wrong.

The special education line item of a school district budget can be misleading because it usually doesn't include salaries, health insurance and pensions for special education teachers, teaching assistants and teacher aides. Many of these employee costs are paid for by grants that fall into another category – federal grants, for example – of the school district budget.

If special education employees are 25 percent of the district's total workforce, they comprise 25 percent of the district's entire health insurance bill. The same applies for pension costs, the employer's share of Social Security costs, etc.

Where's the beef?

We don't ever want to return to the dismal state of special education we had before the IDEA (PL-94-142), but it's important that we put our money into things that improve student achievement.[clxxxvii]

The pendulum has swung too far in the other direction, especially given the fact that special education services don't have a positive impact on student achievement. In fact, quite the opposite. The data shows the more districts spend on special education the worse the results.[clxxxviii]

And, as we put more and more resources into special education it becomes self-perpetuating; the "solution" for students who can't read becomes – "put them in special ed." It's become an academic crutch for students and teachers.

And a boon to the union coffers. In 1969-1970 there were 57,000 teacher aides in schools in the U.S. By 2009, that number had grown to 737,000 teacher aides in U.S. schools.[clxxxix]

Teacher aides work as one-on-one aides for special education students who need toileting, feeding and help with mobility in classrooms and on the bus. Teaching assistants, who in New York State are now required to complete two college courses (yes, two college courses), provide academic help to special education students.

As the number of special education teachers, teacher aids and teaching assistants has increased so have the number of students identified as needing special education services in the U.S.

Between 1976-77 and 2009-10, the number of students identified as needing special education services grew from 3.7 million to 6.5 million and the number of students classified as "learning disabled" grew from 800,000 to 2.8 million during the same years.[cxc] The total student population stayed roughly the same during these years.

More subject specialist teachers (computers, art, music, vocational education, Advanced Placement, etc.) at the elementary, middle and high school levels, decreased class sizes and added English language learner programs also have contributed to lower pupil-to-teacher ratios but to a lesser degree.[cxci]

Some of these added jobs were lost during the 2008 economic meltdown. But recent trends show the additional staffing coming back to schools as the states again add to their budgets with restored state aid lost during the recession.[cxcii]

Unfortunately, the addition of these jobs hasn't produced any significant positive impact on academics as measured by internationally recognized tests.

TODAY VS. 1970

Everything related to adding more teaching staff has contributed to the unsustainability of school district budgets in more ways than one. In 1970, a typical family health insurance plan cost about $700 annually in a high-cost state and $400 or less in a low-cost state. Employers in high-cost states paid the full amount. In low-cost states some school districts paid the full amount and others paid as little as nothing towards employee health insurance.

With the normal inflation factor of 6.46 between 1970 and 2015, the high-cost states' $700 policy would be expected to increase to $4,522 in 2015. In low-cost states the average district health insurance expense of $250 per employee with normal inflation would be expected to increase to $1.615 (6.46 X 250 = 1615).

But as close as I can estimate after looking at several sources, the cost of the same typical family health insurance plan without deductibles and with smaller co-pays (similar to those in place in 1970) today is $20,400[cxciii] in high-cost states. In low-cost states, school districts have generally opted for lower cost high deductible/high co-pay plans that cost about $14,000 per year for a typical family plan.

All school districts pay for a mixture of family health insurance plans, individual plans and two-person plans so the average cost of health insurance per school district employee in high-cost states is $16,000 and in low-cost states the cost of health insurance per employee is $11,000. And low-cost states pay 80 percent of the cost of high deductible/high co-pay plans ($8,800 = 11000 X 0.80), and high-cost states pay an average of 85 percent of the cost of no deductible/low co-pay plans. ($13,600 = 16000 X 0.85).[cxciv]

The No. 1 reason school district health insurance costs have gone up: They hired more staff, teachers, support staff and administrators. In low-costs states there are 20 percent more teachers, 50 percent more support staff and 33 percent more administrators today than there were in 1970.

The entire $8,800 school district health insurance cost for each employee in low-cost states added since 1970, some of whom have retired and still receive health insurance, is part of the $3,549 per pupil cost increase beyond simple inflation spent in low-cost states.

In high-cost states there are 84 percent more teachers, 50 percent more support staff members and 33 percent more administrators. The entire $13,600 in school district health insurance costs per employee/retiree added since 1970 in high-cost states, some of whom have retired and still receive health insurance from the school district, is part of the $13,980 in per pupil cost increase beyond CPI in high-cost states, including New York State.

You get the picture.

TAKE IT ONE STEP FURTHER

Even without employees added since 1970 the cost of health insurance has risen well beyond CPI. The cost of health insurance for the employees who existed in 1970 in low-cost states and the retirees from those positions, which accounts for 80 percent of today's teachers, 67 percent of today's support staff and 25 percent of today's administrators, has increased dramatically.

In low-cost states, $7,185 (8800 − 1615 = 7185) per employee/retiree health insurance cost is part of the $3,549 total per pupil cost increase above and beyond CPI inflation. The $7,185 would have been $1,615 if only CPI were applied.

The cost of health insurance for the employees who existed in 1970 in high-cost states and the retirees from those positions, which accounts for 54 percent of today's teachers, 75 percent of today's support staff and 25 percent of today's administrators, also has increased dramatically.

In high-cost states, $9,078 ($13,600 − $4,522 = $9,078) per employee/retiree health insurance cost is part of the $13,980 total per pupil cost increase above and beyond CPI inflation. The $13,600 would have been $4,522 if only CPI were applied.

Keep in mind health insurance is sometimes more expensive in low-cost states because there are fewer options. Less competition and fewer health care providers drive up the price of health care. School districts in many rural areas see a greater percentage of their budgets focused on health insurance.

Negotiations 101

When we exchanged our negotiating proposals and sat down for our first negotiating session with teachers in mid-October, I was a little uncertain what to expect. I felt good about our team: Tom Garrigus, our business official and numbers guy; Alice Donnelly, our professional negotiator; and myself.

I felt confident about our proposal, which included the graphs and data for salaries and health insurance comparing Mt. Mason with ten neighboring school districts.

Our proposal included:

- *the school board approved salary offer (1 percent new money each year above the step raises built into the existing salary schedule for a five-year contract with no retroactive raises for the five years the district had been without a contract)*
- *moving the district's teacher salary schedule closer to the 11 district average line plus 4 percent over the five-year period. (This extra percent per year meant we would be aiming to hit the area average teacher salary five years out assuming the region continued to give teachers raises averaging 1 percent.)*
- *shift the active teachers into a new and much cheaper health insurance base plan (the old plan would remain available at an extra cost to teachers who wanted to keep it by paying the entire difference)*
- *teachers contribute toward the cost of health insurance in increasing increments of 5 percent for each of the final 4 years of the contract (5 percent, 10 percent, 15 percent and finally 20 percent).*

The latter was designed so that teachers' raises in salary always would exceed their increased contribution to their health insurance.

Our proposal also suggested we form a committee with all the unions and the school board to select a new health insurance consultant the school board would appoint. This mutually agreed upon consultant would help us select our new health insurance base plan.

My uncertainty came from what to expect in the teachers' proposal. My concerns about Sally Anselm's reputation as a difficult negotiator was partially put to rest when I saw that the NYSUT (New York State United Teachers union) representative assigned to help with these negotiations was Charlie Stafford a NYSUT representative I had a decent experience with in the City School District of Albany.

Then I looked at the teachers' proposal. They were asking for 5 percent new money per year (that would mean 25 percent more over five years), no changes to health insurance and in place of a retroactive raise for the five years the district was without a contract a lump sum payment equal to 10 percent of each teacher's salary.

The five teachers on their team smirked almost in unison when I asked Sally Anselm, the teacher union president, if I understood their proposal correctly. We were miles apart. I asked for an opportunity to caucus and discuss their proposal with our team while they did the same with their team and our proposal.

Once we were alone I asked Tom Garrigus if he could add the final year salary the teachers' proposal projected to the graph we put in their packet which showed the teacher area average salary plus 4 percent. Tom said it would take him a few minutes. When he was done, we went back and showed what he had created to the teachers' negotiating team the updated line graph.

Mt. Mason Teacher Initial Salary Proposal

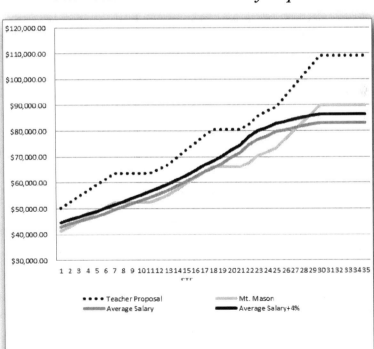

We shared the graph, explained what it meant and shared the data behind the graph.

"Mt. Mason is too small a school district to set the labor contract norm for teachers in our area," I told them. "I'm here for one year and you are not obligated to settle your contract with us in that time period. But given your history there's a good chance that if this contract isn't settled this year it may not settle for many years to come.

I explained to them that Mt. Mason teachers shouldn't be paid significantly less or more than neighboring districts' teachers. Their health insurance plan should also cost about the same as other districts in the area. And they should be contributing towards their health insurance at about the same rate as other teachers in the area.

Then I spoke with the best sincerity I could muster. "I've convinced the school board that we need to look at the local norms to settle this contract," I said. "If you want a significantly better deal than the local norm on salary and health insurance you'll need to wait for the next superintendent to tackle this negotiations process. Your salary offer is clearly well outside the parameters we have for these negotiations. Please reconsider it. I suggest we adjourn for today."

As I gathered my papers and we broke up, NYSUT representative Charlie Stafford signaled me silently to follow him to an adjacent room.

"Look, these guys are used to playing hide the ball and dealing with a school board that lies to them and treats them disrespectfully in private and in public," he said. "I think we can work this out because your offer is reasonable. Give me a week or two and I'll call you about another meeting."

I nodded and smiled. "Charlie, I'm sure you'll try to do your job, but we need to move quickly. I have two other contracts I need to settle this year."

When the school board met in executive session the following Tuesday, Harold was just about singing when he heard what had happened.

"See, I told you these teachers were real bastards," he said. "They'll never settle this contract. You'll see," he said with a combination of venom and joy.

The following day, Charlie Stafford called. "We have a new salary proposal for your team to review. How soon can we meet?" he asked.

Eight days later we were all around the same table again, and Sally Anselm handed me a copy of our proposal with handwritten notes on the side. The notes said:

- *increment plus 2 percent per year on salary*
- *okay to hiring a new health insurance consultant*
- *okay to health insurance base plan idea as long as teachers have some control over what new plan we buy*
- *active teachers move to new base health insurance plan or they pay the difference in cost from the base plan if they stay with BC/BS*
- *retired teachers don't have to make any changes*
- *health insurance contributions of 2 percent, 4 percent, 6 percent and 8 percent for active teachers*
- *zero percent contributions in retirement for teachers who retire during this contract*
- *a one-time payment in place of retroactive raises equal to 3 percent of salary*

We all looked at the notes and I realized our team needed to agree on how best to respond. I wanted to hear what Tom and Alice had to say.

"This is a good starting place. I want to meet with our team separately to discuss how we can best respond. This may take us an hour or so," I said, as respectfully as possible.

When the three of us were in Tom's cramped office with the door shut, Tom spoke first. "This is the best proposal we've seen in six years. The health insurance concessions alone will put us in the black for sure even with lower contributions and 2 percent plus increment salary increases. This is a huge gain for the district," he said.

Alice was sober and thoughtful. "I think we can stretch their health insurance offer a bit. I sense that they would bend more as long as we link it to the area average. They should be contributing more for health insurance, and we need to get the retirees contributing for their health insurance also.

"Let's go back with 4, 8, 12 and 16 percent, and retirees contribute at the rate in effect when they retire," Alice said. "This becomes a bit of a retirement incentive because if they retire sooner they will contribute less for their health insurance in retirement. It also shows movement on our part so they know we're listening to them. And it moves us closer to the area average.

"With the base plan we want and the contributions by teachers that I'm suggesting we'll be saving $2,500 per teacher per year compared to what we are spending. The extra 1 percent on salary they are asking for beyond what we offered amounts to about $600 per teacher per year above what we offered." Alice said.

I knew we could hit the school board's target if we accepted their offer, but I thought we could do better.

"Even with the cumulative effect of adding salary raises over five years we were still well ahead," I said. "The problem is the top step teachers. Two percent per year for them for five years will make that right hand end of the graph, which is already too high, stick out like a sore thumb.

"And our school board does not want retroactive raises, and this one-time, off-schedule payment smells like a retroactive raise but it won't affect the salary schedule," I said.

We all sat quietly. "What if we said to them that we can agree with increment plus 1.75 percent so that it moves every step on their schedule as close as possible to the area average line," Tom said. "That would force them to face the fact that their top step teachers are paid more than they should be. It would also force them to deal with the bumps and flat places in their salary schedule. And it would force them to do the math which I am not eager to tackle."

I laughed. "I knew there was a reason I brought you along on this team. Sounds good to me. Alice?" I turned to Alice. She smiled and nodded.

"The one-time, off-schedule payment is the way NYSUT has been handling districts that haven't settled for a long time around the state. In the end, we'll have to give in on that to some degree. If Tom can find the money in this year's budget to pay for it, I suggest we go back with 2 percent instead of the 3 percent they proposed for the signing bonus," Alice said.

"I'm okay with that," I said.

"Tom, do we have the money?" I asked. Tom nodded and Alice went to work typing up our counter proposal on Tom's computer. Tom printed copies for members of both negotiating teams.

After an hour we returned to the negotiating room and the teacher team members were scattered about the room, reading their phones, gossiping over coffee and reading the newspaper. Once they reassembled Alice handed out a sheet summarizing our counter proposal:

- *Employees pay the difference for any plan more expensive than the base plan for health insurance.*
- *They contribute 4, 8, 12 and 16 percent in years two through five for active employees and future retirees (retire with the contribution rate in effect at that time). Note: We specified years two through five because it's too late to get this new health insurance plan in place for the present year.*
- *1.75 percent plus increment on salary distributed so as to best match the area average plus 4 percent line on the graph in year five of the contract.*
- *2 percent off-schedule, one-time payment in place of a retroactive raise.*

Alice added in her written counter proposal that the agreement (1) must be approved by positive votes from the school board and the union (2) the new health insurance consultant must be approved by the school board with input from all the bargaining units (3) the base health insurance plan to be in effect for years two through five of this five-year contract must be agreed to by the unions and the school board (4) the one-time payment and any retroactive raises for the year in progress (the first year of this five-year contract) would be paid within two weeks of the completion of steps one, two and three in a separate check.

Sally and her team members read our counter proposal carefully. "We'll need some time to digest this and think about it. We also need to meet and discuss how we should respond. I will call you when we are ready to talk further," she said in a very formal manner.

DON'T FORGET RETIREE HEALTH INSURANCE

Health insurance costs for retired employees are as much a concern as they are for present employees when it comes to budgeting. New York State law doesn't allow school districts, cities, towns, villages or counties to unilaterally reduce the health insurance benefits provided to a retired employee and these costs have increased dramatically as have the number of retirees – and their lifespans – and their spouses are frequently provided with health insurance.

Many school districts are rapidly approaching the point where they are paying for nearly as many retiree health insurance plans as they are employee plans. While retirees 65 and over receive Medicare, the insurance plans paid for by the public employers are frequently supplemental to retirees' Medicare with retirees' supplemental plans costing approximately $10,000 or more a year in high-cost states. Many districts also pay for all or part of the retiree's spouse's supplemental health insurance.

THE VAGARIES OF THE STOCK MARKET

Rising employee pension costs also contributed significantly to the 163 percent of increased per pupil expenses beyond simple inflation in New York since 1970.

In New York State, when I began my career as a teacher my employer, the Albany City School District, contributed a percentage of my salary toward my defined benefit pension. I was not required to contribute any-thing to this pension system.

I worked in the system for 35 years and I earned 2 percent per year toward my retirement (2 percent X 35 years = 70 percent) so that when I retired, at 55 years of age, I received a pension equal to 70 percent of the average pay I received in my three highest consecutive years of service.

The pension monies paid into the system in my name by the four dif-ferent school districts in the state where I worked were invested in the stock market by a state oversight committee. With the stock market ups and downs this resulted in wildly fluctuating payments into my pension account by the school district where I worked that guaranteed I would receive this "defined benefit."[cxcv]

In good years when the pension fund stock market investments were growing rapidly the contribution rate was near zero percent for my employer. In an average year the contributions were approximately 8 to 10 percent of my salary. When the stock market tanked the school district's contribution rate would soar to higher than 20 percent of my salary.[cxcvi]

After a few years, legislators who had enacted this system in the 1960s realized they were funding an overly rich pension plan they could never sustain and their solution was to make the employees start contributing a portion of their salary toward retirement but, under public union pressure, they maintained the "defined benefit" aspect of the pension plan.

My 1970 plan with zero employee contributions was designated Tier 1 and the employees who followed – Tiers 2, 3, and 4 – were obligated to contribute to their "defined benefit" plans. Today, the New York Teachers Retirement Fund is totally solvent as are the other support staff and munici-pal retirement funds operated by the state.

However, the wildly fluctuating employer retirement payments con-tinue to be a planning disaster for all the school districts, counties, cities, towns and villages in New York State.[cxcvii]

In low-cost states, the pension contributions have increased but much less rapidly. Most of these states offer "defined contribution" plans similar to a 401-K plan private employers and employees offer. The ups and downs of the stock market and its resultant impact on the future retiree fall on the employee not the employer in these "defined contribution" pension benefit plans.

"Defined contribution" pension plans in low-cost states are simpler and cheaper for school districts. The unions that lobbied for and received the richer "defined benefit" plans in high-cost states have held on tightly to their hard won benefit.[cxcviii]

Today, the school districts in states with "defined benefit" public pension systems like New York are contributing up to 21 percent of employee salaries into these pension funds to make up for the stock market pension fund losses during the recent recession.[cxcvix]

Some New York state school districts have entered extended payment plans that allow them to reduce these immediate onerous costs by spreading the pension payments out over multiple years in hopes that employer contribution rates will again decline.[cc]

In Illinois and New Jersey where payments to the "defined benefit" public employee pension funds are by law made directly out of the state budget by the state legislatures and the governors, the recent recession and the political difficulties of raising taxes have resulted in underpayments to teacher pension funds and the threat of pension fund insolvency.[cci]

In states where school districts pick up the cost of employee pensions, the increases in pension fund expenses has added a cost equal to at least 3 percent to 15 percent of employee salaries for all positions on staff since 1970, according to my best estimate.

In low-cost states this pension contribution amounts to approximately $2,000 per employee per year above and beyond simple inflation for positions already on staff in 1970 and approximately $3,000 per employee per year above and beyond simple inflation for all positions added since 1970.

In high-cost states with higher salaries and larger employer pension contributions to cover the "defined benefit" pensions these numbers increase to an average of $5,000 for positions on staff in 1970 and $10,000 per employee for positions added since 1970 above and beyond simple inflation.

Increasing salaries for teachers, support staff and administrators is a factor in the increase in per pupil expenses above and beyond CPI inflation found in all states and especially in high-cost states, but it is a smaller factor than most of us might expect.

As I noted at the beginning of this chapter starting salaries for teachers in low-cost and high-cost states are roughly in line with CPI inflation expectations. Median and end-of-career teacher salaries are slightly higher than CPI inflation would predict in low-cost states (approximately $5,000 average per teacher higher).

Median and end-of-career teacher salaries in the strong union states are significantly higher than CPI inflation would predict (approximately $17,000 average per teacher higher). But this impact pales in comparison to the 84 percent increase in the number of teachers-per-pupil and the increased cost of health insurance and pension benefits in high-cost states.

Still, none-of-the-above have had any discernible positive impact on student achievement.

Mt. Mason gets a new supporter

Three weeks passed since we exchanged demands with the teachers' negotiating committee. In the interim I had to listen to Harold excoriate me.

"You're giving away the store with big raises and no real concessions on health insurance. You have no idea who you're dealing with here. These people will lie right to your face. We never should have brought you to Mt. Mason. This will be a disaster. You'll see. You promised us increment plus 1 percent; now we're already up to increment plus 1.75 percent and with a big retroactive raise you said we wouldn't have to pay. And that won't be the end. Mark my words."

Near the end of this interminable three-week hiatus in negotiations, school board member Helen Anderson (typically on Harold's side) showed up in my office without an appointment.

I was about to leave with my coat on and my briefcase in hand but I invited her into my office and we sat at a small conference table.

"I just wanted you to know regardless of how Harold votes I will vote to approve this teachers' contract if you recommend it to us," she said.

"I joined this school board two years ago when Harold asked me to. He said we needed to make sure these administrators didn't give away everything to the teachers union because it would send our taxes way up. I believed him.

"The dummies on the school board with Harold and the superintendent here at that time were disrespectful to everyone who dared to raise a question. They didn't have a clue as to what they were doing. But now I can see Harold is just a big bag of wind who doesn't know anything. I just want this to be over with so I can get off this school board," she said.

"I appreciate your support," I told her, "but remember we have two other employee contracts with the support staff and the administrators that need to be negotiated and settled, a budget that needs to be approved and a new superintendent that will need to be hired when I leave at the end of this school year. Please stay until your term ends in June," I said.

Helen sighed. "I'll try. But as soon as Harold finds out that I'm on your side he'll make my life miserable. He can't let this contract be approved. His whole life revolves around playing with this school district like a cat plays with a half dead mouse. His favorite pastime is drinking beer with his buddies at the lodge where he tells tall tales about what a great leader he is.

"I'm sure you realize he creates all these conflicts to make himself look like a hero who repeatedly saves the day for Mt. Mason. And his buddies wind him up every night like one of those toy cars that run on springs."

According to Helen, Harold's buddies laugh when they read about another school board conflict in the local newspaper.

"I used to think it was funny myself but not now," she said. "I just don't want to be part of it anymore. Unlike Harold, I actually have a life and a husband I like to spend time with and hobbies to keep me busy. I've had more than my share of this."

I knew Helen's perspective was accurate. Her life would be miserable when Harold realized she wanted to settle this contract. Only a sense of common decency and maybe a bit of guilt for Helen who had helped perpetuate this unnecessary drama for the past two years could convince her to stay for the rest of the school year and allow me to settle these contracts.

Finally, a response from the teachers union

The next day Sally Anselm called. I held my breath when I picked up the phone. Were our negotiations about to come to a full stop?

Sally sounded reassuring. "I'm sorry it took so long for me to get back to you, but we've been sorting through the math on the salary schedule idea you gave us," she said. "We had to bring in the high level financial types at NYSUT, but I think we have a solution. The upper end of the schedule for the most senior teachers gave us the most headaches."

"We struggled with that as well. We weren't sure how best to solve it. That's why we left it to you." I said laughing.

"When do you want to meet?" I asked.

Sally chuckled, too. "Our team is available next Thursday after school," she said.

When our third negotiating session with the teachers began, Charlie Stafford started things off by handing out a three-page summary of their response to the district's proposal from the last meeting. It included a graph that looked much like the one we had given them with a big change in the teacher salary request that matched the area average much more closely and included raises of increment plus 1.75 percent new money each year for the contract.

The teachers' new graph looked like this:

Mt. Mason Teachers Contract, 2nd Teacher Salary Proposal

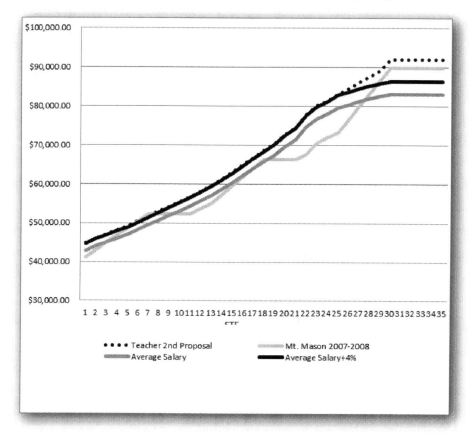

Sally explained the new graph. "Our proposed salaries follow the area average plus 4 percent most of the way out to end of the schedule until tracking that line would mean our teachers would lose money. We're proposing teachers contribute to health insurance costs, and we want to make sure this new proposal gives them real raises after their health insurance contributions at every step except the top step.

"The raises for top step teachers we are proposing are less than what those teachers will be contributing toward their health insurance. This *proposal will bring our top end teachers closer to what we think will be the area average teacher salaries four years out – the black line average plus 4 percent line – than they are right now. You can see that because at the right hand end of the graph the dotted line is closer to the black line than the light gray line is to the dark gray line."*

Tom Garrigus had a question. *"So essentially you're proposing salaries equal to the area average, plus 4 percent, plus an extra $250 for all steps except the last five steps where the dotted line goes significantly above the black line to make certain top end teachers aren't losing money?"* he asked.

"Yes." Sally replied.

Alice Donnelly jumped in. *"If I'm reading your proposal correctly you're anticipating health insurance contributions by teachers in years two through five of the contract at 3.5, 7.5, 11 and 14.5 percent, correct?"* Alice asked.

"Yes, that brings us to the area average and we would agree to the new base plan, the new health insurance consultant and your proposal to make retirees contribute in retirement at the rate they were paying when they retired," Sally said.

"And you are looking for an off-schedule, one-time payment in place of retroactive raises equal to 2.5 percent of teachers' present salaries to be paid this year. And the one-time payment will be made two weeks after we've settled on the health insurance base plan and we have formal approval from the school board and the teachers union, right?" I asked.

"Yes." Sally said.

Once we were in Tom's office for our private caucus Alice smiled broadly. *"This is a very good proposal. It gives us 90 percent of what we wanted. The raises they're proposing will put Mt. Mason teachers slightly ahead of the area average. An extra $250 raise per teacher per year over five years is very little.*

"Their extra ask on the one-time, off-schedule payment is only about $300 per teacher more than we offered. They need to be able to claim victory somewhere and this will give them that victory. They can say Mt. Mason teachers are being paid better than the area average.

"The health insurance givebacks are much bigger and are very close to our proposal. I think we have a deal unless Tom can't find the extra $60,000 we need for the bigger one-time payment in this year's budget," she said, looking at Tom.

"I can find it and I agree this looks like an agreement to me," Tom said, as he turned toward me expectantly.

"I can buy this as an agreement," I said, "but my hard sell will be with the school board. They'll hate the bigger one-time payment, the raises for top-end teachers and the lower health insurance contributions. I wonder what made this union come around so quickly."

"They knew it was now or never," Tom said. "You're only here one year and you're the first superintendent they've dealt with who has some level of control with this school board. This was their first chance to negotiate with Harold Smith out of the room and they wanted to get this done before he wormed his way back into the negotiations."

"And they want that one-time, off-schedule payment as soon as possible. Those teachers stuck on steps that don't go up haven't had a raise for five years. That offer and Harold's absence sealed the deal," Alice said.

We went back in to meet with the teachers again.

WHERE EXACTLY HAS THE MONEY GONE?

Any business dominated by personnel costs like education (lawyers, architects, medicine, etc.) has increased in per employee cost much more than CPI inflation since 1970 because of health insurance costs and pension costs that have jumped upward every time the stock market has dropped even in low-cost states.

With 70 to 85 percent of a typical school district's costs associated with personnel costs it's easy to see where the extra money has gone.

The following data – area of expense of total budget in high-cost and low-cost states – assumes rough school budget expense distributions based on a detailed analysis of fifty 2015-16 school district budgets found online at websites for schools in New York State and around the country in high-cost and low-cost states:

Area of Expense	of total budget in high cost states	of total budget in low cost states
Teacher/Professional staff salaries	30 percent	45 percent
Support staff salaries	7 percent	9 percent
Administrative salaries	3 percent	3 percent
Employer Health Insurance costs	20 percent	22 percent
Employer pension costs	7 percent	3 percent
Employer share of Social Security contributions	3 percent	4 percent
Special/vocational Education Transportation and Tuition Costs	4 percent	3 percent
Other including technology	7 percent	7 percent

(Note: The "of total budget" chart doesn't include 100 percent of school district expenses. I've excluded expenses that track more closely to CPI inflation like utilities, supplies, equipment, bus purchases, etc.)

The rise in low-cost states

School districts in low-cost-per-pupil states have spent $7,490 per pupil or 84 percent ($3,549) more than CPI inflation since 1970.

They added 20 percent new teaching staff, 50 percent new support staff (mostly teacher aides and special education school bus drivers and aides) and 33 percent new administrator staff primarily for special education.

They gave salary increases that were modestly more than CPI inflation, which increased expenditures in salaries and benefits and created a portion of the $3,549 in per pupil costs beyond CPI.

To ameliorate rapidly increasing costs, low-cost state school districts purchased less expensive health insurance plans with greater deductibles and co-pays paid for by their employees. They also contributed less toward employee pensions with "defined contribution" pensions, rather than "defined benefit" pensions.

The following is a breakdown of what percentages went to what out of the $3,549 total increase beyond CPI in per pupil costs in low-cost states since 1970:

- Teacher salaries for new positions (15.9 percent) and for raises beyond CPI inflation (7.9 percent) total 23.8 percent

- Support staff salaries for new positions (6.3 percent) and for raises beyond CPI inflation (1.3 percent) total 7.6 percent
- Administrative salaries for new positions (1.6 percent) and for raises beyond CPI inflation (0.3 percent) total 1.9 percent
- Health insurance costs for new positions (13.9 percent) and for HI inflation beyond CPI inflation (26.5 percent) total 40.4 percent
- Pension costs for new positions (1.5 percent) and for contributions caused by extra raises and increased contribution rates (2.7 percent) total 4.2 percent
- Additional employer Social Security costs for new positions and raises beyond CPI 1.6 percent
- Special and vocational education tuitions and transportation 6.3 percent
- Other 14.2 percent (includes technology growth)

Do the math for the first bullet

How were the low-cost state salary numbers in the first bullet calculated? Low-cost states have added 20 percent more teachers since 1970 so 16.7 percent of today's teacher salary budget is attributable to the teachers added since 1970. (0.20/(1.0 +.0.20) = 0.167)

This 16.7 percent represents 7.5 percent of per pupil costs (0.20/1.20 X 0.45 = 0.075) or 7.5 percent of today's low-cost state per-pupil budget or $562 (0.075 X 7490 = 562) in per pupil expenses.

The $562 is 15.9 percent (562/3549 = 0.159) of the $3,549 in additional expenses beyond CPI in low-cost states.

As for the second part of the first bullet, the teachers already on staff received raises beyond CPI over this 45-year period equal to approximately $5,000 or 10 percent of their present median wage of $50,000. According to my calculations, 83.3 percent of the present teaching staff occupying positions that existed in 1970 accounts for $281 of the $3,549 (0.833 X .45 X .10 X 7490 = $281) or 7.9 percent of the total above CPI during these years (281/3549 = 0.079).

How were the low-cost state health insurance numbers calculated? Health insurance cost increases beyond CPI inflation come in part from newly added employees. In low-cost states 20 percent of teachers, 50 percent of support staff and one-third of administrators were added. In a typical school district between 1970 and 2015, 30 percent of the health insurance contracts the district pays for including retiree health insurance costs are additional.

This amounts to $494 (0.30 X .22 X 7490 = 494) or 13.9 percent of the $3,549 in total costs beyond CPI (494/3549 = 0.139).

In addition, for the 70 percent of health insurance contracts that were there in 1970, 81.6 percent of health insurance expenses represent expenses above and beyond CPI inflation (7185/8800 = 0.816).

This amounts to $941 (0.70 X .22 X 0.816 X 7490 = 941) of the $3,549 total in beyond CPI cost increases since 1970. That $941 represents 26.5 percent (941/3549 = 0.265) of the total $3,549 in cost increases beyond CPI in low-cost states.

UNION PREMIUM STATES

Even if the high-cost states had implemented the exact same changes as the low-cost states their costs would have increased more than the $3,549 beyond CPI increases experienced by low-cost states because everything in the high-cost states costs more. ($3,549 vs. $6,486).

School districts in high-cost per pupil states like New York State have spent a total of $22,552 per pupil or 163 percent ($13,980) more than CPI inflation since 1970. Expenditures above and beyond the type of increases experienced by low-cost states are attributable to the "union premium."

Remember: low-cost states added 20 percent new teachers since 1970. High-cost states added 84 percent new teachers since 1970 so the salary and benefit costs for the extra 64 percent of new teachers in high-cost states beyond the 20 percent added in low-cost states are part of the "union premium."

The union premium teachers represent $2,354 per pupil (0.64/(1.0 + 0.84) = 0.348, 0.348 X 0.30 X 22552 = $2354).

In addition to hiring more new teachers, support staff and administrators, high-cost state school districts have purchased more expensive health insurance plans ($1,591 added to per pupil expenses) and added more teaching employees obligating the school districts to pay for more health insurance plans for the new employees and retirees ($1,019 added to per pupil expenses) than low-cost states.

If high-cost states had used the same strategies as low-cost states to deal with special education population growth, health insurance, salary increases and resultant pension and social security increases, new transportation and special education tuition needs, technology and other cost increases, they would have increased their costs to $15,058 per pupil.

The "union premium" is represented by the difference between the actual cost $22,552 and that $15,058. This difference is $7,494 per pupil annually (22552 − 15058 = 7494).

The following is a breakdown of what percentages went to what out of the $7,494 total increase beyond CPI in per pupil costs attributable to the "union premium" in high cost states since 1970:

- Teacher salaries for extra 64 percent new teaching positions (31.4 percent) and for additional raises beyond CPI (5.9 percent) total 37.3 percent
- Support staff salaries for additional raises beyond CPI (2.2 percent) total 2.2 percent
- Administrative salaries for additional raises beyond CPI (1.1 percent) total 1.1 percent
- Health insurance costs for extra 64% new teaching positions (13.6 percent) and for more expensive HI plans (21.3 percent) total 34.9 percent
- Pension costs for extra new teaching positions (4.6 percent) and for increased employer contribution rates (4.6 percent) total 9.2 percent
- Additional employer Social Security costs for extra new teaching positions and for raises beyond CPI 4.0 percent

* Special and vocational education transportation and tuitions 4.6 percent
* Other 7.0 percent

As to the "other" category on the charts, consider this: When school districts renovate or build new schools they add to their debt service costs in their budget. If the district has added special education teachers, music teachers, AP History teachers, etc., they will be adding classrooms in their renovations and new schools, all of which add to cost increases above and beyond CPI inflation.

Similarly, more teachers will mean more copier and paper expenses, more classroom supplies and textbooks and more heat, AC and lights. In the end more teachers mean more expenses.

It's also worth noting that the total "union premium" of $7,494 represents precisely one-third or 33 percent of the total cost per pupil in NY State (0.33 X 22552 = 7494).

Back to the negotiating table

"I think we have a deal," I said to both negotiating teams, when we returned to the negotiations. "Of course I'll have to convince the school board and we all know that will take a bit of work. And we have to select the new health insurance consultant and choose a new health insurance base plan. But I think all of that can be done over the next few months.

"I'll talk to the school board in executive session next Tuesday and put the approval of this contract on the agenda for the public school board meeting scheduled for the second Tuesday in November. I'm assuming Charlie and Alice can finalize the language by November 12th so I can deliver it to the school board in time for them to review it before our meeting."

Charlie and Alice both indicated they could complete the final contract language by the November 12th.

"How soon can you have the teacher union vote?" I asked Sally.

"Oh, no," she said abruptly. "We've been down that road before. The school board votes first and then we'll vote within a week after they've approved the contract. Four years ago they backed out at the last minute after we approved a contract extension to the existing contract. We'll wait for them this time," Sally said.

"Okay, Tom will prepare for the one-time payment before the February break along with a retroactive check for this year assuming we can select a health insurance consultant and base plan before then," I said.

With everyone smiling we shook hands all around and adjourned.

After five years of acrimony we had come to agreement in three negotiating sessions, less than six hours of total meeting time. Something didn't make sense here. I had a feeling I'd find out what that something was in my next school board executive session.

A stormy executive session

Alice and I carefully prepared for executive session with the school board. We had 90 minutes to explain the agreement. We attempted to anticipate the school board members' questions and misconceptions and decided how best to explain the information. We discussed the roles each of us would take in the conversation.

Alice convinced me that I should explain the math and the numbers and then step back. She would answer the questions, particularly Harold's questions. She noticed that whenever I answered questions from Harold he used the exchange as an opportunity to appear the dominant male by interrupting and attempting to distract me from providing clear and convincing information and logic.

She thought he might be more likely to listen to what was being said if she answered the questions, and the other school board members were less likely to be distracted by the back and forth between Harold and me.

Alice and I also discussed strategy for handling our conversation with the school board that would hopefully make the session more productive.

We agreed I should call Tabitha Conners in advance of the executive session and request that she refrain from engaging Harold in heated verbal exchanges that wasted time, created unnecessary animosity and only created confusion.

When I spoke to Tabitha on the phone to make this request she was reluctant. "He's such an asshole and has created such havoc in this school district for five years. I just can't stand to let him say these stupid disgusting things and not react," she said.

"I understand completely how you feel," I told her. "But if you give Alice and me the first hour of our 90-minute meeting then you're free to say whatever you please in the last 30 minutes," I told her.

She finally agreed.

Harold's reaction when we handed out the summary was predictable. First, he asked for 10 minutes to study the pages we'd distributed before we said anything. We agreed.

Harold scribbled furiously with his pen in the margins of the document while the other school board members read the pages and waited for the explosion.

Here it comes.

"This isn't an agreement this is a surrender. The health insurance contributions are down to 14.5 percent. There's a huge retroactive check for 2.5 percent of each teacher's salary. The top-end teachers who are already overpaid are getting a $3,000 raise. And the language in there about a health insurance base plan is so weak I bet there'll never be a new cheaper base plan and all this 'health insurance savings' will be a smoke screen that never happens," he bellowed.

Alice immediately answered calmly and professionally. "Let's all go through this step by step and make sure everybody understands all the details before you react," she said. Harold stopped for a few seconds to consider what Alice had said.

I entered the conversation to explain the details of the salary portion of the proposed agreement. Harold interrupted about half way through my explanation of the two graphs showing the huge change from the teachers union's initial salary proposal to their second much more reasonable salary proposal.

"Why are those top-end teachers getting a raise? They're already overpaid?" he barked.

Alice answered Harold's questions as we had planned. "We had to give them some kind of raise or they would never approve this contract. They're the teachers on the negotiating team. If you look you can see that the dotted line at the right end is closer to the black line than the light gray line is to the dark gray line. That means over the five years of this agreement Mt. Mason's teachers' salaries will move closer to the area average than they are right now. We can't totally solve this problem in one negotiations, but we've improved.

"Also, those teachers' raises will be significantly less than the $2,600 per year average because each of them will be contributing about $2,000 per year on average toward health insurance at the end of this agreement," she said as calmly and succinctly as possible.

Harold again was stymied and squirming and this gave me a chance to continue my explanation of the proposed contract provisions.

I quickly finished my explanation of the salary graphs and continued with the health insurance base plan and contributions. Again Harold interrupted.

"We were promised 20 percent teacher contributions toward health insurance and now we're down to 14.5 percent. Where did they come up with that crazy number? This is awful." He spat the words out, red-faced and puffing.

Again, Alice answered calmly and professionally as though Harold had not even raised his voice. "I believe the goals the school board adopted were that the combined impact of the health insurance savings and the salary increases were not to exceed 1 percent of the salary base in new money per year.

"This proposed agreement actually saves the district money because the health insurance savings increases each of the last four years of the contract to about $5,000 per teacher per year, in year five, and the total

new money in the salaries increases to about $3,000 per teacher, in year five, counting each year from year one. The district will save more in health insurance than will be given away in salaries."

I could see Tabitha was ready to pounce and rub salt in Harold's open wound with this last bit of information. She realized she could say again that not settling this contract for five years had cost the district millions of dollars and it was Harold's fault. I gave her a look that said clearly, "Not now, please wait."

She understood my look and appeared to physically bite her tongue.

"The 14.5 percent health insurance contribution is the area average for teachers, which is where the negotiations ended," Alice said with a smile. Harold was stymied again.

While he licked his wounds and plotted his next interruption, I jumped back in to explain the one-time payment of 2.5 percent of this year's salary we negotiated in place of a retroactive salary raise. I emphasized that making this a one-time payment meant it did not raise the salary schedule and therefore helped to keep future salary payments lower.

"Whatever you call it, it's a retroactive raise and we said no retroactive raises," Harold shouted. "This is bullshit. You guys are all the same. Empty suits with no ethical standards. You tell us one thing and as soon as our backs are turned you sell us out. I'll never vote to approve this contract," he said, emphatically.

Again, Alice spoke calmly and professionally "This off-schedule, one-time payment is the way NYSUT teacher unions have been settling contracts that expired several years ago around the state. This is roughly the norm for how these long expired contract settlements have gone statewide. And Tom says we have the money to make this settlement in this year's budget without creating a shortfall.

"In addition, even with this one-time payment we're still well within the board's goal of a total of 1 percent new money per year with the health insurance savings in the mix. This agreement will save the school district about $500,000 per year for each of years two through

five of this contract and this one-time payment will only cost the district about $500,000. Overall this contract is a $1.5 million net savings for the district as Tom's summary sheets show."

Harold was steaming. He rose from his chair in a menacing stance and snarled. "This contract will never be approved."

Turning toward me he continued to spew venom. "And your days in this school district are numbered. You're the worst excuse for a leader I've ever met. I'll make sure you're out of here before Christmas."

Only one thing kept me in the room: The boy in the blue parka.

The rest of the school board watched wondering what might happen next as Harold stomped out of the room with Doug two steps behind. Harold stopped at the doorway when he realized Helen hadn't followed.

"Helen, are you coming or not?" Harold barked. It wasn't a question. It was an order.

Helen looked like a deer in the headlights. "I'm staying," she said. "I have some other questions."

Harold's growl was audible as he turned and strode purposefully toward the parking lot and his big black pick-up truck which was parked next to Doug's red pick-up truck.

After Harold left Helen sighed and looked like she might cry. "Will the teachers get their one-time payment before the February break if we approve this contract at our next meeting?" she asked.

"If we can nail down the new health insurance consultant within the next few weeks and get the new health insurance base plan selection process completed by February 1st - — yes," I told her.

"Will the new health insurance base plan go into effect during this school year?" Tabitha asked.

"No, not until next fall," I replied.

"So that's why you're figuring on health insurance savings only for years two through five in the new contract?" Mike asked.

"Yes, that's correct. So, this year with the one-time, off-salary schedule 2.5 percent payment to teachers and their raises for this school year, the district will have a net loss this school year but will more than make up for that in future years with the new health insurance plan and the teacher contributions for active teachers and future retirees," I explained.

"And those graphs and the health insurance data information which we can update when this contract expires should make our next negotiations with the teachers a lot easier," Tabitha said.

"I certainly hope so," I replied with a smile.

Then I realized that with Harold gone this group was behaving like a real school board. They were asking the right questions, being respectful of me and each other, following up on other members' ideas and showing their own intellects and ideas. It made me wonder how much could have been accomplished in the Mt. Mason school district if Harold Smith had never decided to run for the school board.

The school board's public approval

On the day of the next scheduled public school board meeting with the teacher contract vote on the agenda Helen Anderson called me.

"I don't know what Harold is up to, but he's planning something," she said. "He hasn't talked to me except to call me a traitor at the lodge in front of all his buddies when I was there with my husband, John, over the weekend."

"My husband told me Harold was going to show you up good at the meeting tonight and make sure everyone knows you're lying about the numbers. He's also been telling people this contract is going to raise everyone's taxes – big time. John is trying to get me to vote against the contract because all of our friends are backing Harold. But I refuse to budge and so now we're not speaking."

"Don't worry Helen. Our numbers are right. Harold is just grasping at straws because he's about to lose his toy and he's going to lose *his position of importance with his buddies at the lodge. Tom and I will handle whatever Harold throws at us," I replied as reassuringly as possible.*

At 4:30 p.m., immediately after Helen and I spoke on the phone, I held a meeting with the reporters from three local newspapers covering the school district. I handed each a press release detailing the results of the teacher negotiations and a summary sheet regarding the new teacher contract the school board would be voting on that night.

I showed them the line graphs and the health insurance summary data. I carefully explained where Mt. Mason fit into that data with the old contract in place and where it would fit when the proposed contract was approved. I answered every one of their many questions to be sure they fully understood what the school board would be voting on later that night.

It was important this be communicated accurately to the public. I knew if I didn't take the time to meet with reporters before the public meeting their reports would be all about whatever scene Harold created and they'd miss the real story about the details and advantages – of this contract.

The school board meeting started on time and the room was full with 40 audience members including several teachers, the teachers' negotiating team, the three reporters and several of Harold's buddies from the lodge. After about 15 minutes of routine actions we arrived at the point in the process where the school board would first discuss the proposed teacher contract one at a time and then act on the contract.

"I am the school board president and I will take the option of speaking last on this topic before the school board votes," Harold said.

I made certain all the audience members had in their hands the press release I had discussed with the reporters earlier in the day and Tom Garrigus' summary sheets that showed the line graph of the regional teacher salaries and the health insurance data for all the neighboring school districts. I distributed all this information to the school board on Friday before the public meeting.

Tabitha spoke first emphasizing the long and acrimonious negotiations and the fact that with this settlement the district and the teachers were both "winners" financially and that now the district could get back to concentrating on improving academic results for Mt. Mason's children and improving the working relationships that had suffered during the years with an expired teachers' contract.

Mike spoke second and emphasized the health insurance savings, the expanded teacher contributions toward health insurance for active teachers and future retirees in the new contract and the teacher salaries that brought Mt. Mason closer in line with teacher salaries in the surrounding school districts.

Doug as usual just passed. "I'll let Harold speak for me," he said with an embarrassed smile.

Helen was not eager to speak. She cleared her throat three times and then spoke just above a whisper. "This contract saves the district more than $2 million in health insurance costs over five years and it will only cost the district about $1 million in teacher raises over that same five years. It's a good deal and I'll be voting for it," she said.

It was Harold's turn to speak. "Doug and a few of our audience members will have to set up our computer screen projector and while they do that I want to hand out an accurate summary of the financial impact of this proposed contract. Harold pulled out a large stack of copies of a document I had not seen previously and one of his lodge buddies gave copies to everyone at the meeting.

As this man handed me a five-page Excel spreadsheet document he gave me a gleeful smile. "Enjoy. This is the last thing you'll ever be seeing in Mt. Mason."

Doug and two other "helpers" plugged in and turned on a computer and projector while Tom, Alice and I quickly scanned the suspicious document.

Tom whispered so that Alice and I could hear him but not Harold. "I think it's a summary of health insurance costs with inflation estimated at 7 percent per year and it compares our expenses this year with the projected costs under this contract. But I'm not certain."

"Health insurance inflation has only averaged 4 percent per year over the last three years since the Affordable Care Act came in," Alice said.

"Harold is looking for a way to stop this vote. He knows the teacher union would assume the school board was just going to back out again like they did when they thought they had a contract settlement four years ago. The teachers would be on the warpath immediately and this agreement would fall apart," she added.

Harold was speaking now. "As you can see from these numbers the superintendent and Mr. Garrigus have not told us the truth about the real cost of this contract. We all know that health insurance inflation is a real factor and they failed to take inflation into account with their projections of costs and savings.

"In the end this contract will not save the district money; it will cost us more than $1 million over the five years. The teachers will not be contributing 20 percent toward their health insurance as they are in Gloversville and Amsterdam and our highest paid teachers will be paid $5,000 more than similar teachers in nearby districts. Any vote to approve this contract is a sell out for Mt. Mason taxpayers."

Alice, sensing Tom's and my anger at being publicly called liars and doing her best to help us avoid Harold's trap with an overreaction, jumped in before either of us could say anything.

"First, health insurance inflation is averaging 4 percent per year over the last three years not the 7 percent you're using in this spreadsheet. Second, inflation at any rate on the $15,000 base plan this contract requires will be significantly less than the same inflation on the $18,000 per plan the district is paying right now.

"Lastly, bringing this sheet here tonight and springing it on everyone at the last minute is not reasonable. I am guessing your motive is just to stall this vote when what your numbers suggest is not a realistic appraisal of the actual proposed contract," she said professionally but firmly.

Harold glowered at Alice. "Inflation has not been properly taken into account in the financial projections provided to us by Mr. Garrigus. We can't vote on this contract until this information is properly accounted for," he said, triumphantly.

The Mt. Mason school board had a strict rule about public comments at their school board meetings. Previous stormy sessions with verbal and even physical altercations at the meetings had resulted in a school board policy that limited public comments to a short, tightly structured interval at the beginning of the board meetings and a similar short interval at the end of the meetings. A voice in the back of the room from one of the teachers from the negotiating team violated the public comment rules.

"Harold, we all know the inflation on $18,000 is more than the inflation on $15,000. We don't need to stop this vote to study that question," she said. Everyone laughed, even Harold's lodge buddies and Harold's red face became even redder.

Helen Anderson smiled. "I call the question," she said cheerfully. "I second that," said Mike, also smiling. The vote to shut down discussion passed three to two with Harold and Doug voting to continue the discussion and the other three board members voting against.

"I move we approve the proposed teacher contract," Tabitha said, as she read into the school board meeting minutes a long paragraph Alice had prepared in advance that outlined the conditions for the approval, including a new health insurance consultant for the district, the selection of a mutually agreed upon health insurance base plan for the teachers union membership and a payment schedule for the one-time, off-schedule payment to teachers and the raises for the present school year dating back to the beginning of September.

The school board vote to approve the contract passed three to two and the meeting adjourned immediately after the vote. I rushed to reach the three reporters before they dashed to their cars to make sure they understood the smoke screen behind Harold's claim that we hadn't properly accounted for health insurance inflation.

But before I could get to them as they left Sally Anselm grabbed my hand and shook it wildly. "We did it! Thank you for pulling that off. We could have been stuck here without a contract for another ten years," she said with a big smile.

As Sally shook my hand and spoke, Harold Smith walked behind me with his entourage of Doug and his lodge friends carrying their computer equipment. Loud enough for all to hear Harold made a comment that said all that needed to be said about the school board leadership dynamic in Mt. Mason.

"Our superintendent is shaking hands with that asshole teacher union president who has caused our community untold grief. Mr. Palmer is a poor excuse for a leader. He's the worst superintendent we've ever had."

Sally's grip on my hand tightened and her eyes became a steely gray as she glared at Harold over my shoulder. "Nice to see you, Harold. Have a great night at the lodge with your friends," she said.

The next morning I spoke with all three reporters on the phone in an attempt to clarify what had happened at the meeting. Two of the three reporters understood and their reports that came out later that evening reflected the fact that they understood that Harold had provided no real financial data that warranted delaying the vote to approve the new teachers' contract.

However, the third reporter was stuck on the fact that our financial projections for the costs and savings in the new contract had not taken health insurance inflation into account. I explained repeatedly that when health insurance inflation was accounted for the health insurance savings we were projecting in comparison to not settling the contract and keeping the high-priced health insurance plan now in place (which would also be subject to inflation) would be even greater.

I offered to have Tom Garrigus give the reporter a financial projection with the health insurance inflation adjustment in place later that day. But the reporter declined the offer saying that she would miss her deadline if she waited for Tom's new projection.

In the end the news stories were mostly positive. As usual they spent too much print focused on the back and forth between Harold and everyone else in the room. But it was as good as we could hope for given Harold's last gasp attempt to stall the vote with misinformation.

Tom produced a cleaned up version of the financial projections on the contract with health insurance inflation accounted for three days later. It showed the extra savings we all knew would be there when 4 percent health insurance inflation was included in the mix ($500,000) but by then it was old news and no one was interested in reading.

After several meetings and planning sessions Alice and Tom helped me successfully settle the other two negotiations with the support staff (primarily civil service employees who pay dues to the statewide union) and the administrators (principals and assistant principals who pay dues to the statewide union) before the end of the school year.

Their agreements followed the pattern of the teachers with salaries closer to the regional average for their job titles in the neighboring school districts, a switch to a new cheaper health insurance base plan and increasing contributions for their health insurance over five years.

The teachers voted to approve their new contract in November just before the Thanksgiving break. We selected the new health insurance consultant before Christmas and finished the determination of the new health insurance base plan in March...much later than we'd hoped. However, the required tasks were completed and the one-time payments to all union employees and their retroactive checks for the present school year were in their hands before the spring break in early April.

Helen Anderson announced her resignation from the school board effective July 1 at the last school board meeting in March. With Helen's resignation there were three school board member positions up for a vote that May: Helen's position, Harold's position and Mike's position.

Harold and Mike were both running for re-election. Three other new candidates from the community were also on the ballot. One of the potential new members was a friend of Harold's who frequented the lodge. The other two potential new members were parents of school age children and friends of Tabitha and Mike. The school board starting July 1, when I would be leaving the district, could have as many as three new members.

I contemplated writing a letter to the editor in the three newspapers that covered the school district and encouraging the voters not to re-elect Harold to the school board. I also considered endorsing Mike and his two friends who were new potential board members. But in the end I decided that Mt. Mason needed to decide what they wanted from their schools in the future. Did they want more buffoonery from Harold and his type or did they want to turn a corner toward a new kind of leadership in this school district?

The day of the school budget vote and school board member election all five of the present school board members and the three potential new board members plus the same three reporters showed up in the high school gym where the votes were counted.

The budget passed (a big sigh of relief for me). Mike and one of his friends were elected to the school board. Harold Smith garnered more votes than any other school board candidate and was re-elected to the school board.

Harold immediately spoke with the reporters present and claimed this as a victory and a mandate for him to continue to, as he said, "rein in these weak and clueless superintendents and protect the taxpayers of Mt. Mason from their spendthrift ways."

The Mt. Mason school board had partially turned a corner. Harold would still be there making life miserable for the next superintendent, but that new superintendent would have an apparent three-member majority to help smooth the inevitable leadership trials headed toward Mt. Mason.

On June 1, at a special school board meeting the Mt. Mason school board appointed Anastasia Balland to the position of permanent superintendent of schools for Mt. Mason with a three-year contract set to start on July 1.

I did not know Ms. Balland and had not been involved in the superintendent hiring process.

Mike and Tabitha had earlier in the year encouraged me to stay on as the permanent superintendent for the school district. Later they told me that given Harold's anger they thought it best for me to leave at the end of the year.

This was a pattern I had seen before and I understood completely. If I made the changes necessary to move the school district forward as the interim superintendent too many toes would be stepped on to stay on as the regular superintendent. Besides, another long-term superintendent position in a contentious district like Mt. Mason was probably not something my cardiologist would recommend.

In the end Mike, Tabitha and I agreed it was best if I kept my distance from the entire superintendent search process.

I discovered online that Ms. Balland was an elementary school principal from nearby Amsterdam who had no central office experience. When Helen Anderson called me a week after Superintendent Balland's appointment to say goodbye she informed me that Ms. Balland had impressed the school board with her charm and ready smile at the interview. Helen also said she thought Harold Smith would eat her alive.

I met with Superintendent Balland five times in June to help set her up for the best chance of success. My conclusion in the end was the same as Helen's: Superintendent Balland would have a very difficult job and she would need to raise her game significantly to keep Harold Smith in check and move the district forward. But at least she wouldn't have three expired union contacts to deal with on her arrival to the school district.

As I made my final 25-mile drive home from Mt. Mason on June 30 I had very mixed emotions. I felt relieved to be away from Harold, proud that we had settled the contracts and angry that I had wasted a whole year on three labor contracts.

I decided to become a school administrator to improve learning for children not to negotiate contracts. It was sad to think that what we had done in Mt. Mason might well be undone in a couple of short years as a rookie superintendent struggled to get her feet on the ground and keep a tenuous new school board majority moving in a positive direction.

And I wondered what kind of system of contract negotiations and school district leadership might have a real chance to work in a place like Mt. Mason.

WHAT'S THE SOLUTION?

Having each individual school district in New York State, many with fewer than 1,000 students, individually negotiate every single solitary labor contract with multiple unions is a waste of valuable leadership time and resources. It also pits large (Goliath) state level unions armed with negotiations specialists against local school districts (David) armed with the best attorneys they can afford.

Right now, 733 school districts in New York State cannot be fully and effectively concentrating on improving students' educational achievement when they spend so much time focusing on employee contributions for health insurance, salaries for top-end teachers and which bus drivers get the easiest bus runs (all topics of negotiations I have had to deal with). None of these issues will ever contribute to higher student achievement.

A potential solution is state level negotiations for all school district employee pay and benefits with a regional cost adjustment that scales the standard statewide employee salary and benefits agreement to the cost of living and the cost of health insurance in each region of the state.

The state's negotiations team, composed of a few representative school board members, a few superintendents and a small group of lawyers and financial representatives, including a couple of school business officials and a comparable group of representatives from state level teachers union, could settle one negotiations for the entire state.

This idea also applies to villages, towns, cities and counties where multiple levels of government waste resources and time negotiating with local unions representing police, firefighters, nursing home workers, clerical employees, etc.

The need for public union representation and negotiations for pay and benefits is without question. But thousands of local negotiations waste precious taxpayer dollars on lawyers and consultants and waste far too many hours of precious leadership time that should be devoted to improving school and local government effectiveness.

The current bargaining system is inefficient and guarantees schools in particular will spend too much priority leadership time trying to resolve issues that should be handled in a larger arena. And it allows thousands of Harold Smiths to masquerade as leaders while they do nothing more than block progress, including academic progress.

Why do these tiny government outposts still exist when almost every state has tried to consolidate their functions? For a few reasons:

1) The school board members, village council members, mayors, superintendents, etc., want control, power and paychecks.

2) The local folks don't want to lose their beloved Lion as the team mascot. Decisions to consolidate school districts become a threat to individual and group identity. They don't want to lose their seat on the school board, they don't want to lose the elementary school that has the tree they planted in their brother's name out front, etc.

   Local control all too frequently translates into sophisticated systems run by amateur townsfolk with misplaced priorities. And this is an urban, suburban and rural problem.

3) The process of consolidation is frequently blocked by much higher property taxes for one potential participant government entity.

   The solution to No. 3 is actually an easy math problem that can be solved with a fairly simple five to ten year tax rate change phase-in plan with doses of extra state aid to grease the wheels. Many states neglect to incorporate such a phase-in coupled with a state aid boost when they talk about consolidation legislation.

Transitioning to a new system

State level organizations for superintendents, school board members and school business officials could select three representative members each to serve on the state negotiations team for employee salary and benefits.

Three selected representatives of the state education department would join this team. This 12-member team could issue an RFP for an attorney firm to assist with negotiations and a regional cost adjustment process within the state.

Once the team has selected the attorney firm to help them with negotiations, the state level unions representing employees in the school districts would be invited to participate in negotiations starting with the state level teachers union.

If there are multiple state level unions representing teachers, the largest state level teacher union by membership would negotiate first. Once the teacher negotiations were settled and a process of regional cost adjustment for teacher salaries and benefits resolved, separate negotiations would take place first with the state level union representing support staff members and lastly with the state level union representing administrative staff. The same regional cost adjustment would apply to all three types of school district employee.

LOCAL INNOVATIONS

The goal of these negotiations for the state level teams would be to create teacher salary structures that attract and retain good employees (good starting salaries for entry level teachers and a flatter step system with smaller yearly raises for teachers).

These salary schedules would allow for the possibility of teacher career ladders that started teachers at lower pay in teaching assistant roles where they tutor students, teach lessons under the guidance of a certified, tenured and successful teacher and progressed to starting teacher pay with successful completion of this entry level responsibility.

These salary schedules would encourage local innovations that paid teachers extra for assuming leadership roles and for hours during evenings, weekends, summer, and school breaks with students or with their peers working on curriculum improvements and training. In other words, more pay for the best teachers who would assume extra responsibilities and leadership roles.

These negotiations would also move toward benefits packages with higher deductible/higher co-pay health insurance plans than those provided to public employees presently in the high-cost states and "defined contribution" type pension plans similar to those currently found in low-cost states.

Once teacher negotiations are finished the same set of priorities would be the goal for negotiations with support staff and school administrators.

If the teachers' contract in a school district at the time of transition to this statewide system of negotiations provided significantly higher pay or more costly benefits, the newly negotiated state level teacher contract would provide a five-to-ten-year transition period to smooth out the shift to state level negotiations. The same would apply for teachers who were significantly underpaid or whose benefits cost their school districts much less than the benefits package negotiated at the state level.

The examination earlier in this chapter of why school costs increased so dramatically over the past 40 years noted that low-cost states appropriately added fewer staff members to meet the needs of special education. They also, in general, successfully avoided the financial pitfalls of "defined benefit" pension plans and super expensive low deductible and low co-pay health insurance.

School districts in the low-cost states also successfully avoided overpaying their top-end teachers.

But their academic results are unacceptably weak. In many low-cost states, public education serves only poor minority children and poor white children. Parents who can afford it, send their children to private schools. This is not a real solution.

Low-cost state school districts need to spend more on starting teacher salaries to attract more highly qualified teachers. And they need to spend more to help struggling students and poverty students improve their academic performance.

AND WHAT ABOUT THE HIGH COST-STATES?

The high-cost states have wasted huge amounts of money by adding staff that did not improve results. While high-cost states results are better than those of low-cost states, they're still nowhere near acceptable.[ccii]

Additional staff hired since 1970 went to academically unproductive positions in special education in high-cost states. A fraction of these positions were necessary to address the unserved needs of severely disabled students. However, many of these positions were wasted coordinating and implementing a highly regulated and academically ineffective program.

Some of the new teachers helped to reduce class sizes but didn't produce any measurable improvement in academic results. And some of the new teachers went to electives in the visual and performing arts, vocational education and specialized subjects and other curriculum tracks that increased students' enjoyment of school at the middle and high school levels, but did nothing to improve test scores.

As a principal, I have always supported the addition of electives, arts, Advanced Placement and vocational education programs to help students reach their full potential and to motivate students who otherwise would have dropped out of school or never had a chance to shine academically. But first we have to make sure all children can read, write and solve challenging math problems at a level necessary to achieve success in college or in a 21st century career before we contemplate adding these wonderful but nonessential programs.

The high-cost states have also wasted money on unnecessary, bigger raises for more senior teachers, expensive health insurance and costly defined "benefit" pension plans.

However, given the negotiations set-up in high-cost states with local school districts negotiating with state level unions representing teachers, support staff and administrators and laws like the New York State Taylor Law and decisions like the Triborough Decision, these results are to be expected.

HOW SHOULD WE BE SPENDING OUR MONEY TO PRODUCE BETTER ACADEMIC RESULTS?

Below are three strategies I think would improve academic results for students beyond those noted previously in this book. All three will require us to deal more effectively with tough financial choices and difficult politics.

First, in order to create the significant positive academic achievement change we've sought but failed to produce during my career, we have to re-deploy some of the money we have assigned to special education since 1975 in both high-cost states and low-cost states.

High-cost states could fund most of the new expenses I advocate simply by re-deploying unnecessary special education expenses and moving to "defined contribution" pension plans and less expensive health insurance plans for employees. Low-cost states will have to increase taxes and re-deploy special education expenses in order to implement these three improvement strategies.

Many students in the United States leave elementary school two to four years behind expectations in reading, writing and math.[cciii] The massive growth of special education services between 1975 and the present led many educators to believe that special education was at least a partial answer to our educational underperformance issues.

It is not. As more students were placed in special education a pattern emerged. The greater the percentage of students placed in special education in any school district, the lower student achievement levels.

This problem expanded rapidly with the "specific learning disabilities" label for academically struggling students.

Currently, more than 35 percent of students in special education programs and classes are labeled with "specific learning disabilities."

This label gives parents a reason for their children's poor performance in school, but it doesn't help the student read or do math any better, and in the end it becomes a crutch disguising low student expectations and wasting limited educational resources.

Similarly, remedial education (pulling weaker students aside during the school day for small group instruction in reading or math, frequently funded with Federal grants awarded based on student poverty) has not produced results for the same reasons.

The pattern has been consistent: Students are pulled out of challenging regular instruction where they are struggling academically to meet with the remedial teacher or the special education teacher in another room during the school day. Once in this new setting these students face less challenging curriculum and textbooks and other learning materials below their grade level.

This instruction came in much smaller, very expensive classrooms while their desks the regular general education classrooms sat empty. And it produced, in general, few notable academic gains for students.

One of the obvious drawbacks of these "pull-out" programs is that students who are pulled out are missing more challenging regular instruction and falling further behind. And, they never catch up.

And they're being asked to do less challenging work, guaranteeing they go backwards.

What's remarkable is the staying power of this type of intervention as the underperformance of this strategy has been known since the early 1970s. Yet, it still exists in one form or another in many school districts today.

Part of the reason for this strategy's longevity despite its failure is that it created many easier jobs for special education educators and remedial teachers who staffed these low expectation classrooms.

Many of these teachers are regular educators who earned a Master's degree in reading or special education and then semi-retired to their easier jobs. These teachers have fought against giving up less taxing jobs ever since.

These pull-out programs also gave the regular classroom teachers a place to send more challenging learners. The tougher-to-teach students are at least out of their hair for an hour or two a day and this makes their jobs easier. The solution worked for the adults but not for the students and we're still trying to reverse the move to lower expectations, even after 40-plus years of failure.

Additionally, the large percentage of ethnic minority children and children from poverty placed in low performing special education and remedial classes makes them one of the most discriminatory and racist practices in the U.S. education system. Many of us have said uncomplimentary things about George W. Bush but his statement about "the soft bigotry of low expectations" was completely on target.[cciv]

This "pull-out" approach for remedial and special education students fell out of favor in recent years due to persistently low student achievement levels and the social impact of segregating less successful students.

Now in favor is a "push-in" model for special education and remedial education, which puts two teachers in the classroom at the same time with all the students: regular education, remedial education and special education students.

For each lesson one teacher takes a lead instructional role and the other supports the instruction while moving around the room helping students.

This approach has some promise because at least all the students are seeing the same instruction and the same learning materials, and they're all facing the same levels of challenge.

But the "push-in" model suffers from two of the same incorrect assumptions that befell the "pull-out" model.

1. Incorrect assumption: students can learn the same challenging curriculum in the same amount of time.

    Our school day timetable and our school year calendar assumes this to be true. It's not. All U.S. students go to school for approximately seven hours a day for 180 days with very small variations. A few charter schools, a very few public schools and a number of private schools fall outside this norm, but very few regular public schools offer extra instructional time to a subset of their students who need it.

2. Incorrect assumption: The cheapest and most effective way to help students who are struggling academically is to work with them as part of a group of students.

Strategy 1: One-on-one tutoring

The only time a truly struggling student progresses is when they're tutored one-on-one by a certified teacher who is following the curriculum and academic expectations the student is seeing in regular classrooms. I have tutored many students during my career. Their progress in a one-on-one setting can be amazing.

When I needed to, I tutored my own children, but most students don't have a parent who can tutor them at home. Wealthy parents hire the best tutors money can buy when their children struggle in school. But our society has decided without considering the options that students who come from poverty or even working class homes don't deserve the "luxury" of one-on-one tutoring when they're struggling in school.

The first strategy to improve academic achievement in U.S. schools is to add many more hours of one-on-one tutoring from certified teachers delivered outside the regular school day for students who are struggling academically.

We need to shift financial resources dramatically away from traditional learning disabled special education and remedial education teacher salaries and benefits to more certified one-on-one tutors who work in the hours before school, after school, evenings, on weekends, during school vacations and summers.

An effective tutor diagnoses what the student knows, where the learning blockage – or gap – is occurring and how best to remove it. If they have to back up and re-teach something, they can do that and then return to the lesson at hand.

That set of tasks (back up and re-teach one-on-one) is virtually impossible to complete effectively in a classroom with 25 students who are ready to move forward with the instruction when some students lack the skills or background to move forward.

A few gaps in learning caused by unavoidable school absences, chaos at home or in the neighborhood, or normal learning difficulties can create insurmountable obstacles for students.

Planning and teaching lessons in regular classes at three levels, incorporating re-testing and re-teaching opportunities for all students and providing extra challenges for students who are ready for them as advocated elsewhere in this book can significantly decrease the numbers of students needing additional academic intervention.

However, these strategies for regular classroom instruction won't eliminate the need for an effective intervention for a significant percentage of students who will need additional academic support to succeed.

A true special educator with a very high skill set with a caseload of five to ten tutors and 75 to 100 students could help tutors diagnose student learning difficulties and devise strategies for regular classroom teachers, tutors and students to improve learning for students who struggle.

But, in general, these tutors don't need to be special education certified teachers. This program of tutoring for struggling students outside the regular school day would be provided to learning disabled special education students in place of their present special education experience and to students who are struggling academically who lack the special education label.

The tutoring experience I am describing would be flexible and continue only as long as it's needed. The tutoring would be focused heavily on the early grades with 60 to 70 percent of a school district's tutoring support provided in grades K-4. The remaining 30 to 40 percent of tutoring resources should be provided sparingly in the upper grades.

I sat through far too many meetings with parents whose children were struggling in school and heard them ask for one-on-one tutoring outside the regular school day for their child that fit into their family's busy schedule and was paid for by the school district.

These parents were making the right request and almost always I had nothing I could give them. Volunteer tutors are great but a certified teacher who follows the curriculum exactly, coordinates her work with the regular classroom teacher and makes certain the work the student does with the tutor allows them to improve their report card grades in the regular classroom is the best professionally appropriate option.

Would you return to a doctor's or a lawyer's office, where you were given a volunteer assistant to work with – when she has a chance.

Teaching is a profession and we need to treat it as a profession. I have always expected teachers to offer help outside the regular school day for students who are struggling, and I would certainly continue with that expectation.

But the test data indicates that the numbers of students needing one-on-one tutoring (more than 50 percent in the early grades in some high poverty schools) far exceeds the number that can be served by volunteers or dedicated teachers staying after school to help "Johnny learn to read." What I am suggesting will require major resources and significant professional time.

Why haven't we looked at this option before? Special education teachers and remedial teachers do not want to work odd hours in the early morning, late afternoon, evenings, weekends and summers. What I am suggesting would be the end of their present positions. Principals don't want to supervise their schools during these extra hours. Unions don't want full-time union dues paying jobs broken up into multiple part-time positions with odd hours that may or may not pay union dues.

Most regular classroom teachers won't want to work for extra pay and the odd hours being offered with these tutoring assignments. Low-cost state school districts and state legislators don't want to raise taxes.

Is this outside-the-school-day tutoring option affordable? Consider a full-time special education teacher with a case load of 20 learning disabled students in a low-cost state with an average of $50,000 in salary and another $13,000 in benefits (social security, medical insurance and pension).

Certified tutors in these low-cost states average $20 per hour including social security costs. (I am assuming these will be part-time positions without medical or pension benefit costs.)

Currently, $63,000 of total teacher cost for a low-cost school district converts to 3,150 hours of tutor pay at $20 per hour (63000/20 = 3150). If all 20 learning disabled students received three hours per week of tutoring outside the regular school day for the 36 weeks of the school year calendar it would require 2,160 hours of tutoring time.

This would leave 990 hours of tutoring time for summertime, school breaks and students who are not labeled learning disabled. This switch is financially possible and it is much more flexible than the very inflexible special education system we now have in place.

In high-cost states the average special education teacher salary and benefits costs would increase to an estimated total of $98,000 and the tutor rates would increase to $30 per hour with the total number of tutor hours available increasing to 3,267 so it's still affordable in high-cost states.

Too frequently in high-cost states and particularly in underfunded schools serving mostly poverty students the pinch of ever increasing budget costs and local school tax rate concerns collide and school districts make the easiest political decision. They cut the programs and learning opportunities critical for student motivation.[ccv] I am not advocating for more such ill-advised cuts. We need to reallocate money now spent on special education and remedial education, not producing academic gains, to one-on-one tutoring outside the regular school day.

The tutoring I envision would also be administered flexibly from one to five hours per week with an assumed average of three hours per week per student. In the end, if five hours per week of one-on-one tutoring outside the regular classroom and solid regular classroom instruction can't help a student succeed, it is doubtful any financially affordable strategy will work for that child that will lead to a regular high school diploma and passing all the tests required for graduation.

This failure by the school district and the students will become clear for the small group of students and parents (my best estimate 1 to 3 percent of a suburban middle class population, 3 to 6 percent of a high poverty population) who must face the fact that the school district can't find a way for their child to succeed academically and pass all the exams required for a high school diploma.

Those failure rates I'm estimating are significantly lower than the failure rates we're now seeing in school districts across the nation (50 percent failures and higher on Common Core standards in many schools), particularly in districts with high percentages of students who receive free and reduced price lunch and schools struggling to implement the more challenging Common Core level academic expectations.

The sad truth is even our best efforts won't be enough for 100 percent of students, but we need to devise a system that helps as many students as possible succeed academically with challenging standards and within budget.

We can't lower expectations so that every student will succeed. Our high school diplomas will come to mean very little if we lower expectations so that every student "succeeds." And we can't continue to spend as much as we have on outmoded special education and remedial programs to little or no effect.

Our track record since 1970 shows that just throwing money at our educational problems will not work. However, the educational achievement data also shows that lower levels of K-12 education funding correlate to fewer college educated adults in the future.[ccvi] So we need to spend wisely.

When the time comes and parents and students understand a student won't pass all the required tests with the support available, a special education certificate that properly recognizes what the student has achieved should be given to them at graduation time.

The decision of when to give up on the regular diploma and how it should be done should rest solely with the student and parent with support and guidance from the school staff.

STRATEGY 2: EARLY INTERVENTION`

As noted elsewhere in this book, the most successful interventions for academically struggling students and students from poverty take place when students are young. There are two complementary interventions that research indicates would have a significant positive impact on poverty populations.

- Monthly or bi-monthly (six times a year) home visits to the homes of all children aged 0 to 5 in high poverty neighborhoods by trained school district employees following an established calendar and curriculum in their interactions with parents and children.[ccvii ccviii]
- Full-day preschool provided by certified teachers in a well-regulated setting with classes of 15 or fewer students and a full-time classroom aide for all three and four year olds from poverty has also been shown to improve school achievement and later life outcomes for participants.[ccix ccx ccxi ccxii]

Monthly home visits of two hour duration provided by a trained college graduate who is a school district employee or the employee of a community organization partnering with the school district to provide this service would cost approximately $750 - $917 per child per year.

(Note: The caseload for a home visit professional = 60 children with the home visit professional completing three daily visits and 20 visitation days per month. Assuming the home-visit professional's salary, benefits, training and supervision costs equals $45,000 per year in low-cost states and $55,000 in high-cost states, the cost per child would be $750 per child per year in low-cost states (45000/60 = 750) and $917 per child per year in high-cost states.

If school districts across the country added this service for all children ages three and four, it would add students at five new ages (0, 1, 2, 3, 4) to the lists of children receiving services from the school district.

In high-cost states the cost for monthly home visits for all children ages 0 to 5 would add to the existing school per pupil costs (NY state $22,552) $353 per student per year (5/13 X 917 = 353) or 1.56 percent increase in costs. And, of course, delivering this service with bi-monthly home visits to only the 50 percent of students eligible for free or reduced price lunch would cost one-fourth as much.

In low-cost states this would add $288 to the existing annual cost per pupil ($7,490), serving 13 grades K-12 (5/13 X 750 = 288). This represents a 3.85 percent increase in costs which could obviously be split between local school districts and the states.

If this service was provided with bi-monthly visits (6 times per year instead of 12) and provided only to the approximately 50 percent of our student population that qualifies for free or reduced price lunch, cost per child could be reduced by 75 percent.

The least expensive and most effective way to provide full-day preschool for all three and four year olds would involve using existing school bus runs to transport the children, existing schools or nearby low-cost alternative facilities (to eliminate extra costs for more school nurses, food services, administration, etc.) and partnering with a community organization that provides certified, well-trained teachers, class sizes of 15 and a full-time aide for each classroom. And uses an evidence-based preschool curriculum.

Assuming in low-cost states a total teacher expense for salary and benefits of $50,000, for teacher aide salary and benefits $33,000, and $20,000 per classroom for additional required buses due to the extra students, teacher and aide training and supervision, equipment, materials, supplies and utilities, the cost per pupil per year would be $6,867 ((50000 + 33000 + 20000)/15 = 6867).

This pre-school program student population would be two-thirteenths of the regular K-12 school population and it would add $1,056 (2/13 X 6867 = 1056) to the existing $7,490 yearly cost per K-12 pupil.

This $1,056 would represent a 14 percent increase in per school budget costs over the existing $7,490 per pupil cost in low-cost states. These costs could be cut in half if pre-school was only offered to students from families eligible for free and reduced price lunch.

In high-cost states all of the expected costs for a full-day pre-school program for all three- and four-year-old children would increase by approximately 25 percent from the costs anticipated in low-cost states and the expected cost per present K-12 pupil would increase by $1,320 (1.25 X 1056 = 1320), which would represent a school budget and per pupil cost age increase of 6 percent (1320/22552 = 0.06).

It's worth noting that high quality preschool is an excellent economic investment that more than pays for itself in the long run.[ccxiii]

This cost could be reduced one-half by making free pre-school available only to 3- and 4-year-old children from families that qualify for free or reduced price lunch. These numbers might seem like a stretch for local school budgets but some school districts are already doing this with local voter approval.[ccxiv]

It is also worth noting that a switch to "defined contribution" pension plans in high-cost states would eventually save school districts 5 percent of their present per pupil costs. A switch by school districts in high-cost states to less costly health insurance plans with higher deductibles and co-pays like those utilized in low-cost states would eventually save school districts in high-cost states another 15 percent of their present per pupil costs.

School districts in low-cost states need to spend more to pay for home visits for all children ages 0 to 5 and for full-day pre-school for three- and four-year-old children, especially for children from poverty.

STRATEGY 3: EQUITABLE FUNDING

Most states use a combination of state funding, local school property tax funding and a small amount of federal funds to pay for their schools. The biggest problem with this system is wealthier school districts have more to spend per pupil and not just because of local school property taxes. In politics, there is something called "shares" and school aid is distributed on how strong each school district's political lobby is. Generally, wealthier suburban school districts have a stronger political base.

Meanwhile poor children cost more to educate, particularly with new more challenging Common Core standards.

In many states successful lawsuits have effectively pointed out the discrepancy in these funding levels and the need to redirect funding to the districts with the highest percentages of students who receive free and reduced price lunches. But legislators don't want to agitate high-tax-paying suburban parents who show up at the polls.

In many urban and rural areas with larger concentrations of poverty and minority students a greater percentage of the voters are mostly white senior citizens. Given their fixed incomes they won't vote to increase local school property taxes to provide more support for the schools that serve more minority and poverty children.

The result is suburban schools that require less funding actually receive more state aid for education and more local school property tax funding, and school districts serving more minority and poverty students receive less. Most states have a formula that would properly distribute the money but politics subverts the proper implementation of the formula.

The simplest solution to this conundrum is a state-wide property tax coupled with state and federal funding that creates an equitable distribution with more total funding per pupil going to school districts serving poverty students.

How much more per pupil for poverty students? The data from the Campaign for Fiscal Equity lawsuit in New York State indicated at least 25 to 50 percent more per poverty pupil was necessary to level the playing field.

If non-poverty student education is funded at a rate of $10,000 per student per year from all sources including federal, state and local sources, the poverty student funding rate would have to be $12,500 to $15,000 per student per year.

Implementing such a system in New York State and many other states would require a regional cost adjustment. Also, since this funding arrangement is significantly different from the present system in place in most states it would require a multi-year phase-in process.

(Note: Federal funds go mostly to districts serving more poor and minority students. However, federal funding amounts to less than 10 percent of the total money spent on education in the U.S. Federal funds would help states move toward this suggested solution but would be insufficient to fully fund the recommended change.)

I understand completely the political difficulty of what I'm proposing. I also know that some of our politicians are already pushing in the opposite direction.[ccxv] But, I am an educator not a politician and my priority is student learning.

Funding inequity needs to be addressed if we are to improve our schools.

It's been 60 years since Brown vs. the Board of Education ended "separate but equal" education in the U.S. "Separate and *unequal*" doesn't work, either. And there is nothing in the data I've seen that tells me it will ever work.

The natural question is: Should suburban school districts continue to be allowed to raise local taxes to provide "extras" for their students?

No.

If parents and guardians want to shell out money to give their children lessons above and beyond what school districts offer, they should do it on their own and not require schools to do it for them.

Public schools should not be promoting inequality.

Conclusion

● ● ●

I'VE MET AND WORKED ALONGSIDE many exceptional educators and school board members during my 40-plus years in education. Professionals who understand their craft, their students, their parents, their schools and school districts and communities. Professionals who find creative and effective ways to help students achieve at higher levels than some might expect.

In the solutions-based book "Why We Failed: 40 Years of Education Reform" I described some of the key work habits and attitudes these successful professionals exhibited daily. If I did my job as an author effectively, you know by now what separates these exceptional performers from their peers and how you and your school or school district can rise to their high standards.

During my 40-plus years in education I also worked with people who should never have entered the K-12 education arena. Teachers, counselors, support staff, principals, school board members and superintendents who should have worked anywhere but in schools.

I've done my best to accurately describe them and the most common problems they create so that you can more readily recognize them in your school or school district and minimize the harm that they cause. I'm also hoping this book will help you identify when your actions or words are causing you to inadvertently drift into the wrong lane, the same lane where these unhelpful folks regularly spend their work days or school board meeting evenings.

We all have negative impulses and personal agendas that cause us to work toward the wrong goals or work toward the right goals in the wrong way. Recognizing when we drift into the wrong lane, quickly and cleanly admitting the error of our ways and moving back into the proper lane are critical to changing the trajectory of K-12 education.

Much of what ails education today is political and financial: funding formulas that send state aid to districts based on politics; tenure protections for problem performers that haven't changed because of union campaign contributions; charter school laws designed to hurt public schools due to politics; special education rules and procedures designed to appease political pressures from parents; school board members' personal agendas; personnel, budget or student achievement problems for school districts; incompetent or lazy superintendents, principals and teachers; and support staff members hired due to local politics; adding a whole lot of teachers in the strong public union states due to political pressures from unions despite the fact that the extra teachers didn't improve student achievement; setting up local negotiations in strong public union states that pit the Goliath state teachers union against the local David school district.

The list is long.

And all too frequently in the K-12 education arena the politicians come up with bright ideas that might have a real chance to work but implement them on a schedule that fits the politicians' election agenda, not the real agenda schools must follow to properly implement big, complex changes. (Think Common Core and state tests tied to teacher evaluations.)

These political problems are so thorny that the most common reaction I received from people who knew I was writing this book was something like: "Are you kidding me? There is no way to fix that mess. The politics are impossible."

I remain optimistic. I have proposed solutions to some of the most difficult issues we face. Some – most – I know are politically difficult, but we need to remind ourselves that politicians work for us. Many have forgotten this and will need blunt reminders from us to move the ball forward. And we'll need a detailed plan for every issue so that it will be harder for the politicians to run for cover. (See the What We Can Do section at the end of this book.)

I'm also optimistic because during my 40-plus years in education I worked with great teachers, talented and effective department chair people and teacher leaders, excellent principals and assistant principals, outstanding superintendents and assistant superintendents and exceptional school board members. They set the bar high. Their inspiring efforts and successes demanded that everyone around them work harder.

We can't give up despite the difficulty of the task at hand – and it's a difficult one – because the efforts and achievements of these people demand that we match their success.

We also have to continue the fight because of the students. I met hundreds – thousands – of students during my education career. Eddie, my first African American friend – yes, a student can be a friend to a teacher – whose ready smile and sense of humor crossed the racial barriers of my all-white upbringing; Serena, a bright student who resisted learning at every turn; Tommy who survived scoliosis surgery and kept his sense of humor while he participated in classes from his bed at home via radio transmission; Carmen who loved to catch my mistakes and smiled infectiously every time she was right and I was wrong; Danny who made sure bullies never picked on weaker classmates; Diana, who never let her unfamiliarity with the English language stop her from solving the most difficult calculus problems; Ronnie, who made the mistake of bringing a weapon to school and finished high school while working with a school provided tutor and later graduated from college on the dean's list; Tim, with a heart of gold, a gym full of friends and extremely weak reading skills who never gave up and finally passed all the tests and graduated one year later than his peers.

It's a long list.

Every one of these students was special, interesting, valuable and in need of something only a well-run school district, school or classroom can provide: caring, knowledgeable and effective educators who work long hard hours every day to maximize the effectiveness of their talents, to fully utilize the limited available resources and to provide the best learning opportunities they can create for their students. These students and millions like them in school districts across the country deserve no less.

What can we do?

• • •

THE "WHAT CAN WE DO" section has a segment that corresponds with each chapter of the solutions-based book "Why We Failed: 40 Years of Education Reform"

"Common Core is Not the Problem"
What can we do?
<u>**Superintendents, Principals, Teachers and School Boards**</u>

* Lobby State and Federal governments for:
    o Time limits on annual standardized tests (no more than one hour for each grade three to eight math and language arts tests and no more than three hours per subject for required high school exit exams).
    o The option of using authentic assessments selected from a state education department approved bank of authentic assessments for up to 20 percent of each grade three to eight English language arts and math end-of-year assessment and each required high school exit exam. Include a provision for local teachers to gain approval for their own authentic assessments to be added to the bank.
    o Public release of all grade three to eight English language arts and math assessments and all high school exit exams (excluding any field test questions for both) within one month of testing.

○ Release of state, school district, school and individual student test results for grade three to eight English language arts and math tests within one month of testing.

○ Procedures to adjust the inclusion of state test data in the performance evaluations of teachers to include averaging multiple years of student test data and special procedures for tenured teachers with multiple and persistent ratings of "ineffective" or "developing" as outlined in the "Creating Quality with Tenure" chapter of this book.

Superintendents, Principals, Department Chairs and Teachers

* Work together to organize regular public presentations and displays of authentic assessments of student school work from all the academic disciplines and grade levels to create a real audience for students' academic work.

* Work together to increase parent and community understanding of the Common Core standards and the testing and assessment process to gain long-term commitment and support. They should also understand we're attempting to move towards more reasonable testing procedures that include scaled down student time commitments for grade three to eight tests, inclusion of authentic assessments for students in the testing process and adjustments to the teacher evaluations tied to student testing to make them more fair and realistic in their implementation timeframe.

* Use school board meetings, the district website and district newsletters to showcase and report on authentic assessment activities completed by students and teachers. Encourage principals to showcase and report on authentic assessment activities at PTA meetings and community events. Inform the news media of authentic learning activities to maximize the opportunity for positive public relations for the district and for expanding the real audience for students' authentic assessments. Ensure teachers who create authentic

learning opportunities are properly recognized for their contributions in all these venues.

Superintendents and School Boards

* Communicate to parents and the broader community that we are increasing academic expectations to a level we can and should expect our students achieve.

* Help them understand we are trying to move to reasonable testing procedures that include scaled down student time commitments for grades three to eight tests, inclusion of authentic assessments for students in the testing process and adjustments to the teacher evaluations tied to student testing to make them fairer and more realistic in their implementation timeframe. This process will need to be ongoing given the mistakes already made with Common Core implementation in many states.

Superintendents

* Initiate training for principals and teachers on the proper techniques for developing and integrating high quality rigorous authentic assessments that emphasize skills and content in the Common Core curriculum. See "Charter Schools, School Choice and Poverty" and "Politicians Need Not Apply" chapters for advice on finding funding for this training.

* Initiate training for principals and teachers to effectively organize and manage classrooms for open-ended instruction, and train principals to diagnose instructional issues unique to open-ended instruction.

* Work with principals and teachers to develop district-wide teacher observation and evaluation goals and procedures that include:
  o Brief (6 - 15 minute) mini-lectures with focused content and skill goals tied to challenging Common Core standards in

grades three through eight and disciplines that fall outside the Common Core purview.

- o Regular individual and group work with daily corrections of students' written work and verbal and written feedback for students prior to graded unit exams.
- o Teacher graded individual or group practice or prep tests or an equivalent rigorous learning activity prior to the end-of-unit exams with built-in opportunities for students to raise their grades and understand their errors in advance of graded unit exams.
- o Authentic assessment/extended project work for each unit that develops student soft skills, ability to apply their learning, motivation, creativity and independence.
- o Re-testing procedures that encourage students to repeat academic tasks until mastered and measures to incorporate their final success in grades.
- o Planning instruction on three levels to provide extra challenges for students who are ready for them, extension activities for students who need more practice to master the required skills and content and re-teaching and re-learning activities for students who have yet to master basic content and skills.

School Board Members

- ♦ During public school board meetings: Discuss plans to train principals and teachers in your district on the proper techniques for developing and integrating high quality rigorous authentic assessments that emphasize skills and content in curriculum that's tied to the Common Core standards. Ask your superintendent how s/he plans to provide funding for this training.
- ♦ During public school board meetings: Ask your superintendent to explain how s/he plans to train all teachers and principals in your district to effectively organize and manage classrooms for open-ended instruction.

- Ask your superintendent to organize a school board presentation regarding district procedures for teacher observation and evaluation and how this process encourages good instruction.

- Ask your superintendent to provide you with an explanation of how each school in your district provides re-teaching and extra challenges for students and how students are given an opportunity to improve their grades on tests after initial teacher made tests are given.

- Ask your superintendent to share with all board members a schedule of authentic assessment demonstrations open to the public. Attend public presentations and displays of authentic academic assessments from all the academic disciplines and grade levels.

- Encourage your superintendent and school board president to use school board meetings, the district website and any district or school newsletters to showcase and report on authentic assessment activities completed by students and teachers.

- Encourage your superintendent to have principals do the same with academic assessment presentations and displays organized as part of PTA meetings and community events, reported on with articles including pictures and videos on school websites and in school and school district electronic newsletters. Ask your superintendent in public to inform the press of ongoing authentic learning activities to maximize the opportunity for positive public relations for the district and for expanding the real audience for students' authentic assessment work.

- Work with local, regional and statewide school board groups to have discussions and presentations relating to Common Core standards and the testing and assessment process to gain long-term commitment and support.

Principals and Teachers

- Volunteer to work together to develop district-wide teacher observation and evaluation goals and procedures that emphasize the value of: (a) brief mini lectures with focused content and skill goals tied to Common Core level curricula or similarly challenging content and skills in all grades and disciplines (b) lots of student individual and group work with daily teacher corrections of student written work and lots of verbal and written correction feedback for students prior to graded unit exams (c) graded individual or group practice or prep tests or an equivalent rigorous learning activity prior to end-of-unit exams with-built in opportunities for students to raise their grades and understand their errors before graded unit exams are given. (d) authentic assessment/extended project work for each unit that develops students' soft skills, ability to apply what they have learned, motivation, creativity and independence (e) re-testing procedures that encourage students to repeat academic tasks until they are mastered and measures their final success as part of their grades (f) planning instruction on three levels to provide extra challenges for students who are ready for them, extension activities for students who need more practice to master the required skills and content and re-teaching and re-learning activities for those students who are struggling to master the basic content and skills.

Principals

- Ask your school district superintendent for opportunities to receive training on the proper techniques for developing and integrating high quality rigorous authentic assessments that emphasize skills and content in the Common Core standard areas. Use suggestions from chapters "Charter Schools, School Choice and Poverty" and "Politicians Need Not Apply" to help find funding within the funds expended in your building for this training.

- Ask your superintendent for training opportunities on effectively organizing and managing classrooms for open-ended instruction. Offer to organize training on these same topics for principals and instructional administrators in your district. If this training is effective you'll be better able to diagnose instructional issues related to teacher classroom management for open-ended instruction and provide suggestions that will help teachers improve their classroom management strategies.

* Work with teachers to organize regular public presentations and displays of academic authentic assessments from all the academic disciplines and grade levels in your building to create an audience for student academic work while increasing community and parent understanding of the academic challenges faced by students and the achievements of the school's students.

Teachers

* Ask your principal to organize or provide you and other teachers in your school with an opportunity for training on the proper techniques for developing and integrating high quality rigorous authentic assessments that emphasize Common Core skills and content. Encourage your principal to use suggestions from "Charter Schools, School Choice and Poverty "and "Politicians Need Not Apply" chapters in this book to help find funding for this training.

* Ask your principal to find a way to provide training for teachers in your school for effectively organizing and managing classrooms for open-ended instruction.

* Encourage your principal to find funding to support teacher coaches who can help you integrate these innovative strategies into your classroom. These teacher coaches will not be evaluating your work as a teacher; they will be helping you transition to a classroom that more fully emphasizes effective instruction required for success with the Common Core or any other more challenging curriculum.

* Work with your principal, department chair, teacher leaders and other teachers to organize frequent public presentations and displays of students' academic authentic assessments from your classroom to create a real audience for your students' academic work while increasing community and parent understanding of the academic challenges faced by your students.

- Use your classroom and the hallways available nearby, PTA meetings and back to school nights for parents, your school's website and any school or district newsletters to showcase and report on authentic assessment activities completed by students. Include pictures and videos on the school website and in electronic newsletters. Ask your principal to inform the press while all of these authentic learning activities are ongoing in order to maximize the opportunity for positive public relations for your students and for expanding the real audience for your students with their authentic assessment work.

"Politicians Need Not Apply"
What can we do?
<u>Superintendents</u>

- Schedule annual public presentations on academic performance data and academic improvement plans by school principals and special education department administrators. Time presentations to coincide with the budget cycle.
- Schedule similar annual presentations from your school business official and each operational department (transportation, operations and maintenance, food services, technology, etc.) that include improvement plans.
- Share the spotlight at public meetings with members of your administrative team so that the school board better understands the administrative team's essential leadership role in the district.
- Use school district performance data as an incentive to create annual improvement plans that address low performance. Expect the next report from each building or department to show growth and how the improvement plans from year to year create a cohesive overall plan of improvement to prevent a hit or miss approach to problem solving.
- Use the decisions you make every day as an ongoing opportunity to demonstrate your ethics to school district employees, to the school board and to the public. Discuss the ethical aspects of decisions with the school board, with the administrative team, with the staff

and public. When ethical discussions are public there is only one possible answer to most questions.

* Give credit to members of your administrative team publicly at school board meetings and in employee meetings when they've have taken steps that improved academic performance. Provide the praise regardless of where the idea originated.

* Look for "happy accidents" that provide an opportunity for unexpected or unplanned performance improvements. Coach your administrators to look for these opportunities.

* Demonstrate for your leadership team a combination of holistic/artistic thinking and logical/linear thinking about problems. Look for the strengths and weaknesses in your own performance with this balance of perspectives and address the weaknesses with plans for long- term improvement.

* Build a realistic on-the-spot writing task into the interview process for administrators in your school district.

* Use staff retirements and resignations as an opportunity to rethink school district structure and how the resources tied to the position can be used more creatively and effectively to achieve your district's mission.

* Select data-intensive tasks integral to improvement and complete data analysis yourself. If you lack the skills necessary to complete data collection and analysis don't just delegate these responsibilities. Instead, have the staff member you would delegate these tasks to teach you how to complete them independently so you can do them next year or the next time they're needed.

* Learn to write effectively and write all of the key communications essential to the critical aspects of your job. If this is hard for you find a mentor who will help you learn to communicate in writing clearly even If it means paying someone to help you. You will write rough drafts and they will edit them and over time their editing will become less necessary, particularly if you take the time to understand the edits and to question the editor on why they're making changes when they make them.

* Avoid becoming the superintendent who survives by politics. When politics interferes with your work and the work of your school board or administrative team first check your own actions and make sure you haven't allowed something to fester and become a political mess. If you have allowed this to happen fix the mess promptly and move on. If others are responsible, have a private conversation with those involved in creating political turmoil. If that doesn't work, try an executive session discussion with all the players at the table. If that doesn't work bring the issue up in public before it destroys the district's chances of success.
* Don't stand by and watch the district fail academically or financially.
* Be honest about the data. Compare your school district to demographically similar school districts and tell everyone the truth about your district's performance.

School board

* Ask your superintendent to schedule annual academic performance reports with improvement plans from principals, the special education department, the business official and each operational administrator.
* When hiring a superintendent look beyond the candidate who makes you feel most comfortable to the candidate who has a track record of using data to guide improvement efforts, who can write best (include an on-the-spot writing task as part of your interview process), who understands the value of a "happy accident" and can tell you about one s/he has taken advantage of in the past, the candidate who can describe ethical issues s/he has dealt with in the past.
* Avoid using politics to advance your individual goals. Do not make phone calls or send emails to other school board members or employees to lobby for your cause. Use email sparingly for school board issues and when you use it include the full school board and the superintendent in the email distribution. Information that goes

to one member of the school board should go to all members and to the superintendent. (Some basic advice: Your emails about school board issues may be subject to the Freedom of Information Act and may be public documents.)

* Make sure your school board publicly sets consensus goals on an annual basis with input from all board members to identify the most important goals worthy of administrative time and effort. Use past school and school district performance data and demographically similar school and school district performance data to set these goals.

* Encourage your superintendent to use staff retirements and resignations as an opportunity to rethink the structure of the district and how the resources tied up in that position can be used more creatively to achieve your district's mission.

* When politics interferes with your work as a school board member speak individually and privately with those involved to give the people involved a chance to resolve the issue and avoid being embarrassed when the entire leadership team realizes their error. If the school district superintendent has allowed an issue to go unresolved and it's developed into turmoil call the superintendent to discuss your concerns privately. If the private approach fails to resolve the issue, bring it up in executive session with the full school board and the superintendent. If that fails, bring the issue up in a public meeting. Frequently, the motivations that drive private political agendas become useless baggage in a public discussion.

* Model the proper mixture of data intensive work and holistic vision about the school district that you want to see in the administrative team.

* Stick to your role as a school board member. As a member of the school board your role is to work collaboratively with your fellow school board members to set policy and goals for the district and to make sure the superintendent has plans in place and achieves those goals. You may ask for updates and reports regarding the achievement of those goals, but your only personnel decisions relate to the

superintendent's contract terms and whether or not s/he continues in the job. All other personnel decisions belong to the superintendent or her/his designee. The superintendent can't be expected to act on your individual goals unless you convince your fellow school board members that your individual goals should become school board goals.

* Avoid school board member "alliances" that trade achievement of one team's goals for another team's goals. If your school board is involved in such "teams" discuss the issue in executive session and try to agree to end the alliances. If the executive session conversation doesn't work bring it up for public discussion.

* Don't get roped into trying to be a "fixer" for the problems of parents, residents or employees. This is not your role. If you are approached with this kind of concern tell whoever has approached you that you will inform the superintendent of the concern.

* Work with your fellow school board members and the superintendent to enact a "no retaliation" policy that directs all school district employees to refrain from actions that might be seen as retaliation against anyone who reports concerns about district activities to any employee or to any school board member.

* Report all employee, parent, student or resident complaints about the school district immediately to the superintendent and properly identify the source of each complaint. The superintendent should follow up on each complaint and inform the entire school board regarding the problem's resolution.

* Make sure your own behavior and the behavior of those who work with the school board reflects the highest ideals for ethical behavior at all times.

Principals

* Offer to provide an annual presentation of your school's academic performance data and an improvement plan to your school board. If your superintendent agrees be sure to include any budgetary implications and be ready to proceed with the implementation of the

plan with or without additional funding. Whether or not the school board presentation takes place have your superintendent review the plan and approve your presenting the data and improvement plan to staff and parents.

* Improve your own writing skills by writing your own emails, memos, letters, presentations, speeches and press releases. If you need help with this skill pay someone to edit your rough drafts and learn to improve your writing skills by carefully reviewing their edits.

* Identify the most critical data intensive tasks you face every year in your work as a principal. Do these tasks yourself with attention to detail and creativity using technology to enhance the quality your work. If you need additional skills to complete these tasks, recruit a staff member or a consultant to help you with the task as they mentor you toward independence in this skill area. Make sure your staff members know you are taking on this growth/data intensive responsibility as your own.

* Use your work every day with the staff in your school as an opportunity to demonstrate your personal ethics and to support your co-workers as they grapple with ethical issues.

* Share all the available data about your school's performance, both good and bad, with parents and staff members. Use the "bad" data as a reason to develop plans to improve your school's performance. Use the "good" data as an opportunity to publicly recognize the appropriate employees for their positive contributions.

* Always use staff retirements and resignations as an opportunity to rethink the structure of your school and how the resources tied up in the position can be used more creatively to achieve your school's goals.

* Avoid using politics just to keep your job or to hide negative data and weak performance in order to avoid making necessary changes in your school's approach.

* Don't initiate private conversations with individual school board members to improve your political stock with them; it will probably

backfire and it will certainly undermine your superintendent's ability to do her/his job well. If school board members contact you with questions, suggestions or demands, always let them know you will contact the superintendent immediately to report the issue.

* Look for "happy accidents" that present an opportunity, if handled properly and creatively, to improve academic results and your school's operations.

* Keep your ear to the ground to detect growing concerns about the school district or the school among parents or staff members about the pace or nature of change in your school. If you sense resistance to your change efforts have private one-on-one conversations with teachers and parents to hear them out. Be careful not to gravitate toward staff members and/or parents who will tell you what you want to hear or the grumpy ones that are never happy. Select level-headed and mature teachers, parents and staff members who are willing to tell you when you are wrong. If you find out valuable information tell your superintendent and avoid throwing your information source under the bus by identifying her/him publicly.

* Make the contrast between your ethical behavior, your willingness to be honest about data that says your school could be doing a better job, your willingness to tackle data intensive tasks, your willingness to be accepting of advice and opinions that contradict your stated position, your willingness to be both holistic and linear in your thinking at the same time and, most of all, your willingness to avoid the easy political solution; you will be able to move mountains with the support of thankful staff members and parents.

Teachers

* Research examples of academic data analysis and improvement plans exist that are working in other school districts and share what you find with your principal.

* Approach your principal with ideas for improvements to programs and curriculum for better test results. Also share parent and student engagement efforts you think might present promise for your school.
* Whenever individual school board members ask you for support on their personal issues (who should be the basketball coach, for example) or they are looking for "dirt" about your principal, your superintendent, or another district employee, refer them to your principal or superintendent. "I'll make my principal aware of it," and tell them this same thing every time.
* Avoid using the potential minority "alliance" on your school board to get something you or your colleagues want as it will kill any chance for real long-term leadership success in your district.
* Be understanding and supportive when your principal or superintendent uses staff retirements and resignations as an opportunity to rethink the structure of the district and how the resources tied up in that position can be used more effectively to achieve your school's or your district's mission. Don't be afraid to offer suggestions to your principal in this area.
* Provide academic data regarding the program you work with in your district to your school principal to help her/him better understand the issues you face in your classroom. For example, if you teach chemistry and half of your students have already completed algebra and the other half are just taking it now it will significantly increase the complexity of your job, especially if algebra skills are required in your curriculum.
* Let your principal and superintendent know that you noticed and appreciated the route they took when they faced a difficult ethical decision and made the ethical choice despite the difficulties they encountered.
* Support your principal's efforts to keep a balanced perspective in working toward solutions. Use logical/linear approaches and holistic/artistic/creative approaches in tandem by asking the right questions to reframe the issues differently.

* If you see what looks like an ethical lapse by your superintendent or principal bring your concerns to their attention privately. If that doesn't work and you're still sure your view is correct, write a letter to the superintendent regarding the issue with your principal or to the school board president if the issue involves the superintendent. Be certain a "no retaliation" policy is in place in your district before writing these letters. In districts with employee unions sometimes the union leaders can help to deal with these concerns.

* Look for "happy accidents" that might provide opportunities for creative solutions.

* Keep your ear to the ground to identify potential problems in your school, grade level or department and try to be one of those thoughtful, mature voices your principal would seek out when s/he is unsure how best to proceed. Don't be afraid to head to her office and share your thoughts in private if s/he doesn't come to ask for them.

"Creating Quality with Tenure"
What can we do?
Superintendents, School Boards, Principals and Teachers

* Propose the adoption of a modification to the state's tenure law to your state legislators and governor that includes a 2%/5% provision. The provision would allow for limited numbers of summary dismissals of tenured teachers and other tenured school employees who have documented misconduct issues or who have been on improvement plans for at least one year and have not sufficiently improved their performance. The 2%/5% provision could become a 4%/8% provision or 10%/15% provision or higher in districts with poor academic performance (based on where they fall in around the predictor line), decreasing enrollment or charter school implementation that results in teacher layoffs.

   Each year a few of the poor performing tenured teachers and teachers with ugly misconduct issues would be leaving the district at a very slow rate (no more than 1 percent per year average under the 2%/5% numbers) and the remaining teachers who are doing their jobs well and avoiding misconduct problems would be receiving more pay due to the salary redistribution recommendation included in the law's amendment. How much more? In the highest paid districts in the country about $2,000 per year per teacher, in average paying districts $1,300 per year and in the lowest paying districts $750 per year. And the number is negotiable. A properly negotiated dollar value would prevent administrators from using this law change to summarily rid themselves of teachers for personal or budget savings reasons while offering the opportunity to rid the profession of poor performers who drag down the entire profession.

- Ensure the school district budget provides adequate yearly funding for the implementation of effective performance improvement plans for teachers and other tenured employees designated to complete a performance improvement plan by their supervisor. Funding should cover teacher or principal/administrator coaches and teacher substitutes to allow improvement plan teachers to complete school visits. Raise the issues of funding for improvement plans during the school budget development process. This budget should also include annual training for supervisors regarding the most effective tactics for the implementation of improvement plans for teachers and other tenured employees that address both legal issues and teacher/tenured employee performance improvement strategies.

Superintendents and Principals

- Participate in annual training regarding the most effective tactics for the implementation of performance improvement plans for tenured employees, including addressing both legal issues and tenured employee performance improvement strategies.
- Develop and implement improvement plans for one to four teachers/tenured employees per administrator for each school year (superintendents should do the same for any school administrators they supervise). Improvement plans should follow the format noted

in the "Creating Quality with Tenure" chapter that includes: a concise written explanation of the specific performance weaknesses, district-funded training, substitute coverage as needed to attend training and observe peers inside and outside the district who are strong in employee's areas of performance weakness, opportunities for co-teaching and non-evaluative classroom observations with coaches and other colleagues in the district (where appropriate). The plan should include paid teaching coaches who are not supervisors and who would help teachers with plans to develop essential skills in areas of performance deficit. Schedule 20 to 30 brief classroom/work site visits and at least three formal observations of the teacher participating in the improvement plan by the principal or administrator who supervises the teacher and document the entire improvement plan process. Principals should be ready to identify savings within their own schools that can be used to fund this effort.

School Superintendents

* Include in the recommended modifications to the state's teacher tenure law guidelines for distributing any salary savings resulting from the dismissal of the tenured employees and rehiring of their replacements in equal shares to other members of the dismissed employee's bargaining unit. (This effort would be more effective if sponsored by a state or regional superintendents' organization.)

* Report to the school board regarding all administrators who are involved in improvement plans twice a year (fall and spring) detailing ongoing activities and progress. This preliminary communication is necessary to avoid potential surprises for the school board when poor administrative performance requires legal or other action by the school board.

* Once in the beginning of the school year inform the school board in executive session of all tenured employees in the district engaged in improvement plan implementation, the reasons for their

involvement in these plans and the identity of the administrator overseeing the implementation.

* Once in the beginning of the school year invite principals and other administrators to an executive session with the school board for a five-minute discussion regarding any tenured employees involved in improvement plans. These conversations help make principals and administrators accountable for their work in this important area and head off any surprises for the school board should legal or other actions be required as a result of improvement plans.

* In May or at an appropriate earlier date depending on the state's school budget and hiring schedule inform the school board which tenured employees will be dismissed under the 2%/5% provision. These personnel decisions should be made by the superintendent with notification to the school board.

* As soon as possible discuss with your school district attorney all employee misconduct issues. Also, immediately inform the school board in executive session regarding any employee misconduct. Potential strategies and predicted outcomes as well as associated costs for dealing with these misconduct issues should be clarified with the school board in advance of any recommendations to the school board from the superintendent regarding district actions.

School Boards

* Publicly request from superintendents in August/September of each school year a list of tenured employees with performance improvement plans, the reasons for the plan and the names of the administrators responsible for implementing the plans.

* Request an executive session report from the superintendent regarding any administrators involved in improvement plans twice a year (fall and spring) detailing ongoing activities and progress. Request that the superintendent inform the school board about the plans early in the year in the event the school board is required to take legal or other action later on.

- In the early spring publicly request superintendents invite principals and other administrators to an executive session with the school board for a five-minute individual discussion regarding each tenured employee involved in a performance improvement plan. These conversations help make principals and administrators accountable for their work in this important area and help to head off any surprises for the school board should legal or other actions be required as a result of improvement plans.

- Adopt a policy requiring the superintendent and, when necessary, the school attorney to discuss all employee misconduct issues during executive session. Clarify potential strategies and predicted outcomes as well as associated costs for dealing with misconduct issues before the superintendent makes a recommendation on these issues and before the school board is expected to take any actions regarding employees.

Principals

- Report to the superintendent regarding all teachers and other tenured employees who are involved in improvement plans a minimum of twice a year (fall and spring) detailing ongoing activities and progress in creating performance improvements. This preliminary communication is necessary to avoid any potential surprises for the superintendent and school board in the event continued poor tenured employee performance requires legal or other action by the school board.

- Request the opportunity to inform the school board in an executive session through a five-minute presentation/discussion on performance improvement plan progress with any teachers/tenured employees in early spring. These conversations will help head-off any surprises for the superintendent and school board should legal or other actions be required as a result of improvement plans.

- Request approval to participate in annual training regarding the most effective tactics for performance improvement plans implementation for tenured employees that address both legal issues and tenured employee performance improvement strategies.

- Request in advance of budget planning adequate annual funding for the implementation of effective performance improvement plans for teachers and other tenured employees designated to complete a performance improvement plan by a supervisor. This funding should pay for teacher/tenured employee coaches and site visits. This budget should also include training for supervisors regarding the most effective improvement plan implementation tactics for teachers and other tenured employees that address both legal issues and teacher/tenured employee performance improvement strategies. In the event that the superintendent is unwilling or unable to find funding to address this need request the opportunity to develop a funding stream to support this critical activity from within the existing school budget by reallocating funding from other expense areas. Creating this budget change will require using tactics similar to those discussed in "Politicians Need Not Apply" chapter of this book.
- Immediately inform the superintendent regarding all employee misconduct issues and proceed as directed by the superintendent.

Teachers

- Participate willingly and enthusiastically in an improvement plan if you have been designated by your principal/supervisor as a candidate for a performance improvement plan. Ask your principal to follow the format noted in this chapter including: a concise written explanation of the specific performance weaknesses, district-funded training, substitute coverage as needed to attend training and observe peers inside and outside the district strong in areas of your identified performance weakness, opportunities for co-teaching with and non-evaluative observation by teacher coaches and other colleagues in the district (where appropriate). The plan should include paid teacher coaches who are not supervisors and who would help teachers with lesson plans and the development of essential skills in areas of performance deficit. Your principal or supervisor should during the year conduct 20 to 30 brief classroom/work site visits and at least three formal observations of the teacher participating in the improvement plan.

* Volunteer to support teachers with performance improvement plans.
* Report any incidents of employee misconduct that endanger students, fellow employees or the school's reputation.

"Special Education: All Heart and No Head"
What can we do?
Superintendents and School Board Members

* Request from US senators and all local members of the U.S. House Representatives, an amendment to the IDEA law (PL-94-142) that establishes funding caps for totals spent on each child for all services provided by the school district appropriate to children's disabilities. Include language allowing special education students presently diagnosed as having learning disabilities to be provided academic support by either professionals certified in special education or certified in any other area approved by your district's Committee on Special Education. PL-94-142 has been previously modified with amendments and can be modified again without violating any of the core principles of the law requiring the provision of a free appropriate public education for all children with disabilities. A request to the U.S. Congress will have greater effect if it comes in a letter signed by a large group so connect with your state or regional membership organization.

Superintendents

* Assign your school business official and Committee on Special Education chairperson the task of calculating the costs for all special education services provided inside the district by district personnel, provided inside the district by outside organizations or providers and provided outside the district to district special education

students including transportation, legal fees, administrative and clerical support, support services, tuitions, medical support and all other special education bills paid for by the school district. Share this list with all school board members, administrators, special education teachers, regular education teachers, Committee on Special Education Members and parents of special education students. The list should allow each special education student parent to identify clearly the costs for each of the extra services their child is receiving.

* Make a similar list of any special education federal grants or state aid received by the district for all special education services provided including any special education transportation aid. Attach these two lists together, share them with stakeholders and explain the finances involved in special education to anyone who will listen.

* Make sure the Committee on Special Education considers financial costs in its decision-making just as you want to make sure your doctor considers what your insurance will cover and how you can minimize your costs while maintaining or improving your health.

* Ask your state education department to request a waiver from the U.S. Department of Education on requirements related to certification of teachers providing special education services to learning disabled students and time limits and class size limits on special education classes for students designated as learning disabled. Again, this request will have much more effect if it comes in the form of a letter signed by a large group so connect with you state or regional membership organization.

* Provide the entire membership of your district's Committee on Special Education with cost containment training with the goal of meeting the needs of all disabled students in a cost effective manner. Put an administrator in charge of providing leadership for the Committee on Special Education and provide training on cost containment strategies.

* Establish rules for the Committee on Special Education that prevent special education service providers from performing evaluations on students who might be receiving services from the providers completing the evaluations.

* Make sure parents of students who might have a disabling condition, regular education teachers and special education staff members all understand the purpose of the special education label is to formally agree that the student needs less challenging academic expectations than regular students in order to succeed in school. If the student is struggling academically but less challenging academic expectations are not required your school district system should provide that student with the necessary one-on-one tutoring outside the special education arena and outside the school day. Tutoring should not be limited to special education students or to special education certified teachers.

* Hire new college graduates with teaching certifications as teaching assistants at an annual salary that is 60 percent of a beginning teacher's salary as one option to provide one-on-one tutoring for students who are struggling academically. Pay these teaching assistants who are certified as teachers or other certified teachers for student one on one tutoring on an hourly basis (including time before school, after school, evenings, weekends, during school breaks or over the summer). These same teaching assistants may provide extra challenges for students who are ready to move forward. This type of help is much more flexible in its delivery than regulation laden special education services.

* Ensure the school district is maximizing the special state and federal aid available to help offset some of the costs the district bears for services provided to special education students. (Note: In three districts where I worked significant state aid was lost due to inadequate record keeping and document processing related to special education student identifications regarding their disabling conditions, specific program placements and program costs.) Hire a consultant who will work for a percentage of the extra aid they can generate to audit your records in the special education area.

* Analyze data that compares the special education classification rates for all types of disabilities in your district with other districts with similar demographics (poverty rates and resource levels) to make sure you're not over-diagnosing special education. Share the data with the school board at a public meeting, with the administrative team, with

the Committee on Special Education and with the teaching staff. Explain how over-diagnosis lowers school district student achievement in the long run by misdirecting district resources that could produce improved academic achievement in the regular education arena with tutoring for students outside the regular school day.

* Encourage principals and special education administrators to develop plans to provide one-on-one tutoring to all students who are struggling to pass the required state tests using funding saved from reorganization of staff responsibilities. Whenever there is a staff resignation or retirement investigate options to redirect resources. This strategy could work for students who need extra help to pass the required state exams by providing extra pay during staff lunch periods or preparation time, after or before school, on weekends, during school vacations or in the summer. Make sure you use any special education savings for one-on-one tutoring. If superintendents use their administrators' savings plan just to cut the budget, the administrators will never create another real savings/ improvement plan for your review.

* Support your special education administrators and the Committee on Special Education when they deny a request from a parent who demands services not required. Make sure your Committee on Special Education is following proper state required procedures including dates of implementation and all state required guidelines and has properly documented everything before you enter into a legal challenge in the special education arena.

School Board Members

* Review the business official's and special education committee's list detailing the cost of all special education services and the list showing any extra aid that comes to the district to help offset special education costs. Bring this issue up for discussion at a public meeting of the school board to determine whether or not the district wants the administration to commit time to create cost detail and aid lists if they don't already exist.

- Discuss the possibility of the school superintendent contacting your state's education department to request a waiver from the U.S. Department of Education on requirements related to certification of teachers providing special education services to learning disabled students including time limits and class size limits on special education classes for students designated as learning disabled. (Note: Some states are already moving in this direction.)

- Request information regarding any cost containment training received by your district's Committee on Special education.

- Review your school district's administrative organizational chart to determine if an administrator is charged with the responsibility of providing leadership for the Committee on Special Education. If administrative leadership is not clear request an executive session discussion to investigate cost containment measures and over-identification issues related to special education services. Teacher leaders for the Committee on Special Education can come under intense pressure from regular education teacher colleagues who are angling for special education labels for students they don't want impacting their evaluations or from special educators who want more students in special education classes to pad low enrollment numbers that jeopardize special educator jobs.

- Ask your superintendent if your district has guidelines that prevent special education service providers from performing evaluations on students who might end up receiving services from the evaluating providers. Make sure providers, parents and staff members are aware of this rule.

- Make sure parents, regular education teachers and special education staff members understand the purpose of the special education label is to agree formally that a student needs less challenging academic expectations in order to succeed in school.

- Request from your superintendent details for procedures in place to academically support students who are struggling outside the special education arena.

- Ask your superintendent what plans are in place to reduce the special education budget and use the funding saved to hire teaching assistants who are certified teachers and who are starting their careers at an annual salary that is 60 percent of that of a full-time permanent starting teacher. These certified teachers/teaching assistants can provide one-on-one tutoring for students during and outside the regular school day schedule or provide extra challenges for students who are ready for more. This type of help can be much more flexible in its delivery than regulation laden special education services.

* Ask your superintendent if steps are being taken to make sure the district is maximizing the special state and federal aid available to help offset some of the costs the district bears for services provided to special education students. Ask your superintendent if s/he has investigated using consultants who can potentially increase funding in this area for a percentage of the additional funding found by auditing your state filings for special education aid.

* Avoid trying to be the "fixer" of parental concerns about special education placements and staff issues. Report any parental complaints immediately to the superintendent and the entire school board and request updates on the resolution of the parent's concerns.

Principals and Special Education Administrators

* Observe special education classes regularly to ensure the academic challenge level for special education students dovetails with the difficulty of tests they will have to take.

* Make sure teachers who deal with students with weaker skills, including both special education and regular education students, understand fully the content and skills required by the latest standards and tests in your state.

* Monitor and supervise teaching employees to ensure special educators adapt regular student academic expectations and lesson plans to meet the needs of disabled students who are integrated into regular classes. Avoid putting special education students in separate settings where academic expectations may be watered down unless the

student's parents have agreed the student's disability will prevent them from taking required tests or receiving a regular diploma.

* Look for ways in the development of each student's Individualized Education Plans to fully meet the needs of disabled students in a more flexible way.

* Create an opportunity to fund a program to support the academic achievement of students who are struggling to pass the required state tests, including both special education students and regular education students by using any staff retirements or resignations (particularly in the nonteaching areas and the special education department) to put more resources where they are needed with expanded one-on-one tutoring for students outside the regular school day and school year.

* Look for a way to implement a plan that provides one-on-one tutorial support from teachers who (1) fully understand the content and skills required on tests students must pass, and (2) have a high degree of empathy for all students who need help to succeed academically whether designated as a special education student or a regular education student. Consider hiring teaching assistants who are certified as teachers at a pay rate of 60 percent of what your district pays a starting teacher as part of this plan. This plan could include one-on-one tutoring for students who need extra help to pass the required state exams during the school day or tutoring done for extra hourly pay during staff lunch periods or preparation time, after or before school, on weekends, during school vacations or in the summer.

* Minimize turf wars over personnel, budgets and supervision responsibilities between special education and regular education administrators, teachers and support staff. This is a joint responsibility.

* Share with your superintendent any program details regarding new and more cost effective and academically successful delivery systems for special education services in place in other school districts that your colleagues who work in those districts have described to you.

* Complete training for and fully implement the Response to Intervention model in your school and school district.

Teachers

* Special education teachers: If you're co-teaching classes with regular education teachers, become fully knowledgeable about the content and skills required by the state tests. Training or college coursework may be required.

* Regular education teachers: Fully share the teaching responsibilities in co-taught classes with special education co-teachers so that both teachers and all the students view the special educator's role as that of a teacher and not a teaching assistant.

* Teachers: share with principals and special education administrators any inexpensive but effective ideas regarding how best to organize, schedule and implement the delivery of one-on-one tutoring outside the regular school day and year for students who are struggling to pass required state tests, including both special education and regular education students.

* Avoid "turf wars" between special education staff members and regular education staff members.

* Make certain all staff who work with special education students fully understand students' Individualized Education Plans (IEP's) and their responsibility to implement the plans and to suggest any necessary modifications to the IEP's to create flexibility so that the professional with the appropriate knowledge of the content and skills required on the tests theses students must pass and the professional who has necessary empathy and a positive relationship with the student is the person providing one-on-one tutoring to this student on a regular basis.

* Discuss special education delivery systems with colleagues who teach in other districts and if you hear about something that sounds promising share it with your principal and special education administrator.

* If you have the appropriate skill set and available time, let your principal and special education administrator know you're interested in providing one-on-one tutoring to students who need extra help to pass the required state exams for extra pay during your lunch period

or preparation time, after or before school, on weekends, during school vacations or in the summer.

"The Politics of Teaching Reading"
What can we do?
<u>Superintendents</u>

* Complete a public presentation regarding the academic performance data for the school district every year and include charts and graphs that show how the district compares to other districts with the same demographics including the same levels of poverty and the same types of resources per student.
  o Disaggregate the data so that you're comparing your school district to one with the same or a close percentage of students who receive free and reduced lunch.
  o Provide comparisons for groups of children by ethnicity, boys and girls and special education designated students. Avoid comparing your schools/district to other schools/districts with higher or lower levels of student poverty.
* Assign principals with the task of developing annual academic performance improvement plans finalized before the school district budget is set so that additional funding (when available and necessary) can be built into the plans.
* Encourage principals to engineer budget trades within their schools to keep improvement costs from increasing the budget.
* Make sure improvement plans represent the best research regarding school improvement and fit the needs and resources of the school district.
* Have the principals complete a formal dry-run presentation of the plan with you before presenting to the school board, faculty and parents.
* Have principals present improvement plans in public with the involvement of key teacher leaders every year to gain school board, staff and parent understanding and support prior to the plan's implementation. Be sure your principals take into account comments,

suggestions and criticisms and incorporate ideas that will make the final plans more effective.

* Anticipate where there will be employee friction as a result of the implementation of improvement plans and invite principals to school board executive sessions prior to the plan's implementation to discuss the anticipated impact of plan implementation on staff, students and parents.

* If political issues develop during academic improvement plan implementation, invite the school principal into a school board executive session to explain again the plan and answer any questions. Support those principals as best you can.

* Schedule principals for a public school board presentation mid-year to discuss plan implementation progress.

* Look for funding sources within the existing school district budget that can support academic improvement plan implementation and recommend changes to the budget during the budget development process. (See Chapter "Politicians Need Not Apply" for savings ideas.)

* Look for structural changes in your school district that would create an opportunity to fund part or all of your improvement plan, i.e., a custodian in your school district is retiring. Can you get along without a replacement? With a part-time replacement? Never just rehire what you have. Always look for the opportunities to reallocate resources where you need them most and share your ideas with your school board.

* Establish ground rules with your school board regarding every board member and the superintendent having access to the same information at all times including complaints and the sources of those complaints and how the school board and superintendent should deal with those complaints. These ground rules are best established when there is no specific issue waiting to be resolved.

School Board Members

* Request the superintendent provide annual school district academic performance data in comparison to other school districts with similar

demographics and similar resources per student. Request disaggregated data that shows comparisons on performance for children from poverty, groups of students by ethnicity, boys and girls and special education students. Be wary of any data that compares your schools/district to schools/districts with a higher or lower level of student poverty.

- Request the superintendent have principals present their academic improvement plans to the school board at a public session.

- Request the superintendent hold executive session discussions prior to the implementation of academic improvement plans regarding particular employees who will potentially have concerns about the expectations of these plans. Make certain your school board members have agreed in advance on how they will deal with complaints from employees who resist improvement plan efforts.

- Ask the superintendent to schedule principals to report to the school board publicly on improvement plan progress mid-year.

- If any employee, parent or student contacts a school board member with a complaint regarding anything in the school district, share the complaint with the entire school board and the superintendent including the identity of the person making the complaint.

- Adopt a policy that complaints about anything in the school district should be handled through the normal "chain of command" and should not be dealt with by the school board until the superintendent and the administrative staff have had a chance to resolve the concerns.

- Avoid at all costs the role of "fixer" of problems within the school district.

- Support the superintendent and the school board president if one of the members of your school board goes "off the reservation" and becomes a fixer or fails to share complaints and their source as expected by your ground rules including if all else fails voting to support censure or removal of the offending school board member.

- Adopt a school district "no retaliation" policy regarding any employee, parent, student or resident who raises legitimate concerns with a school board member or district employee. Legitimate means the complaint or concern is based on facts and not misinformation. The policy should entrust to the superintendent or her/his designee the responsibility of resolving all complaints and correcting any misinformation while keeping the school board properly informed.

Principals

* Assess the strengths and weaknesses of your school's academic program and report to school staff, parents and the superintendent data showing a comparison of your school's academic performance to similar schools (similar poverty, size and resources per pupil) in your state or region. Disaggregate data to show comparisons based on poverty, ethnicity, gender and special education designation. Avoid bogus comparisons of academic performance with schools or districts with higher or lower levels of student poverty that make the school look good or bad.

* Brainstorm with the entire staff regarding possible academic improvement plan strategies after investigating strategies being used by schools with similar demographics and resources that outperform your school.

* Develop a detailed improvement plan with the help of key teacher leaders in your school. Use a full day retreat or a series of half days to develop the plan if possible.

* Ask for additional funds from the school district to support your improvement plan but be ready to move forward with the plan's implementation with or without additional funding.

* Look for structural changes in your school that would create an opportunity to fund part or all of your improvement plan, i.e., a secretary in your school has moved away and resigned from her position. Can you get along without a replacement? What about a part-time replacement? Never just rehire what you have. Always look for the opportunities to reallocate resources where you need them most and share your ideas with your superintendent.

* Ask your superintendent for an opportunity to present your academic performance improvement plan to the school board at a public school board session.

- Provide your superintendent with a written update on the status of your plan's implementation at mid-year and volunteer to do a public presentation to the school board on the update.
- Hold a faculty meeting discussion on plan progress mid-year.
- Anticipate who among the staff will struggle the most with the plan's implementation and who might raise concerns directly with school board members. Discuss these individuals and their antici-pated concerns with the superintendent and request an opportunity to discuss these issues with the school board in executive session before they hear complaints from staff.
- If problems develop during the implementation of your academic improvement plan, let your superintendent know and collabora-tively develop a plan to address the problem, keeping the school board informed of progress.

Teachers

- Share information about academic improvement plans from other districts with your school's principal.
- Share data comparing relevant school performance with your school's principal.
- Request the opportunity to observe other teachers in your school or other schools who are implementing teaching strategies like those described in Gail Long's classroom.
- Volunteer for a teacher leadership position.
- Attend training on using data to adjust instruction for students who need extra help and for those who are ready for additional challenges.
- Make yourself aware of and fully utilize the online state curriculum resources appropriate to the grade level/courses you instruct that allows you to run a multilevel classroom with extra challenges for those stu-dent who are ready for them and extra support for students who need it.
- Work to implement a successful "push-in" remedial or special edu-cation program in your classroom. If you are a remedial or special education teacher attend training to learn how to use your skills to

make a "push-in" approach work for you and for the other teachers on your grade level team or that you work with in your school.

- Ask your principal to use faculty meetings as an opportunity to discuss teaching strategies and training.

"Charter Schools, School Choice and Poverty"
What can we do?
Superintendents, School Board Members, Principals and Teachers

- Identify misplaced incentives in state laws regarding charter schools, magnet schools and any other school choice options that create rogue, invasive species choice schools and lobby your state legislature to fix these laws. You can identify these misplaced incentives by asking the following questions:
  - Are school choice options created with the approval or involvement of the host public school district's superintendent and school board?
  - Are they draining critical resources from public school districts due to poorly designed funding formulas?
  - Do the laws provide sufficient state funding support to deal with the extra costs associated with implementing a successful charter school/magnet/school choice plan?
  - Do they have special education or English as a second language student exclusion policies?
  - What's the "return rate" of these schools? Is the "return rate" tracked? What happens if the schools have high "return rates"?
  - Do school choice options promote success using test score data that fails to properly take into account student transfers between the choice schools and the regular public schools and the choice schools' exclusion of special education and English as a second language students?
  - Are school districts given the choice of which educators are laid off when a charter school is started and staff is selected?

- o Can school districts lay off educators with documented performance and misconduct issues and hire more effective educators when charter or magnet schools start?

- Approach your state level advocacy group and request they lobby your legislature and your state board of education to hire only state education commissioners who have experience as superintendents in turning around underperforming school districts in your state. Lobby the legislature to ensure the state education department is staffed with individuals with experience as school superintendents, school business officials and principals in school districts and a history of positive turnarounds in school district and school performance. Lobby also for a separate properly staffed division in your state education department charged with takeovers of long-term underperforming school districts.

- For superintendents: Work with your local state legislators to design a law to fund rental subsidies for up to 20 percent of families that live in a high poverty school district in your state. For school board members: Request support from your state level advocacy organization advocating state legislators to pass a law that funds rental subsidies for up to 20 percent of the families that live within the attendance boundaries of a single high poverty school district in your state. For principals and teachers: If your state is considering a student's family rental subsidy law that would allow poverty children to move to a low poverty school district to complete their education, encourage your state level principals' advocacy group to also lobby in support of this law.

  - o Rental subsidy legislation should be designed so that participating families making the move to a wealthier community have children ages 0 to 3 (younger children will benefit the most from rental subsidy relocation funding), be free or reduced price lunch eligible, be residents of the selected school district at the time the rental subsidy program starts and be willing to relocate to one of a select set of nearby low poverty school districts. Eligible families would be required to complete an application with assistance from the receiving school district and enter a true lottery. The rental subsidies would be paid directly to the landlord/property owner/

rental agency and continue only for as long the family is free or reduced price lunch eligible and is a resident of one of the selected target school districts with at least one child aged 0-5 or attending the local public schools in the target district. Once all the rental subsidy families' children have left high school the subsidy ends.

o   Target school districts must have 30 percent or fewer free or reduced price lunch eligible students to receive students with rental subsidies and be performing academically average or above average in comparison to established targets that take student poverty into account (like the scatterplot graphs in this book). School districts will be removed from the list as potential future recipients of rental subsidy families if their academic performance slips below established targets or free and reduced price lunch percentages increase above 30 percent. (Recipient families that had already relocated to the school district would not be required to relocate again at that time and would continue to receive the rental subsidy for as long as they remained in the district and their children had not graduated from high school.

o   School district rental subsidy law should also pay for a long-term (25 years minimum) university study of academic achievement (high school graduation rates, college attendance and graduation rates, test score performance, etc.) and outcomes (income levels, key health outcome rates, incarceration rates, welfare recipient rates, mortality rates, substance abuse rates, unemployment rates, etc.) for the rental subsidy recipient family children and for children from families that applied for the rental subsidy but were denied the subsidy as a result of the lottery system.

* Encourage your state level advocacy group to advocate for the passage of the legislation described above.

* Encourage your state level advocacy group to lobby for passage of laws that provide help and support to families of children living in poverty in your state. If your personal politics leans right encourage your state superintendents group to support Republican strategies for reducing citizen poverty and poverty's negative

impacts on educational achievement at the state and federal levels with expanded Earned Income Tax Credits, expanded preschool opportunities for three- and four-year-old children, home visits by paid professionals for all children ages 0 to 5, more job training, changes in tax laws that promote small business growth and hiring of workers in decent paying jobs, etc.. If your personal politics leans left encourage your state level superintendents group to support Democratic strategies for reducing poverty at the state and federal levels with expanded Earned Income Tax Credits, expanded pre-school opportunities for three and four year old children, home visits by paid professionals for all children ages 0 to 5, sliding scale state supported child care, expanded family leave opportunities, higher minimum wages, etc.

- For school board members: Discuss with your fellow school board members at a public session the need for your superintendent to design school district and school building academic performance comparisons that take into account student poverty levels, student transfers in and out of regular district, charter and magnet schools and exclusion of special education and second language students from choice schools so that more accurate school to school and school district to school district comparisons can be made. For superintendents: Design school district and school building academic performance comparisons that take into account student poverty levels, the boomerang effect (student transfers from regular district schools to charter and magnet schools and back), the exclusion of special education and second language students from choice schools so that more accurate school-to-school and school district-to school district comparisons can be made. For principals: Discuss with your superintendent the need for your school district to design school district and school building academic performance comparisons that take into account student poverty levels, student transfers in and out of regular district, charter and magnet schools and exclusion of special education and second language students from choice schools so that more accurate school to school and school district to school district comparisons can be made. Volunteer to help your superintendent with this task. For teachers: Discuss with your principal the need for your school district to design school district and school building academic performance comparisons that take into account student poverty levels, student transfers in and out of regular district, charter and magnet schools and exclusion of special education and English as a second language students from choice schools so that more accurate school to school and school district to school district comparisons can be made. Suggestions: Use graphical representations showing predicted performance lines like those in this book. Separate out your district's regular education population (exclude special education and English as a second language populations) and compare their performance to the choice schools that exclude special education and/or second language students. Count students who transfer in and out of choice schools as partial students for the district program and partial students for the choice school program with the portions determined by their time spent in each system. Explain and share your performance comparison reports with your school board, colleagues in your state superintendents' group, the state education department and most important with local media covering your school district, making sure they understand the intricacies of this complicated analysis. Volunteer to help your principal with this sharing.

Superintendents and Principals

- Support the position that advocates for greater integration of students by ethnicity, second language and poverty status when discussing and acting on proposed change in laws. It may make your job more challenging but it will also help provide children with the skills they will need to live and work successfully in diverse environments and communities.

Superintendents

- Design proposed changes to your state's choice school laws to address the weaknesses noted above and allow school districts to creatively and effectively implement charter schools and magnet schools as parental choice options. These laws should allow school districts laying off employees due to the initiation of a parental choice school to first lay off those employees with documented misconduct and job performance issues.

- Design charter school laws that encourage improvement of academic performance of all children in the school district, including those who remain in regular public schools.

- Take your proposed law changes to your state level superintendents' organization and work with them to modify your plan so that all superintendents can support it.

- Take the rough draft plan as modified by your state superintendents' group to your state education department and invite them to designate six to eight employees who will become part of the team working to create equitable school choice change plans for your state.

- Invite three teacher union representatives and three representatives of politically conservative groups in your state that are advocating for changes in your state's tenure and seniority laws for educators and for greater accountability for school district superintendents, central administration employees and school boards in school districts consistently performing academically well below predicted performance.

- Encourage this state level school choice improvement planning group (while hopefully continuing your own involvement as a member of the team) to work collaboratively using the rough plan created by your state level superintendents' group as a starting point to design a finalized plan that addresses the school choice law weaknesses noted above.

- Ensure the final plan gives school districts the option, if layoffs are necessary, to lay off a limited number of educators with documented performance or misconduct issues when creating a new charter/magnet school choice plan in districts consistently performing academically well below predicted performance. Ensure the plan requires these select school districts be formally notified by their state education department that their poor performance allows them this special school choice performance improvement opportunity at the outset of a three-year timetable for required improvement. Ensure the plan requires the replacement of superintendents, school boards and high ranking central office administrators with appointees selected by your state education department if the school districts in question fail to show significant student achievement gains (80 percent reduction in the gap between predicted performance and actual performance) within three years of notification.

* Take the collaboratively designed plan created to your governor and to all state level legislators and request their enactment of law changes that will accomplish the plan.

* Establish budgets that provide meaningful training for educators in your district on teaching students from poverty. Participate in this training yourself. Make certain all district policies and procedures coincide with best practices as identified through this training. Include training specifically related to teaching strategies that work most effectively with diverse learner groups.

* When discussing and acting to initiate proposed changes in laws, state education department rules and local school district policies in your state or school district pursue the changes which help to balance student poverty, ethnic minority and English as a second language enrollment percentages between school districts and among schools within school districts.

School Board Members, Principals and Teachers

* Work with your school district or school leadership team to establish policies for your school that avoid the pitfalls and misplaced incentives of rogue, invasive species charter schools. These pitfalls include: such schools are frequently created without the approval or involvement of the host public school district's superintendent or school

board; they drain critical resources from public school districts due to poorly designed funding formulas; laws governing such schools generally provide insufficient state funding support to deal with the extra costs associated with implementing a successful charter school/ magnet school plan. (Charter school/magnet school funding formulas should be designed so that they encourage the improvement of the academic performance of all children in the school district including those who remain in the regular public schools.); they frequently use special education or English as a second language student exclusion policies; they frequently exhibit "return rate" problems so that students struggling with behavioral, academic or school attendance issues, over time, end up concentrated in the regular public schools while the choice schools accumulate a more successful student cohort; they inaccurately promote success using test score data that fails to properly take into account student transfers between the choice schools and the regular public schools and the choice schools and exclusion of special education and second language students; they frequently make it impossible for school districts to initiate viable choice school options because they fail to allow school districts the option of laying off educators with documented performance or misconduct issues when a charter school is started and its staff is selected. School districts should be able lay off educators with documented performance issues who are making inadequate progress with performance improvement plans and educators with a history of documented misconduct issues and hire more effective educators with the installment of a "choice" charter or magnet school.

School Board Members

- Continue to advocate for changes in the laws regarding school choice options with your local legislators and your governor. Attempt to enlist the support of your state level school board member advocacy organization to encourage changes to the law.

- Make certain your school district establishes yearly budgets that provide meaningful training for all educators in your district regarding performing their jobs effectively with students from poverty. Participate in this training yourself. Make certain all district policies and procedures coincide with best practices as identified through this training. Include training relating to teaching strategies that work most effectively with diverse learner groups.

- If your state is considering a student/family rental subsidy law that would allow poverty children to move to a low poverty school district to complete their education while the impacts of the rental subsidy is studied by a university advocate in support of this law and encourage your state level school board members' advocacy group to also lobby in support of this law.

- When discussing or acting as a school board member on proposed changes in laws, state education department rules and local school district policies in your state or school district, laws -- rules and policies that would help to balance student poverty, ethnic minority and second language percentages between school districts and among schools within school districts – support the position that advocates for greater integration. It's the right thing to do and it will improve student achievement for students in schools that provide sound instruction for diverse learning groups. It may make your job more challenging but it will help provide all students with the skills they'll need to live and work successfully in diverse environment and in diverse communities.

Principals and Teachers

- If you are a principal of a non-choice school or the principal of a choice school advocate with your state and regional level principals' organizations to support changes in the laws and rules regarding choice schools in your state that create the misplaced incentives and pitfalls noted above.

- Volunteer to work on a committee for your state or regional level principals' organization tasked with developing realistic options for choice schools that could become a plan of restructuring of choice schools to address the concerns above and could be supported by the state legislators in your state.

- When discussing or presenting information to colleagues, parents and media that compares your school's performance with the performance of other schools in the district or other schools outside the district, act as an educator who enlightens others so they understand the impact of poverty on student achievement or the impact of policies that exclude special education or English as a second language students. Be honest about your school's academic strengths and shortcomings. Don't try to hide weaker-than-hoped-for student academic performance by your students. Explain fully how exclusions of English as a second language or special education students and student transfers in and out of your school impact achievement as a whole. If you are a choice school principal, monitor and publicly discuss your school's "return rate."

Teachers

- Advocate with your principal for adequate annual funding in your school district's budget that provides meaningful training for all educators in your district regarding performing their jobs effectively with students from poverty. Participate in this training yourself. Discuss with your principal school and school district policies that don't align with best practices identified through this training. Advocate training include support for teachers with trainers who can plan with teachers and observe said teachers in their classrooms as they implement their plans designed with teaching strategies that work most effectively with diverse learner groups.

- If your state is considering a student's family rental subsidy law that would allow poverty children to move to a low poverty school district to complete their education while the impacts of the rental subsidy is studied by a university advocate in support of this law and encourage your state level teachers union to lobby in support of this law.

"Where has all the money gone?"
What can we do?
<u>Superintendents, School Board Members, Principals, Teachers</u>

* Work with your state level group to lobby for legislation that supports the following. (Note: While many state level teachers unions and many individual teachers may not support all the items on this list, many can support several of them.)

  In all states:
  o Ban campaign contributions from public unions to state and local legislators (assuming a way can be found to make this constitutional).
  o Change rules and laws for learning disabled special education students so that the students' special education needs can be met with one-on-one tutoring outside the regular school day and school year from any teacher with a certificate appropriate to the student's learning deficits (elementary, math, English, Social Studies, etc., not just special education teachers).
  o Support legislation setting a maximum on spending per pupil for disabled students established by the severity of disability (i.e., for a severely, multiply disabled student = 3.5 X average spending per pupil for regular education student of the same age in the same school district.)
  o Support legislation and state and local funding that pays for home visits by trained school district personnel for all children from birth to age 5 and especially children from poverty.
  o Support legislation and state and local funding for full day pre-kindergarten for all children ages 3 and 4 and especially for children who qualify for free and reduced price lunch.
  o Support legislation that equitably provides a mix of state, local and federal per pupil funding to local school districts. Equitable means extra funding per pupil for children from poverty. Equitable also means a statewide property tax that is distributed to districts based on total enrollment with extra funding

for poverty enrollment. This new system will have to be phased in over multiple years.

In high-cost, strong public union states:

- ○ Reform public union negotiations laws so that step raises and expensive health insurance plans and other contact provisions do not carry forward when a public union contract has expired.
- ○ Establish state level public union negotiations utilizing a statewide representative team of school negotiations attorney specialists, superintendents, business officials, health insurance consultants and a few representative school board members so that the contract negotiated is a statewide contract for all educators with regional cost adjustments for salaries and health insurance costs.
- ○ Move to defined contribution public employee pensions for all public employees in the state who will retire at a set future date at least 10 years from the date of legislation authorizing this switch.
- ○ For all public employees, including school employees, phase in higher deductible and co-pay employee health insurance plans comparable to those found on the Affordable Care Act websites with contributions by employees of at least 20 percent and retirees of at least 50 percent toward the cost of the plan.

- ● In high-cost strong public union states, the committee negotiating for the state must set carefully structured public union negotiations salary and health insurance goals. Each school board in the state would complete a single consensus survey to inform the state level negotiating team of their suggested goals. Goals should be based on salaries and health insurance costs encountered by school districts regionally. Graphs and charts similar to those found in the "Where has all the money gone?" chapter would help create this comparison and these goals. If you are a superintendent and your principal isn't aware of these graphs, share the information from this chapter with her/him and vice versa.

Superintendents

- For superintendents: In small and medium-sized school districts in high-cost, strong public union states, lead the negotiations team in settling contracts until state level negotiations have been established. School board members should be part of setting goals but should not be part of the negotiating team, particularly in districts with a history of protracted and acrimonious negotiations.

- For longstanding and difficult public union contract anomalies (like the top end teacher pay issue in Mt. Mason) work to resolve these issues over multiple contract negotiations.

- As necessary meet individually with specific school board members to tutor them through the complicated details of the math and contract language in public union contract negotiations.

- In high-cost strong public union states, recommend hiring an experienced and effective school district attorney who can help to lead the negotiations effort. The contract and term of this attorney should be reviewed for possible changes every three to five years.

- Recommend hiring an experienced and effective health insurance consultant to aid the district in selecting the best and most cost effective health insurance products, negotiating all insurance related issues in public union contracts and keeping all the employee and retiree groups informed about health insurance costs, effectiveness and the necessity of any potential changes. The contract and term of this health insurance consultant should be reviewed for possible changes every three to five years.

- Compile data on the academic effectiveness of all special education classes and remedial classes (including those funded by Federal grants) for learning disabled students and students struggling academically. If a student starts the school year two years behind her/his grade level peers in reading or math and ends the year more than two years behind that means the program s/he's enrolled in is not working. As Napoleon said, "When your horse dies, dismount." Report this data publicly and use it to support a shift to one-on-one tutoring outside the regular school day for learning disabled students and remedial students as an alternative to traditional special education and remedial education classes.

* If a special education teacher retires or resigns from a position in your district use the funding spent on salary and benefits for that position to pay for hours of part-time, one-on-one tutoring outside the regular school day for learning disabled students and regular education students (one to five hours a week) who are struggling academically. If necessary, make sure the Committee on Special Education Children in your school district approves any necessary changes in the student's Individualized Education Plan, indicating that the student's needs can be met with tutoring by a tutor with a valid teaching certification in the area of the child's academic deficit (NOT required to be a special education teacher).

* If one of your schools has room, encourage the principal to house a before school/after school/early evening child care center funded by parents who would pay for this child care on an income-based sliding scale. Integrate one-on-one tutoring with certified teacher or teaching assistant support for learning disabled and all other academically struggling students into the child care center.

* Pursue any federal, state, local and foundation grants that would help pay for one-on-one tutoring outside the regular school day for learning disabled students and students who are struggling academically and for home visits six to 12 times per year for children from birth to age 5 by trained school district employees following the curriculum of one of the nationally recognized home visit programs and for full day pre-kindergarten for 3- and 4-year-old children.

* Review special education expenses to avoid duplication and potential waste with excess numbers of one-on-one aides assigned to specific special education students and extra special education school bus runs that can be consolidated without creating overly long bus rides for students.

* Gradually move teacher salary schedules toward smaller annual increments that are evenly spaced in dollars (not percentages) for all steps so that teachers start their careers at higher salaries and see smaller salary increases each year. Add a new beginning rung on

the career ladder for certified teachers at lower pay (60 percent of regular teacher starting pay) who would work as teaching assistants with student tutoring responsibilities or teaching lessons under the supervision of an experienced teacher. Allow for extra pay for teachers who assume leadership roles, work extra hours with students, develop curriculum used by a grade level or department or who work extra hours training or being trained with their peers. (Selection of teachers who take on these roles would not be based on seniority.)

* In high-cost strong public union states, communicate directly with the press and the public regarding ongoing public union negotiations to the maximum extent possible under existing law by writing detailed press releases and meeting separately with reporters in advance of public events where negotiations will be discussed to clarify any proposed changes.

* During the local school district budget building process re-allocate funding to the extent possible from positions and expenses that have not improved student achievement (salaries and benefits for learning disabled teachers and remedial teachers, expensive employee health insurance plans, extra legal fees for unnecessarily protracted negotiations, etc.) to expenses that research says will improve student achievement: one-on-one tutoring outside the regular school day for students who are struggling academically, pre-school for 3- and 4-year-old children and home visits by trained school district employees for children from birth to age 5.

School Board Members

* In high-cost strong public union states, encourage your superintendent to work with the school board to set carefully structured public union negotiations salary and health insurance goals agreed to in advance. Goals should be based on salaries and health insurance costs encountered by school districts regionally. Graphs and charts similar to those found in the "Where has the money gone?" chapter will be helpful in creating this comparison and these goals.

* In small and medium-sized school districts in high-cost strong public union states encourage the superintendent to lead the negotiations team in settling contracts. In general, school board members should not be part of the negotiating team particularly in districts with a history of protracted and acrimonious negotiations.

* For longstanding and difficult public union contract anomalies (like the top end teacher pay issue in Mt. Mason) encourage the superintendent to work to resolve these issues over multiple contract negotiations.

* Meet individually with the superintendent as needed to better understand the complicated details of the math and contract language in public union contract negotiations. If one of your fellow school board members needs a one-on-one meeting with the superintendent to explain this information tell your superintendent.

* In high-cost, strong public union states, encourage your superintendent to recommend hiring an experienced and effective school district attorney who can help to lead the negotiations effort. The contract and term of this attorney should be reviewed for possible changes every three to five years.

* Encourage your superintendent to recommend the hiring of an experienced and effective health insurance consultant to aid the district in selecting the best and most cost effective health insurance products, negotiating all public union contracts and keeping employee and retiree groups informed about health insurance costs, effectiveness and the necessity of any potential changes. The contract and term of this health insurance consultant should be reviewed for possible changes every three to five years.

* Encourage your superintendent to compile data on the academic effectiveness of special education classes and remedial classes (including those funded by Federal grants) for learning disabled students and students who are struggling academically. If a student starts the school year two years behind her/his grade level peers in reading or math and ends the year more than two years behind the program s/he's enrolled in is not working. As Napoleon said, "When your horse

dies, dismount." Ask your superintendent to report this data publicly and if academic underperformance for these classes is noted, as it is nationally, encourage your superintendent to use this data to develop plans that support a shift to one-on-one tutoring outside the regular school day for learning-disabled students, remedial students and struggling regular education students as an alternative.

* If a special education teacher retires or resigns from a position in your district, encourage your superintendent to use the funding spent on salary and benefits for that position to pay for hours of part-time one-on-one tutoring hours outside the regular school day for learning disabled students and regular education students (one to five hours per week) who are struggling academically. Caution your superintendent to be certain that the Committee on Special Education Children in your school district approves a change the Individualized Education Plan for any special education students receiving this tutoring to indicate that their needs can be met with tutoring by a tutor with a valid teaching certification in the area of the child's academic deficit (NOT required to be a special education teacher).

* Encourage your superintendent to look for school building space to house one or more before school/after school/early evening child care centers funded by parents who would pay for this child care on an income based sliding scale. Point out to your superintendent that one-on-one tutoring provided to learning disabled and struggling students can be integrated into this child care setting.

* Encourage your superintendent to pursue any federal, state, local and foundation grants which could help to pay for one-on-one tutoring outside the regular school day for learning disabled students and students who are struggling academically, for home visits six to 12 times per year to the homes of all children from birth to age 5 in the school district by trained school district employees following the curriculum of one of the nationally recognized home visit programs and for full day pre-kindergarten for 3- and 4-year-old children.

- Encourage your superintendent to charge one of the district's employees with reviewing all special education expenses to avoid duplication and potential waste with excess numbers of one-on-one aides assigned to specific special education students and extra special education school bus runs that can be consolidated without long bus rides for students.

- Encourage your superintendent to gradually move your teacher salary schedule toward smaller annual increments evenly spaced in dollars (not percentages) for all steps so that teachers start their careers at higher salaries and see smaller salary increases each year and add career ladder pay options for teachers that start the newest teachers at lower pay (60 percent of the pay earned by a regular starting teacher) with reduced responsibilities as tutors for struggling students or teaching lessons under the supervision of an experienced teacher. Allow for extra pay for teachers who assume leadership roles, work extra hours with students, develop curriculum used by a grade level or department or who work extra hours training or being trained with their peers.

- In high-cost strong public union states, encourage your superintendent to communicate directly with the press and the public regarding ongoing public union negotiations to the maximum extent possible under existing law by writing detailed press releases and meeting separately with reporters regarding negotiations and proposed contracts.

- In the local school district budget-building process, work with your superintendent and fellow school board members to re-allocate funding to the extent possible from positions and expenses that have not improved student achievement (salaries and benefits for learning disabled teachers and remedial teachers, expensive employee health insurance plans, extra legal fees for unnecessarily protracted negotiations, etc.) to expenses that research says will improve student achievement: one-on-one tutoring outside the regular school day for students who are struggling academically, pre-school for 3- and 4-year-old children and home visits by trained school district employees for children from birth to age 5.

Principals

- Principals should not be part of the negotiating team particularly in districts with a history of protracted and acrimonious negotiations but should attempt to reduce the negative impact on students and staff of any protracted negotiations in your school district.

- For longstanding and difficult public union contract anomalies (like the top end teacher pay issue in Mt. Mason) help the superintendent explain to everyone involved the necessity of resolving these issues over multiple contract negotiations.

- Meet individually with the superintendent before any public union negotiations as needed to make sure s/he understands any complicated operational details specific to your school building related to the language in public union contracts being negotiated.

- Inform your superintendent of any misinformation circulating in the school district or among the public related to ongoing or planned public union negotiations.

- Compile data on the academic effectiveness of special education classes and remedial classes (including those funded by Federal grants) for learning disabled students and students who are struggling academically in your school. As Napoleon said, "When your horse dies, dismount." Report this data to your superintendent and if academic underperformance for these classes is noted as it is nationally, ask your superintendent for an opportunity to use this data to develop plans that support a shift to one-on-one tutoring outside the regular school day for learning disabled students, remedial students and regular education students who are struggling academically within your school as an alternative.

- If a special education teacher retires or resigns from a position in your school ask your superintendent for an opportunity to use the funding spent on salary and benefits for that position to pay for hours of part-time, one-on-one tutoring hours outside the regular school day for learning disabled students and regular education students (one to five hours per week) who are struggling academically in your school.

Work with your superintendent and the other administrators in your district to make sure the Committee on Special Needs Children in your school district approves a change in Individualized Education Plans for special education students receiving this tutoring to indicate that their needs can be met through tutoring by a tutor with a valid teaching certification in the area of the child's academic deficit (NOT required to be a special education teacher).

* Inform your superintendent that you would be able to house in your school building a before school/after school/early evening child care center funded by parents who would pay for this child care on an income based sliding scale. Point out to your superintendent that one-on-one tutoring provided to learning disabled and struggling students could be integrated into this child care setting.

* Offer to help your superintendent pursue any federal, state, local and foundation grants that could help to pay for one-on-one tutoring outside the regular school day for learning disabled students and students who are struggling academically, for home visits six to 12 times a year to the homes of all children birth to age 5 in the school district by trained school district employees following the curriculum of one of the nationally recognized home visit programs and for full day pre-kindergarten for 3- and 4-year-old children.

* Tell your superintendent immediately if you become aware of any special education expenses or other expenses that could be reduced or consolidated without negatively impacting student outcomes, including but not limited to one-on-one aides assigned to specific special education students and extra special education school bus runs that could be consolidated without creating long bus rides for students.

* Encourage your superintendent to gradually move teacher salary schedules toward smaller annual increments that are evenly spaced in dollars (not percentages) for all steps so that teachers start their careers at higher salaries and see smaller salary increases each year and add a step on the career ladder that starts the newest teachers as tutors for struggling students or for teaching lessons under the supervision of an experienced teacher. Allow for extra pay for

teachers who assume leadership roles, work extra hours with groups of students or tutoring students, develop curriculum used by a grade level or department or who work extra hours training or being trained with their peers. Look for and implement creative ways to use these options in teacher pay as a way to bring out leadership potential for the teachers in your school.

* In the local school district budget building process work with your superintendent and fellow principals toward re-allocation of funding (to the extent possible) from positions and expenses that have not improved student achievement (salaries and benefits for learning disabled teachers and remedial teachers, expensive employee health insurance plans, extra legal fees for unnecessarily protracted negotiations, etc.) to expenses that research says will improve student achievement: one on one tutoring outside the regular school day for students who are struggling academically, pre-school for 3- and 4-year-old children and home visits by trained school district employees for children from birth to age5.

Teachers

* In high-cost strong public union states, encourage your union to set carefully structured public union negotiations salary and health insurance goals. These goals should be based on salaries and health insurance costs encountered by school districts regionally. Graphs and charts similar to those found in this chapter will be helpful in creating this comparison and these goals.

* Support goals that bring employee pay, benefits and working conditions closer to the norm in your region.

* For longstanding and difficult public union contract anomalies (like the top end teacher pay issue in *Mt. Mason*), encourage your negotiating team to work to resolve these issues over multiple contract negotiations.

* In high-cost, strong public union states, teachers' state level union dues, in most cases, provides the services of an experienced labor

relations specialist to help your local negotiating team complete their negotiations. If your contract negotiations are stalled, encourage your local team to utilize the help of this experienced professional. If one of these state level professionals has already been involved and owns part of the responsibility for the excessive delay, ask for a new one. The same goes for the local school district union leadership team and the negotiating team. If the teams in place are not getting the job done after a reasonable amount of time, change the team.

* In all states, encourage your union to support the hiring of an experienced and effective health insurance consultant to aid the district in selecting the best and most cost effective health insurance products, negotiating all public union contracts and keeping all the employee and retiree groups informed about health insurance costs, effectiveness and the necessity of any potential changes. No employees are well served by wasting public dollars on overpriced health insurance products.

* Encourage your principal to compile data on the academic effectiveness of all special education classes and remedial classes (including those funded by Federal grants) for learning disabled students and students who are struggling academically in your school. If a student starts the school year two years behind her grade level peers in reading or math and ends the year more than 2 years behind the program she's enrolled in is not working. As Napoleon said, "When your horse dies, dismount." Encourage your principal to report this data to your superintendent and if academic underperformance for these classes is noted, as it is nationally, encourage your principal to ask your superintendent for an opportunity to use this data to develop plans that support a shift to one on one tutoring outside the regular school day for learning disabled students, remedial students and other students who are struggling academically in your school as an alternative.

* If a special education teacher retires or resigns from a position in your school ask your principal to consider asking the superintendent for an opportunity to use the funding spent on salary and benefits for that position to pay for hours of part time one on one tutoring

hours outside the regular school day for learning disabled students and regular education students (1 to 5 hours per week) who are struggling academically in your school. Caution your principal to be certain that the Committee on Special Education Children in your school district approves a change the Individualized Education Plan for any special education students receiving this tutoring to indicate that their needs can be met with tutoring by a tutor with a valid teaching certification in the area of the child's academic deficit (NOT required to be a special education teacher).

* Encourage your principal to volunteer your school building as a site to house a before school/after school/early evening child care center funded by parents who would pay for this child care on an income based sliding scale. Point out to your principal that one on one tutoring provided to learning disabled and struggling students could be integrated into this child care setting.

* Offer to help your principal pursue any federal, state, local and foundation grants which could help to pay for one on one tutoring outside the regular school day for learning disabled students and students who are struggling academically, for home visits 6-12 times per year to the homes of all children ages 0-5 in the school district by trained school district employees following the curriculum of one of the nationally recognized home visit programs and for full day pre-kindergarten for 3 and 4 year old children.

* Encourage your union and/or your school district leadership to gradually move teacher salary schedules toward smaller yearly increments that are evenly spaced in dollars (not percentages) for all steps so that teachers start their careers at higher salaries and see smaller salary increases each year and add career ladder pay options for teachers that start the newest teachers at lower pay with reduced responsibilities as tutors for struggling students or teaching lessons under the supervision of an experienced teacher and allow for extra pay for teachers who assume leadership roles, work extra hours with students, develop curriculum used by a grade level or department or who work extra hours training or being trained with their peers.

+ In high-cost strong public union states, encourage your union to communicate directly with the press and the public regarding ongoing public union negotiations to the maximum extent possible under existing law by writing detailed press releases and meeting separately with reporters regarding negotiations and proposed contracts.

+ In the local school district budget building process advocate with your superintendent and your school board members to re-allocate funding to the extent possible from positions and expenses that have not improved student achievement (salaries and benefits for learning disabled teachers and remedial teachers, expensive employee health insurance plans, extra legal fees for unnecessarily protracted negotiations, etc.) to expenses that research says will improve student achievement: one on one tutoring outside the regular school day for students who are struggling academically, pre-school for 3- and 4-year-old children and home visits by trained school district employees for children from birth to age 5.

Why We Failed: 40 Years of Education Reform

Lonnie Palmer spent 40-plus years as an educator that included teaching science and math (physics, AP Physics, chemistry, earth science, algebra, geometry, trigonometry and pre-calculus) and serving an assistant principal, principal, assistant superintendent and, finally superintendent of urban, suburban and rural schools in New York State. He also worked as a school turnaround specialist in North Carolina and New York State.

http://www.lonniepalmer.com
@lonniepalmer4

The solutions-based book "Why We Failed: 40 Years of Education Reform" was published by Guaranteed Press. Visit us at http://www.guaranteedpress.net Follow us @guaranteedpress on Twitter and Guaranteed Press on Facebook.

i   Snyder, T.D., and Dillow, S.A. (2012). *Digest of Education Statistics 2011* (NCES 2012-001). *National Center for Education Statistics*, Institute of Education Sciences, U.S. Department of Education. Washington, DC., https://nces.ed.gov/programs/digest/d15/tables/dt15_236.65.asp

ii   Drew Desilver, "U.S. students improving – slowly – in math and science, but still lagging internationally," Pew Research Center, Fact Tank, February 2, 2015, http://www.pewresearch.org/fact-tank/2015/02/02/u-s-students-improving-slowly-in-math-and-science-but-still-lagging-internationally/

iii   Tom Loveless, "2013 Brown Center Report on American Education: How Well Are American Students Learning?," Brookings, March 18, 2013, http://www.brookings.edu/research/reports/2013/03/18-brown-center-report-loveless

iv   Robert C. Bobb, "Standardized tests can help combat inequity," *The Washington Post*, August 28, 2015, https://www.washingtonpost.com/opinions/standardized-tests-can-help-combat-inequity/2015/08/28/0e91e7be-46aa-11e5-8e7d-9c033e6745d8_story.html

v   Harold O. Levy, "The dumbing-down of state testing," *The Washington Post*, October 2, 2015, https://www.washingtonpost.com/opinions/the-standardized-testing-shell-game/2015/10/02/1f16c6f8-690b-11e5-9223-70cb36460919_story.html?postshare=771444001226743

vi   Jessica Bakeman, "State announces high teacher scores, hopes union fears are calmed," *Politico*, October 22, 2013. http://www.capitalnewyork.com/article/politics/2013/10/8534883/state-announces-high-teacher-scores-hopes-union-fears-are-calmed

vii   Kate Taylor, "Cuomo Fights Rating System in Which Few Teachers Are Bad," *The New York Times*, March 22, 2015. http://www.nytimes.com/2015/03/23/nyregion/cuomo-fights-rating-system-in-which-few-teachers-are-bad.html

viii   Motoko Rich, "States Given a Reprieve on Ratings of Teachers," *The New York Times*, August 21, 2014, http://www.nytimes.com/2014/08/22/education/education-secretary-allows-reprieve-on-test-based-teacher-ratings.html?emc=edit_tnt_20140821&nlid=47562199&tntemail0=y

ix   Kate Taylor, "Cuomo, in Shift, Is Said to Back Reducing Test Scores' Role in Teacher Reviews," *The New York Times*, November 25, 2015. http://www.nytimes.com/2015/11/26/nyregion/cuomo-in-shift-is-said-to-back-reducing-test-scores-role-in-teacher-reviews.html

x   Patrick Welsh, "Four decades of failed school reform," *The Washington Post*, September 27, 2013, https://www.washingtonpost.com/opinions/four-decades-of-failed-school-reform/2013/09/27/dc9f2f34-2561-11e3-b75d-5b7f66349852_story.html

xi   Jon Campbell, "Common Core: How much shorter will NY's tests get?," *Poughkeepsie Journal*, February 1, 2016, http://www.poughkeepsiejournal.com/story/news/local/new-york/2016/02/01/common-core-how-much-shorter-nys-tests-get/79645086/

xii   Geoff Decker, "New York ditches controversial test-maker Pearson," *Chalkbeat*, July 9, 2015, http://www.chalkbeat.org/posts/ny/2015/07/09/new-york-ditches-controversial-test-maker-pearson/#.Vxfjy0fIa70

xiii   Alan Singer, "Pearson Education Can Run, But It Cannot Hide," *Huffington Post*, December 15, 2014, http://www.huffingtonpost.com/alan-singer/pearson-education-can-run_b_6327566.html

xiv   Sharon Lurye, "Concerns rising over Pearson, the company behind PARCC and other tests," *Philly Voice*, March 17, 2015. http://www. phillyvoice.com/concerns-rising-over-pearson/

xv   Hiten Samtani, "More Parents Are Saying No to Pearson's Field Tests," *Schoolbook WNYC*, May 23, 2012. http://www.wnyc.org/ story/303153-more-parents-are-saying-no-to-pearsons-field-tests/

xvi   Javier C. Hernandez and Robert Gebloff, "Test Scores Sink as New York Adopts Tougher Benchmarks," *The New York Times*, August 7, 2013. http://www.nytimes.com/2013/08/08/nyregion/under-new-standards-students-see-sharp-decline-in-test-scores.html

xvii   Valerie Strauss, "How come officials could predict new test score results?," *The Washington Post*, August 12, 2013. https:// www.washingtonpost.com/news/answer-sheet/wp/2013/08/12/ how-come-officials-could-predict-results-on-new-test-scores/

xviii   Valerie Strauss, "Why a kindergarten teacher is running for Congress," *The Washington Post*, September 20, 2014, https://www. washingtonpost.com/news/answer-sheet/wp/2014/09/20/why-a-kindergarten-teacher-is-running-for-congress/

xix   Benedict Carey, "Studying for the Test by Taking It," *The New York Times*, November 22, 2014, http://www.nytimes.com/2014/ 11/23/sunday-review/studying-for-the-test-by-taking-it.html? smid=nytcore-iphone-share&smprod=nytcore-iphone

xx   Editorial Board, "D.C. and Maryland test results look bad, but they show the rigor of new standards," *The Washington Post*, October 30, 2015, https:// www.washingtonpost.com/opinions/dc-and-maryland-test-results-look-bad-but-they-show-the-rigor-of-new-standards/2015/10/30/

a894b9e8-7e79-11e5-beba-927fd8634498_story.html?postshare=
9701446324341060

xxi   T. Rees Shapiro, "Common Core educational standards are losing support nationwide, poll shows," *The Washington Post*, August 20, 2014,
https://www.washingtonpost.com/local/education/common-core-
educational-standards-are-losing-support-nationwide-poll-shows/
2014/08/19/67b1f20c-27cb-11e4-8593-da634b334390_story.html

xxii   Valerie Strauss, "Five myths about the Common Core," *The
Washington Post*, December 13, 2013, https://www.washingtonpost.
com/opinions/five-myths-about-the-common-core/2013/12/13/
da05f832-5c40-11e3-be07-006c776266ed_story.html

xxiii   Robert Petrelli, "The RNC on the CCSSI, OMG!," *Thomas B. Fordham
Institute*, April 17, 2013, https://edexcellence.net/commentary/educa-
tion-gadfly-daily/flypaper/2013/the-rnc-on-the-ccssi-omg.html

xxiv   Kyle Schwartz, "A struggle worth having for students," *The Washington
Post*, March 24, 2015, https://www.washingtonpost.com/opinions/a-
struggle-worth-having-for-students/2015/03/24/544cb41e-cf4f-
11e4-8a46-b1dc9be5a8ff_story.html

xxv   Kevin Huffman, "We don't test students as much as people think we do.
And the stakes aren't really that high.," *The Washington Post,* October
30, 2015, https://www.washingtonpost.com/opinions/we-dont-test-
students-as-much-as-people-think-we-do-and-the-stakes-arent-really-
that-high/2015/10/30/3d66de1c-7e79-11e5-beba-927fd8634498_
story.html?postshare=3671446775439749

xxvi   Valerie Strauss, "Kindergarten show canceled so kids can keep studying to become 'college and career ready.' Really.," *The Washington Post*,
April 26, 2014, https://www.washingtonpost.com/news/answer-sheet/

wp/2014/04/26/kindergarten-show-canceled-so-kids-can-keep-work-ing-to-become-college-and-career-ready-really/

xxvii   Eric A. Hanushek, Paul E. Petersen and Ludger Woessmann, "U.S. Students from Educated Families Lag in International Tests," *EducationNext*, Fall 2014, http://educationnext.org/us-students-educated-families-lag-international-tests/

xxviii   Gregory Korte, "The Every Student Succeeds Act vs. No Child Left Behind: What's changed?," *USA Today*, December 11, 2015. http://www.usatoday.com/story/news/politics/2015/12/10/every-student-succeeds-act-vs-no-child-left-behind-whats-changed/77088780/

xxix   Alia Wong, "When Parents Are the Ones Getting Schooled by the Common Core," *The Atlantic*, August 5, 2015. http://www.theatlantic.com/education/archive/2015/08/common-core-schools-parents/400559/

xxx   James Marshall Crotty, "If Massachusetts Were A Country, Its Students Would Rank 9th In The World," *Forbes/Education*, September 29, 2014. http://www.forbes.com/sites/jamesmarshallcrotty/2014/09/29/if-massachusetts-were-a-country

xxxi   Valerie Strauss, "The scary way Common Core test 'cut scores' are selected," *The Washington Post*, April 29, 2014. https://www.washingtonpost.com/news/answer-sheet/wp/2014/04/29/the-scary-way-common-core-test-cut-scores-are-selected/

xxxii   Fareed Zakaria, "Fareed Zakaria: America's educational failings," *The Washington Post*, May 1. 2014, https://www.washingtonpost.com/opinions/fareed-zakaria-americas-educational-failings/2014/05/01/b61eaa22-d15c-11e3-9e25-188ebe1fa93b_story.html?wpisrc=emailtoafriend

xxxiii   Diane Ravitch, "The Common Core Costs Billions and Hurts Students," *The New York Times,* July 23, 2016, http://www.nytimes.com/2016/07/24/opinion/sunday/the-common-core-costs-billions-and-hurts-students.html?emc=eta1

xxxiv   Robert A. Williams, "School Superintendent Selection-NOT most Qualified Protests Planned, *Citizens for Good Government,* May 17, 2016, http://citizensforgoodgovernment.org/online/2014/05/26/school-superintendent-selection-not-most-qualified-protests-planned/ Note: Google search of "school superintendents good old boys" resulted in 752,000 entries.

xxxv   Colin L. Powell, Alma J. Powell and Laysha Ward, "At-risk students need more help from us, not Washington," *TheWashington Post,* August 29, 2014, https://www.washingtonpost.com/opinions/at-risk-students-need-more-help-from-us-not-washington/2014/08/29/130186aa-2e2e-11e4-9b98-848790384093_story.html

xxxvi   National Center for Education Statistics, "Status Dropout rates," *National Center for Educational Statistics,* May 2016, http://nces.ed.gov/programs/coe/indicator_coj.asp

xxxvii   Barbara O'Brien, "Hamburg School Board member faces misconduct charges," *The Buffalo News,* April 28, 2014, http://www.buffalonews.com/city-region/hamburg/hamburg-school-board-member-faces-misconduct-charges-20140428

xxxviii   Michal Rosenberger, "Team Leadership: School Boards at Work," *Technomic Publishing Company,* 1997, ISBN 978-1-56676-5268, p. 76 https://books.google.com/books?id=fnibdp2PVwcC&pg=PA76&lpg=PA76&dq=school+board+member+select+weak+superintendent&source=bl&ots=O2frJ6F7GX&sig=e4h7TciOpXb

hIVyEcjGCx_CNFrQ&hl=en&sa=X&ved=0ahUKEwjqqJi-
peHMAhUIcz4KHaiPDcIQ6AEIITAC#v=onepage&q=school%20
board%20member%20select%20weak%20superintendent&f=false

xxxix   Drew Desilver, "U.S. voter turnout trails most developed countries,"
         Pew Research Center, Fact Tank, May 6, 2015, http://www.pewre-
         search.org/fact-tank/2015/05/06/u-s-voter-turnout-trails-most-devel-
         oped-countries/

xl   Sandra Tan, "Despite high stakes, voter turnout is low for Buffalo
         School Board races," *The Buffalo News,* May 3, 2016, http://www.
         buffalonews.com/city-region/buffalo-public-schools/despite-high-
         stakes-voter-turnout-is-low-for-buffalo-school-board-races-20160503

xli   Jack Cullen and Thomas Geyer, "Low turnout follows Scott County
         school board election trend," *Quad City Times,* September 9, 2015,
         http://qctimes.com/news/local/government-and-politics/elections/
         low-turnout-follows-scott-county-school-board-election-trend/arti-
         cle_cead6a09-bcb8-55ab-99e7-598794f36bc7.html

xlii   Laura McMullen, "Report: School Boards Play Important Role,
         Face Challenges," *US News and World Report,* May 16, 2012, http://
         www.usnews.com/education/blogs/high-school-notes/2012/05/16/
         report-school-boards-play-important-role-face-challenges

xliii   Donna Lowry, "All but one in Atlanta cheating scandal to serve
         time," *USA Today,* April 14, 2015, http://www.usatoday.com/story/
         news/nation/2015/04/14/atlanta-educators-sentenced/25759985/

xliv   John Hildebrand, "NYS takeover of Roosevelt schools failed, some
         say," *Newsday,* June 29, 2013 http://www.newsday.com/long-island/
         nassau/nys-takeover-of-roosevelt-schools-failed-some-say-1.5595650

xlv   Lindsey Layton, "GOP-led states increasingly taking control from local school boards," *The Washington Post*, February 1, 2016, https://www.washingtonpost.com/local/education/gop-led-states-increasingly-taking-control-from-local-school-boards/2016/02/01/c01a8e4e-bad3-11e5-b682-4bb4dd403c7d_story.html?postshare=5811454381903583&tid=ss_mail

xlvi   Katherine B. Stevens, "Tenured Teacher Dismissal in New York: Education Law § 3020-a "Disciplinary procedures and penalties"," *American Enterprise Institute*, October 2014. http://www.aei.org/wp-content/uploads/2014/10/STEVENS_Teacher-Dismissal_Report_DRAFT.pdf

xlvii   New York State School Boards, "NYSSBA ISSUE BRIEF 3020-a Teacher Discipline Reform," *New York State School Boards Association*, 2016, http://www.nyssba.org/index.php?src=gendocs&ref=3020-a%20Teacher%20Discipline%20Reform

xlviii   Frank Eltman, "Firing tenured teachers isn't just difficult, it costs you," *USA Today*, June 30, 2008. http://usatoday30.usatoday.com/news/education/2008-06-30-teacher-tenure-costs_N.htm

xlix   Katherine B. Stevens, "Tenured Teacher Dismissal in New York: Education Law § 3020-a "Disciplinary procedures and penalties"," *American Enterprise Institute*, October 2014. http://www.aei.org/wp-content/uploads/2014/10/STEVENS_Teacher-Dismissal_Report_DRAFT.pdf

l   Susan Edelman, "City pays exiled teachers to snooze as 'rubber rooms' return," *The New York Post*, January 17, 2016. http://nypost.com/2016/01/17/city-pays-exiled-teachers-to-snooze-as-rubber-rooms-return/

li   Frank Bruni, "Toward Better Teachers," *The New York Times*, October 28, 2014, http://www.nytimes.com/2014/10/29/opinion/frank-bruni-toward-better-teachers.html?smid=nytcore-ipad-share&smprod=nytcore-ipad

lii   Valerie Strauss, "A Time magazine cover enrages teachers — again," *The Washington Post*, October 25, 2014, https://www.washingtonpost.com/news/answer-sheet/wp/2014/10/25/a-time-magazine-cover-enrages-teachers-again/

liii   Beth Hawkins, "What to do with an ineffective teacher? St. Paul starts with support, and moves to accountability," *MinnPost*, March 28, 2011. https://www.minnpost.com/learning-curve/2011/03/what-do-ineffective-teacher-st-paul-starts-support-and-moves-accountability

liv   "Teachers Matter: Understanding Teachers' Impact on Student Achievement. Santa Monica, CA: RAND Corporation, 2012. http://www.rand.org/pubs/corporate_pubs/CP693z1-2012-09.html

lv   Natalie Wexler, "Which schools spend the most on poor kids?," *The Washington Post*, October 20, 2014, https://www.washingtonpost.com/blogs/all-opinions-are-local/wp/2014/10/20/which-schools-spend-the-most-on-poor-kids/

lvi   Meridith Broussard, "Why Poor Schools Can't Win at Standardized Testing," *The Atlantic*, July 15, 2014, http://www.theatlantic.com/education/archive/2014/07/why-poor-schools-cant-win-at-standardized-testing/374287/

lvii   Robert David Sullivan, "Two and a half decades of Prop. 2 ½," *CommonwealthMagazine*, January 1, 2005. http://commonwealthmagazine.org/economy/the-geography-of-proposition-2frac12-overrides/

lviii   Alan Singer, "Who Is Charlotte Danielson and Why Does She Decide How Teachers Are Evaluated?," *Huffington Post*, August 10, 2013. http://www.huffingtonpost.com/alan-singer/who-is-charlotte-danielso_b_3415034.html

lix   ROCHESTER CITY SCHOOL DISTRICT, "Teacher Evaluation Guide 2012-13," *Rochester City School District*, 2012, http://www.nctq.org/docs/Rochester_Teacher_Evaluation_Guide_AUGUST_2012.pdf

lx   Michael Cubbin, "TEACHER OBSERVATIONS DON'T WORK... BUT WHY?," *The Business of School Blog*, July 9, 2015. http://thebusinessofschoolblog.com/?p=671

lxi   Valerie Strauss, "Reasonable doubt on teacher evaluation," *The Washington Post*, February 8, 2012. https://www.washingtonpost.com/blogs/answer-sheet/post/reasonable-doubt-on-teacher-evaluation/2012/02/07/gIQACKuzxQ_blog.html

lxii   Valerie Strauss, "Teacher spends two days as a student and is shocked at what she learns," *The Washington Post*, October 24, 2014, https://www.washingtonpost.com/news/answer-sheet/wp/2014/10/24/teacher-spends-two-days-as-a-student-and-is-shocked-at-what-she-learned/

lxiii   Joy Resmovits, "Starting Teacher SAT Scores Rise As Educators Face Tougher Evaluations," *Huffington Post/HUFFPOST POLITICS*, October 30, 2013. http://www.huffingtonpost.com/2013/10/30/teacher-sat-scores_n_4175593.html

lxiv   Dan Goldhaber and Joe Walch, "Gains in Teacher Quality," *EducationNext*, Winter 2014. http://educationnext.org/gains-in-teacher-quality/

lxv Emily Deruy, "Why the Country's Lack of Teacher Diversity Is a Problem," *The Atlantic*, May 14, 2014, http://www.theatlantic. com/politics/archive/2014/05/why-the-countrys-lack-of-teacher-diversity-is-a-problem/430929/

lxvi Lauren Rivera, "Hirable Like Me," *Kellogg Insight, Kellogg School of Management, Northwestern University*, April 3, 2013. http://insight. kellogg.northwestern.edu/article/hirable_like_me

lxvii Steven Sawchuck, "States Slow To Shut Down Weak Teacher Education Programs," *Huffington Post/HUFFPOST POLITICS*, January 2, 2015. http://www.huffingtonpost.com/2014/12/31/teacher-education-school-closures_n_6401316.html

lxviii Sara Mead, "Be Prepared America's approach to teacher prep is broken.," *US News and World Report*, August 6 2015. http://www. usnews.com/opinion/knowledge-bank/2015/08/06/americas-approach-to-teacher-prep-is-broken

lxix U.S. Education Department, "HISTORY Twenty-Five Years of Progress in Educating Children with Disabilities Through IDEA," *U. S. Education Department*, 1990, http://www2.ed.gov/policy/speced/ leg/idea/history.html

lxx Robert L. Osgood, "The History of Inclusion in the United States," *GU Press*, 2005, Chapter 3, ISBN 978-1-56368-318-3, http://gupress. gallaudet.edu/excerpts/HIUS.html

lxxi Tracy Thompson, "The Special-Education Charade," *The Atlantic*, January 3, 2016, http://www.theatlantic.com/education/ archive/2016/01/the-charade-of-special-education-programs/ 421578/

lxxii   Atlas, "Individuals With Disabilities Education Act Cost Impact on Local School Districts," *Atlas*, June 3, 2015, http://atlas.newamerica. org/individuals-disabilities-education-act-cost-impact-local-school-districts

lxxiii   Robert Worth, "The Scandal of Special-Ed," *The Washington Monthly*, June 1999, http://www.washingtonmonthly.com/features/1999/9906. worth.scandal.html

lxxiv   Steve Billmyer, "New York state schools ranked by spending per pupil: Look up, compare any district," *syracuse.com*, May 19, 2014, http://www.syracuse.com/news/index.ssf/2014/05/new_york_state_schools_ranked_by_spending_per_pupil_look_up_compare_any_district.html

lxxv   Ashly McGlone, "Special ed case costs approach $1M," *San Diego Union-Tribune*, August 12, 2014, http://www.sandiegouniontribune. com/news/2014/aug/12/solana-beach-special-ed-case-legal-fees/

lxxvi   Michelle Snell, "Special Education Quality Assurance Special Education Programs & Services Review of the Lake Placid CSD," *The State Education Department/University of the State of New York*, July 30, 2015, http://www.lpcsd.org/site/depts/SPED/2015SPED focusedreview.pdf

lxxvii   Great Schools Staff, "IDEA 2004 Close Up: Disciplining Students With Disabilities," *Great Kids!*, May 20, 2015, http://www. greatschools.org/gk/articles/idea-2004-close-up-disciplining-students-with-disabilities/

lxxviii Allan G. Osborne Jr., Ed. D., Charles J. Russo, J.D., Ed. D., "Attorney Fees, School Boards, and Special Education," *School Business Affairs*, June 2010, http://files.eric.ed.gov/fulltext/EJ904679.pdf

lxxix Gordon Donaldson, "Maine Schools in Focus: The Big Squeeze — Paying for Special Education Services," *UMaine News*, February 18, 2016, https://umaine.edu/edhd/2016/02/18/maine-schools-in-focus-the-big-squeeze-paying-for-special-education-services/

lxxx Jose L. Martin, "Legal Implications of Response to Intervention and Special Education Identification," *RTI Action Network, 2016*, http://www.rtinetwork.org/learn/ld/legal-implications-of-response-to-intervention-and-special-education-identification

lxxxi Thomas B. Parrish, "Who's Paying the Rising Cost of Special Education?," *The Journal of Special Education, Eric,* 2001, http://eric.ed.gov/?id=EJ627943

lxxxii Terri Rothman and Mary Henderson, "Do School-Based Tutoring Programs Significantly Improve Student Performance on Standardized Tests?," Research in Middle Level Education, RMLE Online, 2011, http://files.eric.ed.gov/fulltext/EJ925246.pdf

lxxxiii Stacy M.L. Dawson, "Pull-Out or Push-in Service Delivery Model: Conducive to Students or Teachers?," *St. John Fisher College, Fisher Digital Publications*, August 2014, http://fisherpub.sjfc.edu/cgi/viewcontent.cgi?article=1297&context=education_ETD_masters

lxxxiv Ruth Curran Nield, "Falling Off Track during the Transition to High School: What We Know and What Can Be Done," *The Future of Children, Princeton-Brookings, Journal Issue: America's High Schools Volume 19 Number 1 Spring 2009,* http://futureofchildren.org/publications/journals/article/index.xml?journalid=30&articleid=38&sectionid=84

lxxxv Jim Wright, "Six Reasons Why Students Are Unmotivated (and What Teachers Can Do)," *Intervention Central, RTI Toolkit: A*

Practical Guide for Schools, March 15, 2012, http://www.fehb.org/
CSE/CCSEConference2012/wright_CCSE_Conference_Breakout_
Motiv_Students_15_Mar_2012.pdf

lxxxvi   Robin Chait and Andrea Venezia, "Improving Academic Preparation
for College What We Know and How State and Federal Policy Can
Help," *Center for American Progress*, January 2009, https://www.ameri-
canprogress.org/wp-content/uploads/issues/2009/01/pdf/academic_
prep.pdf

lxxxvii   Steven Zemelman, Harvey Daniels, and Arthur Hyde, <u>BEST
PRACTICE Today's Standards for Teaching and Learning in
America's Schools, Third Edition,</u> *HEINEMANN*, 2005, http://
www.heinemann.com/shared/onlineresources/e00744/sample.pdf

lxxxviii   Hildy Gottlieb, "Why Boards Micro-Manage and How to Get Them
to Stop," *Creating the Future, ReSolve*, 2009, http://www.help4non-
profits.com/NP_Bd_MicroManage_Art.htm

lxxxix   Schoollawesource.tasb.org, "Board Roles and Responsibilities," *TASB
eSource*, https://www.tasb.org/Services/Legal-Services/TASB-School-
Law-eSource/Governance/Board-Roles-and-Responsibilities.aspx

xc   Alexandria Neason, "Half of teachers leave the job after five years.
Here's what to do about it," *The Hechinger Report*, July 18, 2014,
http://hechingerreport.org/half-teachers-leave-job-five-years-heres/

xci   Lynette Halloway, "State Official Paves Way for 5 Charter Schools
to Open in Fall," *The New York Times*, August 6, 1999, http://www.
nytimes.com/1999/08/06/nyregion/state-official-paves-way-for-
5-charter-schools-to-open-in-fall.html

xcii   SUNY Charter School Institute, " January 2014 SUNY Request for
Proposals-Round1 "SpringCycle," *The State University of New York*, June

6, 2016, http://www.newyorkcharters.org/create/request-for-proposals/january-2014-suny-request-for-proposals-round-1

xciii   Herbert J. Wahlberg, "Market Theory of School Choice," *Education Week*, July 12, 2000, http://www.edweek.org/ew/articles/2000/07/12/42walberg.h19.html

xciv   Motoko Rich, "Oakland District at Heart of Drive to Transform Urban Schools," *The New York Times*, March 4, 2016 http://www.nytimes.com/2016/03/05/education/oakland-district-at-heart-of-drive-to-transform-urban-schools.html

xcv   Sarah Reckhow, Matt Grossmann, and Benjamin Chung Evans, "Policy Cues and Ideology in Attitudes Toward Charter Schools," *Michigan State University, College of Education, Education Policy Center,* 2016, http://education.msu.edu/epc/library/papers/AttitudesToward CharterSchools.asp

xcvi   Paul E. Peterson, "African-Americans for Charter Schools," *Wall Street Journal,* August 3, 2010, http://www.hoover.org/research/african-americans-charter-schools

xcvii   Marcus Brandon, "Rep. Brandon: African-Americans must blaze own path on school choice, ed reform," *redefined,* August 5, 2014, https://www.redefineonline.org/2014/08/rep-marcus-brandon-african-americans-must-blaze-path-ed-reform/

xcviii   Stephanie Simon, "Special Report: Class Struggle - How charter schools get students they want," *Reuters,* February 15, 2013, http://www.reuters.com/article/us-usa-charters-admissions-idUSBRE91E0HF20130215

xcix   Andrew J. Rotherham, "The Charter Moment," *U.S. News and World Report,* June 19, 2015, http://www.usnews.com/opinion/articles/2015/06/19/whats-working-and-whats-not-with-charter-schools

c   Edward Cremata, M.A., Devora Davis, Kathleen Dickey, M.S., Kristina Lawyer, M.Ed.T., Yohannes Negassi, M.A., Margaret E. Raymond, Ph.D., James L. Woodworth, Ph.D., "National Charter School Study 2013," *Stanford University, Center for Research on Education Outcomes*, 2013, http://credo.stanford.edu/documents/ NCSS%202013%20Final%20Draft.pdf

ci   Kim McGuire, "Charter schools struggling to meet academic growth," *Star Tribune*, February 17, 2015, http://www.startribune.com/ charter-schools-struggling-to-meet-academic-growth/292139891/

cii   Lynette Halloway, "State Official Paves Way for 5 Charter Schools to Open in Fall," *The New York Times*, August 6, 1999, http://www. nytimes.com/1999/08/06/nyregion/state-official-paves-way-for-5-charter-schools-to-open-in-fall.html

ciii   Clifford J. Levy, "Senate Passes Charter Plan For Schools," *The New York Times*, December 18. 1998, http://www.nytimes.com/1998/12/18/ nyregion/senate-passes-charter-plan-for-schools.html

civ   William Tuthill, "Economic incentive package lures call center to Arbor Hill," *Albany Business Review*, November 16, 1998, http:// www.bizjournals.com/albany/stories/1998/11/16/story4.html

cv   Mike Goodwin, "Disgraced Aaron Dare tells jury how he and popular cop plotted fraud," *Times Union*, March 17, 2010 http://blog. timesunion.com/crime/disgraced-aaron-dare-tells-jury-how-he-and-popular-cop-plotted-fraud/4094/

cvi   Blogspot, "Charter School Scandals," Blogspot, July 2010, http:// charterschoolscandals.blogspot.com/2010/07/new-covenant-charter-school.html

cvii   City of Albany Police Department, "North Station," *City of Albany Police Department, City of Albany, NY,* June 2016, https://city-of-albany-ny-28.hub.biz/

cviii   Robin K. Cooper, "SUNY Trustees vote to close New Covenant Charter School," *Albany Business Review,* March 23, 2010, http://www.bizjournals.com/albany/stories/2010/03/22/daily12.html

cix   Scott Waldman, "Failed school offers lesson," *Times Union,* June 20, 2010, http://www.timesunion.com/news/article/Failed-school-offers-lesson-561951.php?cmpid=email-desktop

cx   Scott Waldman, "Albany district eyes ex-charter school," *Times Union,* September 7, 2012, http://www.timesunion.com/local/article/Albany-district-eyes-ex-charter-school-3849006.php

cxi   Brittany Horn, "Brighter Choice ordered to close," *Times Union,* March 6, 2015, http://www.timesunion.com/news/article/Brighter-Choice-middle-schools-fate-to-be-6118614.php?cmpid=email-desktop

cxii   Alana Semuels, "Why Do Some Poor Kids Thrive?," *The Atlantic,* April 6, 2016, http://www.theatlantic.com/business/archive/2016/04/kids-poverty-baltimore/476808/

cxiii   Pedro A. Noguera and Antwi Akom, "The Significance of Race in the Racial Gap in Academic Achievement," *In Motion Magazine,* June 19, 2000, http://www.inmotionmagazine.com/pnaa.html

cxiv   Lynne C. Huffman, Sarah L. Mehlinger, Amy S. Kerivan, "Risk Factors for Academic and Behavioral Problems at the Beginning of School," *Stanford University, CE-Credit.com,* 2000, http://secure.ce-credit.com/articles/9580/riskfactorsacademic.pdf

cxv   Sam Wood, "Lead poisoning in Pa., N.J. may be worse than Flint," *Philly.com*, February 6, 2016, http://articles.philly.com/2016-02-06/news/70376889_1_lead-exposure-lead-problem-blood-lead-level

cxvi   Nekesa Mumbi Moody, "New York Accused of Racism on Incinerator Site : Albany: Blacks were told the plant posed no hazard. Blackened snow at governor's mansion brought action.," *The Los Angeles Times*, March 6, 1994, http://articles.latimes.com/1994-03-06/news/mn-30611_1_environmental-racism

cxvii   George Will, "The sobering evidence of social science," *The Washington Post*, July 6, 2016, https://www.washingtonpost.com/opinions/the-sobering-evidence-of-social-science/2016/07/06/4a3831f8-42dd-11e6-bc99-7d269f8719b1_story.html?tid=ss_mail

cxviii Lindsay Tepe, "The Common Core Is Driving the Changes to the SAT," *The Atlantic*, March 10, 2014, http://www.the-atlantic.com/education/archive/2014/03/the-common-core-is-driving-the-changes-to-the-sat/284320/

cxix   Robert Bifulco, Randall Reback, "Effect of New York Charter Schools on School District Finances" *The New York State Education Department*, December 31, 2011, http://cpr.maxwell.syr.edu/efap/Papers_reports/Bifulco/Report_3.pdf

cxx   Kate Taylor, "At a Success Academy Charter School, Singling Out Pupils Who Have 'Got to Go'," *The New York Times*, October 29, 2015, http://www.nytimes.com/2015/10/30/nyregion/at-a-success-academy-charter-school-singling-out-pupils-who-have-got-to-go.html

cxxi   Followthemoney.org, "NEW YORK STATE UNITED TEACHERS has given $17,374,628 to 509 different filers over 20 years.,"

Followthemoney.org, August 2016, http://www.followthemoney.org/entity-details?eid=19234

cxxii   Natalie Wexler, "High-poverty schools need better teachers, but getting them there won't be easy," *greatergreaterwashington.org*, February 20, 2015, http://greatergreaterwashington.org/post/25826/high-poverty-schools-need-better-teachers-but-getting-them-there-wont-be-easy/

cxxiii   James J. Heckman, "The American Family in Black and White: A Post-Racial Strategy for Improving Skills to Promote Equality," *Daedalus Special Issue*, February 2011, http://heckmanequation.org/content/resource/american-family-black-and-white-post-racial-strategy-improving-skills-promote-equal

cxxiv   Kimberly G. Noble, "How poverty affects children's brains," *The Washington Post*, October 2, 2015, https://www.washingtonpost.com/opinions/no-poor-child-left-behind/2015/10/02/df86c56e-4048-11e5-9561-4b3dc93e3b9a_story.html?postshare=6721444002009734

cxxv   Robert Samuelson, "Are we No. 1? It depends," *The Washington Post*, October 21, 2015, https://www.washingtonpost.com/opinions/are-we-no-1-it-depends/2015/10/21/6d7f997c-7807-11e5-b9c1-f03c48c96ac2_story.html

cxxvi   David Bornstein, "Overcoming Poverty's Damage to Learning," *The New York Times*, April 17, 2015, http://opinionator.blogs.nytimes.com/2015/04/17/overcoming-povertys-damage-to-learning/?emc=edit_tnt_20150417&nlid=47562199&tntemail0=y

cxxvii   Dian Schaffhauser, "The Problem Isn't Teacher Recruiting; It's Retention," *The Journal*, July 17, 2014, https://thejournal.com/articles/2014/07/17/the-problem-isnt-teacher-recruiting-its-retention.aspx

cxxviii   Marlene Sokol, "High-poverty schools continue to wear on teachers, surveys show," *Tampa Bay Times*, May 24,2015, http://www.tampabay.com/news/education/k12/high-poverty-schools-continue-to-wear-on-teachers-surveys-show/2230928

cxxix   Jim Tankersley, "High inequality makes poor kids drop out more," *The Washington Post*, March 10, 2016, https://www.washingtonpost.com/news/wonk/wp/2016/03/10/high-inequality-makes-poor-kids-drop-out-more/?postshare=5801457914836066&tid=ss_mail

cxxx   Motoko Rich, "Percentage of Poor Students in Public Schools Rises," *The New York Times*, January 16, 2015, http://www.nytimes.com/2015/01/17/us/school-poverty-study-southern-education-foundation.html

cxxxi   Brad Plumer, "Here's how the safety net has — and hasn't — reduced poverty in the U.S.," *The Washington Post*, December 10, 2013, https://www.washingtonpost.com/news/wonk/wp/2013/12/10/heres-how-the-safety-net-has-and-hasnt-reduced-poverty-in-the-u-s/

cxxxii   Kirsten Andersen, "The number of US children living in single-parent homes has nearly doubled in 50 years: Census data," *LifesiteNews.com*, January 4, 2013, https://www.lifesitenews.com/news/the-number-of-children-living-in-single-parent-homes-has-nearly-doubled-in

cxxxiii   Aparna Mathur, Had Fu and Peter Hansen, "The Mysterious and Alarming Rise of Single Parenthood in America," *The Atlantic*, September 3, 2013, http://www.theatlantic.com/business/archive/2013/09/the-mysterious-and-alarming-rise-of-single-parenthood-in-america/279203/

cxxxiv   Emily Badger, "The unbelievable rise of single motherhood in America over the last 50 years," *The Washington Post*, December 18,

2014, https://www.washingtonpost.com/news/wonk/wp/2014/12/18/the-unbelievable-rise-of-single-motherhood-in-america-over-the-last-50-years/

cxxxv   Dexter Mullins, "Six decades after Brown ruling, US schools still segregated," *Aljazeera America*, September 25, 2013, http://america.aljazeera.com/articles/2013/9/25/56-years-afterlittlerockusschoolssegregatedbyraceandclass.html

cxxxvi   Richard Rothstein, "Segregated Housing, Segregated Schools," *Education Week*, March 25, 2014, http://www.edweek.org/ew/articles/2014/03/26/26rothstein_ep.h33.html

cxxxvii Emma Brown, "On the anniversary of Brown v. Board, new evidence that U.S. schools are resegregating," *The Washington Post*, May 17, 2016, https://www.washingtonpost.com/news/education/wp/2016/05/17/on-the-anniversary-of-brown-v-board-new-evidence-that-u-s-schools-are-resegregating/?tid=ss_mail

cxxxviii Andrew Joseph Parr, "A Quantitative Study of the Characteristics of Transient and Non-Transient Students in Nevada Elementary Schools, *Eric*, 2010, http://eric.ed.gov/?id=ED518783

cxxxix   Edward Cremata, Devora Davis, Kathleen Dickey, Kristina Lawyer, Yohannes Negassi, Margaret E. Raymond, James L. Woodworth, "National Charter School Study 2013," *Center for Research on Education Outcomes Stanford University*, 2013, http://credo.stanford.edu/documents/NCSS%202013%20Final%20Draft.pdf

cxl   Julia Schwenkenberg, James VanderHoff, "Why Do Charter Schools Fail? - An Analysis of Charter School Survival in New Jersey," *Rutgers University*, March 2013, https://www.searchlock.com/search?q=national+failure+rate+for+charter+schools&tsrc=y

cxli Scott Waldman, "The education model that fell apart," *Politico*, April 3, 2015, http://www.politico.com/states/new-york/albany/story/2015/04/the-education-model-that-fell-apart-021065

cxlii NY Times Editorial, "More Lessons About Charter Schools," *The New York Times*, February 1, 2013, http://www.nytimes.com/2013/02/02/opinion/more-lessons-about-charter-schools.html

cxliii Debra Bruno, "D.C.'s Education in School Reform," *Politico*, July 16, 2015, http://www.politico.com/magazine/story/2015/07/charter-schools-dc-what-works-120222

cxliv Erica Frankenburg, Genevieve Siegel-Hawley, Jia Wang, "Choice without Equity: Charter School Segregation and the need for Civil Rights Standards," The *Civil Rights Project/Proyecto Derechos Civiles, UCLA Graduate School of Education & Information Studies, January 2010*, https://civilrightsproject.ucla.edu/research/k-12-education/integration-and-diversity/choice-without-equity-2009-report/frankenberg-choices-without-equity-2010.pdf

cxlv Emily Badger, "The one thing rich parents do for their kids that makes all the difference," *The Washington Post*, May 10, 2016, https://www.washingtonpost.com/news/wonk/wp/2016/05/10/the-incredible-impact-of-rich-parents-fighting-to-live-by-the-very-best-schools/

cxlvi Ben DuBose, "Urban vs. suburban: the high school graduation gap," *The Los Angeles Times*, April 2, 2008, http://articles.latimes.com/2008/apr/02/nation/na-schools2

cxlvii- Gregorio Caetano and Vikram Maheshri, "School Segregation and the Identification of Tipping Behavior," *University of Rochester and University of Houston,* December 30. 2015, www.gregoriocaetano.net/resources/Research/caetano_maheshri_tipping.pdf

cxlviii   Justin Wolfers, "Why the New Research on Mobility Matters: An Economist's View," *The New York Times, The Upshot*, May 4, 2015,http://www.nytimes.com/2015/05/05/upshot/why-the-new-research-on-mobility-matters-an-economists-view.html?action=click&contentCollection=U.S.&module=RelatedCoverage&region=EndOfArticle&pgtype=article

cxlix   Motoko Rich, "Percentage of Poor Students in Public Schools Rises," *The New York Times*, January 16, 2015, http://www.nytimes.com/2015/01/17/us/school-poverty-study-southern-education-foundation.html

cl   Maya Brennan, "The Impacts of Affordable Housing on Education: A Research Summary," *Center for Housing Policy, May 2011*, http://www.nchh.org/Portals/0/HHFF_Impacts_of_Affordable_Housing.pdf

cli   Najya Hannah-Jones, "Choosing a School for My Daughter in a Segregated City," *The New York Times Magazine*, June 9, 2016, http://www.nytimes.com/2016/06/12/magazine/choosing-a-school-for-my-daughter-in-a-segregated-city.html?_r=0

clii   Eric Chyn, "Moved to Opportunity: The Long-Run Effect of Public Housing Demolition on Labor Market Outcomes of Children," *Department of Economics, University of Michigan*, July 1, 2016, www.hha.dk/nat/larss/CAFE2015/EChyn.pdf

cliii   George Theoharis, "Racial achievement gaps were narrowest at the height of school integration.," *The Washington Post*, October 23, 2015, https://www.washingtonpost.com/posteverything/wp/2015/10/23/forced-busing-didnt-fail-desegregation-is-the-best-way-to-improve-our-schools/?postshare=7061445656067189

cliv   Eliza Shapiro, "Upper West Side becomes latest school integration battleground," *Politico*, June 29, 2016, http://www.politico.com/

states/new-york/city-hall/story/2016/06/upper-west-side-becomes-latest-school-integration-battleground-103345

clv   Richard V. Reeves and Edward Rodrigue, "Five Bleak Facts on Black Opportunity," *Brookings*, January 15, 2015, http://www.brookings.edu/blogs/social-mobility-memos/posts/2015/01/15-mlk-black-opportunity-reeves

clvi   Nick Anderson, "SAT scores at lowest level in 10 years, fueling worries about high schools," *The Washington Post*, September 3, 2015, https://www.washingtonpost.com/local/education/sat-scores-at-lowest-level-in-10-years-fueling-worries-about-high-schools/2015/09/02/6b73ec66-5190-11e5-9812-92d5948a40f8_story.html

clvii   Lindsay Layton, "U.S. students lag around average on international science, math and reading test," *The Washington Post*, December 3 2013, https://www.washingtonpost.com/local/education/us-students-lag-around-average-on-international-science-math-and-reading-test/2013/12/02/2e510f26-5b92-11e3-a49b-90a0e156254b_story.html?tid=a_inl

clviii   Catherine Rampell, "Americans hate all public schools, except the ones their own kids attend," *The Washington Post*, September 22, 2014, https://www.washingtonpost.com/news/rampage/wp/2014/09/22/americans-hate-all-public-schools-except-the-ones-their-own-kids-attend/

clix   Snyder, T.D., and Dillow, S.A. (2012). *Digest of Education Statistics 2011* (NCES 2012-001). *National Center for Education Statistics, Institute of Education Sciences, U.S. Department of Education. Washington, DC.*, https://nces.ed.gov/programs/digest/d15/tables/dt15_236.65.asp

clx   Snyder, T.D., and Dillow, S.A. (2012). *Digest of Education Statistics 2011* (NCES 2012-001). *National Center for Education Statistics, Institute of*

Education Sciences, U.S. Department of Education. Washington, DC., https://nces.ed.gov/programs/digest/d15/tables/dt15_236.65.asp

clxi   Snyder, T.D., and Dillow, S.A. (2012). *Digest of Education Statistics 2011* (NCES 2012-001). *National Center for Education Statistics, Institute of Education Sciences, U.S. Department of Education. Washington, DC.,* https://nces.ed.gov/programs/digest/d15/tables/dt15_236.65.asp

clxii   Snyder, T.D., and Dillow, S.A. (2012). *Digest of Education Statistics 2011* (NCES 2012-001). *National Center for Education Statistics, Institute of Education Sciences, U.S. Department of Education. Washington, DC.,* https://nces.ed.gov/programs/digest/d15/tables/dt15_236.65.asp

clxiii Richard Rothstein and Karen Hawley Miles, "Where's the Money Gone? Changes in the Level and Composition of Education Spending," *Economic Policy Institute,* 1995, http://www.epi.org/publication/books_wheremoneygone/

clxiv   James W. Guthrie, "School Finance: Fifty Years of Expansion," *School Finance,* Winter 1997, http://www.ncbi.nlm.nih.gov/pubmed/10892463

clxv   David Umhoefer, "Did FDR oppose collective bargaining for government workers?," *Politifact,* August 13, 2013, http://www.politifact.com/wisconsin/statements/2013/aug/13/scott-walker/Did-FDR-oppose-collective-bargaining-for-governmen/

clxvi   Daniel Desalvo, "The Trouble with Public Sector Unions," *National Affairs,* Fall 2010, http://www.nationalaffairs.com/publications/detail/the-trouble-with-public-sector-unions

clxvii   Thomas B. Edsall, "Republicans Sure Love to Hate Unions," *The New York Times*, November 18, 2014, http://www.nytimes.com/2014/11/19/opinion/republicans-sure-love-to-hate-unions.html

clxviii   Thomas McGinty and Brody Mullins, "Political Spending by Unions Far Exceeds Direct Donations," *Wall Street Journal*, July 10, 2012, http://www.wsj.com/articles/SB1000142405270230478240457748858 84031850026

clxix   Chris Bragg, "The Labor Loophole," *Albany Times-Union*, June 13, 2015, http://www.timesunion.com/tuplus-local/article/The-labor-loophole-6325922.php

clxx   E. J. McMahon, "Taylor Made: The Cost and Consequences of New York's Public-Sector Labor Laws," *Empire Center*, NY Torch Blog, October 17, 2014, http://www.empirecenter.org/publications/taylor-made-the-cost-and-consequences-of-new-yorks-public-sector-labor-laws/

clxxi   Associated Press, "As organized labor shrinks, unions representing government workers grow," *MPR News*, July 5, 2014, http://www.mprnews.org/story/2014/07/05/union-members-have-ties-to-government

clxxii   Neil King Jr., Thomas M. Burton and Kris Maher, "Political Fight Over Unions Escalates," *Wall Street Journal*, February 22, 2011, http://www.wsj.com/articles/SB1000142405274870380020457615888 51079665840

clxxiii   Steven Greenhouse, "The Friedrichs case: A time bomb for unions," *The Washington Post*, January 15, 2015, https://www.washingtonpost.com/opinions/the-friedrichs-case-a-time-bomb-for-unions/2016/01/15/

f4ff39da-bac3-11e5-829c-26ffb874a18d_story.html?postshare=12614
52913720370&tid=ss_mail

clxxiv   Karlee S. Bolanos, "Understanding Triborough: It's Not Just a Complex of Bridges in the City," *NYMuniBlog*, June 28, 2012, http://www.nymuniblog.com/understanding-triborough-it-is-not-just-a-complex-of-bridges-in-the-city/

clxxv   Hunter Schwarz, "5 maps that show the best states for teachers," *The Washington Post*, September 3 2014, https://www.washingtonpost.com/blogs/govbeat/wp/2014/09/03/5-maps-that-show-the-best-states-for-teachers/

clxxvi   Albany City School District, "Teacher Contract 2007-2011," *PERB*, 2011, www.google.com/webhp?sourceid=chrome-instant&ion=1&espv=2&ie=UTF-8#q=Albany+NY+City+School+District+teacher+salary+schedule

clxxvii   Ramin P. Jalishgari, "3 Law Firms Dominate Contracts for Teachers," *The New York Times*, February 16, 1997, http://www.nytimes.com/1997/02/16/nyregion/3-law-firms-dominate-contracts-for-teachers.html?pagewanted=all

clxxviii   Warren Fiske, "Brat: U.S. school spending up 375 percent over 30 years but test score remain flat," *Politifact*, March 2, 2015, http://www.politifact.com/virginia/statements/2015/mar/02/dave-brat/brat-us-school-spending-375--over-30-years-/

clxxix   James Marshall Crotty, "7 Signs That U.S. Education Decline Is Jeopardizing Its National Security," *Forbes*, March 26, 2012, http://www.forbes.com/sites/jamesmarshallcrotty/2012/03/26/7-signs-that-americas-educational-decline-is-jeopardizing-its-national-security/#7112b1659993

clxxx   Reid Wilson, "Best State in America: Connecticut, for its teachers," *The Washington Post,* September 5, 2014, https://www.washington-post.com/opinions/best-state-in-america-connecticut-for-its-teachers/2014/09/05/8e11ac88-3457-11e4-8f02-03c644b2d7d0_story.html

clxxxi   Snyder, T.D., and Dillow, S.A. (2012). *Digest of Education Statistics 2011 (NCES 2012-001). National Center for Education Statistics, Institute of Education Sciences, U.S. Department of Education. Washington, DC.,* https://nces.ed.gov/programs/digest/d15/tables/dt15_236.65.asp

clxxxii   Snyder, T.D., and Dillow, S.A. (2012). *Digest of Education Statistics 2011 (NCES 2012-001). National Center for Education Statistics, Institute of Education Sciences, U.S. Department of Education. Washington, DC.,* https://nces.ed.gov/programs/digest/d15/tables/dt15_236.65.asp

clxxxiii   Snyder, T.D., and Dillow, S.A. (2012). *Digest of Education Statistics 2011 (NCES 2012-001). National Center for Education Statistics, Institute of Education Sciences, U.S. Department of Education. Washington, DC.,* https://nces.ed.gov/programs/digest/d15/tables/dt15_236.65.asp

clxxxiv   Snyder, T.D., and Dillow, S.A. (2012). *Digest of Education Statistics 2011 (NCES 2012-001). National Center for Education Statistics, Institute of Education Sciences, U.S. Department of Education. Washington, DC.,* https://nces.ed.gov/programs/digest/d15/tables/dt15_236.65.asp

clxxxv   Richard Rothstein, "Where's the Money Gone? Changes in the Level and Composition of Education Spending," *Economic Policy Institute,* http://www.epi.org/publication/books_wheremoneygone/

clxxxvi   Richard Rothstein, "Where's the Money Gone? Changes in the Level and Composition of Education Spending," *Economic Policy Institute,* http://www.epi.org/publication/books_wheremoneygone/

clxxxvii Ann M.Hocutt, "Effectiveness of Special Education: Is Placement the Critical Factor?, *Future Child*, 1996 Spring, http://www.ncbi.nlm.nih.gov/pubmed/8689263

clxxxviii DanLips,ShaneaWatkins,Ph.D.andJohnFleming,"DoesSpendingMore onEducationImproveAcademicAchievement?," *TheHeritageFoundation*, September 8, 2008, http://www.heritage.org/research/reports/2008/09/ does-spending-more-on-education-improve-academic-achievement

clxxxix Snyder, T.D., and Dillow, S.A. (2012). *Digest of Education Statistics 2011 (NCES 2012-001). National Center for Education Statistics, Institute of Education Sciences, U.S. Department of Education. Washington, DC.*, https://nces.ed.gov/programs/digest/d15/tables/dt15_236.65.asp

cxc Snyder, T.D., and Dillow, S.A. (2012). *Digest of Education Statistics 2011 (NCES 2012-001). National Center for Education Statistics, Institute of Education Sciences, U.S. Department of Education. Washington, DC.*, https://nces.ed.gov/programs/digest/d15/tables/dt15_236.65.asp

cxci Jeanne Batalova and Margie McHugh, "Number and Growth of Students in U.S. Schools in Need of English Instruction, 2009," *Migration Policy Institute*, August 2010, http://www.migrationpolicy. org/research/number-and-growth-students-us-schools-need-english-instruction-2009

cxcii Dan Goldhaber, "Research vs. Conventional Wisdom II: Teacher Jobs Lost During the Great Recession," *Education Week*, August 12, 2015, http://blogs.edweek.org/edweek/rick_hess_straight_ up/2015/08/research_vs_conventional_wisdom_teacher_jobs_lost_ great_recession.html

cxciii Citizens' Budget Commission, "Pass Governor's Proposal to Reform State Retiree Health Insurance Benefits," *Citizens Budget Commission*,

March 14, 2016, http://www.cbcny.org/cbc-blogs/blogs/pass-governorpercentE2percent80percent99s-proposal-reform-state-retiree-health-insurance-benefits

cxciv Robert Costrell and Jeffery Dean, "The Rising Cost of Teachers' Health Care," *Education Next*, Spring 2013, http://education-next.org/the-rising-cost-of-teacherspercentE2percent80percent99-health-care/

cxcv E. J.McMahon, "Defusing New York's Pension Bomb," *Empire Center, NY Torch Blog*, June 7, 2006, http://www.empirecenter.org/publications/defusing-new-yorks-pension-bomb/

cxcvi E. J.McMahon, "Defusing New York's Pension Bomb," *Empire Center, NY Torch Blog*, June 7, 2006, http://www.empirecenter.org/publications/defusing-new-yorks-pension-bomb/

cxcvii E. J.McMahon, "Defusing New York's Pension Bomb," *Empire Center, NY Torch Blog*, June 7, 2006, http://www.empirecenter.org/publications/defusing-new-yorks-pension-bomb/

cxcviii US Department of Labor, Bureau of Labor Statistics, "Retirement costs for defined benefit plans higher than for defined contribution plans," *US Department of Labor, Bureau of Labor Statistics*, December 2012, http://www.bls.gov/opub/btn/volume-1/retirement-costs-for-defined-benefit-plans-higher-than-for-defined-contribution-plans.htm

cxcix E. J. McMahon and Josh Barro, "New York's Exploding Pension Costs," *Empire Center for New York State Policy, Manhattan Institute*, December 2010, http://www.empirecenter.org/publications/new-yorks-exploding-pension-costs/

cc   E. J. McMahon and Josh Barro, "New York's Exploding Pension Costs," *Empire Center for New York State Policy, Manhattan Institute*, December 2010, http://www.empirecenter.org/publications/new-yorks-exploding-pension-costs/

cci   Rob Steyer, "COLA clashes in spotlight as public plans, participants tussle," *Pensions and Investments*, May 2, 2016, http://www.pionline.com/article/20160502/PRINT/305029991/cola-clashes-in-spotlight-as-public-plans-participants-tussle

ccii   John C. Osborne, John Fensterwald and Matt Levin, "STATES IN MOTION: VISUALIZING HOW EDUCATION FUNDING HAS CHANGED OVER TIME," *Edsource, States in Motion*, November 6, 2015, https://edsource.org/2015/states-in-motion-school-finance-naep-child-poverty/83303

cciii   Roland G. Freyer and Steven D. Levitt, "Falling Behind," *Education Next*, Fall 2004, http://educationnext.org/fallingbehind/

cciv   James Hohmann and Elise Vieback, "The Daily 202: The soft bigotry of low expectations, revisited," *The Washington Post*, July 7, 2015, https://www.washingtonpost.com/news/powerpost/wp/2015/07/07/the-daily-202-the-soft-bigotry-of-low-expectations-revisited/

ccv   Valerie Strauss, "An eighth-grade boy's 'outrageous' class schedule," *The Washington Post*, September 12, 2015, https://www.washingtonpost.com/news/answer-sheet/wp/2015/09/12/an-eighth-grade-boys-outrageous-class-schedule/

ccvi   Thomas C. Frohlich, Michael B. Sauter, Evan Comen and Samuel Stebbins, "America's Most and Least Educated States: A Survey of All

50," *24/7wallstreet.com*, September 23, 2015, http://247wallst.com/special-report/2015/09/23/the-most-and-least-educated-states/

ccvii Shelley Peacock, Stephanie Konrad, Erin Watson, Darren Nickel and Nazeem Muhajarine, "Effectiveness of home visiting programs on child outcomes: a systematic review," *Bio Med Central*, January 9, 2013, http://bmcpublichealth.biomedcentral.com/articles/10.1186/1471-2458-13-17

ccviii Nicholas Kristof and Cheryl WuDunn, "The Way to Beat Poverty," *The New York Times*, September 12, 2014, http://www.nytimes.com/2014/09/14/opinion/sunday/nicholas-kristof-the-way-to-beat-poverty.html

ccix W. Steven Barnett, "Preschool Education and Its Lasting Effects: Research and Policy Implications," *Arizona State University, Colorado University at Boulder*, September 2008, http://www.readingrockets.org/articles/researchbytopic/33827

ccx Lawrence J. Schweinhart, "Lasting Benefits of Preschool Programs," *Eric Digest*, 1994, http://www.ericdigests.org/1994/lasting.htm

ccxi Richard Perez-Pena and Motoko Rich, "Preschool Push Moving Ahead in Many States," *NY Times*, February 3, 2014, http://mobile.nytimes.com/2014/02/04/us/push-for-preschool-becomes-a-bipartisan-cause-outside-washington.html?referrer=

ccxii Jared Bernstein, "The biggest public policy mistake we're continuing to make, year after year," *The Washington Post*, February 1, 2016, https://www.washingtonpost.com/posteverything/wp/2016/02/01/the-biggest-public-policy-mistake-were-continuing-to-make-year-after-year/?postshare=771454355779258&tid=ss_mail

ccxiii   Lyndsey Layton, " Study: High-quality early education could reduce costs," *The Washington Post*, February 3, 2015, https://www.washingtonpost.com/local/education/study-high-quality-early-education-could-reduce-costs/2015/02/03/b714bcee-ab6f-11e4-abe8-e1ef60ca26de_story.html

ccxiv   Emily Badger, "Voters in Seattle just taxed themselves to pay for preschool for the poor," *The Washington Post*, November 5, 2014, https://www.washingtonpost.com/news/wonk/wp/2014/11/05/voters-in-seattle-just-taxed-themselves-to-pay-for-preschool-for-the-poor/

ccxv   Kevin Casey, "Why G.O.P. and Teachers Are Uniting to Stop Obama Effort to Help Poor Schools," *The New York Times*, May 17, 2016, http://www.nytimes.com/2016/05/18/upshot/why-poor-districts-receive-less-government-school-funding-than-rich-ones.html?emc=edit_tnt_20160517&nlid=47562199&tntemail0=y

The solutions-based book "Why We Failed: 40 Years of Education Reform" was published by Guaranteed Press. Visit us at http://www.guaranteed-press.net Follow us @guaranteedpress on Twitter and Guaranteed Press on Facebook.

38078361R00312

Made in the USA
Middletown, DE
12 December 2016